# THE POLITICS OF
# REVELATION AND REASON

## RELIGION AND CIVIC LIFE IN
## THE NEW NATION

John G. West, Jr.

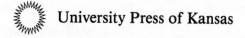

University Press of Kansas

Published by the University Press of Kansas (Lawrence, Kansas
66049), which was organized by the Kansas Board of Regents and
is operated and funded by Emporia State University, Fort Hays
State University, Kansas State University, Pittsburg State
University, the University of Kansas, and Wichita State University

Library of Congress Cataloging-in-Publication Data

West, John G.
The politics of revelation and reason : religion and civic life in
the new nation / John G. West, Jr.
p.   cm. — (American political thought)
Includes bibliographical references and index.
ISBN 0-7006-0780-3 (hardcover)
1. Religion and politics—United States.   2. Church and state—
United States.   3. Faith and reason—History of doctrines.
I. Title.   II. Series.
BL2525.W424   1996
322'.1'097309034—dc20                                      95-51171

British Library Cataloguing in Publication Data is available.

Printed in the United States of America

10 9 8 7 6 5 4 3 2 1

Produced digitally by Lightning Source Inc.

For my parents
John and Sophie West

# CONTENTS

# PREFACE

"We disapprove of the measures adopted by a certain party, styling themselves the Christian party in politics," declared the petition from a citizens' group. The document went on to indict Christian political activists for advocating policies that were "infusing a spirit of religious intolerance and persecution into the political institutions of the country, and which, unless opposed, will result in a union of church and state."

Given present controversies, the petition could have been written last week. Instead, it was issued in 1831. Those who believe that religion in politics is somehow a recent phenomenon in America should reexamine the history books. Religion has been an integral part of the nation's politics from the early years of the republic, and in this book, I try to explain why. I also seek to illuminate both the opportunities and the dangers religion poses for politics in a representative democracy.

As a political scientist interested in current affairs, I initially considered writing about contemporary conflicts over faith and politics in America. The more I studied the early years of the United States, however, the more I realized that present controversies are simply a continuation of arguments that have been going on since the nation began. The questions debated during the early years of America are hauntingly familiar: Does religion have a political role, and if so, what should it be? What are the advantages of religion in politics? What are the dangers? And how can people of faith bring their religious beliefs to bear on public issues without dividing citizens along religious lines and infringing on the liberty of conscience of those who do not share their religious views?

Exploring how these questions were answered in the past can help clarify what is at stake at present. Indeed, examining the debate over religion and politics more than a century and a half ago may provide more illumination than looking at current conflicts over abortion, school prayer, gay rights, or any number of other issues. Contemporary controversies often cloud our judgment because we have a direct interest in their outcome. When we are able to examine the same fundamental disputes at a distance, however, we are more likely to grapple with the real merits of the respective arguments.

That is what I hope can happen here, for there is much we all can learn from the way religion became involved in politics in the early United States. Those who criticize the role of faith in politics today might gain a better understanding of how and why religion can play a beneficial role in our politics, and those who champion religion's political role might gain a deeper appreciation of the dangers as well as the possibilities of religious political activism. Finally, evangelical Christians might rediscover part of their heritage, for much of this book is the story of how their forebears first became involved in politics in America. Politically active evangelicals of today might profit from both the mistakes and the successes of their nineteenth-century predecessors.

Few achievements in life are solitary efforts, and I would like to acknowledge the many people who have enabled me to write this book. First, since this work began as my doctoral dissertation, I would like to recognize the four persons who served on my dissertation committee: Charles R. Kesler, a gifted scholar and teacher who first persuaded me to go to graduate school and then made it possible for me to do so; Harry V. Jaffa, a brilliant political philosopher whose understanding of the American Founding underlies the entire book; Leonard W. Levy, one of the nation's foremost constitutional historians, who has influenced my views on church-state matters more than he may realize; and William B. Allen, now dean of James Madison College at Michigan State University, whose insights and encouragement I continue to cherish. I am equally grateful to American Political Thought series editors Lance Banning and Wilson Carey McWilliams, who along with Robert Calhoon provided excellent suggestions as to how to strengthen the manuscript. They were also understanding when some of the revisions took longer than anticipated, as was University Press of Kansas' fine director Fred Woodward, whose enthusiasm about the manuscript from the start was heartening.

At Discovery Institute, the late Kathryn Flower lent her meticulous research skills, which were indispensable in the later phases of the project. This was one of Kathryn's last projects at the institute; her untimely death at the end of 1995 was a tremendous blow to all of us who knew and worked with her. I regret that she did not live to see this book in print. Also at Discovery Institute, President Bruce Chapman encouraged me to pursue this project despite the many other things that I should have been doing. At Seattle Pacific University, both Kathy Cissna and Sheralee Priem provided needed help, and Edythe Porpa assisted with the index. Historian Richard John, meanwhile, made Chapter 3 much easier to write by his fine journal article on the Sunday mails and by his willingness to share with me some of the unpublished petitions he had already unearthed. The able staffs of the interlibrary loan office at the Claremont Colleges, the Henry Huntington Library in San Marino, California, and the National Archives in Washington, D.C., also aided my research considerably. After writing this book, I have a much keener appreciation of the role of libraries and their staffs in the world of scholarship. Finally, I wish to thank the Dora Haynes Foundation and the Claremont Graduate School, which awarded me a Haynes Dissertation Grant in 1990–1991, which greatly facilitated both the research and the writing of the core text.

# INTRODUCTION
## RELIGION'S PERSISTENT PRESENCE IN
## AMERICAN POLITICS

"The American clergy stands aloof from public business. That is the most striking, but not the only, example of their self-restraint. Religion in America is a world apart in which the clergyman is supreme, but one which he is careful never to leave."[1] So observed Alexis de Tocqueville when describing the political role of religion in the early American nation. According to Tocqueville, religion may have been the first of America's political institutions, but its influence was indirect at best; it helped fashion society's morals but did not actively participate in matters for legislation. Indeed, American clergy were "at pains to keep out of affairs and not mix in the combinations of parties."[2]

Tocqueville's account of religion in America is widely cited today and just as widely admired.[3] Given the present upheavals caused by religion in American politics, one can readily understand why. Many Americans no doubt yearn for religion to have no effect on politics, and the era Tocqueville depicted probably sounds to them like a golden age.

The problem with golden ages, of course, is that they are almost always imaginary. This one is. Religion has never been kept out of politics in America, and the period during which Tocqueville lived was no exception. From the election of 1800 to the beginning of the Civil War, evangelical Christians converged on the political arena en masse, producing a political movement that in many ways paralleled the New Christian Right that arose during the 1980s. That Tocqueville missed this political phenomenon is all the more incredible considering that evangelical political activism reached a fevered pitch while he was on American soil in 1832.

A little more than a year before Tocqueville came to America, evangelicals began peppering Congress with memorials against the removal of the Cherokee Nation from Georgia. Congressman (later Governor) Wilson Lumpkin of Georgia denounced what he termed the "Christian party in politics" and complained of the books and pamphlets being "written and circulated extensively by Northern ministers and some missionaries of the Cross—misrepresenting and perverting every fact connected with this Indian subject."[4] By the time Tocqueville arrived, the battle had shifted to the courts with the cases of *Cherokee Nation* v. *Georgia* (1831) and *Worcester* v. *Georgia*

(1832). Both cases attracted widespread national attention; the latter one was hotly debated in the press, and nearly sixty members of Congress left their seats in order to hear oral arguments in the case before the Supreme Court.[5] That Tocqueville was aware of the American policy of Indian removal is clear, for he spent several pages criticizing it, but he nowhere alluded to the great political controversy surrounding the policy or the political activities of churches and missionaries on behalf of the Indians.[6]

Tocqueville also failed to notice the bitter struggle raging over the Sunday mails. The origins of this conflict dated back to 1810, when Congress passed a law requiring post offices to be open every day of the week that mail arrived. In the larger towns and cities this meant that the post offices would be open Sundays. Almost immediately petitions began to trickle into Congress asking that the law be repealed. During the next several decades, the trickle became a torrent. Petitions poured in from nineteen states, the Territory of Michigan, and the District of Columbia; signatories included former governors, current justices of state supreme courts, past and present members of Congress, lawyers, merchants, and numerous postmasters.[7] Petitions in favor of repeal in turn spurred a number of petitions opposed to the action, and the flurry of petitions on both sides of the question led to several congressional reports being issued on the subject. When Tocqueville arrived, petitions were still circulating. As with Cherokee removal, a key point of contention in the Sunday mails debate was the question of how involved churches should be in politics. Those arguing for repeal of the Sunday mails were invariably tied to religion, and their opponents lost no opportunity to attack what they saw as a dangerous combination of church and state.[8]

The Sunday mails and Cherokee removal were the two major national issues involving religion in politics in the late 1820s and early 1830s; but even they represented only a portion of the total picture. Evangelical ministers and laity were equally active at the state and local levels, spearheading crusades against lotteries, dueling, prostitution, and intemperance.[9] This involvement of evangelicals in the American political process raised fundamental questions about the role of religion in a free society. Perhaps in no time was the debate over the role of religion in politics more vigorous or articulate.

In our own day, of course, the debate over religion and politics has resumed with a vengeance, reawakened in part by the return of evangelicals to the political arena in the late 1970s. Most evangelicals steered clear of political entanglements after the demise of Prohibition.[10] When they suddenly and recently came

back to the political arena, reaction was often nasty. Within the religious community evangelicals were chided by more liberal Christians for confusing political conservatism with Christianity and for adopting, in the words of one observer, "the kind of attitude which in previous eras led to holy wars."[11] Outside
the religious sphere, groups such as People for the American Way and the
American Civil Liberties Union attacked newly politicized evangelicals as un-
democratic and un-American.[12] Patricia Harris, secretary of health and human
services in the Carter administration, implied that they might even produce an
American Ayatollah Khomeini.[13] Similarly hostile refrains continue in the
1990s; indeed, attacks on the Christian Right formed a key part of the Demo-
crats' electoral strategy in the 1994 elections.

   That the controversy over religion and politics in America is a recurring
one indicates the fundamental nature of the conflict. There is a permanent
tension here, one that has been called by some the "theological-political
problem."[14] Simply stated, the theological-political problem is a variation of
the old question of dual loyalty. As a nation of immigrants, we are most familiar with this question when framed in terms of national origin and ethnicity. Throughout our history doubts have been raised about whether certain ethnic groups can really be loyal Americans during times of national
crisis. But the dual loyalty question posed by national origin and ethnicity is
trifling compared to the one posed by religion. Imagine a group of citizens
who claim to be citizens of both the United States and some other country.
Imagine further that they claim their citizenship in this other country is
more important than their U.S. citizenship. Indeed, they will risk torture, disaster, and death on behalf of their other country. Moreover, if ever asked to
choose between the United States and the other nation in some controversy
they will invariably choose to follow the other country. If you can picture
this, you have grasped the fundamental challenge that religion has posed to
politics since at least the rise of Christianity in the Roman Empire.

   In the ancient world (that is, the world before Christianity), the tension
between faith and government was less profound because political and religious obligations largely coincided. There were several reasons for this.
First, ancient religions were particular rather than universal. Each state had
its own state religion, and adherence to that religion was part of patriotism
toward one's country. As a citizen of one state, one could not believe in a religion of another state—precisely *because* it was a religion of another state.
Political obligation and religious obligation were thus identical; to be impi-

ous was to be disloyal.[15] Second, religion in the ancient city constituted an integral part of the way rulers governed. Priests sent armies off to war, offered sacrifices for national transgressions, and consulted the gods for advice in national emergencies. Religious rituals were preeminently civic ceremonies and tied the members of the political community closer together.[16] Finally, religion in the ancient city was this-worldly; it stressed the attainment of fame in this world more than it pointed to eternal felicity in the hereafter. Religion in the ancient world was so tied to temporal affairs that one might even regard it as a mere tool of state that rulers employed for their own ends. Niccolò Machiavelli took this view, shrewdly lauding the flexibility of pagan religions because rulers could use them to sanction whatever policy they wanted to pursue at any given moment.[17]

The advent of Christianity changed matters decisively. For the first time one had a religion not tied to a particular race or nation. Christians preached that all men could now be brothers—children of the same God—regardless of race or economic station. "There is neither Jew nor Greek, there is neither slave nor free, there is neither male nor female; for you are all one in Christ Jesus."[18] Similarly, instead of being united to the governing authorities, Christianity began its life radically separated from the state. Forswearing all temporal power, the church existed in its first centuries as a self-governing, self-perpetuating institution that relied on the voluntary patronage of its members.[19] Finally, instead of prizing this-worldly fame and gratification, Christianity stressed the relative unimportance of the affairs of the present world in comparison with those of the world to come.[20] As the apostle Paul wrote to the church at Philippi, "Our citizenship is in heaven."[21]

Now one might think that a religion that forswore temporal power and glory could never constitute a threat to the state. But it is precisely for this reason that Christianity was so incredibly dangerous. Because the church was separate from the state, it acted as an independent authority outside the control of the state; and because the church anchored its authority in a transcendent God rather than in any temporal ruler, its demands naturally took precedence over the claims of temporal authority. Once religion and state were separated, obedience to God became more important than obedience to the state. This stance was bound to create political problems, particularly when the Christian understanding of morality clashed with the morality of the Roman ruling class.[22] Only in Christianity's universal outlook, which paralleled that of the Roman Empire, did the church coincide with the surrounding political situation. But given the church's independence, even this parallelism made the church seem a threat because the church appeared to be setting itself up as an alternative to the empire. It was only a matter of time before politics and Christianity began to clash in very practical ways, as historian Philip Schaff noted in his *History of the Christian Church:* "The conscientious refusal of the Christians to pay divine honors to the emperor and his statue, and to take part in any idolatrous ceremonies at public festivities, their aversion to the imperial military service, their disregard for politics and depreciation of all civil and temporal affairs as compared with the spiritual and eternal interests of man, their close brotherly union and frequent meetings, drew upon them the suspicion of hostility to the Caesars and the Roman people, and the unpardonable crime of conspiracy against the state."[23]

The virulent, bloody persecution of Christians by Rome that resulted becomes understandable in light of the theoretical challenge to the empire posed by Christianity. That challenge was finally resolved on terms intelligible to the ancient city: Christianity became the state religion of the Roman Empire.[24] Once again there was one God for one city—only now the city was universal. But as matters turned out, this development did not solve the theological-political problem; it merely reformulated it.

In the ancient city theology had been subordinated to politics. Now Christianity began to subordinate politics to theology. Heresy was transformed into a state crime, and infidelity to God became disloyalty to the state. In a very real sense the situation that had existed in the ancient city was now stood on its head. In the ancient city the preeminent function of religion was to inspire political obedience and loyalty.[25] All religion was political religion. Hence, religious belief per se was not nearly as important as political loyalty. But Christianity had not begun as a political religion—indeed, it began with the devaluation of politics—and so for the church political loyalty could never be more important than doctrinal loyalty. The result was that doctrinal loyalty increased in importance while political loyalty diminished. Harry Jaffa points out the result: "The Christian empire made belief central to fidelity, and heresy assumed an unprecedented gravity as an offense not merely against the good order of civil society, but of the world. While belief was elevated to an unprecedented level, obedience sank correspondingly. The decline and fall of the ancient empire replaced centralized Roman administration with the most decentralized, and most lawless, of regimes—feudalism."[26]

With the breakup of the Roman Empire into smaller states, the theological-political problem assumed yet another form. Since one government for all of Christendom proved to be impossible, the problem now became "how to discover a source of law for particular political communities, within the larger framework of the cosmopolis of the city of God."[27] The preliminary solution—the divine right of the king, any king who happened to be in power—again called for a union between church and state.

There is no need to recount here the battles between church and state that followed the establishment of Christianity as the official religion of the Roman Empire. It is sufficient to note that the struggles involving religion and politics implicated both sides. Rulers tried to control churches, and churches tried to dominate states.[28] The consequences these struggles had for America were far-reaching. First, many colonists fled to America to escape religious persecution brought about by state churches in Europe.[29] Second, and somewhat paradoxically, state churches in the Old World set the pattern for church-state relations in the New. Most colonists hated particular state churches because they disagreed with them, but many did not hate the idea of state aid to churches. When they set up their own governments, they often secured funding for religion by law.[30] The persecution of religious dissenters that resulted had not yet disappeared by the time of the Revolution. Virginia still punished dissenting ministers during the 1770s, causing James Madison to complain in 1774 about the "diabolical Hell conceived principle of persecution" after learning that dissenting clergy had been jailed in an adjacent county for (in his words) "publishing their religious Sentiments which in the main are very orthodox."[31]

Even though conflicts between religion and politics in colonial America were tepid compared to what had occurred in the Old World, they were potent enough to make the relationship between these two forces a continuing and pressing concern. Consequently, the quest for a solution to the theological-political problem animated much of early American political thought. George Washington, Benjamin Franklin, Thomas Jefferson, James Madison, and others spent a great deal of time reflecting on religion and its role in society and on how to prevent the strife and bloodshed caused by the mixture of religion and politics in other countries. Many of the Founders' most profound theoretical statements dealt with the relationship between religion and state: Washington's Farewell Address and its delineation of the mutual connections among religion, morality, and domestic felicity; Jefferson's Statute of Religious Liberty and its majestic declaration that "God hath created the mind free"; and Madison's "Memorial and Remonstrance," with its lucid arguments about why government support of ministers corrupts religion just as much as it does government.

This book's purpose is to explore how the Founders tried to solve the theological-political problem and to determine whether their solution worked in practice in the early decades of the new nation. To answer these questions requires not only a reexamination of the thought of the Founders on the subject of religion, which has been done often enough before,[32] but also a thorough and thoughtful investigation of what occurred in the generation following the enactment of the Constitution. The latter investigation focuses on evangelical political activism from the election of 1800 to 1835.[33] This activism is worthy of study not only because evangelicals were the period's most politically active religious adherents but also because they provide the most stringent test of any proposed solution to the theological-political problem.

To understand why this is the case, one first must have a clear grasp of precisely who evangelicals were in early-nineteenth-century America. Unfortunately, recent scholarship has spread more confusion than enlightenment in this area. The tendency has been to label as "evangelical" any nominally Christian group typified by religious enthusiasm, populism, and revivalism. Yet this definition distorts the traditional meaning of the term. It includes as evangelicals many who would not have been considered as such in nineteenth-century society; and it excludes groups that definitely considered themselves evangelicals during the period.

The way out of the confusion is to recognize that in the nineteenth century those who called themselves evangelical defined themselves primarily by adherence to a common body of doctrines, not by a common mode of worship or a common method of church organization. All Protestants who adhered to historic Christian doctrines such as the Trinity, salvation by grace, and the atoning death and bodily resurrection of Christ were regarded as evangelicals.[34] Hence, in the nineteenth century the term included Presbyterians and Episcopalians just as much as it did Methodists and Baptists. However, it did not include preachers—no matter how popular in their orientation— who enunciated doctrines outside the framework of historic Protestant theology.

Once the traditional definition of evangelicalism has been restored—as adherence to a particular set of doctrines rather than as a particular style of

worship or church organization—it becomes clear why nineteenth-century
evangelicalism exacerbated the friction between theology and politics. The
problem was that evangelical Christianity undercut the common ground between citizens of different religious persuasions. Unlike Unitarianism or uni-
versalism, two other modes of belief during the early nation period, evangelicalism taught that salvation in no way depends on what a person does. It is
based solely on faith in Christ and his death on the cross as an atonement
for one's sins. Everyone who fails to accept Christ's atonement—no matter
how moral—will be eternally damned, for no one is good enough to justify
himself before God on the basis of his own works. In the moral sphere, evangelicalism taught that true morality can be achieved only by those who live
in obedience to the dictates of the Bible under the power of God's Holy
Spirit.[35]

Although these doctrines do not necessitate social conflict, they do create
the conditions for friction. If evangelicals are the only ones with true knowledge about morality, if evangelicals are the only ones who can live truly
moral lives, one can see how evangelicals might be tempted to rule over nonbelievers for their own good. Hence, nothing can present itself as the solution to the theological-political problem—at least as it has been manifested
in America—if it does not effectively deal with the challenge posed by evangelicalism.

Something should be said about the scope of this book's examination of
nineteenth-century evangelicals. First, the focus is on evangelical efforts *in
politics*. Thus, unlike several other books, this one does not concentrate on
the intricacies of evangelical theology, and it does not explore the divisive
conflict that arose during this period within the Presbyterian Church on the
finer points of Calvinism. These theological issues have limited utility in
helping explain evangelical political theory. In evangelical political writing
of the era, issues of disestablishment, social disintegration, and the proper
conception of virtue were far more prominent than theological controversies
about, say, the conversion process. Accordingly, evangelical theology is discussed only insofar as it informed evangelical political theory and practice.
The emphasis is on the common moral and political principles underlying
evangelical reform.

Second, this book focuses only on the first wave of evangelical reform in
the new nation, which is dated here from 1800 to 1835. It is true that evangelical social and political activism took place in the new nation before 1800,

but that activism tended to be subsidiary to larger secular movements. In the 1790s, for example, many New England evangelicals were active in politics simply as partisans of the Federalist Party. Only after the election of 1800 and the selection of Thomas Jefferson as president did most evangelicals better understand that they could exercise a significant *independent* voice in the political and social arena. The end date of 1835 points to the regrouping that occurred among evangelical activists in the mid-1830s. Prior to this date the Sunday mails and Cherokee removal campaigns had served as national focal points; after these campaigns failed, evangelicals had to find a new focus, and thereafter slavery became the dominant concern. Because the intention here is to examine the formative stage of evangelical activism (before slavery became the all-encompassing issue), the book purposely stops after the Sunday mails and Cherokee removal campaigns.[36]

Third, this book necessarily focuses on those evangelicals who were most involved in politics, not on those who were not. Consequently, the book gravitates toward evangelicals from the Presbyterian/Reformed theological tradition because members of this theological tradition exercised a political influence disproportionate to their numbers. They were the evangelicals most active in leading—and explaining—evangelical reform during the period in question.[37]

Finally, the approach herein is idea oriented. This book is not primarily social history or even religious history. It is an account of political ideas and of how political actors understood themselves and justified their actions within the public arena. The argument advanced in the following pages is that the political leaders of the Founding generation understood the political role of religion in a certain way and that their intellectual frame of reference was ultimately reflected in the debates over religion and politics engaged in by evangelical reformers and their critics.

This is an unabashedly old-fashioned approach to religion and politics, one that purposely deemphasizes the kind of sociological analysis of religion pioneered by H. Richard Niebuhr in *The Social Sources of American Denominationalism* (1929).[38] To be sure, sociological analysis has it uses. Intellectual history that does not take into account social and cultural forces can be one-dimensional and naive. But social history that seeks to explain all intellectual disputes in terms of the social and economic status of the disputants is equally distorted. Human beings are reasoning creatures, and the reduction of political debates to a clash of interests and status undermines the intellectual enterprise itself. The unending quest to "see through" the beliefs and ideas of others to get at the subrational "root causes" of political movements is ultimately self-defeating. "If you see through everything, then everything is transparent," C. S. Lewis once aptly observed. "But a wholly transparent world is an invisible world. To 'see through' all things is the same as not to see."[39]

Niebuhr himself eventually recognized the limitations of the sociological approach when it came to the realm of ideas. Writing in *The Kingdom of God in America* (1937), he perceptively explained his dissatisfaction with his previous book:

> Though the sociological approach helped to explain why the religious stream flowed in these particular channels [i.e., race, class and sectional interests] it did not account for the force of the stream itself; while it seemed relevant enough to the institutionalized churches it did not explain the Christian movement which produced these churches; while it accounted for the diversity in American religion it did not explain the unity which our faith possesses despite its variety; while it could deal with the religion which was dependent on culture it left unexplained the faith which is independent, which is aggressive rather than passive, and which molds culture instead of being molded by it.[40]

I argue that the sociological approach to religion is of limited utility when one is trying to understand the intellectual debate over the political role of religion in the new nation. This book does not ignore social factors, but they are admittedly of secondary interest. The primary purpose is to describe and understand intellectual arguments, not identify sociological causes. In line with this purpose, Chapter 1 reexamines the ideas of key Founders on the subject of religion and its role in society. Chapter 2 recounts how evangelicals became involved in politics in the early nineteenth century and compares the Founders' view of the political role of religion with the theories offered by such prominent evangelicals as Timothy Dwight, Lyman Beecher, and Francis Wayland. Chapters 3 and 4 provide case studies of the controversies over the Sunday mails and Cherokee Indian removal. Finally, the Epilogue summarizes the enduring lessons of both evangelical reform and the Founders' understanding of religion's proper role in politics.

# ONE

## RELIGION AND THE AMERICAN
## FOUNDING REVISITED

The Constitutional Convention had been meeting for only a few weeks when the crisis erupted. The four small states demanded equal representation in the Senate, fearful that their rights would be trampled on without it. The larger states balked, and the small states threatened to walk out. Tempers flared, delegates exchanged angry barbs, and deliberations deadlocked.

Just as the convention seemed about to disintegrate, the oldest delegate rose to speak. At eighty-two, Benjamin Franklin was already the stuff of which legends are made, and he was accorded more than a little deference by the rest of the convention. "The very heavens obey him, and the clouds yield up the lightning to be imprisoned in his rod," wrote fellow delegate William Pierce in awe.[1]

The doctor proposed a three-day adjournment to cool tempers, supplemented by the hiring of a chaplain, who would "introduce the business of each day by an address to the *Creator of the universe,* and the Governor of all nations, beseeching Him to preside in our council, enlighten our minds with a portion of heavenly wisdom, influence our hearts with a love of truth and justice, and crown our labors with complete and abundant success!"[2]

The account of the youngest delegate at the convention, twenty-seven-year-old Jonathan Dayton from New Jersey, continues the story:

The words of the venerable Franklin fell upon our ears with a weight and authority, even greater than we may suppose an oracle to have had in a Roman senate! A silent admiration superseded, for a moment, the expression of that assent and approbation which was strongly marked on almost every countenance; I say *almost,* for *one* man was found in the Convention, Mr. H——, from ——, who rose and said, with regard to the first motion of the honorable gentleman, for an *adjournment,* he would yield his assent; but he protested against the second motion, for the appointment of a chaplain. He then commenced a high-strained eulogium on the assemblage of *wisdom, talent* and *experience,* which the Convention embraced . . . and concluded by saying, that therefore he did not see the necessity of calling in *foreign aid!*[3]

Ignoring "this impertinent and impious speech," according to Dayton, Washington and the rest of the convention immediately ratified both the call for a chaplain and an adjournment. The subsequent recess was spent in "free and frank" consultations, the result of which appeared in the morning session three days later. As soon as the chaplain had closed his prayer, a compromise was secured on the organization of the Senate according to the present plan.

Thus occurred the miracle at Philadelphia. At the very point the convention was about to break apart, passion and self-interest gave way to reflection and choice as delegates humbled themselves before the Supreme Lawgiver of the Universe. Or so it was supposed by those who read the preceding account, which first appeared in the respected *National Intelligencer* in 1826.[4] Evangelicals quickly appropriated the story to vindicate the pious character of the Founding. Here was positive proof that the Framers had remembered the Supreme Being while drafting the Constitution. It almost made up for their having left God out of the Preamble.

That prayers were initially proposed by a deist, rather than a Christian, proved but a minor irritant. Evangelical Thomas Grimké equated Dr. Franklin with the biblical Cornelius, the Roman centurion in the New Testament who believed in one God.[5] Grimké added that subsequent events at the convention bore witness that God had heard the delegates' prayers. "The result must convince us, that the supplications of our Cornelius and of his fellow-worshipers, were 'had in remembrance before God,'" declared Grimké in a Fourth of July oration in 1833. "Order arose out of chaos; Light, out of darkness; Discord was exchanged for Unanimity; the jealous, proud and selfish States, became bound to each other, as by the indisoluble bond of perpetual wedlock . . . [and] that Constitution under the blessing of Heaven, has hitherto secured to us, at home, liberty, safety and prosperity; abroad, independence, respect and admiration, altogether unexampled in the history of the world."[6]

There was only one problem with this account, as James Madison pointed out to Grimké in a letter in 1834: It was not true.[7] Franklin had made the speech, but his proposal for prayers had been tabled.[8] But in one respect the truth or falsity of the narrative was irrelevant. The extraordinary thing was that Americans should even be interested in prayer at the Constitutional Convention. The Constitution expressly forbade religious tests for national office, and by the 1820s disestablishment had occurred in every state but one; yet, paradoxically, Americans remained insatiably curious about the religious beliefs of the Founders. Indeed, one of the raging debates of the 1830s focused on whether George Washington was a Christian. In the pages of the *New York Free Inquirer,* Robert Dale Owen claimed Washington was a deist,[9] and in lecture halls Frances Wright boldly asserted, "Washington was not a Christian. He believed not in the priest's God, nor in the divine authority of the priest's book."[10] Defenders of Washington's piety responded in 1836 with *The Religious Opinions and Character of Washington,* a 414-page tome by E. C. McGuire that depicted the general as devoted to constant prayer, the frequent taking of Communion, and the diligent observance of the Christian Sabbath.[11]

An intervening century did nothing to dampen the enthusiasm for inquiries into the Founders' religion. In 1919 William Johnson published a defense of Washington's orthodoxy titled *George Washington the Christian;* and in 1959 historian Paul Boller sought to lay to rest such accounts with his *George Washington and Religion.* More recently, there have been omnibus books dealing with the religious beliefs of several Founders at once, including John Eidsmoe's *Christianity and the Constitution: The Faith of Our Founding Fathers* (1987) and Edwin Gaustad's *Faith of Our Fathers: Religion and the New Nation* (1987). There has even been an anthology of selections from the Founders themselves titled *"In God We Trust": The Religious Beliefs and Ideas of the American Founding Fathers* (1958).[12]

Even though such books may appear unseemly in an ostensibly secular republic such as ours, they serve a serious purpose. Questions about the religious beliefs of the Founders are important because they point the way to a far more significant concern: At the deepest level these questions constitute an inquiry into the place of religion in America's constitutional order. Americans want to know how the Founders viewed religion because they seek assurance that American republicanism is not incompatible with American religion. Put another way, Americans want to know about religion and the Founders because they are interested in how the Founders resolved the theological-political problem.

Broadly speaking, there are three ways the Founders could have resolved it. They could have subordinated the state to religion (the approach adopted by present-day Iran). They could have subordinated religion to the state (the ancient solution to the problem, typified by Greece and Rome). Or they could have attempted to place religion and the state on some sort of equal footing, each independent within its own particular sphere.

Each of these solutions has been ascribed to the Founders by various writers. John Whitehead adopts the first view when he suggests that according to the Framers, "Biblically revealed higher law offers the only reliable guide to personal and national health."[13] Walter Berns advocates the second position when he claims that America's "solution of the religious problem consists in the subordination of religion."[14] And Harry Jaffa stakes out the third view when he writes that "the American Founding . . . provided for the coexistence of the claims of reason and of revelation in all their forms, without requiring or permitting any political decisions concerning them."[15]

Determining which of these alternatives the Founders actually embraced requires the careful consideration of several questions. What did the Founders think was the proper relationship between religion and society? Did they envision the churches as serving a vital political function in the new republic? Did they believe that reason and revelation differ substantially in the content of morality? Did they believe that the churches had to be made safe for republican government? These are the pressing queries that must be answered before any conclusions can be reached about whether the Founders developed a coherent solution to the theological-political dilemma, and these are therefore the questions that animate our investigations here.

Something should be said from the outset about the selection of Founders to be discussed. The reasons for choosing James Madison and Thomas Jefferson are obvious to anyone conversant with their writings and the period; with some justification they are the figures most readily cited in judicial discussions of religion and the Founding.[16] Both were tireless supporters of the freedom of the mind in general and the freedom of religion in particular. Madison's "Memorial and Remonstrance" and Jefferson's Statute of Religious Liberty are justifiably celebrated for their lucid and elegant exposition of the principles of religious liberty. In addition, Jefferson and Madison were perhaps the most distinguished proponents of a strict separation of church and state during the Founding. Alexander Hamilton and John Adams provide an interesting counterpoint to the views of Jefferson and Madison, for both spoke more of religion's public role than of religious freedom. Benjamin Franklin and George Washington prove much harder to pigeonhole. They believed in the freedom of the mind as much as Jefferson and

Madison, but along with Hamilton and Adams they also saw the need for what Franklin termed "Publick Religion."[17]

The remaining figures—John Witherspoon, John Jay, and James Wilson—are less remembered today, but all three had significant things to say about religion and society, and equally important, all were major national political figures in their own time. Witherspoon served as president of the College of New Jersey and as a member of the Continental Congress. Jay was the nation's premier diplomat and the first chief justice of the Supreme Court. Wilson, also a justice of the Court, was arguably the most comprehensive thinker on American constitutionalism during the Founding period.

The focus here is on those who supported the new constitutional system, not on those who opposed it. Thus, the selection of Founders to be discussed does not include any Anti-Federalists. Yet Anti-Federalist views on the public role of religion were not fundamentally different from the views of Federalists such as Washington and Wilson. Anti-Federalists certainly differed with Federalists over whether the new Constitution would subvert the strength of religion at the local level; but both sides agreed that vibrant religion is necessary for the survival of the social order—and ultimately—representative democracy.[18]

## THE REVOLUTIONARIES: FRANKLIN AND WITHERSPOON

### Benjamin Franklin (1706–1790)

If George Washington was the father of his country, Benjamin Franklin was its elder sage, its first philosopher, and—one might add without any intended disrespect—its preeminent wit. Indeed, sometimes it is difficult to take Franklin seriously, for he had a penchant for treating almost everything as a joke. Yet beneath Franklin's wit lay cool, deliberate thought. As with Jonathan Swift or Samuel Johnson, Franklin's jokes invariably had a serious point.

Discovering the precise nature of Franklin's beliefs, however, can be a taxing endeavor. This is particularly the case in the realm of religion. One must remember that the Founders lived during an era when the clergy still held a place of social importance and when open disbelief in Christianity ignited fierce opposition. Those who ignored this social reality did so at their own peril, as Thomas Paine discovered after he wrote *The Age of Reason* in Europe in 1794. A blistering attack on Christian revelation, *The Age of Reason* offended even American deists such as John Adams. On returning to America, Paine faced ridicule by opponents and ostracism by friends.[19]

Franklin, unlike Paine, was acutely aware of the problem that philosophers and statesmen face when their own beliefs contradict well-settled public opinion, and so he decided early on to abandon all "abrupt contradiction and positive argumentation, and put on the humble inquirer and doubter." According to Franklin, this indirect method of disputation was particularly helpful given his religious beliefs. Having become "a real doubter in many points of our religious doctrine, I found this method safest for myself and very embarrassing to those against whom I used it."[20]

In later years Franklin became even more circumspect in advancing his own opinions, and to this tentative manner of speaking Franklin attributed much of the respect with which he was accorded. He retained, he said, "only the habit of expressing myself in terms of modest diffidence. . . . This habit, I believe, has been of great advantage to me when I have had occasion to inculcate my opinions and persuade men into measures that I have been from time to time engaged in promoting."[21] This is one of the most explicit passages in which Franklin spoke of the necessity of subterfuge in public discourse, but there are others where the same point is conveyed more subtly, as when he cautioned his daughter in a letter after she apparently entertained thoughts of staying away from church in 1764. Franklin counseled her against such a move more on grounds of prudence than piety: "You know I have many Enemies. . . . It is therefore the more necessary for you to be extremely circumspect in all your Behaviour, that no Advantage may be given to their Malevolence. Go constantly to Church whoever preaches."[22] In other words, those who seek the confidence of the public must be willing to accommodate the public's prejudices.

If a statesman must be careful not to needlessly offend the public by his actions, however, he must be equally scrupulous not to give unnecessary offense in his writings. In this regard Franklin noted the difficulties his friend evangelist George Whitefield suffered after publishing some of his opinions. According to Franklin, Whitefield would have been wiser to confine himself to the spoken word. Then his "unguarded expressions, and even erroneous opinions delivered in preaching, might have been afterwards explained or qualified by supposing others that might have accompanied them, or they might have been denied."[23]

Hence, if a person should be timid in what he says and does, he should be even more careful in what he writes. A corollary to this is that when an individual does feel compelled to admit something unpopular in writing, he should do so privately—and swear the correspondent to silence. Thus, when Franklin at last acknowledged his doubts about the divinity of Christ at the request of Reverend Ezra Stiles, president of Yale, Franklin also pledged his friend to secrecy.[24]

Given Franklin's mild-mannered approach, it would be simplistic—if not simpleminded—to take many of his statements at face value. One must pay particular attention even to those arguments he put forth with hesitation and diffidence; for given his manner of discourse, these may have been his most important arguments. With this caution in mind, we may proceed to examine what Franklin had to say in the area of religion and morality.

On the surface, at least, Franklin extolled both morality and piety. Franklin's moralism of thrift and industry is so etched in the American imagination that many of his proverbs continue to be quoted even today—"God helps them that help themselves," "There are no Gains, without Pains," and, of course, "Early to Bed, and early to rise, makes a Man healthy, wealthy and wise."[25] As for piety, Franklin regularly donated money for the support of ministers and the erection of churches.[26] And when Franklin drafted a plan for the education of youth, he noted that the study of history "will . . . afford frequent Opportunities of showing . . . the Mischiefs of Superstition . . . and the Excellency of the CHRISTIAN RELIGION above all others antient or modern."[27] To be sure, Franklin himself rarely attended services;[28] and his own statements of religious belief—when he made them—were not at all evangelical, ranging instead from Unitarian to polytheistic.[29] Regardless of his private theology, however, Franklin usually appeared in public as a sincere believer in God. On occasion he could even rise to a kind of spiritual grandeur, as with his remarkable speech at the Constitutional Convention advocating prayers to open the daily sessions. As noted at the beginning of this chapter, Franklin delivered this speech at a time when delegates had deadlocked over how to constitute the national legislature; though Franklin's proposal was ultimately tabled, some scholars speculate that the speech helped pave the way for the Great Compromise by steering the delegates away from their preoccupation with local interests.[30] Whatever the actual truth of the matter, Franklin's speech certainly stands out as a superior piece of theological-political rhetoric. One cannot fail to be struck by the eloquence of his remarks, the seeming sincerity of the arguments, and the facility with which Franklin handled his scriptural texts.

Franklin began by painting a dire portrait of the convention's situation and by pointing to divine wisdom as the only measure not employed thus far. He then reminded his colleagues that prayers had not been forgotten during the equally dire days of the Revolutionary War: "In the beginning of the Contest with G. Britain, when we were sensible of danger we had daily prayer in this room for the divine protection.—Our prayers, Sir, were heard, & they were graciously answered."[31]

Franklin's invocation of the Revolution was perhaps the most powerful empirical argument he could have raised at the time on behalf of God's providence. All of the men who were gathered in that room in Philadelphia—the very room where the Continental Congress had convened and issued the Declaration of Independence—knew the sheer improbability of what America had achieved. Despite deep internal divisions, despite a ragtag and ill-supplied army of civilians, the United States had defeated the world's reigning military power. Thus, Franklin did not have to prove the existence of divine providence to these men; he merely had to recall to their memories the facts they themselves knew. As he told them: "All of us who were engaged in the struggle must have observed frequent instances of a superintending providence in our favor."[32]

Moving from the events of history to the pages of the Bible, Franklin next wove together a tapestry of scriptural texts with the adeptness of a New England divine. He began with a gloss on Christ's statement in Matthew 10:29 that not a sparrow "shall fall on the ground without the Father." If a sparrow cannot fall without God's notice, Franklin asked, can an empire rise without His aid? In answer to this rhetorical question, Franklin turned to the Old Testament, quoting Psalm 127: "Except the Lord build the house, they labour in vain that build it." It is not without significance that the Psalm Franklin quoted is ascribed in its inscription to Solomon, the most celebrated political ruler in the Old Testament, who was praised for his all-encompassing wisdom. Nor is it unimportant that Franklin contrasted the advice of Solomon with story of the Tower of Babel from Genesis 11, perhaps the preeminent tale of man trying to build a city without God. Franklin declared that just as God had confounded the builders of Babel, He would confound the Framers of the new constitution if they did not seek recourse to Him. Invoking still more biblical language—this time terms used most often in the Bible to describe Israel's punishment for apostasy—Franklin claimed that America could become a "reproach and bye word down to future ages."[33] Given these rich scriptural motifs, Franklin's speech would not have been out of place in a Congregationalist meeting house. Nevertheless, one suspects that the piety on Franklin's part was more pretense than reality.[34]

It is true that Franklin wrote in his autobiography that he had "never doubted" the basic tenets of his religious creed.[35] But other writings tell a different story. In a revealing letter to Madame Brillon in France, Franklin in 1778 supplied a fable that may indicate the true extent of his religious skepticism.[36] Franklin recalled to Madame Brillon that once at her house he had been shown "numberless Skeletons of a kind of little Fly, called an Ephemere, all whose successive Generations we were told were bred and expired within the Day."[37] Franklin then whimsically remarked that, while walking in Madame Brillon's garden one day, he had happened on a company of ephemera engaged in conversation atop a leaf; and since he understood "all the inferior Animal Tongues," he had paused to listen. He told Madame Brillon that he had been particularly struck by the soliloquy of a certain "old greyheaded" ephemeron, who had lamented that he would not be able to enjoy the fruits of his arduous labors to benefit his race. Franklin then reprinted the soliloquy, which was rather obviously the lament of Franklin himself as he felt the futility of his own achievements. "My Friends would comfort me," wrote Franklin, "with the Idea of a Name they say I shall leave behind me. . . . But what will Fame be to an *Ephemere* who no longer exists? And what will become of all History in the 18th hour, when the world itself . . . shall come to its End, and be buried in universal Ruin?"[38]

What indeed will fame mean to someone who no longer exists? If death is the final end of one's personal identity—and if all history will end in cataclysm—where is the ultimate use of one's good works in this life? This bleak view seems to contradict not only Franklin's supposed beliefs in personal immortality and divine providence but also his public teaching of the efficacy of good works in the present life. Franklin's conclusion to his letter stepped back from this nihilistic view of the cosmos, but only a half step. Franklin noted that "after all my eager Pursuits, no solid pleasures now remain, but the Reflection of a long life spent in meaning well."[39] Here, then, is a limited defense of morality in this life: Even if one cannot achieve any permanent good in this world, even if one is not rewarded in the hereafter, one can have the satisfaction of a life lived well. In other words, virtue is its own reward. One can be happy to have led a virtuous life because it was the right and fitting thing to do. But though Franklin here rescued virtue, he did not do the same for immortality or providence. Franklin's remaining pleasure was his reflection on good deeds now past; there was no expectation of future immortality.

Additional evidence of Franklin's profound spiritual doubts can be found in a curious essay he wrote against monarchy titled "The Levee."[40] A standard eighteenth-century argument against monarchy was that no man is so wise and so good as to merit absolute power over another human being; only God is so omniscient and virtuous that he is fit to be king. In "The Levee," Franklin stood this argument on its head. Franklin first noted that temporal monarchs invite corruption because they are surrounded by designing courtiers "who seek to obtain favor by whispering calumny and detraction, and thereby ruining those that distinguish themselves by their virtue and merit."[41] The heavenly monarch, it turns out, is no different. Recalling the story of Job in the Old Testament, Franklin reminded the reader of how Satan turned God against his faithful servant Job by implying that Job served God only because God had blessed him. The moral of the story according to Franklin: "Trust not a single person with the government of your state. For if the Deity himself, being the monarch, may for a time give way to calumny, and suffer it to operate the destruction of the best of subjects; what mischief may you not expect from such power in a mere man?"[42] Thus, God himself is an imperfect ruler, giving into the lies of designing courtiers; and if God is not fit to be king, man is even less worthy to fill the role. This is not the way a pious man, even a pious Unitarian, spoke.[43]

Given the possibility of radical religious skepticism on the part of Franklin, one must approach with caution his statements about the importance of religion to society. Now it is true that Franklin thought that morality is necessary to the well-being of society. In his own words, "Only a virtuous people are capable of freedom."[44] It is also true that Franklin on several occasions mentioned the role churches could play in promoting morality.[45] But these comments raise several critical questions. First, does religion in fact promote the type of virtue championed by Franklin? If it does not, one must challenge Franklin's seriousness when he talks of the moral function of religion. Second, even if religion *does* promote the morality that Franklin envisioned, what is the precise relationship between religion and morality in society? Is religion somehow *necessary* for the development of virtue among the citizenry? Or is it merely helpful?

As to the question of whether Franklin's account of morality can be squared with the morality of the Bible, one must first emphasize the subsidiary place of revelation in Franklin's thought. Franklin did not regard the Bible as in any sense authoritative. As he pointed out in his autobiography, "Revelation indeed had no weight with me as such."[46] Nevertheless, Franklin still "entertained an opinion that, though certain actions might not be bad *because* they were forbidden by it, or good because it commanded them, yet probably these actions might be forbidden *because* they were bad for us, or commanded *because* they were beneficial to us in their own natures, all the circumstances of things considered."[47] So although reason, rather than revelation, supplied the foundation of morality for Franklin, he also maintained that reason and revelation converge on the same precepts. Certain acts may not be good or bad because the Bible praises or condemns them; but according to Franklin, it so happens that the Bible praises those things worth praising and condemns those things worth condemning. Or so Franklin suggested in this passage.

Thomas Pangle, for one, cannot believe that this is Franklin's real view of morality; Pangle speaks of the "zest for life that breathes through almost every page of the *Autobiography* and that is obviously intended to charm the reader out of every sort of Christian or post-Christian gloom."[48] If Pangle means here that Franklin did not believe in the Calvinist doctrine of total depravity, he is surely right. But if Franklin did not teach total depravity, neither did he teach anywhere that moral perfection is obtainable in this life. Franklin may have been cheerful; but he was not a Pollyanna. Indeed, if one reads Franklin carefully, one finds as an underlying theme the tenacity of human imperfection.

At one point in his life, for example, Franklin fancifully embarked on "the bold and arduous project of arriving at moral perfection."[49] But he soon discovered that he "had undertaken a task of more difficulty than I had imagined. While my care was employed in guarding against one fault, I was often surprised by another; habit took the advantage of inattention; inattention was sometimes too strong for reason."[50] In an effort to improve his success, Franklin adopted a somewhat comical regimen of diligently keeping track of all his failures in a book.[51] He again failed of perfection. His conclusion: "I never arrived at the perfection I had been so ambitious of obtaining, but fell far short of it, yet I was, by the endeavor, a better and happier man than I otherwise should have been if I had not attempted it."[52] Therefore, one should strive for moral perfection without expecting to achieve it; it will be a struggle, according to Franklin, but one will be better for it. If this line of thought is not identical with the Christian doctrine of man's sinfulness, it is still for the most part compatible with that view. This is not where the real problem with Franklin's morality lies from the standpoint of revelation.

The real difficulty with Franklin's morality vis-à-vis the Bible is its emphasis on man rather than God. Biblical morality of necessity finds its consummation in the character of God; one's highest duty is not to "love thy neighbor as thyself," but to "love the Lord thy God with all thy heart, and with all thy soul, and with all thy mind. This is the first and great commandment."[53] From this vantage point moral duties include faithful observance of the Sabbath, diligent prayer and study of the Bible, and efforts to save lost souls for Christ. These are not the sort of moral precepts Franklin had in mind. In fact, emphasis on such spiritual duties is precisely what Franklin found objectionable in the churches of his era. In his autobiography he recalled expectantly attending a worship service where the minister was to preach on Philippians 4:8: "Finally, brethren, whatsoever things are true, honest, just, pure, lovely, or of good report, if there be any virtue, or any praise, think on these things." Franklin listened to the sermon but was gravely disappointed because it stressed spiritual duties such as keeping the Sabbath, reading the Bible, and attending public worship rather than fulfilling civic duties.[54] For Franklin, "doing good to man" was the "most acceptable service of God"; hence, civic morality was to be the churches' main concern. Franklin therefore accorded less respect to those churches that stressed articles of religion "which, without any tendency to inspire, promote or confirm morality, served principally to divide us, and make us unfriendly to one another."[55]

Franklin seems to have envisioned an all-encompassing religion of civic morality, a religion without theological dogmas and creeds to which every citizen could subscribe. This new religion of morality would likely develop strong ties to politics as churchmen refocused their sights from the hereafter to the here and now. Thus, Franklin praised his friend the Reverend Samuel Mather when Mather commented in a tract on the growing controversy between America and Great Britain. Franklin wrote to Mather: "The Remarks you have added, on the late Proceedings against America, are very just and judicious; and I cannot at all see any Impropriety in your making them tho' a Minister of the Gospel. This Kingdom is a good deal indebted for its Liberties to the Publick Spirit of its ancient Clergy, who join'd with the Barons in obtaining Magna Charta."[56] Here we see the natural implications of Franklin's scheme of things: In Franklin's vision of society the clergy would be prized more highly for their public spirit than for their piety. Churches would be valued for their politicial utility rather than their spiritual necessity, and their primary function would shift from evangelization to the production of good citizens.

This view of religion is incompatible with any sort of evangelical Christianity or any sort of orthodox religion for that matter. Franklin's preoccupation with civic morality is problematic from the standpoint of revelation precisely because he wanted the churches to share that preoccupation to the detriment of their primary calling. One might therefore conclude that Franklin solved the tension between revelation and politics by subordinating revelation to politics, the solution of the ancient city. But this conclusion would be unwarranted. Franklin may have thought that civic morality was the churches' most important task, but he never really urged them to change their ways. Indeed, Franklin maintained a respectful stance even toward those churches whose dogmas he found divisive because they, too, preached civic morality. As long as a church upheld civic duties, it was helpful to the commonwealth, notwithstanding the other doctrines it also taught. And as long as a church was helpful to the commonwealth, it behooved statesmen to treat that church with respect and to do nothing to promote disrespect toward its doctrines. As Franklin wrote: "This respect to all, with an opinion that the worst had some good effects, induced me to avoid all discourse that might tend to lessen the good opinion another might have of his own religion; and as our province increased in people, and new places of worship were continually wanted, and generally erected by voluntary contribution, my mite for such purpose, whatever might be the sect, was never refused."[57]

It is this willingness to respect even sectarian religions that makes an equitable solution to the theological-political problem possible. Franklin may not have liked orthodoxy in religion; but he was not willing to wage war—in either word or deed—against orthodox religions. Religious adherents had nothing to fear in Franklin's political commonwealth. They would be left free and unhindered not only from restrictive laws but also from statements of disapprobation by those in authority.

One issue remains. Franklin wished churches to promote civic morality, but this still does not tell us the precise connection between religion and morality in Franklin's thought. Are churches somehow necessary to promote morality in civil society? Or might not the civic morality that Franklin sought be better promoted through secular means? Given that Franklin believed one could know morality through reason alone, and given that he thought most churches needlessly emphasized spiritual duties to the exclusion of civic ones, we must wonder why society should rely on such an imperfect teacher as religion to impart morality to its citizens.

Franklin could have answered that although the wise do not need religion to teach them morality, the great mass of humankind does. This was a standard argument of the period, one made by John Locke (regardless of whether he believed it) and by many others as well.[58] In 1757 Franklin embraced this argument in a letter to a young friend who had written a manuscript attacking particular divine providence. Franklin responded that religion must not be undercut because religion is practically necessary for the inculcation of moral habits. He suggested that the youth turn his reasoning to some "less hazardous Subject. . . . For among us, it is not necessary, as among the Hottentots that a Youth to be receiv'd into the Company of Men, should prove his Manhood by beating his Mother."[59]

Despite the clarity with which Franklin expressed this sentiment in 1757, whether he continued to maintain this view later in life remains unclear. Nearly three decades later, in the second part of his autobiography, he offered seemingly contradictory advice for making the average man moral. Franklin there discussed a book he proposed to write called *The Art of Virtue,* and religion played almost no part in his formulation, except for providing a ritualistic invocation to a vague higher power.[60] The heart of Franklin's new method of inculcating morality was embodied in the maxim "Nothing [is] so likely to make a man's fortune as virtue."[61] As Franklin explained: "In this piece [*The Art of Virtue*] it was my design to explain and enforce this doctrine, that vicious actions are not hurtful because they are forbidden, but forbidden because they are hurtful, the nature of man alone considered; that it was, therefore, every one's interest to be virtuous who wished to be happy even in this world; and I should, from this circumstance . . . have endeavored to convince young persons that no qualities were so likely to make a poor man's fortune as those of probity and integrity."[62]

One might easily conclude from this passage that Franklin made material self-interest the foundation of virtue: If we want to obtain wealth, we ought to be good.[63] Yet another interpretation is also tenable: Franklin may have believed in using self-interest to prod people onto the path of virtue, even while hoping that once they began to practice the virtues, they would eventually recognize that virtue was good for its own sake.[64] Hence, although self-interest might be the beginning of Franklin's moral system, it need not be its end.

Regardless of whether self-interest is the end or the beginning of Franklin's moral project, however, the problem for religion remains the same. If one can adequately convince people to practice the virtues because of rational self-interest, why should one continue to stress the moral function of religion? Religion may perhaps be helpful, but it can in no sense be necessary to civil society. Strangely enough, Franklin never seems to have reached this conclusion, perhaps because he never completed his grand moral project. He never wrote *The Art of Virtue;* and his secret society for the promotion of virtue among young men, The Society of the Free and Easy, was adopted by only two youths before Franklin abandoned the scheme.[65] Also, Franklin seems to have recognized in his later years that self-interest alone may not succeed in inculcating proper habits. The same year he wrote the second section of his autobiography Franklin acknowledged his own debt to Cotton Mather's religious tract *Essays to Do Good,* writing to Mather's son that it "gave me such a turn of thinking, as to have an influence on my conduct through life . . . and if I have been, as you seem to think, a useful citizen, the public owes the advantage of it to that book."[66] Three years later, in 1787, Franklin resorted to a religious appeal in the already discussed speech delivered at the Constitutional Convention.[67]

These actions at least call into question whether the aged Franklin really thought that civic virtue could be maintained without some public recourse to religion. One suspects that the eclectic father of American philosophy never saw reason and revelation as mutually exclusive. He probably thought that both are helpful in fostering morality and that therefore both ought to be encouraged. In his own words, "If Men are so wicked as we now see them *with Religion* what would they be if *without it?*"[68]

## John Witherspoon (1723?–1794)

If anyone spoke from the vantage point of revelation during the American Revolution, it was the Reverend John Witherspoon. Born and educated in Scotland, Witherspoon first rose to prominence battling theological moderates in the Scottish Presbyterian Church, and his religious statements reverberated with the doctrines of historic Christianity.[69] Witherspoon emigrated to America in 1768 to accept the presidency of the College of New Jersey (later known as Princeton).[70] He plunged into colonial politics a few years thereafter, becoming a member of the Somerset County Committee of Correspondence in 1774. Two years later he was elected to the Continental Congress, where he signed the Declaration of Independence and served with distinction on more than one hundred committees. He left Congress only after victory had been assured and the Articles of Confederation had been ratified, returning to Princeton to rebuild his war-ravaged college in 1782. From 1783 to 1789 he served in the New Jersey legislature, and in 1787 he was selected as a delegate to the New Jersey ratifying convention. He remained a respected and influential national figure until his death in 1794.[71]

Witherspoon's most profound impact on the new republic probably came in his role as teacher rather than statesman. As president of his college, he taught the required course in moral philosophy to each senior class, and his students included twenty future senators, twenty-five future congressmen, three future justices of the United States Supreme Court, thirteen future governors, and one future president—James Madison, who remained at Princeton after graduation to pursue further studies under Witherspoon.[72] Additional evidence of Witherspoon's influence can be culled from the list of persons who subscribed to the four-volume editions of his works published in 1800–1801 and 1802, respectively. Subscribers included George Washington, John Adams, Thomas Jefferson, John Jay, Benjamin Rush, and the presidents of most of the nation's major colleges and universities. A curious exception to the subscription list was Witherspoon's most famous student, James Madison.[73]

Witherspoon was an evangelical, yet his comments about the relationship between religion and society curiously paralleled those of Benjamin Franklin, the inveterate skeptic. It is not just that Witherspoon and Franklin both believed civic virtue to be the necessary foundation of society and public policy; it is that Witherspoon agreed with Franklin that churches had an obligation to produce good citizens and not just good Christians.

According to Witherspoon, churches were obligated to promote civic morality in return for the state's guarantee of religious liberty: "By our excellent [state] constitution, [religious societies] are well secured in their religious liberty. The return which is expected from them to the community, is that by the influence of their religious government, their people may be the more regular citizens, and the more useful members of society."[74] In Witherspoon's view, then, churches became the vanguard in the battle to inculcate civic virtue, which was well and good because "virtue and piety are inseparably connected . . . [and] to promote true religion is the best and most effectual way of making a virtuous and regular people."[75] Invoking the example of antiquity, Witherspoon further suggested that the churches had inherited the function of the Roman *censor morum,* who had the power of regulating the manners and morals of the people: "In ancient times, in great states the censorial power was found necessary to their continuance, which inspected the manners of men. It seems probable, that supporting the religious sects in modern times answers this end, for the particular discipline of each set, is intended for the correction of manners."[76]

But if morality is necessary for political prosperity and churches are necessary for morality, should not the government do everything in its power to promote religion? Witherspoon recognized that this question naturally arises from this line of reasoning, but he also understood the difficulties such a question poses for the rights of conscience, which he regarded as natural and unalienable.[77] According to Witherspoon, the government "ought to defend the rights of conscience, and tolerate all in their religious sentiments that are not injurious to their neighbors."[78] Even in cases where persons hold sentiments deemed subversive, the government should probably forgo interference:

It is commonly said . . . that in case any sect holds tenets subversive of society and inconsistent with the rights of others, that they ought not to be tolerated. On this footing Popery is not tolerated in Great Britain; because they profess entire subjection to a foreign power, the see of Rome. . . . But however just this may be in a way of reasoning, we ought in general to guard against persecution on a religious account as much as possible; because such as hold absurd tenets are seldom dangerous. Perhaps they are never dangerous, but when they are oppressed. Papists are tolerated in Holland without danger to liberty. And though not properly tolerated, they are now connived at in Britain.[79]

Hence, we arrive at an apparent paradox: Religion is necessary for the good society, but so is religious liberty. So the government is limited in what it can do to promote religion.

Nevertheless, Witherspoon believed that government could—and should—take certain actions to enable religion and morality to prosper, even while guaranteeing the rights of conscience. Government's first action should be to protect the right of conscience itself, for "the greatest service which magistrates or person in authority can do with respect to the religion or morals of the people, is to defend and secure the rights of conscience in the most equal and impartial manner."[80] Witherspoon never fully developed this thought (his student James Madison did years later in the "Memorial and Remonstrance"), but the idea seems fairly clear: Churches have the best chance to prosper when the government does not interfere with their affairs.

Now if Witherspoon had ended here, one could consider him a soulmate of James Madison and Thomas Jefferson. But Witherspoon went further in proposing government support for religion. He argued first that government officials "ought to encourage piety by [their] own example, and by endeavoring to make it an object of public esteem."[81] Next, he maintained that they ought to punish immorality, which for Witherspoon included profanity and impiety.[82] Finally, Witherspoon implied that a public tax could be levied to support ministers without violating the rights of conscience, though he did not expressly endorse such a tax—and New Jersey did not have one.[83] Here Witherspoon apparently envisioned the sort of arrangement that gradually prevailed in the New England colonies whereby public taxes went to support the religious denomination of the majority of citizens (in New England's case, Congregationalism) but whereby members of other denominations were often exempted from the taxes.[84]

Witherspoon's proposed measures would no doubt pose difficulties for religious liberty as understood today. But they did not necessarily contradict the rights of conscience as understood in Witherspoon's time. For example, a tax-supported church would be clearly unconstitutional today; but Witherspoon likely thought that exemption of dissenters from the tax would square the scheme with religious liberty, for this would guarantee that no one could be compelled to pay for a religion that went against his or her conscience.

As for laws against acts of profanity and impiety, one must first determine what these acts are to ascertain whether they would violate the rights of conscience. In the context of both the passage and the times, these acts likely included profane swearing and blasphemy. The criminalization of such forms of speech would undoubtedly contradict the rights of conscience in a society characterized by nearly unlimited freedom of expression; but eighteenth-century America was not such a society. Freedom of speech at that time largely meant freedom from prior censorship, and publishers were prosecuted for all sorts of injudicious statements after publication.[85] A firm distinction prevailed between liberty and licentiousness, and uncivil discourse—against either God or man—could land a person in jail. Given this situation, one need not accuse Witherspoon of a contradiction in his own mind if he supported laws punishing profanity and blasphemy. Within his own framework Witherspoon could logically grant a man's right to disagree with his neighbor about religion without conceding his right to propagate this belief in whatever intemperate language he so chose.

More difficult to square with Witherspoon's stated support of the rights of conscience is his insistence that government officials ought to encourage piety by their own example. If he meant merely that officials ought to encourage those who were already church members to persevere in their quest for piety and virtue, one might be able to see the propriety of Witherspoon's point. Regardless of an official's personal theological beliefs, he could praise churches for their moral function. This was Franklin's position. But if Witherspoon also meant that public officials were obligated to demonstrate their own piety in public by prayer, church attendance, and other actions, then clearly a difficulty exists here. The right of conscience protected most fundamentally a person's "right to judge for himself in all matters of religion,"[86] and public demands that anyone—either public official or private citizen—be pious seems to encroach on this right.

One might wonder, then, whether Witherspoon resolved the theological-political problem in favor of revelation after all. This suspicion seems to gain further credence from Witherspoon's belief that religion and morality are inseparably connected and that churches ought to be the primary teachers of morality. Precisely what connection links religion and morality, according to Witherspoon? Must one be a Christian to know right from wrong? Is revelation the only adequate foundation for civic morality? But if this is the case, the theological-political problem returns with a vengeance. If one must be moral to be a good citizen and a Christian to understand morality, then membership in the City of Man and membership in the City of God are again confounded and dissenters from the accepted religion must be cast from the fold.

That Witherspoon did not adhere to this position, however, becomes clear in his *Lectures on Moral Philosophy.*[87] In his first lecture Witherspoon tackled the question of how one comes to know morality, and he explicitly rejected the position of those Christians who maintained that revelation supplies the only foundation for morality. "Moral philosophy," Witherspoon announced at the start the lecture, ". . . is an inquiry into the nature and grounds of moral obligation by reason, as distinct from revelation."[88] Witherspoon acknowledged that some Christians had spurned such a pursuit as "reducing infidelity to a system,"[89] but, he replied, "if the Scripture is true, the discoveries of reason cannot be contrary to it; and therefore, it has nothing to fear from that quarter."[90]

Vigorously maintaining the unity of truth, Witherspoon here sought to show those who would base morality solely on revelation that a recourse to reason will enhance revelation's authority rather than diminish it and that proof of the morality of the Bible by reason may be a powerful way to convince skeptics of the trustworthiness of Scripture. To those who would still maintain that revelation supplies the only legitimate knowledge of morality, Witherspoon added: "The whole Scripture is perfectly agreeable to sound philosophy; yet certainly it was never intended to teach us every thing. The political law of the Jews contains many noble principles of equity, and excellent examples to future lawgivers; yet it was so local and peculiar, that certainly it was never intended to be immutable and universal."[91] In other words, the Bible may teach us the first principles of morality, but it cannot show us what to do in every particular situation—hence the need for moral philosophy.

Throughout these *Lectures* Witherspoon acted as the great harmonizer, papering over seemingly divergent intellectual positions to reach the broad common ground.[92] Witherspoon's implication seemed to be that reason, revelation, experience, tradition, and the moral sense all converge on the same moral precepts. Now if one read only the *Lectures on Moral Philosophy,* one might be tempted to conclude that Witherspoon had a rather facile grasp of

the subject matter, failing to recognize or delineate apparent tensions between revealed and natural morality, tensions that someone like Franklin apprehended quite readily. But such a conclusion would be wrong, for we
know from other writings that—whatever Witherspoon implied to the contrary in *Lectures*—he had a deep and sophisticated grasp of the tension between revealed and natural morality. Like Franklin, he thought that reason
and revelation agree substantially on many duties; but also like Franklin, he
had a keen awareness that autonomous human reason and divine revelation
diverge on what are ultimately the most praiseworthy virtues.

Witherspoon's serious reservations to the syncretist approach he adopted
in *Lectures on Moral Philosophy* came out most clearly in two addresses
first given in 1775. Significantly, both addresses were delivered on the Sabbath prior to the graduation of the senior class, which meant they were presented after the conclusion of Witherspoon's course in moral philosophy for
that year. The first was a sermon preached in Princeton titled "Christian
Magnanimity"; the second, Witherspoon's final address to the senior class.[93]
Both speeches cautioned against an overreliance on natural morality. It was
as if Witherspoon had decided suddenly that his students needed a corrective to his course on moral philosophy.

One can indeed know the basic precepts of morality through reason,
Witherspoon again told his students in these speeches; one can even live a
decent life without being a Christian, for one's own temporal happiness to
some degree dictates good behavior.[94] Nevertheless, the practice of these
temporal virtues alone is insufficient. To be truly virtuous, one must be
"born again" in Christ and pursue "the exercises of piety, a life of prayer
and communion with God. This is the source from which a real Christian
must derive the secret comfort of his heart, and which alone will give beauty,
consistency, and uniformity to an exemplary life."[95]

Witherspoon was not merely saying that Christianity completes natural
morality by adding to it; he was also arguing that sometimes Christian virtue
and worldly virtue seem to be fundamentally different. Nowhere is this difference more apparent than with regard to the virtue of magnanimity, or
greatness of soul. In classical morality magnanimity characterizes the best
man. As Aristotle said in the *Ethics,* "What is great in each virtue would
seem to be the mark of a magnanimous man. . . . Magnanimity thus is the
crown, as it were, of the virtues: it magnifies them and cannot exist without
them."[96] Thus, the magnanimous man practices all the rest of the virtues,

performing noble and difficult tasks, even at the risk of his life.[97] The problem magnanimity poses for Christianity becomes evident when one reads in Aristotle that a man is magnanimous "when he thinks he deserves great things and actually deserves them" and that the magnanimous man merits the sort of praise usually accorded to the gods.[98] In short, magnanimity elevates to a virtue that which Christianity condemns as the most damning of all sins—pride. Hence (in the words of Witherspoon), "the gospel seems to stand directly opposed to it. The humility of the creature, the abasement and contrition of the sinner, the dependance and self-denial of the believer, and above all, the shame and reproach of the cross itself, seem to conspire in obliging us to renounce it."[99]

And yet Witherspoon could not bring himself to renounce magnanimity, perhaps because he felt he had to answer the infidel philosophers who charged that "Christianity . . . by its precepts of meekness, humility, and passive submission to injury, has destroyed that nobleness of sentiment, which rendered the ancients so illustrious, and gives so much majesty and dignity to the histories of Greece and Rome."[100] So instead of denouncing magnanimity as a sin, Witherspoon radically reinterpreted it to make it compatible with both Christianity and American republicanism.[101]

According to Witherspoon, Christianity is the religion of true magnanimity because it requires the greatest and most difficult actions and seeks the highest and most noble possessions. It requires the greatest and most difficult actions because it commands us to "subdue every corrupt and sinful passion, however strongly the indulgence is solicited by the tempting object, or recommended by the artful seducer." And it demands that every believer "live for the glory of God, and the good of others"; endure the world's derision and scorn; and accept a martyr's death rather than deny the faith.[102] Christians likewise seek the highest end because their ambition is not temporal felicity but "the inheritance incorruptible and undefiled, and that fadeth not away."[103]

Witherspoon's master stroke came at the very end when he suddenly turned the tables on those who charged Christianity with the impoverishment of classical republicanism. He now implied that classical magnanimity contradicts the bedrock principle of *American* republicanism—equality:

Worldly magnanimity is what always requires such talents, as do not fall to the lot of many, and such opportunities for its exercise, as seldom occur. The road to heroism is not open to every man. But that magnanimity, which is the fruit of true religion . . . may be attained by persons of mean talents and narrow possessions, and in the very lowest stations of human life. In fact, there have been, and are daily examples of it in every rank. We see the heroic fortitude of the martyrs, as manifest in those of early years, and the weaker sex, as in any other; and whoever will visit the solitary walks of life, may find, in the lowest stations, humility, thankfulness, patience under affliction, and submission to Providence, such as would do honor to the most approved virtue, and the most enlightened mind.[104]

So here is the true religion for the new order, a religion of equality where all can achieve glory by their actions, whatever their station in life. Here "the honor which is chiefly desirable, is equally open to the rich and to the poor, to the learned and to the unlearned, to the wise and to the unwise, as it cometh from God, who is no respecter of persons."[105]

This is a fairly brilliant resolution to the problem, but it poses certain difficulties of its own. The implied message is that Christian morality is ultimately more conducive than natural morality to American republicanism. But if this is the case, public morality again becomes confused with religious duties, and the common ground between reason and revelation erodes. That Witherspoon's system indeed raises this difficulty becomes even more obvious in the Thanksgiving sermon he preached after the conclusion of the Revolutionary War. Speaking of how society ought to go about suppressing vice, Witherspoon identified the source of all immorality as "impiety against God" and demanded that the magistrates strike at the root and punish this impiety.[106] What is this remark but a demand that revelation be the authoritative guide in politics? Yet this is not what Witherspoon was arguing. One must note carefully the various vices he listed as he elaborated what he meant by impiety. He included such crimes against religion as "sabbath breaking" and "blasphemy"—but he also listed "idleness," "sloth," "luxury," "strife," "drunkenness," and "rioting."[107] In short, the majority of the vices that Witherspoon considered impious are also civil vices that unassisted human reason could condemn.

Nevertheless, that Witherspoon framed the issue in terms of impiety—and then included Sabbath breaking and blasphemy as among the fundamental causes of social distress—helps illumine the potentially uneasy relationship between religion and reason in the area of public morality. As long as political battles center on areas where revelation and unassisted human reason can reach common conclusions, the theological-political problem will be sublimated, for churchmen and statesmen alike can appeal to a common standard of morality. But what happens when public disputes erupt over such things as Sabbath breaking or blasphemy? During the Founding almost every state maintained laws on both subjects; they were accepted almost without question.[108] Yet their propriety would almost inevitably become controversial once the liberal ideas propagated by Franklin, Paine, and others began to attract followers.

Even if political battles remain properly focused on moral questions where reason and revelation can reach agreement, the sort of Christianity preached by Witherspoon still seems to foster tension between religion and politics. This is the case because for Witherspoon the decent man without religion is almost more dangerous to a believer than the man who is openly immoral. Witherspoon sternly advised his students to "shun, as a contagious pestilence, the society not only of loose persons, but of those especially whom you perceive to be infected with the principles of infidelity, or enemies to the power of religion—Many of these are much more dangerous to pious persons than open profligates."[109]

But if this is so, how ought one to deal with fellow citizens who are not Christians? Are Christians permitted to act in concert only with other Christians in politics? Then the theological-political problem recurs again. Political parties would form along sectarian lines, and Christians would feel obliged to vote only for those candidates who openly propagated Christianity. Religious strife once again would translate into political strife. That the potential for such an outcome is inherent in Witherspoon's position seems apparent from some of his comments on the kind of rulers that citizens ought to elect. He warned that "those . . . who pay no regard to religion and sobriety, in the persons whom they send to the legislature of any state, are guilty of the greatest absurdity, and will soon pay dear for their folly."[110] In a related area Witherspoon vigorously defended the right of ministers to seek political office, which would seem even more likely to inject sectarian strife into the political process.

Yet in the final analysis, Witherspoon's system probably would not lead to sectarian strife in politics because of certain important caveats. First, when discussing the qualifications of rulers, he emphasized moral character in general rather than piety. Nor did he demand that a ruler be extraordinarily pious; Witherspoon merely suggested that it would be inappropriate to have someone "known to be a blasphemer or an infidel" as a magistrate, implying that an inquiry into a candidate's specific religious beliefs need not be prosecuted unless he chooses himself to raise the matter by injecting religion into his public life.[111] In other words, quiet skeptics might be acceptable; one should refuse to vote only for those who openly scoff at Christianity—which, after all, would be not only impious but also unbefitting a gentleman. As for Witherspoon's advocacy of the right of ministers to run for public office, he never presumed to argue that ministers have a right to public office derived from their spiritual authority; instead, he based his argument squarely on the fact that ministers are also citizens and therefore ought to enjoy the same rights and privileges as every other citizen.[112] As a practical matter Witherspoon thought ministers involved in public life ought to keep their religious and public duties separate. As a general rule he did not think ministers should preach politics from the pulpit. There are exceptions to almost every rule, of course, and Witherspoon did note that sometimes during great crises ministers might have to act otherwise, as he himself did on at least two occasions.[113] But the general principle of a separation between spiritual and civic duties remained.

One must also understand the limited extent of Witherspoon's strictures against the formation of friendships with nonbelievers. He did not apply this maxim to civic friendships. Indeed, directly after he implored his students to shun those who lead decent lives but are impious against God, Witherspoon counseled against "pharisaical pride and superciliousness, far less, a rash and presumptuous judging of the state of others. It is not only lawful, but our duty, to have a free communication with our fellow-citizens, for the purpose of social life: it is not only lawful, but our duty to be courteous, and to give every proper evidence of respect and attention to others."[114]

That this does not completely resolve the tension between religion and politics may be granted. Witherspoon spoke from the standpoint of revelation, and he could never deny its ultimate primacy. Reason was the handmaiden of revelation for Witherspoon, just as religion was subordinate to reason in the mind of Franklin. But even so, both men were able to moderate their claims on behalf of civil harmony. They could agree to disagree about the highest matters so they could join together to find solutions to earthly matters. Thus, one already sees glimmers of the Founders' solution to the theological-political problem.

## THE FEDERALISTS: WASHINGTON, WILSON, HAMILTON, ADAMS, AND JAY

### George Washington (1732–1799)

No one who reads either the public or private writings of George Washington can seriously doubt that he devoutly held at least certain rudimentary religious beliefs. The doctrine of God's providence, in particular, suffuses almost everything he wrote, from public addresses to private correspondence. Commenting on the successful completion of the Revolution, he noted in a letter to the Reformed German Congregation of New York: "Disposed, at every suitable opportunity to acknowledge publicly our infinite obligations to the Supreme Ruler of the Universe for rescuing our Country from the brink of destruction; I cannot fail at this time to ascribe all the honor of our late successes to the same glorious Being."[115] Responding to a report that his crops were failing because of drought, Washington calmly wrote his manager at Mt. Vernon, "At disappointments and losses which are the effects of Providential acts, I never repine; because I am sure the alwise disposer of events knows better than we do, what is best for us, or what we deserve."[116] And on learning that a friend had just lost three children, Washington gently advised him, "I participated in the sorrows which I know you must have felt for your late and heavy losses. But [it] is not for man to scan the wisdom of Providence. The best he can do, is to submit to its decrees."[117]

Washington's religious convictions as expressed in his writings are almost identical with the tenets listed by Franklin in his letter to Ezra Stiles. Like Franklin, Washington articulated his belief in one God who rules the world by his providence, the efficacy of good works, and the immortality of the soul. The crucial difference between Washington and Franklin on these matters is one of sincerity: Whereas Franklin's real beliefs are at best a mystery, there is little reason to doubt that Washington actually subscribed to this basic creed. But what else Washington believed remains unclear. The evidence on the subject is partial, contradictory, and, in the end, unsatisfactory.

On the one hand, Washington was a regular member of an evangelical denomination, the Episcopal Church of Virginia; and he served faithfully in that church in the lay office of vestryman, an office that would have required him to take an oath of loyalty to the doctrinal confession of the church.[118] Moreover, in his circular to the states in 1783 Washington referred to Christ as "the Divine Author of our blessed religion."[119] On the other hand, Washington refused the sacrament of Holy Communion during at least some parts of his life, and his statement about Christ in the circular was one of his only specifically Christian doctrinal statements.[120] Usually he appeared to regard differences in theology as irrelevant, commenting at one point, "Being no bigot myself to any mode of worship, I am disposed to indulge the professors of Christianity in the church, that road to Heaven, which to them shall seem the most direct plainest easiest and least liable to exception."[121] In his letter to the Hebrew congregation at Newport, Rhode Island, Washington went further, implying that eternal felicity is open to good people from all religions. At the end of that letter, Washington prayed that "the father of all mercies scatter light and not darkness in our paths, and make us all in our several vocations useful here, and in his own due time everlastingly happy."[122] Had Washington ended his letter with an invocation of temporal felicity only, the theological question would not have been broached. But by adding the request for eternal bliss ("everlastingly happy"), Washington held out the prospect that all good men, regardless of religion, can be saved.

One does not need to untangle the subtleties of Washington's personal piety, however, to understand his view of the role of religion in society. Whatever the ambiguities of his private theology, Washington's political theology was far from ambiguous. Like both Franklin and Witherspoon, Washington embraced the moral function of religion, and like Witherspoon, Washington expected churches to produce good citizens in grateful return for religious liberty. He wrote to the General Assembly of Presbyterian Churches in 1789: "While all men within our territories are protected in worshipping the Deity according to the dictates of their consciences; it is rationally to be expected in return that they will be emulous of evincing the sanctity of their professions by the innocence of their lives and the beneficence of their actions; for no man, who is profligate in his morals, or a bad member of the civil community, can possibly be a true Christian, or a credit to his own religious society."[123] As can be seen from this passage, Washington saw a convergence between Christianity and civic morality: Civic morality and Christian morality were the same.

Like the rest of the Founding generation, Washington believed steadfastly that reason and revelation agree on the basic precepts of morality. Unlike Franklin and Witherspoon, however, Washington almost never probed the parameters of this agreement. He chose not to worry about the areas where reason and revelation might disagree, though he certainly knew that such disagreements were possible, as in the case of Quakers who refused to take up arms in defense of their country.[124] Washington's unwillingness to concentrate on the disagreements between reason and revelation is understandable. He was a statesman, and his preeminent concern was not speculation but practice. His purpose was to lay the solid foundations on which a republic could be built, and exploration of the tensions between reason and revelation would have detracted from this purpose.

For most of his life Washington also steered clear of the controversy over whether religion is necessary to promote civic virtue. When he finally broached the subject in the famous passage in his Farewell Address, he treated it with his usual moderation. Washington at first characterized the idea "that morality can be maintained without religion" a "supposition," indicating his sympathy with the churchmen. Nevertheless, Washington also met the rationalists halfway: He argued that even if one concedes that education alone can instill morality, it can do so only in "minds of peculiar structure," for "reason and experience both forbid us to expect that National morality can prevail in exclusion of religious principle."[125] In other words, even if the morality of the ruling class does not depend on religion, morality among the general citizenry does; hence, religion remains a *political* necessity, if not an intellectual one.

Although often treated as a proof text, this passage on religion and morality was far more than empty rhetoric on Washington's part. It was a summary of how he had lived his public life. Indeed, the full meaning of this section of the Farewell Address can be understood only in light of Washington's actions as a statesman. Throughout his public career he actively promoted piety as essential to temporal political prosperity. As a general during the Revolution, he issued frequent orders encouraging his soldiers to attend worship services and to cease taking God's name in vain.[126] Washington also declared days of thanksgiving for the army after major victories;[127] and after the war concluded, he applauded a minister's proposal that Congress present a Bible to every soldier in the Continental Army, though he noted that the proposal came too late to be put into effect because most of the soldiers had already been discharged.[128]

Returning to private life in Virginia, Washington embraced Patrick Henry's assessment bill that would have taxed citizens to support Christian ministers of their choice. After it became clear that the assessment was attracting a great deal of opposition, however, Washington wished the measure a swift death because he thought enacting it over the wishes of a "respectable minority" would be "impolitic."[129] As president Washington continued to advocate a public role for religion, issuing two national thanksgiving proclamations, the first after the adoption of the Constitution at the recommendation of Congress and the second in 1795 after Jay's Treaty had been negotiated with England and the Whiskey Rebellion had been successfully put down.[130]

In trying to summarize Washington's view of the public role of religion, one must remember several things. First, unlike Franklin, Washington saw no difficulty in incorporating religious duties such as Sabbath observance and reverence toward the name of God into civic morality. In the latter case profanity against God was forbidden by "decency and order" as well as by revelation.[131] This view was undoubtedly in part a product of Washington's gentlemanly code of civility; but it was also a manifestation of his all-encompassing belief in providence. Washington stressed time and again that the nation's prosperity depended on God's providence, which implied that impiety would make us the objects of God's wrath rather than the recipients of his mercy.[132] In this Washington clearly echoed the political theology of evangelical ministers such as Witherspoon.

Despite Washington's support of the civil obligation of certain religious duties, however, one must remember that for him (as for Franklin) religion was defined less by its theological doctrines than by its moral code. Hence, for Washington "religion" was not synonymous with Protestant Christianity or even with Christianity in general. In his view any religion that promoted civic morality was entitled to the protection of the state: "As mankind become more liberal, they will be more apt to allow, that all those who conduct themselves as worthy members of the community are equally entitled to the protection of civil government."[133] This position he reiterated in his letters to congregations of evangelicals, Catholics, and Jews. These letters demonstrate not only his steadfast commitment to religious liberty for all but also his amazing ability to appear pious to members of even rival religions. To Presbyterians he spoke like a God-fearing Protestant,[134] to Methodists he implied his support for revivals in religion,[135] to Jews he invoked the Old Testament,[136] and to American Catholics he wrote that they were "animated alone by the pure spirit of Christianity."[137] Perhaps there is no greater testament to Washington's rhetorical skills in this area than the fact that after his death competing sects, from Catholics to Unitarians, sought to claim him as their own.[138]

But if Washington's definition of religion as morality extends the scope of religious liberty, it also raises a question about religion's proper limits. If the political function of religion is civic morality, what happens if a religion does not promote civic morality? What happens if a religion promotes self-indulgence rather than self-sacrifice? Does that religion also have the right to exist? Or what happens if a religion disagrees in principle with necessary state functions such as the waging of war?

In his letters to various churches, Washington made a point of stressing the need for church members to obey the government and to fulfill all their obligations as citizens.[139] Indeed, he seemed to make religious liberty for a sect contingent on the good citizenship of its members. To the Quakers he wrote in 1789, "*While* men perform their social duties faithfully, they do all that society or the state can with propriety demand or expect; and remain responsible only to their Maker for the religion, or modes, of faith which they may prefer or profess."[140] The implied corollary is that when men do not perform their social duties faithfully because of religious objections, they must answer to the government as well as to God. Of course, this is precisely what worried the Quakers, who were pacifists. They did not want to be persecuted for their refusal to fight during wartime; yet the very connection Washington drew between religious liberty and a religion's usefulness to the state seemed to invite persecution of religious adherents who could not in good conscience agree with state policy.

But Washington sought to circumvent this conclusion with a caveat. After observing that the Quakers were "exemplary and useful citizens" except for "their declining to share with others the burthen of the common defense," he added: "I assure you very explicitly, that in my opinion the conscientious scruples of all men should be treated with great delicacy and tenderness; and it is my wish and desire, that the laws may always be as extensively accommodated to them, as a due regard to the protection and essential interests of

RELIGION AND THE AMERICAN FOUNDING    41

the nation may justify and permit." Ever the gentleman, Washington assured the Quakers that even they merited protection from the government whenever possible, for religious objections to general laws ought to be accommodated as long as they do not contradict "a due regard to the protection and essential interests of the nation."[141] In this passage one finds a distant anticipation of the "compelling state interest" test adopted by the Supreme Court in the twentieth century for use in religious liberty cases.[142]

Washington appears to have applied this same sort of reasoning to the Virginia assessment bill. In a letter defending his initial support for the bill, Washington argued that non-Christians did not have to be penalized by its provisions because they could "declare themselves Jews, Mahometans or otherwise, and thereby obtain proper relief."[143] Here again Washington acknowledged the need for religious exemptions to a generally applicable law. Thus, Washington prized religious freedom even above the uniform application of the laws, as long as the essential interests of the nation did not dictate otherwise.

## James Wilson (1742–1798)

Although all but forgotten in the popular imagination today, James Wilson was viewed by contemporaries as one of America's greatest minds in the area of political and legal theory. To cite the words of Major William Pierce, a fellow delegate with Wilson to the Constitutional Convention of 1787: "Mr. Wilson ranks amongst the foremost in legal and political knowledge. . . . No man is more clear, copious, and comprehensive. . . . He draws the attention not by the charm of his eloquence, but by the force of his reasoning."[144] Given Wilson's reputation, it is no surprise that he played a key role in forging the fundamental political institutions of our country. Wilson was a member of the Continental Congress and signed the Declaration of Independence; he actively participated in the Federal Constitutional Convention of 1787, the Pennsylvania Ratifying Convention, and the Pennsylvania State Constitutional Convention of 1790. On the ratification of the Constitution, he served as an associate justice of the Supreme Court. Wilson also became the first lecturer in law at the College of Philadelphia, and his inaugural lecture was attended by such luminaries as George Washington, John Adams, and Thomas Jefferson. Wilson desired to be chief justice of the Supreme Court, and had his various financial speculations not tarnished his character (at the end of his life he was literally in flight from creditors), President Washington probably would have granted Wilson's wish.[145]

Despite the dubious ethics of some of Wilson's business dealings, in the realm of the mind he clearly was the equal of any of the other Founders. His law lectures rivaled *The Federalist* in their comprehensive exposition of the principles of American government; indeed, the lectures self-consciously tried to supplant William Blackstone's *Commentaries* as the authoritative exposition of law in America.[146] Of all the Founders, Wilson provided the most comprehensive discussion of the nature of law. Drawing heavily from "the sagacious Hooker," Wilson first noted that there are several "different kinds" of law.[147] "All, however, may be arranged in two different classes. 1. Divine. 2. Human laws. The descriptive epithets employed denote, that the former have God, the latter, man, for their author."[148] Divine law can be broken down further into four subcategories. First is the "law eternal," which Wilson defined as "that law, the book of which we are neither able nor worthy to open. Of this law, the author and observer is God. He is a law to himself, as well as to all created things."[149] In other words, this part of divine law relates to God's providence: God's secret counsels and plans that cannot be known unless He chooses to reveal them. Second is the "law celestial," by which God governs heaven. Third are the physical "laws of nature," that is, those rules "by which the irrational and inanimate parts of the creation are governed." Fourth—and most important with regard to politics—is the divine law, as it respects men and nations. This is

that law, which God has made for man in his present state; that law, which is communicated to us by reason and conscience, the divine monitors within us, and by the sacred oracles, the divine monitors without us. . . .

As promulgated to men, it has been denominated the law of nature; as addressed to political societies, it has been denominated the law of nations.

But it should always be remembered, that this law, natural or revealed, made for men or for nations, flows from the same divine source: it is the law of God.

Wilson did not claim—and no previous adherent of natural law had ever maintained—that natural law tells us everything. But it does, according to him, supply us with the fundamental maxims of morality, such as "No injury should be done" and a "Lawful engagement, voluntarily made, should be faithfully fulfilled." These maxims in turn lay down the only legitimate foundation for human law: "What we do . . . must be founded on what he [God] has done; and the deficiencies of our laws must be supplied by the perfections of his. Human law must rest its authority, ultimately, upon the authority of that law, which is divine."[150]

Wilson's framework, at least on the surface, was thoroughly consistent with the historic Christian conception of natural law, and someone like John Witherspoon would have recognized it as such. Unlike Franklin, Adams, and Jefferson, all of whom rejected the Bible as revelation but nevertheless maintained that it provides a true expression of moral law through the teachings of Jesus, Wilson argued that reason and revelation converge on the same moral law because *both* are authoritative routes to the divine mind. In other words, the Bible is authoritative not merely because it happens to coincide with what reason and the moral sense tell us but also because it embodies the "sacred oracles" of the omnipotent God.

But if reason and revelation are both authoritative guides to moral law, what is their practical relation in the realm of politics? Is one a better guide than the other? And what is the proper function of religion in society? Wilson never answered these questions quite as explicitly as some other Founders, but answers are nevertheless forthcoming for those who read him carefully.

First, although Wilson maintained that reason and revelation are both authoritative routes to the divine mind, he did not say that they are equally authoritative. Instead, again adhering to the traditional Christian position, Wilson argued that revelation is superior because it is more explicit; moreover, it is needed because reason and conscience alone are imperfect.[151] Thus, where the Bible is clear, according to Wilson, there is no need for further debate; the question is decided presumptively in favor of the Bible. Of course, part of the difficulty is that answers to political questions are not always evident in the Scriptures, as even an evangelical such as John Witherspoon readily acknowledged. So, according to Wilson, "whoever expects to find, in them [the Scriptures], particular directions for every moral doubt which arises, expects more than he will find. They generally presuppose a knowledge of the principles of morality."

As a practical matter, then, revelation cannot help us decide many actual political questions; it can only reaffirm with a louder voice certain basic precepts of natural law. This does not imply that religion—and, subsequently, revelation—is unnecessary for the well-being of society. According to Wilson, reason, conscience, and revelation all work together, and by their combined efforts move society in the right direction: "The information with regard to our duties and obligations, drawn from these different sources, ought not to run in unconnected and diminished channels: it should flow in one united stream, which, by its combined force and just direction, will impel us uniformly and effectually toward our greatest good."[152] All three springs of morality are necessary to society; and all three must speak with one voice in the realm of morality.

Expanding on this argument in a later lecture, Wilson announced that his "humble task [will] be to select and make such observations concerning our powers, our dispositions, our principles, and our habits, as will illustrate the intimate connexion and reciprocal influence of religion, morality, and law."[153] After making this announcement, however, Wilson set off in another direction, and he never explicitly made the promised comparison. But he did so implicitly, for throughout his remaining lectures he introduced major themes by quoting scriptural texts and then showing how reason and the moral sense correspond to the view propounded by Scripture.[154] By continuing throughout his lectures to refer to Scripture as well as the deductions of reason and the inductions of moral sense, Wilson further drove home his message that reason, conscience, and revelation are mutually reinforcing in the realm of politics.[155]

These passages demonstrate how closely Wilson agreed with Washington's view of the public role of religion. According to Wilson, religion provides the bedrock of society, and government therefore has the responsibility to encourage religion, even while keeping the rights of conscience inviolate.[156] This position echoed Witherspoon as well as Washington, but unlike Witherspoon, Wilson never discussed what it means to encourage religion while at the same time protecting religious liberty.

Notwithstanding Wilson's clear teaching that reason, revelation, and moral conscience agree on the nature of morality, some critics have dismissed this argument as mere rhetoric. They contend that Wilson, following the lead of Thomas Hobbes and John Locke, ultimately reduced moral law to the instinct for self-preservation. If this interpretation is correct, Wilson's moral system would be clearly incompatible with both Christianity and classical political philosophy, and the avowed synthesis he sought to achieve between reason and revelation would disintegrate.[157]

But to make this argument, one must radically reinterpret much of what Wilson himself said. Far from demonstrating an affinity for Hobbes and Locke, Wilson explicitly attacked the views of both as destructive of morality and religion. And far from promoting self-preservation as man's highest end, Wilson contended that "the moral sense displays peculiar inflexibility: it dictates that we should submit to any distress or danger, rather than procure our safety and relief by violence on an innocent person."[158] Self-preservation, in other words, must be tempered by the restraints of the moral law.

Nevertheless, there *are* certain tensions within Wilson's moral system that cannot be overlooked. Wilson did employ the terminology of modern philosophy (i.e., of Hobbes and Locke), even though he hearkened back to an older conception of the universe. He did on occasion go too far in arguing for the compatibility of private interest with public virtue. And he did gloss over those areas where reason, the moral sense, and biblical morality might differ— though when discussing coerced confessions, he implicitly acknowledged the possibility of disagreement. Citing the famed Cesare Beccaria, author of *Crimes and Punishments* (1764), Wilson argued that to compel someone to testify against himself under oath creates an unconscionable rift between revealed morality and the "natural sentiments of mankind."[159] "Can a man think himself obliged to contribute to his own destruction? Why should he be reduced to the terrible alternative of doing this, or of offending against God? For the law, which, in such a case, requires an oath, leaves him only the choice of being a bad christian, or of being a martyr."[160] In other words, when a man testifies falsely after swearing an oath to God, he invites divine retribution; but if he tells the truth, he guarantees his punishment by civil authorities, which makes testifying contrary to the natural desire for self-preservation. The solution, according to Wilson, is for the law not to put a citizen in such an untenable situation. As Wilson emphasized throughout his law lectures, reason, conscience, religion, and law ought to move together in the same direction, mutually reinforcing one another. When they do not, something is fundamentally wrong with the nation's laws.

## Alexander Hamilton (1755?–1804)

Arrogant, yet in his own way gallant and magnanimous, Alexander Hamilton was full of paradoxes. Born the illegitimate son of a West Indies merchant, he rose to the pinnacle of America's ruling class and was accused by opponents of advocating an American aristocracy.[161] A fierce and sometimes ruthless politician, Hamilton could nevertheless treat political enemies with remarkable charity. During the Revolutionary War he befriended the Tory president of King's College, later rescuing him from a mob of patriots who had gathered outside his house.[162] After the war, when it became all too popular to deprive former Tories of their property in violation of the peace treaty, Hamilton publicly defended their civil rights.[163]

Hamilton's private life had contradictions of its own. Tender as a father, usually devoted as a husband, he committed adultery while secretary of the Treasury, a sorry episode that he later publicly exposed to exculpate himself from false charges that he had used his federal office for private financial gain.[164] Accused of being both heartless and calculating, Hamilton time and again acted with great kindness. When a comrade in arms was killed during the Revolutionary War, leaving an orphan daughter, Hamilton took the girl into his own home and raised her as his own. When friends were in debt, Hamilton intervened with their creditors or tried to find some way to raise the needed money.[165]

The same kinds of inconsistencies cropped up in Hamilton's religious life. Hamilton's first known published essay, written at the age of fourteen, was a theological meditation on a hurricane that had devastated the island of Saint Croix.[166] His first patron was Presbyterian minister Hugh Knox, who helped Hamilton begin his education in America.[167] As Hamilton became older, however, his religious devotion appears to have significantly diminished, though there is no indication that he ever became a deist.[168] Unlike some other Founders, Hamilton's lack of evangelical piety was less the result of intellectual doubts than of a lapse in fervor. Near the end of his life, the fervor seemed to return, and he renewed his attachment to the religion of his youth, perhaps spurred on by the death of his eldest son in a duel in 1802.[169]

Whatever the perambulations of his private piety, Hamilton was consistent in championing the political efficacy of religion throughout his life. He was largely responsible for Washington's Farewell Address,[170] and the comments contained therein regarding the political necessity of religion described his own view as well, though Hamilton was undoubtedly more cynical on the subject. Hamilton perceived the political uses of religion early, recording in his commonplace book in 1776 the following quote from Plutarch's *Life of Numa Pompilius:* "He [Numa] was a wise prince and went a great way in civilizing the romans. The chief engine he employed for this purpose was religion, which could alone have sufficient empire over the minds of a barbarous and warlike people to engage them to cultivate the arts of peace."[171] Years later Hamilton would write a memo to William L. Smith arguing for a national fast day on much the same grounds, though in this case Hamilton looked to religion to prepare a nation for war with France rather than peace. Even as Hamilton sought to utilize religion for political ends, however, he maintained that reason and revelation could independently agree on the course of action to be pursued. The "philosopher" *and* the "Christian" should be able to recognize the need for a "rational appeal to Heaven for protection."[172] The politician, who has his own distinct reasons for wanting a day of prayer, appears here as the common broker between philosophy and religion—the great harmonizer who forges a union between philosophy and religion in defense of the national interest.

A year after writing to Smith, Hamilton followed his own advice about advancing Federalist foreign policy by an appeal to religion, and as part of a series of newspaper articles attacking France, he publicly denounced the French Revolution's efforts to undermine Christianity. There were similarities in theme between these essays and Washington's Farewell Address. Again, religion and morality are described as inseparably connected; they are the "venerable pillars that support the edifice of civilized society." And the "politician who loves liberty" equally with the "pious and the moral" regrets the example set by France.[173] Unlike in Hamilton's draft of the Farewell Address, however, there is no longer any concession to the "effect of refined education in minds of a peculiar structure." Instead, "morality *must* fall with religion."[174] And unlike the calming eloquence of the Farewell Address, the tone here is savage; the purpose, undeniably partisan.[175]

One suspects that Hamilton was using religion in this essay more as a rhetorical ploy than as a genuine principle of political action, which suggests that Hamilton, perhaps more than any other Founder, embraced the political theology of the ancient city. Whereas both Washington and Wilson stressed the good that churches could do as independent actors in society, Hamilton tended to reduce religion to a tool to be employed by skillful politicians. One of Hamilton's friends, the Reverend John Mason, helped spearhead an attack by the clergy on presidential candidate Thomas Jefferson during the election campaign of 1800;[176] and in 1802 Hamilton himself proposed a "Christian Constitutional Society" that would have connected Christianity, benevolence, and political action.[177] Historians Douglas Adair and Marvin Harvey labeled this latter proposal a "rather terrifying project" that would have "blow[n] up the fires of religious intolerance."[178] Yet this is probably a misrepresentation. Hamilton, like every other Founder, believed that the basic moral principles on which political arguments rest are sanctioned by reason as well as revelation.[179] Hence, had Hamilton organized the Christian Constitutional Society, the group would have been less likely to stress sectarian religion than the basic principles of morality that were shared across denominational lines.

Despite Hamilton's tendency to make religion subservient to politics, this was not the whole of his political theology. His view of the relationship between religion and politics was neither as principled as some of his public pronouncements suggested nor as Machiavellian as some of his critics have charged. Despite his personal vanity and sometimes overweening ambition, Hamilton usually tried to live in accordance with his stated principles of action. The events leading up to his death show how gravely he took his oft-stated connection between religion and public action, at least in the final portion of his life.

Late in the morning on June 18, 1804, Aaron Burr sent the first of what would become a series of notes to Hamilton. Burr demanded that Hamilton confirm or deny allegations advanced by Charles Cooper that Hamilton had made unspecified attacks on Burr's character.[180] Hamilton at first refused to issue such a blanket acknowledgment or denial but indicated that he was "ready to avow or disavow promptly and explicitly any precise or definite opinion, which I may be charged with having declared of any Gentleman."[181] Burr renewed his inquiry several times, however, and Hamilton finally relented in part and gave assurance that "the conversation to which Doctr Cooper alluded turned wholly on political topics and did not attribute to Colo. Burr, any instance of dishonorable conduct, nor relate to his private character."[182] Unsatisfied, Burr expanded his demands. He now insisted that Hamilton issue a blanket denial that would "wholly exclude the idea that [any] rumors derogatory to Col: Burr's honor have originated with Genl. Hamilton as have been *fairly* inferred from any thing he has said."[183] Hamilton again tried to meet Burr halfway, indicating that he was "not conscious that any charges that are in circulation to the prejudice of Col. Burr have Originated with him."[184] But Hamilton added that he could not be more definitive unless Burr himself was more specific in describing the content of the alleged rumors. At this point Burr challenged Hamilton to a duel.

Hamilton found himself in a prickly position. As a matter of personal principle, he felt he could not supply a blanket apology because he thought his criticisms had been on the whole proper and correct. As a matter of political prudence, he felt he could not refuse the challenge because to do so would brand him a coward and diminish his political effectiveness among the ruling class in which he held sway.[185] Hamilton therefore calculated that he had to accept Burr's demand for satisfaction. But there was something besides honor and politics at stake in Hamilton's decision: his Christianity. Hamilton understood that the teachings of Christianity were incompatible with dueling.[186] Therein lay his difficulty. His own calculations of political prudence and principle (however misguided they might have been) told him to meet Burr on the field of honor; his Christian convictions demanded that he refuse. In the end Hamilton tried to have it both ways. He accepted the duel but wrote his wife that he would not fire at Burr.[187] Thus he would retain his fidelity both to Christianity and his politics of reason, but only by greatly increasing the prospects of his own death.

What actually happened on the morning of the duel is still the subject of considerable debate. Hamilton's second claimed that Burr had fired first and that Hamilton's gun had subsequently discharged involuntarily as Hamilton was falling to the ground.[188] Burr and his second alleged that Hamilton had fired first and that Burr had responded several seconds later.[189] Physical evidence at the scene, as well as the testimony of the dying Hamilton, suggested that Hamilton—in one last act of staggering gallantry—had reserved his fire.[190] If so, his death confirmed the extraordinary lengths he had been willing to go to in defense of the agreement between revelation and reason.

## John Adams (1735–1826)

John Adams complained to Benjamin Rush in 1811 that critics charged him with hypocrisy any time he tried to speak on behalf of religion.[191] Yet there were certainly grounds for this charge. In private he was a thoroughgoing deist; in public he strove to appear an orthodox Christian, even going so far as to issue fast day proclamations that embodied the trinitarian conception of God.[192] Clearly his public and private lives contradicted each other, regardless of whether Adams wished to acknowledge that this was so. Writing privately to Jefferson in 1813, he intimated as much. Quoting a proverb from Hesiod that one should "honor the gods established by law," Adams commented, "I know not how We can escape Martyrdom, without a discreet Attention to this præcept. You have suffered, and I have suffered more than You, for want of a strict if not a due Observance of this Rule."[193] The religion of the masses was evangelical Christianity, and Adams—like Franklin—knew that to survive he had to accommodate himself to the public's prejudices.

This is not to suggest that Adams's numerous statements on behalf of religion were merely cynical attempts to curry public favor. Adams sincerely regarded himself as a pious Christian, but what he meant by Christianity was something far different than what was in the mind of the average minister or layman. For Adams Christianity was preeminently the religion of "reason, equity, and love,"[194] and any of its doctrines that could not be verified independently by human reason had to be jettisoned—or, at the very least, doubted. True, Adams believed that Christianity was a revelation from God, but his definition of revelation was more than a little slippery. He wrote to Jefferson that "phylosophy which is the result of Reason, is the first, the original Revelation of The Creator to his Creature, Man. When this Revelation is clear and certain, by Intuition or necessary Inductions, no subsequent Revelation supported by Prophecies or Miracles, can supercede it."[195] Adams did not deny that God could perform miracles, but at best he thought they could only prepare the mind of the masses to accept the reasonings of philosophers.[196] By extension, when supposed revelations appear to conflict with human reason, they ought to be rejected outright—no matter how well authenticated they are by miracles or prophecies. As Adams wrote Jefferson: "We can never be so certain of any prophecy, or of any miracle, as we are from the revelation of nature, that is, Nature's God, that two and two are equal to four. Miracles or prophecies might frighten us out of our wits; might scare us to death; might induce us to lie, to say that we believe that two and two make five. But we should not believe it. We should know the contrary."[197]

In sum, Adams's God was much more the theoretical anchor of the universe than a living being active in history. Unlike Washington, Adams presented no clear picture of a God who actively rules the world by his providence. Adams instead reduced religion to a series of ethical injunctions, thereby making it indistinguishable from moral philosophy. In Adams's system reason and revelation always agree in the area of morality, but this is so because revelation itself has been swallowed by autonomous reason.

Given Adams's belief in the primacy of reason, one might suppose that he, like Franklin, would be ambivalent about whether churches and religion are necessary for morality in society. But in fact he was not. Unlike Franklin, who saw education as at least a partial substitute for religion, Adams nowhere indicated that he believed religion to be dispensable in the cultivation of social mores. He instead agreed with Washington that religion and religious institutions are necessary to inculcate virtue among the citizenry. As Adams wrote in his diary on August 14, 1796:

> One great Advantage of the Christian Religion is that it brings the great Principle of the Law of Nature and Nations, Love your neighbour as yourself, and do to others as you would that others should do to you, to the Knowledge, Belief, and Veneration of the whole People. Children, Servants, Women and Men are all Professors in the science of public as well as private Morality. No other Institution for Education, no kind of political Discipline, could diffuse this kind of necessary Information, so universally among all Ranks and Descriptions of Citizens. The Duties and Rights of The Man and the Citizen are thus taught from, early Infancy to every Creature. The Sanctions of a future Life are thus added to the Observance of civil and political as well as domestic and private Duties. Prudence, Justice, Temperance, and Fortitude, are thus taught to be the means and Conditions of future as well as present Happiness.[198]

Like Washington, Adams believed that any religion that makes men good is socially beneficial, though he still liked to insist that Christianity alone is the best religion in the world. But this was hardly a contradiction in his system, for he defined every good man as a *de facto* Christian. He wrote the Reverend Samuel Miller in 1820, "I believe with Justin Martyr, that all good men are Christians, and I believe there have been, and are, good men in all nations, sincere and conscientious."[199]

Adams was more outspoken than Washington in championing an avowedly political role for religion, though he was somewhat contradictory on the subject. Adams castigated as corrupt the state-appointed clergy in other countries who meddled in politics to the detriment of society, and he worried that America might someday suffer the same fate.[200] He nevertheless praised American clergy—who were independent of the state—for speaking out on the pressing moral issues of the day.

Perhaps his clearest exposition of the political role he envisioned for ministers came just before the outbreak of the Revolutionary War when a Tory writing under the pseudonym "Massachusettensis" attacked Massachusetts ministers for mixing religion and politics. "When the clergy engage in a political warfare," wrote the Tory, "religion becomes a most powerful engine, either to support or overthrow the state. What effect must it have had upon the audience to hear the same sentiments and principles, which they had before read in a newspaper, delivered on Sundays from the sacred desk, with a religious awe, and the most solemn appeals to Heaven, from lips which they had been taught from their cradles to believe could utter nothing but eternal truths!"[201]

Adams replied that he found Tory's view of the clergy curious, to say the least. If a minister preached absolute submission to the government and its policies, the Tories lavished praise on him. "But if a clergyman preaches Christianity, and tells the magistrates that they were not distinguished from their brethren for their private emolument, but for the good of the people; that the people are bound in conscience to obey a good government, but are not bound to submit to one that aims at destroying all the ends of government,—Oh Sedition! Treason!"[202] Adams added that the clergy were naturally "disposed to be on the side of the government as long as it is tolerable." But there came a point when ministers had to break silence to uphold the law of God:

> It is the duty of the clergy to accommodate their discourses to the times, to preach against such sins as are most prevalent, and recommend such virtues as are most wanted. For example, if exorbitant ambition, and venality are predominant, ought they not to warn their hearers against these vices? If public spirit is much wanted, should they not inculcate this great virtue? If the rights and duties of christian magistrates and subjects are disputed, should they not explain them, shew their nature, ends, limitations and restrictions, how much soever it may move the gall of Massachusettensis?[203]

As this passage attests, Adams drew an explicit connection between religion's role in inculcating morality and the churches' role in politics.[204] He saw that if morality was the domain of the churches and politics was inextricably connected to morality, then it was almost a forgone conclusion that ministers and their congregations would be involved in politics. It was somehow appropriate that Adams should be the one to recognize this fact so clearly. Raised in the land of the Puritans, where election sermons were an annual tradition dating back to the founding of the New England plantations, Adams had experienced religion in politics firsthand. It was fitting that he should grasp the practical result of making the churches the repository of morality.

## John Jay (1745–1829)

Governor of New York, secretary of foreign affairs in the Confederation, first chief justice of the United States Supreme Court, John Jay was unquestionably the most prominent evangelical during the Founding, eclipsing even John Witherspoon in stature. During the battle for the ratification of the Constitution, Jay contributed five essays to *The Federalist,* and during the second term of the Washington administration, he negotiated a crucial treaty with Great Britain in 1794. In his declining years Jay devoted more time to religious benevolences, serving for many years as president of the American Bible Society and being elected to the governing body of the American Board of Commissioners for Foreign Missions (ABCFM).[205]

Like other Founders, Jay insisted that reason and revelation agree in the area of morality. However, he also attempted to highlight the differences between natural and revealed morality. "The moral or natural law," wrote Jay, "was given by the Sovereign of the universe to all mankind. . . . Being founded by infinite wisdom and goodness on essential right, which never varies, it can require no amendment or alteration. Divine positive ordinances and institutions, on the other hand, being founded on expediency, which is not always perpetual and immutable, admit of, and have received, alteration and limitation in sundry instances."[206] The natural law, then, is inviolable; and being natural, rather than revealed, it must be apprehendable by men regardless of their religious professions. Divine positive ordinances, however, can be altered by God and cannot be discovered by reason or conscience alone; they require faith in revelation.

Once one makes this distinction between the natural moral law and divine positive law, one must determine which social institutions and precepts fall into which category. Accordingly, Jay described the nature of divine positive law with more specificity. "There were several Divine *positive* ordinances and institutions at very early periods," he said. "Some of them were of limited obligation, as circumcision; others of them were of universal obligation, as the Sabbath, marriage, sacrifices, the particular punishment for murder."[207] Unlike George Washington, Jay did not include the keeping of the Sabbath as a part of civic morality. It is a divine positive ordinance; so, too, are the availability of divorce and the institution of the death penalty.[208]

But if these matters are revealed ordinances rather than a part of natural morality, what status do they have in political society? Might one conclude from Jay's argument that, whereas the natural moral law applies to all men because all men have access to it through reason or conscience, divine positive ordinances cannot necessarily be applied to all people because only persons of faith can know them? Perhaps. But Jay himself did not draw this conclusion. Indeed, in a letter to Edward Livingston in 1822 Jay suggested that laws enforcing the Sabbath and inflicting capital punishment are necessary to civil society because both the Sabbath and capital punishment are divine institutions sanctioned by the Bible.[209] This view seems to imply that divine positive laws and the dictates of natural morality are *equally* binding on civil society, a position that would exacerbate, rather than solve, the theological-political dilemma.

But Jay himself circumvented this implication by muddying his original distinction between divine positive law and natural law. Although Jay continued to maintain that some social institutions are revealed by the Bible rather than by nature, he added that all "positive laws or ordinances established by Divine direction, must of necessity be consistent with the moral law."[210] From the other side of the fence, Jay said that he did not "know of any action done according to the moral law, that is censured or forbidden by the gospel. On the contrary, it appears to me that the gospel strongly enforces the whole moral law, and clears it from the vain traditions and absurd comments which had obscured and misapplied certain parts of it."[211]

In other words, although divine positive ordinances are promulgated by God through revelation, they are also consistent with the natural moral law. This argument implies that, although one might not be able to *discover* divine positive ordinances without revelation, once revelation declares these ordinances, they can be seen to be in harmony with the natural moral law. This distinction is crucial because it determines the political status of divine institutions such as the Sabbath and marriage. If divine positive ordinances are congruent with natural morality, then political arguments on their behalf can be offered apart from revelation. For example, even though the Sabbath is a divinely revealed institution, a statesman might argue that the good of society requires that a particular day be reserved for rest and moral edification.[212]

If Jay agreed with other Founders about a morality shared by reason and revelation, he also agreed with them about the necessity of the rights of conscience. In a charge delivered to a grand jury several months after the adoption of the New York Constitution in 1777, Jay declared that the "rights of conscience and private judgment . . . are by nature subject to no control but that of the Deity, and in that free situation they are now left [by the new state constitution]."[213] Nevertheless, there were limits to Jay's religious tolerance. Firmly believing that liberty is not the same as license, he secured passage of a qualifying clause in the state constitution according to which "the liberty of conscience hereby granted, shall not be construed to encourage licentiousness, or be used in such manner as to disturb or endanger the safety of the State."[214]

Jay also sought to include in the New York Constitution a loyalty oath for "professors of the religion of the church of Rome."[215] This provision would have compelled Catholics to declare that "no pope, priest or foreign authority on earth, hath power to absolve the subjects of this State from their allegiance to the same" or forfeit their civil rights.[216] In the end all Jay could obtain approval for was a requirement that aliens seeking naturalization renounce allegiance "to all and every foreign king, prince potentate and state, in all matters ecclesiastical as well as civil."[217] Richard Morris sought to explain this display of anti-Catholicism by pointing out Jay's Huguenot ancestry.[218] But even apart from Jay's family history, it was not uncommon during this period for Protestants to regard Catholicism and the rights of conscience as antithetical.[219] Catholicism had a sorry history of state-enforced persecution, and Protestants had long memories, even if their sects had engaged in some of the same practices.

It is also true that Jay's fear of clerics exercising government authority extended well beyond Catholicism. During the Revolutionary War he objected to the hiring of a chaplain for the Continental Congress because of the diversity of religious opinions prevalent in the body.[220] If one takes the New York Constitution as reflective of his views, he also opposed the election of

ministers to public office.[221] During the presidential election campaign of
1812, Jay even discouraged efforts by clergyman John Mason to act as an
agent for his friend De Witt Clinton. Mason sought to line up Federalist
support for Clinton's presidential candidacy in hopes of forging a coalition
that could defeat James Madison. The clergyman subsequently arranged a
meeting between Clinton and old-line Federalists Gouveneur Morris, Rufus
King, and John Jay. Mason planned to attend the meeting, but Jay reportedly objected to the idea, declaring, *"No priest, no Priest."*[222]

Jay's opposition to a connection between government and clergy did not
mean that he opposed all connections between government and religion. He
supported public days of thanksgiving and laws enforcing the Sabbath;[223]
and, like John Adams, he perceived a political function for ministers as independent actors in society. "Although the mere *expediency* of public measures may not be a proper subject for the pulpit," Jay wrote the Reverend
Jedidiah Morse in 1813, "yet, in my opinion, it is the right and duty of our
pastors to press the observance of all moral and religious duties, and to ani-
madvert on every course of conduct which may be repugnant to them."[224]
Ministers have a duty to influence public opinion on questions of public morality because here politics and religion meet on common ground.


## THE REPUBLICANS: JEFFERSON AND MADISON


### Thomas Jefferson (1743–1826)

Like Benjamin Franklin and John Adams, Thomas Jefferson was an unrelenting champion of autonomous human reason, and his religious beliefs
were thoroughly demystified. Jefferson rejected the Trinity, scoffed at the
miracles recorded in the Bible, and commented that Jesus suffered from a
delusion if he truly thought he was the Son of God.[225] Also like Adams and
Franklin, Jefferson tended to reduce religion to moral philosophy; his God
was more a theoretical construct than an actor in history. Jefferson further
agreed with Adams and Franklin that reason and Christian revelation converge on the same moral precepts only because true Christianity is the religion of reason and that Jesus is to be revered not because he had some special revelation from God but because he proclaimed to the world with

unexcelled clarity the moral precepts already delivered to us by reason and the moral sense.

If there was a major difference between Jefferson, on the one hand, and Franklin and Adams, on the other, it involved the political utility of religion. Adams believed that churches are necessary to perpetuate the moral character of the citizenry, and although Franklin might have preferred to substitute "helpful" for "necessary," he generally concurred with Adams's sentiment. Jefferson's views on this matter are much more difficult to unravel.

Part of the difficulty is practical. Jefferson, the prudent realist, was never very consistent in translating his theory on church-state separation into action. On the one hand, he advocated disestablishment in Virginia, he eliminated apostasy and heresy as punishable crimes in Virginia's criminal code, and he generally fought against the introduction of religion into public education.[226] As president he steadfastly refused to issue federal prayer day proclamations.[227] On the other hand, when rewriting Virginia's legal code during the Revolution, Jefferson provided for the punishment of Sabbath breaking, as well as proposing a law for the declaration of state fast days.[228] Similar inconsistencies persisted after Jefferson was elected to the presidency. President Jefferson signed bills authorizing federal chaplains, supplying financial aid to missionary societies working among the Indians, and granting a tax exemption to a church in the District of Columbia.[229] Even Jefferson's political rhetoric often failed to square with his separationist creed. Jefferson may have opposed federal days of thanksgiving, but he invoked the theme of providence in his public utterances nearly as often as his predecessors.[230] In his second inaugural address, he even asked Americans to join with him in prayer. The rhetoric was almost indistinguishable from the thanksgiving day proclamations that Jefferson opposed.[231]

If these contradictions on the field of action are not enough, there are also theoretical ambiguities in Jefferson's writings that make it difficult to peg his precise views on religion's social role. In *Notes on the State of Virginia*, Jefferson put forth an argument that at first appeared to echo John Witherspoon's comments about the role of churches as the *censor morum* of modern society. Jefferson argued that religion flourishes where religious freedom is protected, "of various kinds, indeed, but all good enough; all sufficient to preserve peace and order."[232] This statement seems to suggest that Jefferson accepted the role of churches as the preservers of societal morality; and, in fact, Jefferson contended several sentences earlier that "the several sects perform the office of a Censor morum over each other."[233] But notice the precise wording of this earlier statement: Jefferson did not say that churches act as a censor morum over *society* (as Witherspoon had contended) but merely over *each other*. Jefferson's real meaning becomes explicit when one reprints the sentence preceding his *censor morum* comment: "Difference in opinion is advantageous in religion." In other words, Jefferson was not really arguing that churches maintain the moral order of society but only that the sheer diversity of sects fostered by religious liberty will prevent any one sect from dominating the rest of society.[234] Religious liberty protects society from the domination of any one church by employing the mutual jealousies of competing sects. Jefferson's subsequent comment about the diversity of churches being "sufficient to preserve peace and order" likely carries substantially the same meaning.

A somewhat less equivocal statement about the political usefulness of churches came in Jefferson's first inaugural address, where he commented that Americans were "enlightened by a benign religion, professed, indeed, and practiced in various forms, yet all of them inculcating honesty, truth, temperance, gratitude, and the love of man; acknowledging and adoring an overruling Providence, which by all its dispensations proves that it delights in the happiness of man here and his greater happiness hereafter."[235] Jefferson in this passage explicitly connected social morality and the multiplicity of sects. Yet even here one must remember the context in which this statement was made. Jefferson had just been through a bruising presidential campaign, and he was attempting to heal the nation's wounds and win over (or at least placate) the opposition.[236] This intention can be seen most clearly in the address's remarkable declaration that "every difference of opinion is not a difference of principle. We have called by different names brethren of the same principle. We are all Republicans, we are all Federalists."[237] Jefferson's statement on religion was undoubtedly of similar character.

Since one of the major criticisms put forth by Jefferson's opponents had been that he was an infidel who would seek to decimate Christianity once in office, Jefferson's comments here were probably a public effort to soothe these fears rather than an impartial statement of his own principles.[238] After all, Jefferson elsewhere repeatedly emphasized that the most humble person has direct access to the moral law through the moral sense and that, at most, the moral sense only needs secular instruction in moral philosophy to be complete.[239] Religion has very little to do with the process. In fact, Jefferson wrote his nephew not to worry if he arrived at the conclusion "that there is no God" because "you will find incitements to virtue in the comfort and pleasantness you feel in its exercise, and the love of others which it will procure you."[240] If this is true, however, surely there could be little public need for religion to teach morality, particularly once Jefferson's ideas on public education were implemented.[241]

But here again one faces another set of contradictions. If Jefferson really believed in the complete efficacy of the moral sense and secular education, then why did he spend the last years of his life preoccupied with the moral teachings of the Gospels? In later years Jefferson urged Joseph Priestly to write a comparison between the morality of Jesus and the moral teachings of other ancient philosophers that would show the supremacy of the morality of Jesus. Meanwhile Jefferson himself created two separate compilations from the Gospels seeking to present the moral wisdom of Jesus shorn of the Gospels' supernaturalism.[242] But if moral philosophy and the moral sense are sufficient to propagate morality, then why was Jefferson so interested in the moral teachings of Jesus? One answer might be that, although he regarded evangelical religion as destructive to the state, he thought that a religion transformed into moral philosophy *could* form an important part of the social fabric.

There is a considerable amount of evidence that this was Jefferson's real view. Jefferson wrote John Adams, for example, that the question of whether the world would be better off without religion depended on one's definition of religion:

If by religion we are to understand sectarian dogmas, in which no two of them agree, then your exclamation on that hypothesis is just, "that this would be the best of all possible worlds, if there were no religion in it." But if the moral precepts, innate in man, and made a part of his physical constitution, as necessary for a social being, if the sublime doctrines of philanthropism and deism taught us by Jesus of Nazareth, in which all agree, constitute a true religion, then, without it, this would be, as you again, say, "something not fit to be named, even indeed, a hell."[243]

In other words, even though the world would be better off if sectarian religion was exterminated, Jefferson's demythologized Unitarianism was an essential part of the commonwealth. This preferential view of Jefferson's own religious beliefs raises certain questions about the genuineness of his public commitment to religious liberty for all. Today Jefferson is remembered, understandably, as a vigorous advocate of the rights of conscience. But although in his public statements Jefferson was as charitable as George Washington toward those who differed with him in religion, his private writings rarely corresponded with these public pronouncements.

In fact, Jefferson's private letters overflowed with vituperation against both the beliefs and the character of the evangelical Christians with whom he disagreed. His attacks on Christian revelation were unsparing. He labeled Christ's disciples a "band of dupes and impostors," of which "Paul was the great Coryphaeus, and first corruptor of the doctrines of Jesus."[244] The writers of the Gospels were "grovelling authors" who supplied "a ground work of vulgar ignorance, of things impossible, of superstitions, fanaticisms, and fabrications."[245] Jefferson was equally savage in his assessment of the character of nineteenth-century evangelicals. He suggested that those who believe in the Trinity prove that "man, once surrendering his reason, has no remaining guard against absurdities the most monstrous, and like a ship without rudder is the sport of every wind. With such persons, gullability which they call faith takes the helm from the hands of reason and the mind becomes a wreck."[246] Jefferson likewise mocked the emotionalism of religious revivals, complaining about "fanaticism" among the women of Richmond: "They have their night meetings and praying parties, where, attended by their priests, and sometimes by a hen-pecked husband, they pour forth the effusions of their love to Jesus, in terms as amatory and carnal, as their modesty would permit them to use to a mere earthly lover."[247]

But Jefferson saved his harshest tirades for Presbyterians and Congregationalists, or the "dogmatists of Athanasius and Calvin" as he sometimes called them.[248] He accused them of being "the false shepherds, foretold as to enter, not by the door into the sheep-fold, but to climb up some other way. They are mere Usurpers of the Christian name, teaching a Counter-religion made up of the deliria of crazy imaginations, as foreign from Christianity as is that of Mahomet. Their blasphemies have driven thinking men into infidelity."[249] Elsewhere he ascribed "fanaticism" in Pennsylvania to "the growth of Presbyterianism. The blasphemy and absurdity of the five points of Calvin, and the impossibility of defending them, render their advocates impatient of reasoning, irritable, and prone to denunciation."[250]

Nowhere did Jefferson's intolerance of evangelicals come out more clearly than in the controversies surrounding the University of Virginia. When a Presbyterian minister attacked the appointment to the institution as professor of English-born Unitarian Thomas Cooper, Jefferson responded with epithets and distortions. In a letter to close friend William Short, Jefferson claimed that evangelicals objected to Cooper solely because he was a Unitarian, and Jefferson denounced Presbyterian clergy as "the loudest, the most intolerant of all sects, the most tyrannical, and ambitious; ready . . . to put the torch to the pile, and to rekindle . . . the flames in which their oracle Calvin consumed the poor Servetus. . . . They pant to re-establish *by law* that holy inquisition, which they can now only infuse into *public opinion.*"[251] Not satisfied with labeling his opponents theocrats in the tradition of the Inquisition, Jefferson added that they exercised too much influence over public opinion, darkly suggesting that it might be wise for society to abolish the institution of the Sabbath.[252]

The radical disjunction between the views expressed here and Jefferson's public stance can be seen in Jefferson's earlier bill for establishing religious freedom. There he argued that that for public officials to intrude into the field of public opinion and restrain religious ideas "on supposition of their ill tendency" is subversive of all religious liberty because public officials will invariably make their own religious opinions the "judge of that tendency."[253] Yet in his letter to William Short, this is the course of action that Jefferson himself suggested. Disestablishment had been in place in Virginia for several decades by the time Jefferson wrote this letter, so his comments cannot be construed as a condemnation of official church influence over society. Instead, his point was that even voluntary church influence over public opinion is dangerous because it allows the clergy to mold the minds of the citzenry "as wax in the hollow of their hands."[254]

Jefferson's comments also manifestly distorted the actual position of his evangelical critics. Contrary to Jefferson's intimations, evangelicals were concerned about much more than Thomas Cooper's Unitarianism. This came out in a lengthy article in the *Virginia Evangelical and Literary Magazine* that critiqued Cooper's suitability for the position.[255] The article, written by Presbyterian clergyman John H. Rice, reviewed a lengthy appendix Cooper had written to the published memoirs of his father-in-law, Joseph Priestly.[256]

Rice said he was not impugning the personal character of Dr. Cooper but did take exception to his moral and philosophical views. Rice first objected to Cooper's claim that neither atheism nor a rejection of an eternal state of punishments would undermine societal morality.[257] Rice further attacked Cooper's philosophy of the human mind, which seemed to strip man of his dignity. Cooper was a materialist, and according to Rice, he reduced the faculties of the mind to the physical processes of the brain and rejected the existence of a personal soul and freedom of the will.[258]

Rice's most damning criticism, however, focused on Cooper's intolerance. Cooper promoted his views with an unrelenting dogmatism that seemed to exclude other viewpoints from fair consideration. He misrepresented the views of his opponents when he claimed that trinitarians believe in three separate gods.[259] And in one passage he suggested that those who disagreed with him were no longer entitled to publicly air their ideas: "The time seems to have arrived, when the separate existence of the human soul, the freedom of the will, and the eternal duration of future punishment, like the doctrines of the Trinity, and Transubstantiation, may be regarded as no longer entitled to public discussion."[260] Cooper added that he would not even examine the hypotheses of major Scottish thinkers such as Thomas Reid because of "the perfect *oblivion* into which these writers have fallen, and [because] the utter insufficiency of such young gentlemen and lady's philosophy as they have adopted, has secured them from further amnidiversion."[261] According to Rice, this open intolerance on Cooper's part made him unfit to teach at a publicly funded university.[262]

Thus, when Jefferson attacked evangelicals for being obsessed with Cooper's Unitarianism, he was bludgeoning a straw man. Since Jefferson knew about the article in the *Evangelical and Literary Magazine,* he cannot be excused for his remarks on account of ignorance.[263] Either his anger blinded his perceptions, or he consciously chose to ignore the evangelicals' real objections.

Whichever was the case, Jefferson continued to misread his evangelical opponents. In another letter on the University of Virginia controversy, this time to Cooper himself, Jefferson accused critics of falsely charging that the University was "not merely of no religion, but against all religion."[264] Here again Jefferson appears to have played fast and loose with the views of his opponents. The precise charge made by evangelicals was not that the university was against all religion but that it was being used to propagate Jefferson's own demythologized religion of Unitarianism.

Joseph Cabell told Jefferson this as early as 1821, writing him that the Presbyterian clergy "believe, as I am informed, that the Socinians [i.e., Unitarians] are to be installed at the University for the purpose of overthrowing the prevailing religious opinions of the country."[265] This view was lent credence by the fact that after Cooper's relationship with the university was severed, two more Unitarians were sought for appointment.[266] Under the circumstances it was not too unreasonable for evangelicals to conclude that trinitarian Christians were being excluded from the new institution. Early in 1822 Joseph Cabell informed Jefferson that evangelicals now had an additional piece of evidence in support of their claims: "They have heard that you have said they may well be afraid of the progress of the Unitarians to the South. This remark was carried from Bedford, to the Synod, beyond the Ridge, last fall. The Bible Societies are in constant correspondence all over the continent, and a fact is wafted across it in a few weeks."[267]

Regardless of whether Jefferson made this particular remark, he certainly voiced other opinions that suported the evangelicals' interpretation of his actions. Perhaps most revealing were his comments at the end of his letter to William Short, which implied that the purpose of the university was in some sense to save students from the clutches of the evangelical clergy. After attacking the influence that evangelical ministers had on public opinion, Jefferson added: "But, in despite of their fulminations against endeavors to enlighten the general mind, to improve the reason of the people, and encourage them in the use of it, the liberality of this State will support this institution, and give it fair play to the cultivation of reason."[268]

As Jefferson considered evangelical religion ipso facto unreasonable, it is not improbable to conclude that for him "the cultivation of reason" at the University of Virginia encompassed the propagation, however indirect, of Unitarianism. Although the University of Virginia did not have a chair in divinity, it did have one in moral philosophy.[269] Hence, even though the university would not have supported sectarian Christianity in any way, the type of moral deism that Jefferson espoused likely would have been taught in courses on moral philosophy. It is difficult to escape the conclusion that Jefferson intended the University of Virginia to reform the religious views of its students. This intention would have been perfectly congruent with his hopes for the ultimate triumph of Unitarianism. In letter after letter to fellow Unitarians, Jefferson made explicit his hopes that Unitarianism would supplant evangelicalism as the dominant religion in America. As he wrote to Benjamin Waterhouse in 1822, "I trust that there is not a *young man* now living in the US. who will not die an Unitarian."[270]

One might conclude from all this that the real reason Jefferson supported religious liberty was that he thought it would bring about the triumph of his own demythologized Unitarianism. This undercurrent is plainly present in Jefferson and much more so than many realize. He wrote to Jared Sparks, for example, that "if the freedom of religion, guaranteed to us by law *in theory,* can ever rise *in practice* under the overbearing inquisition of public opinion, truth will prevail over fanaticism, and the genuine doctrines of Jesus, so long perverted by his pseudo-priests will again be restored to their original purity."[271] Yet to reduce Jefferson's support for religious liberty to a cynical ruse to subvert evangelical religion is unwarranted. Support for freedom of religion does not logically imply support for every kind of religious belief or even for the continued existence of every religious sect. What it does imply is that controversies over religion should be resolved through civilized debate rather than by public coercion. Hence, Jefferson's private hopes for the triumph of Unitarianism did not contradict his public support for religious liberty for all regardless of creed. He could logically support religious freedom for all, even while wishing certain ideas to triumph in the long term through the process of free debate. And although Jefferson's harsh denunciations of his religious opponents may have been ungentlemanly, to some degree he was responding in kind because he himself had suffered harsh attacks for his own supposed religious beliefs. In addition, on several occasions Jefferson was willing to admit the good citizenship of those he disagreed with, even when writing to other Unitarians. To Unitarian pamphleteer James Smith, for instance, Jefferson added this caution after attacking the irrationality of trinitarians: "I write with freedom, because, while I claim a right to believe in one god, if so my reason tells me, I yield as freely to others that of believing in three. Both religions I find make honest men, and that is the only point society has any authority to look to."[272] Reverting to the civility of Benjamin Franklin and George Washington, Jefferson acknowledged that even trinitarian sects upheld social morality by producing honest men, and he indicated his unwillingness to use his station to publicly urge the adoption of his own religious views.

Jefferson's private writings regarding the University of Virginia are admittedly more difficult to square with his belief in religious freedom. It is worth noting, however, that Jefferson eventually modified his plans with regard to religion at the University of Virginia. In 1822 he and the Board of Visitors adopted a principled and carefully crafted plan that would "give . . . sectarian schools of divinity the full benefit of the public provisions made for instruction in the other branches of science" while keeping such schools "independent of the University and of each other."[273]

In this plan Jefferson and the board acknowledged that the lack of direct provision for religious instruction had created "a chasm in a general institution of the useful sciences" such as the University of Virginia.[274] Jefferson and the board did not seek to defend this huge gap in instruction as good in itself; they merely suggested that keeping the university out of religious instruction constituted the lesser of two evils. They thought that making no direct provision for religious instruction had created "evils of less danger than a permission to the public authorities to dictate modes or principles of religious instruction, or than opportunities furnished them by giving countenance or ascendancy to any one sect over another."

But now, suggested Jefferson, they no longer had to choose between the lesser of two evils because a "remedy . . . has been suggested of promising aspect, which, while it excludes the public authorities from the domain of religious freedom, will give to the sectarian schools of divinity the full benefit of the public provisions made for instruction in the other branches of science." The remedy involved the establishment of independent schools of theology "on the confines of the University." Certain "pious individuals" were advocating such a proposal so that their students studying for the clergy might have the benefits of both a secular and a religious education.[275] But "the further and greater advantage" of the plan, according to Jefferson and the board, was its benefit to *regular* students of the university. It would remedy the deficiency in their education by "enabling the students . . . to attend religious exercises with the professor of their particular sect."[276] Jefferson concluded his report by declaring that this "arrangement would complete the circle of the useful science embraced by this institution, and would fill the chasm now existing, on principles which would leave inviolate the constitutional freedom of religion."[277]

Two years after Jefferson drafted this report, he framed—and the Board of Visitors ratified—regulations that substantially agreed with the 1822 proposal. These regulations allowed the university to invite religious sects to "establish within, or adjacent to, the precincts of the University, schools for the instruction in the religion of their sect." The regulations further stipu-

lated that "the students of the University will be free, *and expected* to attend
religious worship at the establishment of their respective sects, in the morning, and in time to meet their school in the University at its stated hour."[278]
The regulations also provided for the use of one of the university's "large
eliptical rooms on its middle floor . . . for religious worship."[279]

Historian Leonard Levy discounts Jefferson's reformulated scheme for religion at the University of Virginia as political damage control. Levy argues
that Jefferson's efforts to provide for religious education at the university
were "concessions" made to those who opposed "the secular character of
the university."[280] Levy also points out that after the adoption of much of
the 1822 report as university regulations, Jefferson still refused a request to
conduct Sunday services on university grounds in 1825.[281]

Levy is probably correct.[282] Nevertheless, whatever Jefferson's subjective
reasons for proposing religious accommodation at the University of Virginia, the arguments he offered on behalf of his plan constituted an important amplification of his public views of the status of religion in society. One
might even argue that Jefferson's plan of accommodation was necessitated
by his own previous rhetoric of religious liberty. Jefferson objected to state
financial assistance for ministers because "to compel a man to furnish contributions of money for the propagation of opinions which he disbelieves
and abhors, is sinful and tyrannical."[283] But for evangelicals the same point
applied with peculiar force to education at the University of Virginia: Here
the state was appropriating funds to propagate a type of education that they
found unconscionable. At best the university would belittle the importance
of religion by making it the only part of human life that would not be addressed by the curriculum; at worst the university would actively subvert
evangelical religion by promoting in its place deism under the guise of moral
philosophy. If Jefferson seriously believed in his own arguments as outlined
in the Virginian Statute of Religious Liberty, then he was almost compelled
to square what he was doing at the University of Virginia with his earlier arguments.

Heretofore the discussion has focused on Jefferson's views of religious liberty and on whether he thought churches were necessary to foster social morality. But even if he did believe in full liberty for all sects and in their importance in the cultivation of civic virtue, this does not mean that he thought
churches should become active in politics. Indeed, much evidence indicates
the contrary. When revising the constitution of the state of Virginia, Jeffer-

son initially wanted to bar ministers from holding public office;[284] and when he was made the brunt of vigorous clerical attacks during the campaign of 1800, Jefferson frequently complained about the interference of religious sects in politics, as he did again when evangelicals protested his policies at the University of Virginia.[285] Of course, in these cases Jefferson's stated objection was the attempt to make certain theological doctrines the standard for political action; he might have had a different view of churches engaging in political activities on behalf of shared principles of civic morality. At a bare minimum Jefferson did eventually recognize that ministers should not be legally barred from public office. Once disestablishment had occurred, ministers were set on an equal footing with every other profession, and so there was no longer any need to deny them the equal rights to which other citizens were entitled. As Jefferson wrote to Jeremiah Moor in 1800, "The clergy here seem to have relinquished all pretension to privilege and to stand on a footing with lawyers, physicians, etc. They ought therefore to possess the same rights."[286]

## James Madison (1751–1836)

Perhaps even more than Jefferson, James Madison is the central figure mentioned in present-day discussions of the Founding's understanding of religion and politics. Yet in many ways Madison was unrepresentative of his generation when it came to religion. First, unlike every other Founder discussed here, Madison in later years expressed very little personal interest in religion; indeed, his mature writings are devoid of almost any inkling of his private religious beliefs. George Washington, as nonsectarian as he was, wrote time and again about God's providence. Jefferson and Adams, skeptics though they were, relished attacking the religious beliefs they found foolish and enjoyed discussing with each other their own ideas about God and his attributes. Even the ever-secretive Franklin discussed religion in a variety of ways. But in Madison the silence on spiritual matters is deafening. In his early years he had expressed an almost evangelical zeal for religion, as exhibited in his letters to college friend William Bradford.[287] But after the early 1770s Madison almost never discussed his own religious beliefs. When late in life Frederick Beasley sent him a "tract on the proofs of the Being and Attributes of God," Madison did respond ably, but he also intimated that he had not thought about the subject for some time and did not plan to do so again in the future. He wrote Beasley that "to do full justice" to his work "would require not only a more critical attention than I have been able to bestow on it, but a resort to the celebrated work of Dr. Clarke, which I read fifty years ago only, and to that of Dr. Waterland also which I never read."[288] Given Madison's adult indifference to religion, he, more than any other major Founder, was the forerunner of the modern secularist; it is perhaps fitting, then, that he is so often cited today.

A second characteristic that distinguished Madison from the rest of his generation was that he almost never articulated a belief in the moral role of churches during his public career. Even Thomas Jefferson was willing to publicly acknowledge as president that churches fostered civic morality; and in private he urged the transformation of religion into moral philosophy so that morality would become its sole object. But Madison, at least during his political career, seemed to deprecate the role of organized religion in fostering morality. In an outline of a speech he delivered against Virginia's general assessment, Madison listed "laws to cherish virtue," "administration of justice," "personal example," and "the education of youth" as the proper remedies to social problems—not a proliferation of churches.[289] In *Federalist* no. 10 he argued that "neither moral nor religious motives can be relied on as an adequate control" of factional strife; indeed, religion is more likely to precipitate such conflict than extinguish it.[290]

Near the end of his life, however, Madison appears to have revisited his earlier views. In a letter to Edward Everett in 1823, Madison echoed Witherspoon's understanding of churches as the *censor morum,* reporting that in Virginia "the settled opinion . . . is . . . that rival sects, with equal rights, exercise mutual censorships in favor of good morals."[291] But even here Madison distanced himself from the viewpoint he was expressing. He spoke of the view that connected religion and morality as "settled opinion," that is, settled *public* opinion—which may or may not have been synonymous with Madison's private opinion. Three years later Madison was less coy. Writing to Frederick Beasley, he baldly acknowledged that "the belief in a God All Powerful wise & good, is so essential to the moral order of the World & to the happiness of man, that arguments which enforce it cannot be drawn from too many sources nor adapted with too much solicitude to the different characters & capacities to be impressed with it."[292] In the last several weeks before his death, moreover, Madison appears to have discovered another political function for religion in the United States. Reflecting on the prospects of the Union, he found hope in the existence of national religious associations, believing that "the 4 great religious Sects, running through all the States, will oppose an event placing parts of each under separate Governments."[293]

If Madison during his public career was more reticent than others in making the connection between religion and civic morality, he was the most vocal among the Founders in believing that there should be no official encouragement of religion. Madison did not merely oppose state funding of ministers or the proclamation of state prayer days.[294] He opposed tax exemptions for church buildings.[295] He objected to government chaplains, both in the legislative branch and in the army.[296] He even questioned whether the government should supply chaplains on naval ships, where men might not otherwise have the opportunity for spiritual guidance.[297] And with startling prescience of future controversies,[298] Madison challenged the use of churches to carry out charitable activities on behalf of the government. While president he vetoed an act incorporating a church in the District of Columbia in part because "the bill vest[ed] in the said incorporated church an authority to provide for the support of the poor and the education of poor children of the same, an authority which, being altogether superfluous if the provision is to be the result of pious charity, would be a precedent for giving to religious societies as such a legal agency in carrying into effect a public and civil duty."[299]

Nevertheless, Madison's public arguments on behalf of church-state separation were not based on any avowed hostility toward religion. Indeed, one of the most remarkable facts about his arguments against Virginia's general assessment is that many of them were made from the standpoint of revelation as well as reason. In the "Memorial and Remonstrance" Madison argued not only that establishments of religions were not necessary for civil government but also that they had a devastating effect on religion:

> Ecclesiastical establishments, instead of maintaining the purity and efficacy of Religion, have had a contrary operation. During almost fifteen centuries, has the legal establishment of Christianity been on trial. What have been its fruits? More or less in all places, pride and indolence in the Clergy; ignorance and servility in the laity; in both, superstition, bigotry and persecution. Enquire of the teachers of Christianity

for the ages in which it appeared in its greatest lustre; those of every sect, point to the ages prior to its incorporation with Civil policy.[300]

Even Madison's reluctance to treat religion as the propagator of civic morality may be perceived in religious terms. In remonstrance number five he argued that it was "an unhallowed perversion of the means of salvation" to "employ Religion as an engine of Civil policy."[301]

Several historians have pointed out that the arguments in the "Memorial and Remonstrance" closely paralleled earlier arguments made against the assessment scheme by a wide array of evangelicals, including Baptists, Presbyterians, Methodists, Quakers, and Lutherans.[302] As Thomas Buckley explained, these evangelical dissenters supported disestablishment not because they wanted to privatize religion but because they wanted to "preach the word without hindrance from civil government. For their work they required no assessment; revivals and itineracy sufficed."[303] These evangelicals grounded their belief in religious liberty on their scriptural understanding of "the relationship between God and the individual believer. Every man had to be free to respond in faith and worship as God would draw him. The intervention of the state in any fashion hindered the purity of that relationship and was unwarranted interference in God's work."[304]

Robert Calhoon perceptively points out that Madison "brilliantly combined two different kinds of arguments" in the "Memorial and Remonstrance": "One was drawn out of [the] scores of anti-assessment petitions" filed by evangelicals; "the other came from his own and Jefferson's reading in Enlightenment history and philosophy on the evils of state-sponsored religion."[305] The result was a skillful "blending of the secular and spiritual concerns. . . . The rhetoric subtly mixed evangelical fears of secular impurity with rationlist aversion to encroachments on private judgment."[306]

Madison's effective use of religious arguments persisted throughout his life. After disestablishment had occurred in Virginia, he liked to point out that religious instruction flourished far more after disestablishment than before.[307] Even in the "Detached Memoranda," which contained his most extreme statements on church and state, he carefully maintained that "reason *and* the principles of the [Christian] religion" supported his views on religious liberty and the separation of church and state.[308] Some might argue, of course, that this type of rhetoric tells us more about those whom Madison was trying to persuade than about Madison's own beliefs. Even though

Madison undeniably framed his arguments to persuade religious adherents, there is every reason to suppose that Madison himself agreed in private with his public arguments. Certainly Madison saw no contradiction between religion and religious liberty during his own period of religious fervor as a young man. Even in those early years he railed against what he called the "Hell conceived principle of persecution."[309]

Nevertheless, despite Madison's continued insistence that reason and revelation agree when it comes to the separation of church and state, one could suspect him of a certain degree of hostility toward religion. Unlike the Virginian evangelicals who supported disestablishment, Madison feared organized religion, a fear that became increasingly evident in later years as he vigorously attacked in private the ability of churches to hold and acquire property as corporations.[310] This stance appeared to contradict Madison's earlier arguments. Recall that he previously had maintained that churches did not need state support because they could rely on private support and that voluntary contributions would themselves weed out corrupt churches and indolent clergy because parishoners would donate their money elsewhere. But once disestablishment had occurred in almost every state,[311] Madison began to attack private support for churches as well. Madison's professed devotion to complete religious freedom appears to have disintegrated as he hinted that government should now curtail private donations to religious groups.

Yet one should not try to pin too much on this inconsistency. Whatever fears Madison may have harbored about organized religion in some areas, they did not substantially diminish his support for religious liberty. Even though he could not have appreciated the attacks mounted against himself and Jefferson by some evangelicals, for instance, he never retracted his belief that ministers should be able to run for public office.[312] And like both Thomas Jefferson and George Washington, he looked dimly on government intervention against religious groups even when those groups might be pursuing policies contrary to the best interests of society. According to Madison, "if new sects arise with absurd opinions or overheated imaginations, the proper remedies lie in time, forbearance and example. . . ."[313] Madison even implied that it would be better for the government to allow religious sects to disturb the social order than for that same government to exercise any authority over religious affairs: "The apprehension of some seems to be that Religion left entirely to itself may run into extravagances injurious both to Religion and to social order; but besides the question whether the interference of Govt. *in any form* wd. not be more likely to increase than controul the tendency, it is a safe calculation that in this as in other cases of excessive excitement, Reason will gradually regain its ascendancy. Great excitements are less apt to be permanent than to vibrate to the opposite extreme."[314]

It is also true that Madison's objection to ecclesiastical wealth had as much to do with his economic theories as his religious views. He voiced similar concerns about the accumulation of property by individuals and nonreligious corporations.[315] After condemning the power of religious corporations to hold property in perpetuity in "Detached Memoranda," Madison added, "The power of all corporations, ought to be limited in this respect. The growing wealth acquired by them never fails to be a source of abuses."[316]

In addition, Madison displayed a willingness to accommodate religious activities in the public university setting. As rector of the University of Virginia after Jefferson's death, Madison helped overturn the policy forbidding the use of the university rotunda for religious worship.[317]

Finally, Madison's overall political theory is extremely conducive to the continued existence of evangelical religion. Unlike Jefferson, who looked forward to the day when all men would become Unitarians, Madison saw the political necessity of continued sectarianism. Madison might have publicly complained about animosities and jealousies among competing sects, but privately he was grateful for it. Shortly before he castigated Virginia's general assessment bill in "Memorial and Remonstrance" for fanning the fames of sectarian strife, he wrote Thomas Jefferson: "The presbyterian clergy, have at length espoused the side of the opposition, being moved either by *a fear of their laity* or a *jealousy of the episcopalians.* The mutual hatred of these sects has been much inflamed by the late Act incorporating the latter. *I am far* from being *sorry for it,* as *a coalition between them* could *alone endanger our religious rights,* and a tendency to *such an event had been suspected.*"[318] Here is the kernel of the argument that later became central to Madison's political thought: Animosity among competing sects protects liberty by preventing an unjust coalition that could endanger fundamental rights.

Three years later during the ratification debates, Madison incorporated this argument into his larger defense of the extended republic in *Federalist* no. 10 and no. 51. Now the multiplicity of sects he envisioned encompassed not only those espousing differing religious beliefs but also those holding differing amounts of wealth and those advocating differing ideas about politics. In each of the latter cases,

> the security for civil rights must be the same as that for religious rights. It consists in the one case in the multiplicity of interests, and in the other in the multiplicity of sects. The degree of security in both cases will depend on the number of interests and sects. . . . In the extended republic of the United States, and among the great variety of interests, parties, and sects which it embraces, a coalition of a majority of the whole society could seldom take place on any other principles than those of justice and the general good.[319]

At the Virginia ratifying convention, Madison again applied this scheme of republicanism to religious factions in particular.[320]

Madison's solution to the problem of religious faction thus presupposed the continued existence of doctrinal differences among sects. If sects do not continue to disagree on doctrine, they may be tempted to form a majority faction to impose their shared doctrinal views on society or to extract special favors from the government on the basis of their religious beliefs. Republican harmony therefore demands that sectarianism flourish because this makes it far less likely that religious groups will try to use the government to promote their doctrinal views.

## CONCLUSION

By now certain common themes should be evident. First and foremost is the Founders' attachment to religious liberty. Evangelicals such as Witherspoon and Jay, no less than freethinkers such as Franklin and Jefferson, believed in the right of all sects to worship God as their consciences dictate. Regardless of personal religious preferences, none of the Founders wished the *government* to interfere with the religious opinions of the citizenry—to promote either evangelical orthodoxy (in the case of Witherspoon and Jay) or a rational Unitarianism (in the case of Franklin and Jefferson). All were content to allow competing sects to flourish in America free from government encumbrance. Religious obligation was considered separate and distinct from civic obligation, though it was not regarded as inferior to it. In this one area at least, James Madison supplied the common sense of the subject in the "Memorial and Remonstrance":

> It is the duty of every man to render to the Creator such homage, and such only, as he believes to be acceptable to him. This duty is precedent both in order of time and degree of obligation, to the claims of Civil Society. Before any man can be considered as a member of Civil Society, he must be considered as a subject of the Governor of the Universe: And if a member of Civil Society, who enters into any subordinate Association, must always do it with a reservation of his duty to the general authority; much more must every man who becomes a member of any particular Civil Society, do it with a saving of his allegiance to the Universal Sovereign. We maintain therefore that in matters of Religion, no man's right is abridged by the institution of Civil Society, and that Religion is wholly exempt from its cognizance.[321]

Here in its simplest form is the Founders' solution to the theological-political dilemma. The Founders eliminated the problem of dual allegiance to God and government by removing God from the authority of the government. Religious wars would no longer be fought with civil weapons because the civil government no longer had any legitimate weapons with which to fight religious battles. Church and state would constitute their own separate polities, each independent of the other.

This solution to the theological-political problem in theory, however, required a major corollary to work in practice: a belief that church and state would agree on the moral basis of political action. It is well and good to speak of absolute freedom of religion, but the Founders knew perfectly well that absolute freedom could be accorded only to religious belief and opinion, not to actions. Yet religion encompasses the realm of action as well as belief. Hence, what happens if a church inculcates duties contrary to civil policy and its adherents act accordingly? Will not the government have to intervene against those religious adherents to preserve social order? And will not this very intervention subjugate religion to the state, thus reintroducing the theological-political problem? Only if church and state can agree on the moral standard for political action can this result be avoided. In other words, reason (the operating principle of civil government) and revelation (the ultimate standard for religion) must concur on the moral law for the Founders' solution to work.

The Founders, of course, agreed with this proposition. Evangelicals such as Witherspoon and Jay, no less than champions of the Enlightenment such as Jefferson and Franklin, concurred that the morality of revelation is largely coincident with the morality of reason and conscience. This conceit that reason and revelation agree on the moral law so permeated the Founding era that the modern reader may miss it because authors of the period more often assumed this proposition than demonstrated it. When citing authority for fundamental propositions, writers of the Founding era appealed to both reason and revelation as a matter of course. One finds this conceit restated and reformulated in countless ways in the letters and documents of the era. George Washington appealed to "religion and morality,"[322] "Reason, Religion, and Philosophy,"[323] "religion, decency, and order,"[324] and "Prudence, Policy, and a true Christian Spirit."[325] In his Farewell Address, he referred to "the mere politician, equally with the pious man."[326] John Adams appealed to "revelation, and . . . reason too,"[327] "the bible and common sense,"[328] "human nature and the christian religion,"[329] and "God and Nature."[330] John Jay cited "experience and revelation."[331] James Madison invoked "reason and the principles of the [Christian] religion."[332] Hamilton noted that the moral doctrines of Hobbes were "absurd" [i.e., against reason] as well as "impious" [i.e., against revelation].[333] Even Thomas Jefferson in later years saw fit to appeal to the "obligation of the moral precepts of Jesus"[334] as coincident with the morality of conscience and reason. The major public documents of the period resounded with this same convention. The Declaration of Independence appealed to "Divine Providence" and the "Supreme Judge of the World" as well as the "laws of Nature and Nature's God" [i.e., the laws decreed by the reason and nature of things]. The Northwest Ordinance spoke of "religion, morality, and knowledge." And the Constitution of 1787 was signed both "in the Year of our Lord one thousand seven hundred and Eighty seven" and in the twelfth year "of the Independence of the United States of America" [the republic whose Constitution embodied human reflection and choice].

This pervasive belief that reason and revelation agree on morality undercuts the claim that, according to the Founders, sectarian religion had to "be reformed and rendered harmless" by the spread of Unitarianism if their scheme of republican government was to succeed.[335] Politics in the new republic depended on a shared morality rather than a shared theology. There was little reason for the government to be concerned about continued theological differences. As long as competing religious sects promoted the same reasonable morality, they helped, rather than hindered, republican government. Whatever theoretical grounds certain Founders might have had for opposing sectarian theology, they saw no pressing *political* reason to supplant sectarianism with Unitarianism. If anything, Founders such as James Madison *wanted* sectarian religion to flourish because they knew that continued differences in theology would make a tyrannical combination of religious sects more difficult.

But if the Founders' belief in a morality shared by both reason and revelation undercuts the idea that they wanted to eradicate sectarian religion, it also undermines the claims of those who advocate the "Christian America" thesis. The existence of a common moral order shared by Christians and non-Christians makes a peculiarly "Christian" republic largely unnecessary, particularly when the government of the republic has no say over theology. Civil society can be founded on God's general revelation to all men through the law of nature rather than on tenets peculiar to the Bible. Hence, it is understandable that evangelicals among the Founders mostly eschewed rhetoric tying the American regime to Christian revelation.

This being said, one must not claim too much for the Founding's rapprochement between reason and revelation. The Founders never claimed that autonomous reason and divine revelation could agree on everything, even in the realm of morality. To the contrary, most recognized that one's conception of civic morality would differ somewhat depending on the respective status one accorded reason and revelation. Franklin, Jefferson, and Adams viewed revealed morality through the eyes of autonomous reason; hence, they rejected that part of biblical morality that could not be justified apart from revelation or a belief in God. For Jefferson this meant excising from the civil law crimes such as Sabbath breaking and blasphemy and positive duties such as the appointment of state prayer days. If Franklin and Adams were more favorable toward such practices as prayer days, it was only because they thought that reason dictated their political utility, not because they believed in the validity of revelation. Witherspoon, Jay, and Wilson saw reason in the light of God and his revelation, and hence they had much less difficulty incorporating certain religious duties into civic morality. The same was true for Washington and Hamilton, who may not have entirely accepted the authority of revelation but nonetheless deferred to it because they believed that strong churches were necessary for the maintenance of social morality.

In addition to understanding that reason and revelation might sometimes differ about what duties the government should enforce, the Founders also recognized that on occasion certain churches might engage in actions or preach doctrines directly contrary to civil policy. In these cases, even though the government might have the power to interfere in the activities of those churches, the Founders were doubtful about whether the government should intervene. Washington, Madison, and Jefferson all indicated that the government should not interfere with a religious group unless absolutely necessary for the safety of society. Wilson implied the same by stressing that reason, revelation, and conscience all move together in the same direction for the benefit of society; the government should therefore try to prevent situations where reason and revelation might disagree.

Thus, the Founders' understanding of the relationship between theology and politics was far from superficial. The Founders well knew that religion and unassisted reason might sometimes disagree on the course of civic action and that independence between theology and politics might therefore be difficult to maintain. But knowing this, they still insisted that the area of agreement between reason and revelation was sufficiently broad that both church and state might benefit by being institutionally separate. In Madison's view the practical results of disestablishment in Virginia proved this fact beyond a reasonable doubt.

Yet if the Founders' solution to the theological-political problem was coherent and workable, their political science also contained the seeds of further strife between religion and politics. This becomes apparent when one recognizes the nearly universal opinion during the Founding that morality is necessary to politics[336] and that churches are either necessary or helpful in the creation of that morality: "necessary," according to Washington, Adams, Hamilton, Jay, Witherspoon, and perhaps even Franklin; "helpful" according to Jefferson and Madison during their later years. But if religion is necessary for morality and morality is necessary for politics, then it constitutes no great leap of logic to conclude that religious groups themselves should become involved in politics—at least insofar as politics intersects with morality.

Admittedly, this conclusion was not something most of the Founders thought a great deal about, though some of them certainly foresaw it. Franklin, Witherspoon, Jay, and Adams clearly understood the connections among religion, morality, and politics. Wilson implied that he did, too, though he never explicitly delineated what a political role for churches might mean. Hamilton, forever seeing the political uses of religion, also understood the connections, though he saw the church less as an independent actor in society than as an appendage to an existing political party. And even though Madison and Jefferson may have wished to keep religion out of politics as much as possible, they at least understood that neither clergymen nor churches could be legally prohibited from exercising their political rights.

The result was that even as the Founders defused the conflict between church and state, they created the conditions for the conflict to rise again in another form. Regardless of whether intended, the Founders' solution to the theological-political problem issued a de facto invitation to the nation's churches to enter politics as the sacred defenders of civic morality. What this would mean for the nation—and for its churches—became sharply evident in the first decades of the next century, beginning with the bitter election of 1800.

# TWO

## EVANGELICALS AND THE POLITICS OF REVELATION AND REASON, 1800–1835

A new century was about to dawn, and America found itself embroiled in an angry presidential campaign. Four years earlier, in 1796, Federalist John Adams had narrowly escaped defeat at the polls at the hands of Thomas Jefferson. This time Adams would not be so lucky. Disliked by many within his own party, portrayed as a haughty aristocrat by his enemies, Adams was in an unenviable situation in 1800. Yet the Federalists were not about to buckle without a good scrap. Tainted by the unpopular Alien and Sedition Acts, they tried to shore up their support among the masses by making religion one of the defining issues of the campaign.

Although Jefferson for the most part hid his religious beliefs, rumors swirled about that he was actually a "howling athiest."[1] Federalists subsequently presented the upcoming election as a stark choice between "God and a Religious president" and "Jefferson and no God."[2] Evangelicals aligned with the party did their best to fan the flames of fear. In September a pamphlet appeared in New York titled "The Voice of Warning to Christians, on the Ensuing Election of a President of the United States." The anonymous author was evangelical firebrand John M. Mason, thirty-year-old pastor of the Reformed Church on Cedar Street and friend of Alexander Hamilton. One of the great pulpit orators of the day, Mason would become provost of Columbia College in 1811 and in 1821, president of Dickinson College in Pennsylvania. Mason was so vehement in his orations that during one sermon a blood vessel burst in his nose and blood spurted out. He continued the oration unperturbed.[3]

In "The Voice of Warning," Mason bore down on Jefferson with all possible eloquence. Delivering an exacting exegesis of Jefferson's one published book, *Notes on the State of Virginia,* Mason rebuked Jefferson for undercutting the biblical account of the universal deluge, for implicitly denying that the Jews are God's chosen people, and for asserting that atheism has no ill political consequences.[4] Mason further castigated Jefferson for his ambivalent speculations about blacks, accusing him of hinting that blacks are actually subhuman.[5] Mason acknowledged that Jefferson appeared to back away from this conclusion because (in Jefferson's words) "as a circumstance of great tenderness" it "would degrade a whole race of men from the rank in the scale of beings which their Creator may perhaps have given them." But this qualification infuriated Mason, who attacked Jefferson's "very '*tenderness*'" as being "tinctured with an infidel hue."[6] At best, Jefferson merely acknowledged that blacks "perhaps" were on the same level of being as whites. Such waffling was in flagrant contradiction to divine revelation, according to Mason.

For Mason the facts of the matter were indisputable. Jefferson may not have been an atheist, but he was certainly an open infidel. "This point being settled," one should "have no difficulty about the rest."[7] The "first and highest obligation" of civil officers is to rule in the fear of God, and Christians are thus obliged to seek as their rulers "such men as answer [this] . . . description; and if, unhappily, they are not to be had, for such as come nearest to it." To do otherwise would be treason against God. By elevating an open infidel to the nation's highest office, Mason continued, Christians would show contempt for all they claimed to espouse.[8]

By making theology the locus of the election campaign, Mason threatened to rip apart the Founders' solution to the theological-political problem. Politics was supposed to be the common ground shared by Christians and infidels alike, but Mason sought to turn it into a religious battlefield. To be sure, some of the issues he cited—such as slavery—were within the domain of a natural morality shared by reason and revelation. But Mason fit even these issues into an explicitly theological framework. Out to make the election a referendum on Christian orthodoxy, he ended up confusing the functions of civil and religious authority.

Mason's jeremiad against Jefferson constituted the last gasp of a long campaign by evangelicals to counter the onslaught of the Jeffersonians. Not all evangelicals were Federalists, but many of the evangelical leaders most openly involved in politics were.[9] These tended to be clergymen from among the Congregationalists and Presbyterians. In the years leading up to the fateful election of 1800, their sermons had repeatedly warned about the scheming proponents of infidelity who wished to reenact the bloody French Revolution on American soil. In 1798 the Reverend Jedidiah Morse identified these national traitors as members of a vast subversive organization known as the Illuminati.[10] Yale president Timothy Dwight succinctly summarized the objectives of this secret group as "the overthrow of religion, government, and human society civil and domestic."[11] Federalist evangelicals left few doubts about which political party wished to enact the Illuminati's program in America; nor were they reluctant to prescribe partisan solutions to the problem. On the day of the national fast proclaimed by President Adams in 1799, the Reverend Nathanael Emmons ended his sermon with an open call for his congregation to support both the Alien and Sedition Acts and the administration's unpopular tax program.[12]

As the election campaign of 1800 entered its final months, some Federalist evangelicals hoped for a miracle. The Reverend Thomas Robbins wrote in his diary that Jefferson would probably become president but added, "Blessed be God that all things are in His hands, and may He avert such an evil from this country for His name's sake. I do not believe that the Most High will permit a howling atheist to sit at the head of this nation!"[13] God apparently had other ideas, and though the election in the Electoral College was close, Jefferson was elected in the end.

The aftermath was a great anticlimax as far as evangelicals were concerned. Contrary to the apocalyptic predictions of one Boston newspaper, Jefferson's election did not place "the *seal of death* . . . on our holy religion" or result in the installation of "some infamous prostitute, under the title of the Goddess of Reason . . . [to] preside in the sanctuaries now devoted to the Most High."[14] In fact, once in office the "howling atheist" from Virginia hid his religious views more furtively than before. He signed laws funding both military chaplains and missionaries among the Indians, and he was ever careful to make pious appeals to providence in his public speeches.[15] His public concessions to his private scruples were few and largely symbolic: He apparently invited Tom Paine to dine at the White House in 1802, and he refused to declare federal days of prayer as both Washington and Adams had done, though here Jefferson covered himself by justifying his action in terms of states' rights as well as religious liberty.[16]

Nevertheless, Federalist clergy remained stubbornly reluctant to relinquish their past fears. A month after Jefferson took office, Nathaniel Emmons continued to warn of the coming disaster.[17] It never came—but there were false alarms. In 1802 the clerics' worst nightmares appeared to come true when a mysterious fire broke out at the College of New Jersey at Princeton, one of the remaining bastions of both evangelicalism and Federalism. The conflagration gutted Nassau Hall, consuming most of the college's library and damaging scientific equipment. A board of inquiry convened by the college concluded that the fire had been set,[18] and President Samuel Stanhope

Smith knew where to assign blame. Writing to the Reverend Jedidiah Morse of Boston, Smith complained that the fire was the responsibility of a "small sect" of "jacobinal and anti-religious principles."[19] Despite Smith's suspicions, no one was ever prosecuted for the fire, though several students were expelled.[20]

Bleak as conditions may have appeared to Federalist evangelicals after the election of 1800, two events were already under way that would revive the political fortunes of evangelicalism well into the nineteenth century. The first was the Second Great Awakening. Thirty years before the American Revolution, the original Great Awakening had returned thousands to active piety and revived the influence of evangelical churches in America. But in the initial decades after the Revolution, evangelical religion had fallen under seige from eighteenth-century rationalism. The "Age of Reason" reigned, and Unitarianism captured the former bastions of the Puritans.[21] Now the tide turned. As the end of the century neared, a revival of evangelical religion began in selected parts of both the North and the South, spreading in subsequent years throughout the eastern seaboard and, ultimately, to the western frontier.[22] This sustained evangelical revival was connected to—but not identical with—the broader rise of popular religion during the period described by Nathan Hatch and others. As pointed out in the Introduction, not all of the popular religious movements in early-nineteenth-century America were "evangelical" in the strict doctrinal sense of the term. But certainly many of them were, and these replenished the beleaguered evangelical churches and reinvigorated evangelical clergy.

Precisely how many Americans became evangelicals during this period is open to dispute, in part because more people attended evangelical churches than actually joined them. Accordingly, calculations of religious adherents vary dramatically. In 1832 English lawyer William Gore Ousely estimated that there were roughly 1.3 million Americans attached to various evangelical denominations, if only communicant members were counted. Using a broader definition, however, he estimated that more than 8.4 million Americans were somehow affiliated with evangelical churches.[23] Nineteenth-century historian Robert Baird provided a similarly two-tiered estimate in 1855, reporting that, whereas 4.2 million Americans were members of evangelical churches, some 17.8 million were "more or less under the influence of the evangelical denominations."[24] Whatever the actual numbers, religious adherence rates jumped sharply during this period, and evangelicals unquestionably made up the vast majority of the adherents.[25] Needless to say, the political potential of this pool of like-minded individuals was substantial.

The second event critical to the success of evangelical politics during this period was one that Congregationialists in New England had fought tooth and claw to prevent: disestablishment. It was a case of not knowing what was in one's own best interest. The triumph of the Republicans in state and local elections in New England all but assured an eventual end to what had become known as "the standing order," and the day of reckoning finally arrived when establishments came to an end in Connecticut in 1818 and New Hampshire in 1819.[26] In Massachusetts, meanwhile, a controversy was brewing that would ultimately force Congregationalists in that state to rethink their position on the issue. Over the objections of church members, voters in Dedham Parish had voted to install a Unitarian minister in the town's state-supported church. In 1821 the Massachusetts Supreme Court approved the election, holding that the state bill of rights "secure[d] to towns, not to the churches, the right to elect the minister in last resort."[27] As a result, Congregationalists lost an estimated eighty-one churches to the Unitarians. Seeing establishment turned against orthodox congregations, Congregationalist support for the establishment in Massachusetts withered. In 1823 Congregationalists joined with Republicans to elect a reform legislature that significantly liberalized the Massachusetts establishment; and in 1833, with Congregationalist support, the standing order was abandoned altogether.[28]

Disestablishment was important because it removed the chief obstacle to an evangelical united front on social issues. The standing order had driven a wedge between Congregationalists and other evangelicals, obscuring the fact that they otherwise occupied much common ground. Baptists and Methodists opposed infidelity as much as Congregationalists and Presbyterians did. Baptists and Methodists adhered to a strict moral code based on piety and the Bible. They also supported fast days and the strict observance of the Sabbath.[29] Now that state support of ministers had come to an end, these common beliefs about social order rose to the surface. The door was thrown open to joint action on behalf of common social ends; the only question was whether evangelicals would walk through the opening. They did, and no man did more to coax them onward than Presbyterian divine Lyman Beecher. Among all the evangelicals of the period, Beecher was perhaps the one who most keenly understood changing conditions and what evangelicals needed to do if they were to exert a dominant influence on American society.

He became the most powerful proponent of moral reform in the early nine-teenth century, and he was the chief, though not the sole, architect of what one historian termed America's " 'voluntary establishment' of religion."[30]

## LYMAN BEECHER AND THE ORIGINS OF EVANGELICAL REFORM (1803–1812)

Lyman Beecher remains one of the most intriguing figures of American his-tory.[31] He is remarkable not only for his own achievements, which were con-siderable, but for the accomplishments of his many children. The Beecher family was so prolific in such a variety of ways that someone once quipped that the human race consisted of "men, women, and Beechers."[32] There was more than a kernel of truth to the comment. Most of Beecher's children at-tained distinctions of one sort or another: Henry Ward became a famous ab-olitionist and champion of liberal Congregationalism; Edward assumed the presidency of Illinois College; Charles became Florida's superintendent of public schools; Catherine pioneered education for women, though she obsti-nately opposed women's suffrage; her sister Isabella, as if in rejoinder, be-came a prominent suffragette; and Harriet fanned the flames of abolition in 1852 with *Uncle Tom's Cabin*.[33]

The interests and activities of the children reflected the multidisciplinary talents of their father, who was schoolmaster, sparring partner, and comrade in arms all at once. As Charles Beecher recalled after his father's death: "The law of his family was that, if any one had a good thing, he must not keep it to himself; if he could say a funny thing, he was bound to say it; if a severe thing, no matter—the severer the better, if well *put*. . . . To look upon some hotly-contested theological discussion, a stranger might have said the doctor and his children were angry with each other. Never; they were only in earnest."[34] Beecher inspired fierce devotion in his children, who adored their father even when exasperated by him. Their exuberant attachment to him comes out best in his autobiography, which was turned into a collective fam-ily effort after Beecher became unable to complete it because of his deterio-rating mental faculties.[35]

Beecher's close relations with his children stood in stark contrast to his own upbringing. His mother died two days after childbirth, and his father, a blacksmith, handed him over to his uncle and aunt to be raised. Beecher labored on his uncle's farm into his teenage years, a modest beginning that gave him a lifelong empathy for the working classes.[36] At eighteen Beecher entered Yale and found in President Timothy Dwight a replacement for a distant father. "I loved him as my own soul," Beecher wrote later, "and he loved me as a son. And once . . . I told him that all I had I owed to him. 'Then,' said he, 'I have done a great and soul-satisfying work. I consider myself amply rewarded.' "[37]

Beecher's subsequent career was long and turbulent. His first pastorate ended abruptly when he sought a salary increase and the majority of the church refused him. He then removed to a church in Litchfield, Connecticut, where he labored during the next a decade and a half. In 1826 he assumed the pulpit at the Hanover Street Church in Boston, where he waged war against the Unitarians who had come to dominate both the city's politics and its churches. Beecher was so disliked by Boston Unitarians that when the Hanover Street Church caught fire in 1829, firemen stood idly by and sang in derision, "While Beecher's church holds out to burn; / The vilest sinner may return."[38] In 1832 Beecher became president of Lane Theological Seminary in Cincinatti, Ohio. Envisioned as an evangelical beachhead in the burgeoning west, Lane was soon decimated from within by a split between abolitionist students and a conservative board of directors. In 1835 Beecher was charged with heresy for not adhering to some of the finer intricacies of Calvinist theology. Tried before the Presbyterian synod, he was eventually exonerated. He lived to see the nation engulfed by the Civil War, dying in 1863 after a long enfeeblement.[39]

Beecher originally became interested in moral reform during his first pastorate, in East Hampton, Long Island. He was not the first American evangelical to spearhead reform efforts,[40] but he soon became the most prominent—and the most far-seeing. Possessed by a keen sense of justice, Beecher told his daughter Harriet that he "didn't set up for a reformer any more than this: when I saw a rattlesnake in my path I would smite it."[41] Some of the first rattlesnakes to catch Beecher's attention were whites who mistreated the local Indians on Long Island and preyed on their thirst for liquor. One white merchant would sell whiskey to the Indians until they had given him all their corn. When winter came, the Indians had to buy it back or starve. "Oh, it was horrible, horrible!" recalled Beecher later. "It burned . . . in my mind, and I swore a deep oath to God that it shouldn't be so."[42]

About the same time Beecher was confronted by the plight of the Indians, he was reading accounts in the *Christian Observer* "of efforts in London to repress immorality, drunkenness, and Sabbath-breaking."[43] Realizing that the methods employed by British reformers could be transferred to America, Beecher began to collect his thoughts on the subject. In February 1803, after he preached a sermon, the Moral Society of East Hampton was organized by local citizens "for the suppression of vice, and the promotion of virtue, and useful knowledge."[44] Six months later Beecher appeared before the association to deliver a call to arms.

## Beecher's First Call for Reform (1803)

Beecher's address before the group was titled "The Practicality of Suppressing Vice by Means of Societies Instituted for That Purpose." In it Beecher decried the moral decay of society and warned that if reformation did not occur, the nation's doom was assured because "sin is in its nature anti-social. It will sunder the ties of society; lead us to bite and devour; to be hateful, and to hate one another. God has cursed a departure from the laws and institutions of this government with discord and misery. There is no peace, saith my God, to the wicked."[45] Notice that instead of threatening direct heavenly retribution for vice, Beecher articulated the idea that virtue and vice have natural rewards and punishments in the here and now. In the present life virtue is its own reward, and vice is its own worst punishment. God need not destroy a vicious nation by direct action; he may simply allow it to destroy itself.

Although Beecher vigorously attacked the moral decay of society, he did not condemn most citizens as immoral. If immorality was spreading like contagion, this was occurring less because the majority was corrupt than because the majority was befuddled. Indeed, according to Beecher, the majority started out moral. But this moral majority proved powerless to stop the advancement of vice because sin often masquerades "under the name of virtue" and people are slow to recognize its true aspect.[46] By the time they do recognize the problem, they are often too late. Like the disorganized democracies that appeased Adolf Hitler in the 1930s, the disorganized public faced by immorality will dawdle until disaster is overwhelming.

Hence, organization is necessary. If society is to be reformed and rendered safe for republican government, citizens must unite together in associations to expose the designs of the vicious and prosecute efforts for the promotion of the public good.[47] Once formed, the most important objective of a reform association, according to Beecher, is to shape "public opinion" because it "has in society a singular influence; if vice can in any instance enlist that opinion on its side, it triumphs. But let the weight of that opinion be laid upon any vicious practice, and it will most inevitably sink under it." Moral associations may further influence opinion and habits by promoting moral and religious education among "the rising generation," which will ensure that the next group of citizens will "fill usefully the spheres in which they are called to move."[48]

To those who might have considered this scheme impractical, Beecher responded with a description of successful reform efforts that had begun in London in 1697. If the English could reform London then, when vice was "intrenched, bold, open and daring; religion despised, ridiculed, and, to appearance, almost extinguished," American Christians ought to be able to reform their towns and cities, where conditions were considerably brighter. To those who might object that moral reform would cause dissention in society, Beecher replied that, even if it did, unrestrained immorality would cause more.[49]

As necessary as moral associations are for society's improvement, they are not the whole solution, according to Beecher. Alone, he warned, they could not transform society. "They are to be considered rather as an addition to existing means, and calculated to impart to them additional efficacy." Chief among these "existing means" is "our religion."[50] Beecher conceded that irreligion and immorality are not the same thing, but he contended that one feeds into the other. Irreligion undermines civic morality by removing from the populace the fear of God and his future retribution against evildoers.[51] Thus, without religion civic morality cannot long survive: "Let the sabbath be annihilated, and the sanctuary abandoned; let irreligion and vice be extended through the mass of our nation, and our liberties cannot be preserved. We may form free constitutions, but our vices will destroy them; we may enact laws, but they will not protect us."[52]

In talking about religion as a political virtue, Beecher framed the issue in terms the Founders would have understood; he accordingly cited neither the Bible nor another cleric as the irrefutable authority on the subject. He instead invoked George Washington, father of the country, quoting from the celebrated passage on religion and morality in Washington's Farewell Address. Beecher's underlying implication was clear: If Washington recognized that "a national morality" cannot "prevail in exclusion of religious principles,"[53] surely no other American could dare brand this idea as the un-American product of meddlesome priests. Beecher had played the ultimate trump card; he was staking his theory squarely on the grounds of American republicanism.

If Beecher was hopeful about the prospects for reform in America, however, he was not utopian. He made clear that he expected incremental change, not a revolution. After all, "we are not angels, but men"; nevertheless, "if we can gradually improve ourselves, and improve the society in which we live, though in a small degree, it is an object not to be despised."[54] Beecher's vision of the organizational apparatus of moral reform was equally modest. His strategy in 1803 was one of unadulterated localism. He wanted each town to have a general reform association that would tackle all the moral evils prevalent in the local community. He apparently envisioned thousands of independent moral societies springing up in towns and hamlets across America, each waging the battle against corruption in its own backyard. To assist other communities in their efforts, Beecher had his sermon on moral reform printed as a pamphlet, with the constitution of the East Hampton society supplied as an appendix.

For the most part these thousands of societies never materialized. Over the next decade only a handful of voluntary associations formed, and most of these focused on propagation of the Gospel rather than moral reform. Even if one includes efforts to promote the Gospel as part of moral reform, the results were less than spectacular.[55] Nevertheless, from small beginnings great movements often grow, and during this period an event occurred that sparked an important trial run for the national reform movements that would come later.

## The Antidueling Crusade (1804–)

Ten months after Beecher's sermon in East Hampton, Vice President Aaron Burr shot down Alexander Hamilton in a duel. The two men had been rowed across the Hudson River early in the morning on July 11 to a field in New Jersey. Burr apparently fired first, and Hamilton's gun went off into the air as he was knocked backward to the ground. Hamilton was removed to the house of friend William Bayard in New York, where he lingered between life and death for another day. "His sufferings . . . [were] almost intolerable," his doctor, David Hosack, wrote later. He died at two o'clock in the afternoon on July 12.[56]

Hamilton's death seared the national conscience and provoked America's first national reform movement of consequence. The barbaric custom of taking another's life to avenge an insult was practiced by the most distinguished members of society, and it was far from uncommon in nineteenth-century America. Burr's murder of Hamilton supplied an opportunity to forge a public consensus against the practice, and the nation's ministers seized the occasion to do just that.

Eighteen days after the duel, Presbyterian clergyman Eliphalet Nott— soon to assume the presidency of Union College—condemned dueling in a eulogy of Hamilton delivered before the North Dutch Church in Albany. Dueling "originated in a dark and barbarous age," said Nott. "The polished Greek knew nothing of it. The noble Roman was above it. Rome held in equal detestation the man who exposed his life unnecessarily, and him who refused to expose it when the public good required it. . . . But though Greece and Rome knew nothing of dueling, it exists among us the most rash, the most absurd, and the most guilty practice, that ever disgraced a Christian nation."[57]

Two days later, on July 31, in a funeral oration before the New York State Society of the Cincinnati, John Mason was equally indignant. "The grave of HAMILTON speaks," he declared. "It charges me to remind you that he fell a victim not to disease or accident; not to the fortune of glorious warfare; but, how shall I utter it? to a custom which has no origin but superstition, no aliment but depravity, no reason but in madness." Mason went on to argue that dueling contradicts every moral precept held dear by honorable men: "Is it honorable to serve your country? That man cruelly injures her, who, from private pique, calls his fellow citizen into the dubious field. Is fidelity honorable? That man forswears his faith, who turns against the bowels of his countrymen, weapons put into his hand for their defence." Mason added that if Americans failed to heed the clear dictates of morality and abolish dueling, they invited God's judgment on the nation.[58]

Two weeks later in South Carolina, Baptist minister Richard Furman told his own state's Society of the Cincinatti that "it would be inexcusable in the conduct of a gospel minister" to pass over the "cruel custom" of dueling during a eulogy for Hamilton. Furman went on to attack the practice as a barbarism that gratified "the inhuman passion" for murder and revenge. He

acknowledged that the protection of one's reputation "is of vast consequence to man" but argued that it should be protected "by such means
*alone,* as are worthy of a rational, immortal creature." He further noted the
irony of trying to defend one's reputation by a duel because even if the in-
sulted man prevails and lives, he will "suffer the censure and contempt of all
wise and good men, as well as the reproach of his own conscience."[59]

On September 9, Yale president Timothy Dwight joined the growing cho-
rus of critics, but with nary a mention of either Hamilton or Burr. Dwight,
who was Burr's first cousin, shied away from even alluding to the late conflict, prefacing his sermon with the disclaimer that it would "not intention-
ally apply to any facts of person; it being the Preacher's design to examine
principles, and not to give characters."[60]

Dwight declared that he would show the "THE FOLLY, THE GUILT, and THE
IMPIETY" of dueling, and he proceeded to knock down every conceivable argument on the practice's behalf. As punishment for an offense, dueling is
"absurd" because it places the innocent party in equal jeopardy with the
guilty. As reparation for an evil done, it is even less rational because it can
never repair the damage done to one's reputation. People will not believe a
libel less just because the libeler was killed in a duel. "Truth and falsehood
must, if evinced at all, be evinced by evidence; not by fighting." Nor does
dueling in any way demonstrate a man's good character. It does not prove
that a man has the virtue of bravery because "[b]ravery is honourable . . .
only when exerted in a just, useful, rational cause; where some real good is
intended, and may hopefully be accomplished. In every other case it is the
courage of a brute." Neither does dueling show that a man is truly honorable, for "there is neither delicacy nor honour, in giving or taking affronts
easily and suddenly; nor in justifying them on the one hand, nor in reveng-
ing them on the other. Very little children do all these things daily, without
either honour or delicacy, from the mere impulse of infantine passion.
Those who imitate them in this conduct, resemble them in character; and are
only bigger children."[61]

Finally, said Dwight, the claim that dueling is supported by public opinion is both false and irrelevant. The general public has never justified dueling in any civilized country, and in America the public voice is clearly
against the custom. Only duelists themselves pronounce the practice to be
anything but contemptible.[62] Even if the general public did favor dueling,
however, every decent man would be obliged to condemn it. "No man is

truly great, who has not resolution to withstand, and will not invariably and undauntedly withstand, every false and ruinous public opinion. . . . He who will not do this, when either the worship of a stock, the immolation of a human victim, or the murder of his fellow men, is justified by public opinion, is not only devoid of sound principles, but the subject of miserable cowardice."[63] In short, dueling does nothing its defenders claim it will do, and it violates the most fundamental precepts of the moral order. It is therefore an abomination before both God and man.

Driving his discourse to its inexorable climax, Dwight appealed to the prospective duelist to come and see the dreadful effects of his crime. If cold reason could not persuade him to abandon his scheme, perhaps vividly seeing its aftermath in his mind's eye would. Dwight asked the duelist to visit the newly dug grave of his victim, to step inside the house of his victim's family, to see the tears of his parents, wife, and children.[64] But if the duelist has inflicted such terrible sufferings on the loved ones of his victim, he himself can expect even more horrible tortures on the other side of the grave. Few ministers have drawn as terrifying a picture of damnation as Dwight drew here: "At the great and final day, your country will rise up in judgment against you, to accuse you as the destroyers of her peace, and the murderers of her children. Against you will rise up in judgment all the victims of your revenge, and all the wretched families, whom you have plunged in hopeless misery."[65]

In the last few sentences of this passage, Dwight effectively abandoned his promise of not applying his sermon to particular cases, chastising the hypothetical duelist for abandoning his Christian upbringing from "the moment of birth." This was all but a direct slap at Burr, who, like Dwight, was a grandson of the famous New England divine Jonathan Edwards and whose own father was a promiment minister and president of the College of New Jersey from 1748 to 1757.[66] Dwight's message was clear even if it was cloaked: Burr had repudiated his godly ancestry by instigating and carrying out a duel; he had thus condemned himself to an eternity of intolerable punishment.

A few evangelicals were more compassionate toward Burr. A tract appeared in New York a few days later that sought to offer the vice president a chance at redemption. Put in the form of a letter to Burr, the pamphlet promised him that he could yet avoid the fires of hell if he would only repent and accept God's forgiveness through Christ's death on the cross. To spur

Burr to reflection and repentence, the author, who wrote under the pseudonym "Philanthropos," examined the multifaceted evils of dueling at considerable length, showing that it violated the precepts of reason as well as revelation.[67]

As powerful as these several assaults on dueling were, the polemic most instrumental in making dueling a serious public issue came from Lyman Beecher. When Beecher read about the duel between Hamilton and Burr in the newspaper, he was filled with indignation, and for six months he worked on a sermon condemning the practice.[68] Beecher titled his address "The Remedy for Dueling," and in it he went well beyond other ministers by proposing that citizens withhold their votes from candidates who have participated in duels. Beecher regarded this as the only effectual method of removing the blight of dueling from the land, and he contended that it was a course of action sanctioned by both revelation and reason.[69]

Beecher argued that revelation excludes duelists from public office because it demands that rulers be just men who fear God. But duelists could never "answer this description" for "when arrested by the fatal challenge, no plea of reverence for God, of respect for human law, of conscience, of innocency . . . is for one moment admitted. All obligations are cancelled; all ties are burst asunder; all consequences are disregarded. . . . The obedient subjects of a law so impious, so unmerciful and unjust, God has denounced as unfit to govern men."[70]

But even if "the word of God" does not require the exclusion of duelists from public office, "the abhorrence of murder should exclude from confidence these men of blood." It is a bold affront to the moral law to elevate a murderer to an honored position as ruler, and according to Beecher, every duelist should be regarded as a murderer because every duelist declares his intention to murder, even if he does not actually succeed.[71]

Public safety likewise demands that duelists be kept from public office. "When we intrust life and liberty and property to the hands of men, we desire some pledge of their fidelity." But duelists can offer none because they have demonstrated their rejection of the principles of both religion and morality. They cannot be trusted to act justly. Nor can they be trusted to stay at the helm of the country in times of crisis: "What security have we that the duelist will not, if intrusted with our liberties, desert us in the hour of danger? What security can we have, when it is in the power of every factious rival who can shoot straight to compel him to the field; and, by destroying his life, to derange, perhaps to annihilate, the government?" The election of duelists to public office further undercuts the public safety by confounding "in the public mind, the distinctions between virtue and vice, and weakens that abhorrence of crime which is the guardian of public morality. Elevate swindlers to office, and who shall guarantee the integrity of the common people? Elevate adulterers, and who will punish incontinence? Elevate murderers, and who will be the avengers of blood?"[72]

Equally important, the election of duelists fosters "the destruction of civil liberty" because it honors those who adhere to a system incompatible with republican government. "A free government is a government of laws, made by the people for the protection of life, reputation, and property. A despotic government is where life and all its blessings are subject to the caprice of an individual."[73] The Code Duello inculcates despotism by promoting the idea that disputes ought to be settled by combat rather than by law. Duelists in public office also undermine civil liberty by restraining the freedom of speech:

> The people have a right to investigate the conduct of rulers, and to scrutinize the character of candidates for office. . . . But who will speak on this subject, who will publish, when the duelist stands before him, with pistol at the breast? . . . What should we think of a law that forbade the people to speak of the immoralities of candidates for office,— which made death the penalty of transgression, and which produced annually as many deaths as this nefarious system of dueling? We should not endure it a moment.[74]

Finally, from the standpoint of the voter, voting for a duelist is immoral because it indirectly encourages dueling. "Laws in republics depend for their prompt execution upon a correct and efficient public sentiment." By accepting duelists as officials, the public sends a message to law enforcement that it need not vigorously prosecute the crime of dueling. If, however, voters refuse to elect duelists, their opposition "will tend to annihilate the practice, by arraying public opinion against it in such a manner that the real, unavoidable disgrace of fighting, will be greater than that of refusing to fight."[75]

Beecher denied that any partisan motives lay behind his proposal. He contended that dueling was a great issue of national morality and that his comments applied equally to members of every party. "It is vain to cry out 'priestcraft,' or 'political preaching'; these watch-words will not answer here. The crime we oppose is peculiar to no party; it is common to all. It is a crime too horrid to be palliated, too threatening to be longer endured in officers of government. Any political effect would be the consequence merely, not the object of our exertions."[76]

Although Beecher delivered his antidueling address in churches, he did not expect church members to fight the battle by themselves. For Beecher, dueling was not a peculiarly religious issue; it was a moral issue, and morality applied to all citizens. Thus, "churches will not be left to stand alone. In every part of the nation there are multitudes, conscientious and patriotic, whose zealous cooperation may be expected. Voluntary associations may be formed, correspondences may be established, and a concert of action secured."[77]

Despite this hopeful prediction of the movement's prospects, the immediate effects of the antidueling campaign were less than momentous. Dueling continued to be sanctioned by a significant proportion of the ruling class, and an array of prominent figures in years to come participated in duels, including Stephen Decatur (who died in a duel), Henry Clay (whose duel ended without injury to either party), and Andrew Jackson (who killed a man in one duel and participated in several others). Even Alexander Hamilton's son James sent a challenge in 1809 to someone who had criticized his father in a speech, in stark violation of the elder Hamilton's deathbed condemnation of the practice. When the recipient of the younger Hamilton's challenge refused to accept it, he was branded a coward by the press.[78]

Despite the lingering popularity of dueling, sermons continued to be preached against the practice, resolutions condemning it continued to be enacted by religious bodies, and gradually both public opinion and the laws began to change.[79] In New York the Reverend Asahel Hooker read Beecher's sermon and founded an antidueling association with the assistance of John Mason.[80] Beecher himself subsequently presented a resolution "recommending the formation of societies against dueling" at a Presbyterian synod meeting in Newark, New Jersey. He later recalled how he had mistakenly thought there would be no opposition. A minister who came from a parish where several prominent political men supported the practice promptly demanded that the resolution be dropped. "He came into the house and made opposition, and thereupon others joined, and it suddenly raised such a storm as I never was in before nor since," wrote Beecher. "The opposition came up like a squall, sudden and furious, and there I was, the thunder and lightning right in my face; but I did not back out. When my turn came, I rose and knocked away their arguments, and made them ludicrous. Never made an argument so short, strong, and pointed in my life. I shall never forget it. . . . I was only thirty, a young man nobody had ever heard of. . . . Oh, I declare! if I did not switch 'em, and scorch 'em, and stamp on 'em!"[81]

In 1805 the General Assembly of the Presbyterian Church took a stand on the issue, encouraging its ministers to refrain from attending to the funerals of those who died in duels; it further urged them to refuse the privileges of the church to those who sent or accepted challenges. In 1809 the Convention of Congregational Ministers in Massachusetts pressed its state legislature to enact more effective laws on the subject. In 1810 Virginia disqualified those who sent and received challenges from public office and required all public officials to take an oath against dueling before assuming office. In 1818 Connecticut's new constitution denied duelists the right to vote. The same year the constitution of Alabama gave the state legislature the power to disqualify duelists from public office, and in 1834 Tennessee's constitution actually did so. Tennessee's prohibition was particularly broad, denying public office to "any person who shall . . . fight a duel, or knowingly be the bearer of a challenge to fight a duel, or send or accept a challenge for that purpose, or be an aider or abettor in fighting a duel."[82]

Antidueling legislation was also proposed at the national level. In 1806 Congress passed a law regulating the armed forces that forbade the sending and receiving of challenges or the giving of any assistance to the dueling parties.[83] In 1819 after the death of General John T. Mason in a duel, David Morril proposed that the president be requested to dismiss duelists from the armed services. Failing to win approval for this measure, Morril suggested that a law be passed punishing dueling in the District of Columbia, a proposal that also went nowhere. A year later Stephen Decatur met his death in a duel, and Senator Morril renewed his call for the removal of duelists from the armed forces. Less than a month after Decatur's death, Morril offered a resolution stating "that the President of the United States would be justifiable in striking from the rolls of the army, the names of all persons thereon who have been, or hereafter may be, directly or indirectly, engaged in a duel, or who may have been, or hereafter may be, in any way or manner accessary thereto."[84] This proposal was likewise scuttled. From 1819 to 1822 the House of Representatives considered strengthening the prohibition against dueling in the armed forces but ultimately did nothing.[85] In 1831 Congress again considered prohibiting dueling in the District of Columbia, but it was not until 1839—after a notorious duel between two congressmen that resulted in one of their deaths—that the prohibition actually passsed.[86]

Even though the antidueling campaign failed to achieve immediate results, it was nevertheless an important milestone in the history of American evangelical political activism. It proved that American evangelicals could be more than mere creatures of the existing political order. Previous efforts to expose the conspiracies of Jacobins and the irreligious character of Jefferson had been inextricably intertwined with the party competition between Federalists and Republicans. The campaign against dueling, however, stood on its own merits. Dueling was a moral issue that cut across party lines, and concern over the issue later ended up hurting candidates from both major parties.[87]

The antidueling crusade further demonstrated that evangelicals could enter politics without making religious doctrines the focus of their efforts. During the unseemly Jefferson-Adams contest, Federalist clergy had been obsessed with the theology and piety of the two candidates. The dueling campaign broadened the evangelicals' political horizon. Ministers did not rely exclusively, or even primarily, on the Bible for their arguments against dueling. To be sure, they talked about God's impending judgment because of dueling; but they also stressed moral principles ascertainable by reason and common sense. Eliphalet Nott declared that even pagan Rome and Greece did not embrace dueling, indicating that one need not be a Christian to recoil at the practice. John Mason argued that dueling contradicts patriotism, fidelity, generosity, and humanity. Richard Furman intimated that the practice is unbefitting a "rational, immortal creature." Timothy Dwight condemned dueling's "folly" as well as its "impiety," and Lyman Beecher sought to prove that the custom is a menace to both public safety and civil liberty. In sum, according to evangelical critics, "reason, no less than revelation, remonstrates against" the practice.[88] Evangelicals thus argued the issue within the framework laid down by the Founders. They entered the field of politics on the solid ground of moral principles accessible to both reason and revelation.

But the antidueling campaign was only a first step, a shadow of things to come. By the second decade of the new century, Beecher's vision of thou-

sands of reform associations remained unfulfilled, and in his view the pre-
cipitous moral decline of society continued. Now a minister in Litchfield,
Connecticut, Beecher looked around him and saw a commonwealth rife
with profanity, intemperance, and Sabbath breaking. The old laws against
immorality had fallen by the wayside, and the fate of Connecticut's establishment of religion was as precarious as that of the Federalist Party. Something had to be done. Society had to be reformed, and the churches had to
be prepared for the time when the standing order supporting religion might
fall. "It was the anticipation of the impending revolution and downfall of
the standing order that impelled me to the efforts I made at that time to
avert it, and to prepare for it in all possible ways," he observed later.[89]

Beecher's solution to the crisis was the one he had latched onto in East
Hampton back in 1802: voluntary associations for evangelism and moral reform. Voluntary associations could promote public support for the enforcement of the laws, and, more important, they could operate where the laws
could not reach. Beecher quickly set about organizing a statewide association to suppress immorality, and in October 1812 the Connecticut Society
for the Suppression of Vice and the Promotion of Good Morals was
founded in Hartford.[90]

## Beecher's Second Call for Reform (1812)

Beecher used the occasion to deliver a revised version of his reform sermon
from 1802, "The Practicality of Suppressing Vice by Means of Societies Instituted for That Purpose." He now called the talk "A Reformation of Morals Practicable and Indispensable."[91] The new title indicated the greater ur-
gency of the times. Moral reformation was now not merely practical; it was
also indispensable. Beecher painted the situation of Connecticut in stark
colors. He complained that magistrates had failed to enforce the laws
against immorality for so long that soon the public would not tolerate their
enforcement by magistrates who wanted to do so.[92]

If Beecher was more fearful of the state of society than in 1802, he was
also less sanguine about the general public. In his earlier sermon he had said
that the majority starts out moral and that it allows immorality to proceed
through ignorance of its designs. But here he vigorously criticized the public
for laying down obstacles to reform.

Some citizens lament the prevalent evils, said Beecher, "but if a voice be raised or a finger be lifted to attempt a reformation, they are in a tremor lest the peace of society be invaded. Their maxim would seem to be 'Better to die in sin, if we may but die quietly, than to purchase life and honor by contending for them.'" Others, the bane of a commercial republic, are too preoccupied with their own selfish pursuits: "If *their* fields bring forth abundantly, if *their* profession be lucrative, if *they* can buy and sell and get gain, it is enough. Society must take care of itself. Distant consequences are not regarded, and generations to come must provide for their own safety. The stream of business hurries them on, without the leisure of a moment, or an anxious thought concerning the general welfare." Still others wring their hands and lament that nothing can be done: "It seems never to have occurred to them, that if we cannot do great good, it is best to do a little; and that, by accomplishing with persevering industry all that is practicable, the ultimate amount may be great surpassing expectation."[93] And some pious citizens simply pray and wait for God to deliver them. Benjamin Franklin would have fully approved Lyman Beecher's retort to this excuse, which was a variation of Poor Richard's counsel that *"God helps them that help themselves."*[94] Said Beecher: "Upon this principle, we may pray and wait forever, and the Lord will not come. The kingdom of God is a kingdom of means; and though the excellency of the power belongs to him exclusively, human instrumentality is indispensable."[95]

Finally, there are those citizens who stake out the comfortable middle ground. They are neither hot nor cold. They are the popularity seekers, and they will not join one side until its success is imminent. This group encompasses politicians in particular, and its prevalence in American society is one of the less savory consequences of republican government: "They will not oppose the work, for perhaps it may be popular; and they will not help the works, for perhaps it may be unpopular. . . . This neutral territory is especially large in a republican government, where so much emolument, and the gratification of so much ambition, depend upon the suffrages of the people."[96]

Despite this array of obstacles, Beecher argued that reform not only must be prosecuted but also might succeed. He recalled the accomplishments of previous reformers, such as the abolition of the slave trade in England. "Reformations great and difficult have been achieved."[97] All that Americans needed was a practical plan of action, and Beecher quickly supplied one.

First, public attention must be captured, and the public must be convinced of the magnitude of the evils. This would be no easy feat, for

> [a] small portion only, of the whole mass of crimes, is seen at any one point. A few tippling-shops are observed in a particular place, impoverishing families; and rearing up drunkards; but it is not considered that thousands, with like pestilential influence, are at work all over the land, training up recruits to hunt down law and order. A few instances are witnessed of needless travelling, or labor, or amusement, on the Sabbath, which excite a momentary alarm. But it is not considered that a vast army,—probably three millions of people,—are assailing, at the same time, this great bulwark of Christian lands.[98]

Second, reformation must start within the churches themselves. "If we would attempt . . . the work of reformation, we must make the experiment first upon ourselves. We must cease to do evil, and learn to do well, that, with pure hands and clear vision, we may be qualified to reclaim others."[99] Third, attention must be given to the religious education of the young. Morality will not flourish without religion, and if the rising generation is to be moral, it must learn about God and duty at both home and school.[100]

Finally, laws against immorality and vice must be promptly enforced. Moral suasion alone will not work. "Much may be done in the way of prevention; but, in a free government, moral suasion and coercion must be united."[101] However, this last objective could not be achieved at once because of the dissolute state of society. Laws could not be enforced without public support, and the public increasingly did not accept the laws against intemperance and Sabbath breaking. Thus, before these laws can be enforced, the people must be persuaded that they are just. Here is the critical function of voluntary associations. They must work to create public support for good laws. "They [will] awaken the public attention, and by the sermons, the reports, and the conversation they occasion, diffuse much moral instruction. . . . They have great influence to form correctly the public opinion, and to render the violation of the law disgraceful, as well as dangerous."[102] When vice is again abhorred by society, when reprobates are again shunned and looked on with shame, then the laws will at last prevail. But this result can be achieved only if the people themselves are convinced of its propriety, for in republican regimes persuasion must proceed coercion.

This time Beecher's ideas began to take hold. Voluntary associations of every kind conceivable soon sprang up around the country, supplemented by a growing network of evangelical periodicals that provided an outlet for their views.[103]

## THE RISE OF EVANGELICAL REFORM
## (1812–1835)

Some of the new voluntary associations were local, of the character originally envisioned by Beecher in the Moral Society of East Hampton on Long Island. Within a year after the formation of the Connecticut Society for the Suppression of Vice, thirty local societies were organized in that state alone.[104] Such local associations could draw support from a variety of churches, as the Moral Society of East Haddam, Connecticut, attested. In 1817 its members included Baptists, Presbyterians, and Episcopalians.[105] After disestablishment in Connecticut and New Hampshire and the *Dedham* decision in Massachusetts, interdenominational cooperation increased further. As Lyman Beecher later wrote about the situation in Connecticut: "The consequence [of disestablishment] unexpectedly was . . . that the occasion of animosity between us and the minor sects was removed, and infidels could no more make capital with them against us, and they then began themselves to feel the dangers of infidelity, and to react against it, and this laid the basis of cooperation and union of spirit."[106]

Cooperation among evangelicals at the grass roots continued to flourish during the early part of the nineteenth century. Sometimes the spirit of unity that resulted was profound. In Rochester, New York, Methodists seeking to rebuild a church that had burned down and Baptists seeking money for their own church building received financial aid from Presbyterians and other evangelicals. Moreover, during Rochester's 1832 revival "Baptist, Methodist, Presbyterian, and Episcopal ministers preached from the same pulpit, and the place of meeting shifted indiscriminately between churches."[107]

Such interdenominational cooperation did not stop at the local level. It was also key to the development of interdenominational associations at the state and national levels that focused on particular issues.[108] By the 1820s the push for national reform groups that could coordinate efforts around the country had become inexorable, and the result was what one historian has called "a passion for merger, consolidation, and monopoly such as swept the business world some seventy years later under similar conditions."[109] These larger national associations included the American Bible Society, the American Tract Society, the American Colonization Society, the American Temperance Society, and the American Sunday School Union. A nonsectarian spirit prevailed among most of these groups, and the boards of many of them boasted members from the all the major Protestant denominations. Evangelical unity became so marked at the national level that several of the major associations began holding their annual meetings together each May in New York City.[110]

As the number of voluntary associations grew, so did the scope of their activities. Some associations still concentrated on evangelism, but many others now explicitly engaged in moral reform, attacking poverty, war, intemperance, Sabbath breaking, prostitution, and slavery. Admittedly, the line between evangelism and moral reform was sometimes hazy in these groups. Evangelicals regarded reformation in the present life as one of the most important fruits of the Gospel—hence, moral reform was regarded as an integral part of evangelism, and the Bible was seen as a textbook of ethics as well as theology.[111] Nevertheless, there was a definite division between the explicitly evangelistic groups and those engaged in moral reform.

## Voluntary Associations Focusing on Evangelism

Many of the explicitly evangelistic associations focused on Bible distribution and instruction. Beginning in 1812 new Bible societies were formed in New York, Maryland, New Jersey, Rhode Island, Connecticut, Delaware, Pennsylvania, Louisiana, Vermont, and Virginia. By 1816 Yale president Timothy Dwight was estimating that there were 150 such societies across the nation. The American Bible Society (established in 1816) soon became the largest and most influential of these, and former Chief Justice John Jay assumed its presidency in 1821.[112] From 1829 to 1830 systematic efforts were made to supply a Bible to every American family without one. By May 1855, reported nineteenth-century historian Robert Baird, "more than eleven and a half million copies of the sacred Scriptures, in whole or in part, had been issued by the Bible Societies in the United States."[113] In the sphere of religious instruction, the American Education Society (established in 1816) provided scholarships for students who wanted to enter the ministry, the American

Tract Society (established in 1825) published religious tracts and books, the American Seamen's Friend Society (established about 1830) looked after the spiritual and temporal interests of sailors, and the American Sunday School Union (established in 1824) taught both children and adults to read and instructed them in the principles of morality and evangelical religion.[114]

Sunday schools merit special notice because of their widespread influence. During a time when public education was virtually nonexistent in many areas (particularly on the western frontier), Sunday schools of neccessity formed the backbone of education in many communities. Given the great need in this area, Sunday schools experienced phenomenal growth. In 1828 an estimated 127,000 pupils attended Sunday classes; by 1835 that figure had spiraled to 1 million. To accommodate such large numbers required an extensive infrastructure of 16,000 Sunday schools and from 130,000 to 140,000 teachers, all of whom volunteered their time without remuneration. Some of the more prominent Sunday school teachers in antebellum America included President William Henry Harrison and U.S. attorney general Benjamin Butler.[115] The vast majority of Sunday schools were affiliated with the American Sunday School Union. Because of its size and resources, the union provoked considerable controversy in some parts of the country; but it also attracted support from influential quarters, as can be seen from its list of vice presidents, which included two sitting members of the Supreme Court—Chief Justice John Marshall and Justice Bushrod Washington, nephew of George Washington. The union spearheaded an aggressive program to spread Sunday schools into new areas of the country, and it published vast quantities of reading material in hopes of reforming the character of American children's literature. By 1830 the union had produced at least 250 separate works; 46 of these had been released within the previous year, adding over 6,000 pages of new reading material.[116]

Missionary societies were also prominent among the evangelical voluntary associations, and they exerted a profound influence on American foreign policy, for as mission efforts increased, so did evangelical interest in international affairs.[117] When the Turks tried to quell the Greek uprising in the 1820s, for example, pulpits around the country resounded with appeals to help Greek rebels in their fight against the Ottoman Empire. By this time American missionaries had a significant presence in the Mediterranean, and the religious undercurrents of the Greek crisis were unmistakable. The Greeks were Christians and the Turks were Moslems; thus, American evangelicals saw the Greeks as fighting not only for their political freedom but also for their right to worship as Christians.[118]

In 1826 missions supporters were aroused even more by an outrage in Hawaii that implicated an American naval officer. Missionaries sponsored by the American Board of Commisioners for Foreign Missions had succeeded in converting many of the Hawaiian chiefs, and one result was that they began to enact laws based on the Ten Commandments. One of these laws forbade prostitution and was particularly unpopular with foreigners, setting the stage for a major conflict between shipping interests and the Hawaiian government. The situation exploded early in 1826 when the naval schooner the USS *Dolphin* arrived at Honolulu, commanded by Lieutenant John "Mad Jack" Percival. On hearing of the antiprostitution law, Percival went before Hawaiian leaders and denounced the prohibition, arguing, among other things, that prostitution was not forbidden in America. The next Sunday a mob consisting of sailors from the *Dolphin* and other ships disrupted the natives' morning worship service and demanded that the law be relaxed; failing to obtain the desired results, they smashed the windows of the meeting hall and proceeded to wreak similar damage on the houses of the missionaries. The Reverend Hiram Bingham, head of the missionary station, narrowly escaped being clubbed and knifed by the mob. The missionaries quickly wrote their missions board back in Massachusetts, and its officials demanded an investigation. A lengthy court of inquiry was held in Massachusetts in 1828, but it cleared Percival, and he was never punished. Nevertheless, the protests had two beneficial effects. First, they showed how American evangelicals could defend their religious interests in the political arena by relying on their equal rights as citizens rather than by demanding preferential treatment from the government. Second, the protests succeeded in preventing similar clashes from arising in the future. The next American naval vessel to arrive in Hawaii carried a letter from President John Quincy Adams that all but apologized for the incident, and thenceforth American naval officers helped, rather than hindered, the missionaries on the islands.[119]

The rise of evangelical voluntary associations to spread the Gospel signaled the evangelicals' willingness to adhere to the Founders' solution of the theological-political problem. Even those evangelicals who had supported establishments of religion in the past were learning that their religion could survive—and thrive—within the voluntary system advocated by the Founders. They realized that they could propagate their faith far better through their own private associations than through any government-funded entity. To prosper, the evangelicals needed only a level playing field.

Yet on occasion even these voluntary efforts at evangelization could raise serious questions about the evangelical commitment to equal rights for all. Perhaps the clearest example of this came in the early 1830s with the rise of associations and publications denouncing Catholicism.[120] These attacks went far beyond theological disputation; they condemned Catholicism as inherently dangerous to American society. On the surface at least, evangelical anti-Catholicism seems to contradict the evangelicals' commitment to a level playing field for all citizens. When examined more closely, however, the issue turns out to be considerably more complicated.

Evangelicals claimed that far from contradicting American republicanism, their attacks on Catholicism were demanded by it. There was more to this argument than mere hysteria. To understand evangelical reasoning on the subject, one must first grasp the larger challenge then facing the nation. By the 1830s America was beginning to receive substantial numbers of emigrants from Europe.[121] Many came from countries where civil liberties and self-government by the people were circumscribed at best. Because evangelicals believed with the Founders that the success of republicanism ultimately depended on the character of the people, they knew that these emigrants posed a problem for America's constitutional system. The emigrants had to be educated in republicanism so that they might take their equal place beside American-born citizens.[122]

Foreign-born Catholics were seen as part of this larger problem posed by emigration. Unlike American-born Catholics, who had grown up in the midst of American liberty and had acquired its habits, many foreign-born Catholics had been raised in countries where an explicit connection between church and state was encouraged and where Catholic political doctrines had not been moderated by republican institutions. The problems this could create for America were displayed in a papal encyclical issued in 1832. In that document Pope Gregory XVI attacked the "absurd and erroneous proposition which claims that *liberty of conscience* must be maintained for everyone. [This doctrine] spreads ruin in sacred and civil affairs, though some repeat over and over again with the greatest impudence that some advantage accrues to religion from it."[123] In the same encyclical the pope condemned the "harmful and never sufficiently denounced freedom to publish any writings whatever and disseminate them to the people, which some dare to demand and promote with so great a clamor."[124] A more forthright attack on the principles of American republicanism could not have been offered. Given these teachings, which presumably bound priests and communicants in America as well as elsewhere, the concerns that evangelicals raised about Catholicism vis-à-vis republicanism were understandable, if not entirely legitimate. The American system would face grave problems if large numbers of citizens began to espouse the political theories articulated by the pope. And evangelicals were not the only ones to perceive a threat to republicanism from Catholicism. As Morton Borden has pointed out, universalists castigated the Catholic faith in publications such as *Priestcraft Unmasked,* and a "number of Jewish spokesmen . . . joined in nativist attacks upon Catholics."[125]

None of this excuses the occasional mob violence directed against American Catholics during this period.[126] But it is not clear that such violence can be blamed on evangelical reformers. It is one thing to vigorously—even intemperately—criticize the ideas of a certain group in open debate. This activity is a natural consequence of the freedom of speech. It is quite another matter to incite persecution or violence against those with whom one disagrees. Mainstream evangelical leaders were careful to note the distinction. In the midst of the anti-Catholic *A Plea for the West,* for example, Lyman Beecher maintained that he would not "consent that the civil and religious rights of the Catholics should be abridged or violated. As naturalized citizens, to all that we enjoy we bid them welcome, and would have their property and rights protected with the same impartiality and efficacy that the property and rights of every other denomination are protected; and we should abhor the interposition of lawless violence to injure the property or control the rights of Catholics as vehemently as if it were directed against Protestants and their religion."[127]

Beecher also distinguished between the antirepublican tendencies of certain Catholic doctrines and the decency of the vast majority of ordinary Catholics. Catholics "are not to be regarded as conspirators against our liberties," he said. "Their system commits its designs and higher movement, like the control of an army, to a few governing minds, while the body of the people may be occupied in their execution, unconscious of their tendency."[128]

The main object of evangelical anti-Catholic appeals during this period was increased support for evangelical education and missionary efforts. Beecher's *A Plea for the West* had as its main objective raising money for Lane Seminary in Ohio.[129] Beecher wanted to counter Catholic missionary efforts with Protestant ones. Samuel F. B. Morse adopted the same approach. At the end of his virulently anti-Catholic tract *Foreign Conspiracy Against the Liberties of the United States,* Morse noted that the "weapons" to be employed in the contest were Bible and tract societies, Sunday schools, "common schools for all classes, the college and university for all classes, [and] a free press for the discussion of all questions."[130] On a more practical level, evangelicals worked to supply basic social services to foreign emigrants.[131]

Thus, mainstream evangelical reformers did not advocate violence against Catholics or the denial of their civil rights. Moreover, when violence broke out, reputable evangelical leaders condemned it. On the burning of the Ursline convent in Charlestown, Massachusetts, for instance, orthodox Congregationalist and Baptist publications both denounced the attack and urged that the perpetrators be brought to justice.[132] They also printed, at the convent's request, a list of missing valuables owned by students, so that if the articles were found, they might be returned.[133]

That legitimate concerns existed about certain Catholic doctrines does not justify the hysterical approach adopted by some evangelicals in their attacks on Catholicism, particularly their abetting of the wild stories of imposters who claimed to have escaped from convents.[134] Nevertheless, evangelical leaders were not guilty of blatant self-contradiction in their efforts against Catholicism. In this case at least, they did not use their own religious freedom to deny the rights of others.

## Voluntary Associations Focusing on Moral Reform

In addition to all the groups focusing on evangelism were the evangelical associations devoted explicitly to moral reform. Among these groups temperance societies predominated. Evangelical lawyer Jeremiah Evarts was one of the early architects of efforts in this area. Like Lyman Beecher, Evarts was a graduate of Yale and a good friend of its president, Timothy Dwight. While editor of the *Panoplist,* one of the most influential of the evangelical journals, Evarts began writing against the evils of intemperance in 1810, and in 1811 and 1812 he helped organize Presbyterian and Congregationalist clergy on the issue. Lyman Beecher began to work on behalf of temperance at about the same time, and in 1827 he preached an influential series of lectures on the subject. By 1828 more than 400 temperance societies had been established across the United States, including statewide societies in New Hampshire, Vermont, Pennsylvania, Virginia, and Illinois.[135] These societies sought to educate the public about the extent of the problem and to pressure retailers to refrain from dealing in alcoholic beverages. Sometimes pressure was exerted through a boycott of recalcitrant retailers. In other cases citizens urged elected officials to deny liquor licenses to retailers. The temperance society in North Stonington, Connecticut, employed the latter approach with considerable success. As a result of its efforts, only three of the town's eleven dealers in spirited liquors even sought renewal of their licenses, and none of the three that sought a new license obtained one. Many local societies pointed to significant drops in liquor consumption as proof of their effectiveness.[136] The American Temperance Society, a national group organized in 1826, encouraged the formation of new local societies and disseminated information on intemperance around the country. Its officers and members were almost wholly composed of prominent evangelical ministers and laymen, and its constitution explicitly made the connection between temperance efforts, "Christian morality," and "Christian churches."[137]

Poverty was another social problem that attracted the attention of evangelical reformers. Many local groups focused on helping and educating the poor, including the Andover South Parish Charitable Society (established about 1816), the Rockingham Charitable Society in New Hampshire (established in 1817), the Society for Employing the Poor in Boston (established in 1820), the Society for the Education of Poor and Indigent Children of the Parish of Orange, New Jersey, and a society for the relief of the poor in New Haven, Connecticut.[138] This last group was spurred on in its efforts by Lyman Beecher, who proposed to its members a fairly stringent regimen of "workfare" for the able-bodied poor. Appropriating the rhetoric of modern republicanism, Beecher argued that self-interest and moral principle alike require that the plight of the poor be rectified. If one will not support efforts to eradicate poverty because of a benevolent spirit, one should do so out of mere self-preservation. "The poor will be with you always," said Beecher, "and if you do not educate them, and stop the contagion of vice, they will . . . pilfer from you ten times the amount you would need to give to render them useful and happy. . . . Give, then, if thou hast no bowels of compassion, upon principles of covetousness."[139]

But explicit efforts to help the the hard-core poor were only a small part of the evangelical antipoverty agenda. Workingmen who were drawn into evangelical churches found they now had access to a variety of resources that could help them improve their economic status, as Paul Johnson's study of the revivals in Rochester has shown. Wealthy church members in Rochester organized a savings bank for the benefit of the working classes and provided capital for budding entrepreneurs among Christian workingmen by forming business partnerships with them.[140] As a result of these measures (and the personal discipline and industry instilled by evangelical theology), converts from the working classes experienced a profound upward mobility: "For those who wished to move up [the economic ladder], the most sensible step was to acquire skills and thus move into better-paying and more secure employment. Two-thirds of the laborers who joined churches [in Rochester] made that step between 1827 and 1837. Non-church members in the same occupation moved out of Rochester three times as often and those who stayed rose at about half the rate attained by church members."[141] Likewise, "of the clerks who joined churches during the revivals and who remained in Rochester in 1837, 72 percent became merchants, professionals, or shopkeepers. Most non-churchgoing clerks left Rochester. Of those who stayed, half skidded into blue-collar jobs."[142]

Similar efforts were made to assist poor women. Key associations in this area included New York's Association for the Relief of Respectable, Aged, Indigent Females (established in 1814), the Society for Employing the Female Poor in Cambridge, Massachusetts (established in 1825), and the Magdalen societies in both New York and Philadelphia that sought to rescue women from prostitution.[143] Female reform societies served as a kind of "informal employment agency" for needy young women. Wealthy female members of the societies sought to find positions for young girls in the households of friends.[144]

Yet another reform championed by American evangelicals during this era was the proper observance of the Christian Sabbath. The issue was one with long roots in American and English history, dating back to the Puritan revival of strict Sabbath observance in England during the latter part of the sixteenth century.[145] When the Puritans came to America, they brought with them their stringent sabbatarianism, which was undergirded by a sophisticated theory of the connections among religion, morality, government, and society. "The Puritan Sabbath exerted a profound influence in nearly all of

the colonies and remained a vital aspect of national life well into the twentieth century," writes Winton Solberg. "The reason is readily compre-
hended. . . . At stake was not simply the religious observance of a state day
of the week, but a whole way of life involving man's relations with God and
the entire realm of work and play."[146] Because the Sabbath was considered
crucial in promoting civic morality and rest, as well as piety, most colonies
enforced its observance by law.[147]

These Sabbath-breaking statutes remained on the books in the new nation, but they were often ignored. Evangelical reformers were determined to
rectify the problem. Initial efforts by Lyman Beecher and others focused on
the resurrection of local Sabbath-breaking laws. But soon attention turned
toward Congress, which in 1810 had passed a law requiring many post offices to deliver mail to their customers every day of the week, including Sundays.[148] This deliberate desecration of the Sabbath by the federal goverment
rankled many evangelicals to no end, and between 1811 and 1816 they sent
Congress more than 300 petitions on the subject, inscribed with over 13,000
signatures.[149] These petitions attacked not only the opening of post offices
on Sunday but also the transportation of the mails on the Sabbath by mail
coach, which had gone on without criticism for many decades. The evangelical petitions were respectfully written, and they were just as respectfully received. For a time it appeared that action might be taken. Even though the
House postal committee could not agree to end the transportation of the
mails on Sunday, its members did concede that the opening of the post offices was not necessary and indicated a willingness to go back to previous
practice.[150] Yet in the end nothing was done, and evangelicals dropped the
matter.

When evangelical efforts to promote Sabbath observance revived in the
1820s, there was a distinct shift in tactics. Instead of pressing for the enforcement of local Sunday laws, the General Union for Promoting the Observance of the Christian Sabbath, formed in 1828, emphasized persuasion and
economic boycotts as the best method to increase Sabbath observance. This
shift to a more voluntary approach probably occurred more out of political
prudence than moral principle. Local enforcement of Sabbath laws would
likely engender more controversy than piety. As one General Union report
explained, "We have not the madness to think of coercion merely."[151] Lyman
Beecher again played a pivotal role, drafting the union's first address to the
American people.[152]

The Sabbath observance movement was largely a cultural crusade designed to reinvigorate the social position of the churches in fostering societal morality. Much more openly political was antimasonry, which produced the pugnacious, if rather short-lived, Anti-Masonic Party. Antimasonry swept New England after the kidnapping of William Morgan in 1826. Morgan, a former Mason, had promised to expose the darkest secrets of the Masonic lodge; but before he could publish all his revelations, he disappeared. His body was never discovered. The Morgan disappearance helped spark a wave of antimasonic activity, and for a brief period the Anti-Masonic Party attracted significant support across New England.[153] Although antimasonry derived its support from evangelicals, the movement also split them. The evangelical *Boston Recorder* justified its exclusion of the controversy from its pages by observing: "We cannot engage in a discussion where the *facts* of the case are involved in such deep obscurity. We cannot consent to be ranked among the Anti-Masons, on account of their heat and violence, and the scurrility too often employed in their publications."[154] Even some who supported the antimasonic movement's goals chose to stand aloof from the movement because of its divisiveness. Characteristically, Lyman Beecher was one of these, though he did sanction the cause eventually at an antimasonic meeting in 1831. A year earlier he had counseled his son William not to "preach or talk much openly about Masonry, though I have no doubt it will and ought to come down."[155]

But if antimasonry divided American evangelicals, there was one issue that proved even more bitterly disruptive in coming decades: slavery. Although several years passed before abolitionism eclipsed all other reform efforts, it had already begun to attract notice in the early 1800s. These initial efforts to end slavery focused largely on colonization schemes. In 1816 the American Colonization Society was created to establish a colony in Africa to which the freed slaves could emigrate. Liberia was subsequently founded in 1822 with a group of freed American slaves.[156] From the start the Colonization Society was backed by a precarious coalition of slave-owning Southerners and antislavery Northerners. Many Southerners supported colonization to rid their states of free blacks, whom they viewed as a threat to the continued existence of slavery. Free blacks diminished the market value of slave labor, and they served as an ever-present reminder to enslaved blacks that they might aspire to something better. Southerners were so frightened of free blacks staying in the South that some southern states enacted laws compelling freed slaves to leave their borders or be reenslaved.[157] Northerners who supported the Colonization Society were aware of the less than savory motives of some of their southern allies but persisted in the alliance because they could see no better alternative.[158] They hoped to eventually persuade Southerners that emancipation was the only moral course of action.

The Northerners failed in that objective. The Colonization Society placated slave interests so completely that in the end it accomplished very little. But historian George Dangerfield goes too far when he calls the society "a visible formulation not only of the prevailing racist myth but also of its dismal corollary: that America, 'man's last best hope,' was literally incapable of educating the Negro for freedom and equality."[159] This characterization flatly contradicts the view of the northern evangelicals who supported colonization. They may have believed that America was incapable of educating black Americans for freedom, but this was because they thought America was in the grip of an irrational prejudice against blacks, not because they regarded blacks as racially inferior. Evangelical Theodore Frelinghuysen, a longtime vice president of the Colonization Society, drove this point home in a speech he delivered in 1824. In an address to the New Jersey Colonization Society, Frelinghuysen castigated those who claimed

that the African was incapable of improvement. . . . We enslave, degrade, and oppress a people through many generations—shut out from them all the avenues to skill and science . . . and then we merely let them go, merely say to them, "now live and breathe for yourselves, without our aid or countenance; and because they cannot enter upon, and maintain a career, which white men have learned to course by the unremitting cares and labours of the nursery, the school, and the college, they are put down as blanks in creation. It is as unjust, as it is unreasonable.[160]

Frelinghuysen added that if a selected group of white men were treated in the same unconscionable manner as American blacks had been, "in what rank in the scale of moral existence, think you, five generations, would place them?" Frelinghuysen then challenged anyone who dared judge the black man as inferior to first "give the African fair play. Let his functions have full scope; enlarge his sphere of enterprise; open to his elevated views, the road to fame, and honourable distinction; and then judge, whether his head or his heart be below our standard." But this challenge was more rhetorical than real because Frelinghuysen already believed that enough evidence had been gathered to prove that blacks were equal to whites: "Let Toussaint, Christophe, Petion, and scores of other distinguished men in science, let the flourishing Colony of Sierra Leone, where *fifteen thousand* souls are now living under the influence of Gospel Light and rational liberty, enjoying the privileges of the most favoured civilized Societies; and exhibiting in domestic and public life, talents and virtues, that would not disgrace any village in America; silence forever this cruel prejudice."[161]

According to Frelinghuysen, then, the reasons for colonization and gradual emancipation had nothing to do with the supposed natural inferiority of blacks; it had everything to do with the prejudices of white America—and with the practical problem of dealing with a vast uneducated class of men who had been willfully kept in subjugation and ignorance. Blacks had to be emancipated gradually to prevent a bloodbath in the South, and they had to be colonized to give them an opportunity for full social and political equality. They would not have that opportunity for equality in the United States because of the intransigent prejudice against blacks. This prejudice prevailed even in the North. Frelinghuysen noted that free blacks had lived for years in several northern states, but despite the best efforts of the best men, these blacks were still a "separate, degraded, scorned, and humbled people." This was even the case in states such as New York and Pennsylvania, where the "pulpits have justly brought to bear on the subject that holy charity, which hails a brother in every child of Adam. Their rostrums have echoed with the equal rights of man. Their text has been taken from the Charter of American Liberty [the Declaration of Independence]."[162] But all these efforts had been employed in vain.

Frelinghuysen's position in favor of colonization was the one embraced by many northern politicians, including Henry Clay and Abraham Lincoln,[163] but it was not the only view. By the late 1820s many evangelicals had become convinced that gradual emancipation and colonization could not work and had withdrawn their support from the Colonization Society. Evangelical businessman Lewis Tappan—previously a supporter of colonization—began to agitate for immediate abolition. Disgusted with the Colonization Society's ineffectiveness, he supplied funds to start the American Anti-Slavery Society in 1834. He hoped it would replace the American Colonization Society as the nation's primary antislavery organization, and it did.[164]

A few evangelicals tried to bridge the growing chasm between radical abolitionists and colonizationists. Lyman Beecher, the unfailing champion of evangelical unity, was one of those who made the attempt at reconciliation. Writing to Arthur Tappan in 1833, he declared, "I am not apprised of the grounds of controversy between the Colonizationists and the Abolitionists. I am myself both, without perceiving in myself any inconsistency."[165]

Beecher was soon forced to put this attempt at synthesis to the test. As president of the newly formed Lane Theological Seminary, he found himself in charge of a class of forty earnest and strong-willed students, all of whom became radical abolitionists. Beecher allowed the students to engage in extensive debates over slavery, to organize antislavery societies, and to sponsor a school and a lyceum for the black inhabitants of the city. But he worried that his students were pressing too far too fast given prevailing social prejudices, and he counseled them to act with more caution; in particular, he advised them to avoid social intercourse with the blacks they sought to educate, lest they find themselves "overwhelmed" by the prejudiced part of the community.[166]

This advice was dictated by Beecher's sense of prudence rather than by any racial prejudice on his part. Beecher supported a color-blind admission policy at Lane, and a former slave was admitted as part of the first class.[167] But despite Beecher's best efforts at peacemaking, the seminary disintegrated. While Beecher was visiting the East Coast on a fund-raising trip during summer break, Lane's Board of Trustees gave into its fears of local opposition and issued harsh regulations designed to curtail all antislavery activity by students. By the time Beecher finally returned to the school, the breach was irreparable. Almost none of the seminary's students returned for fall term.[168]

Despite the debacle at Lane, Beecher continued to press for unity among slavery opponents. Indeed, while the crisis at Lane was brewing, he and others had been working to reunify the antislavery movement on a national level. In January 1835 these efforts bore fruit with the launching of the American Union for the Relief and Improvement of the Colored Race. Like the American Anti-Slavery Society, the union openly favored both an end to slavery and the adoption of positive measures to educate and improve the social state of American blacks. But it also embraced colonization as a helpful option for those blacks who wanted to take part in it.[169] Seeking to stake out a reasonable middle ground on an increasingly polarized issue, the union refused to attack either the American Colonization Society or the American Anti-Slavery Society. It announced instead that "so far as our views of justice, and benevolence, and wisdom will allow, we shall be ready to cooperate with either [group], or with both, for the attainment of objects common to them and to us."[170] This appeal for moderation on both sides fell on deaf ears, however, and the American Union soon disbanded.[171]

As northern evangelicals struggled with how best to dismantle slavery, southern evangelicals did their best to ignore the evil.[172] Some even denied that it was an evil. As early as 1822 South Carolina Baptists had accepted Richard Furman's scriptural justification of slavery, and many more would embrace such arguments as time went on.[173] Nevertheless, the notion of slavery as a positive good would not wipe away all evangelical scruples on the subject for several years. Perhaps the major problem during this period was not that southern evangelicals did not know that slavery was wrong but that they were unwilling to do anything about it. Given the harsh southern laws discouraging antislavery activities, such reticence was understandable but not justifiable.[174] Admirably, a few evangelicals in slave states refused to capitulate. Antislavery clergyman John Dixon Long labored in Maryland until 1856, when he finally removed to Philadelphia for the sake of his family.[175] Other evangelicals accepted slavery but refused to parrot the claims of southern spokesmen that blacks were subhuman.[176] On the whole, however, southern evangelicals acquiesced—and then supported—the social system in which they found themselves. The controversy over slavery demonstrated that all evangelicals did not walk in lockstep. It also showed how one's religious convictions could be tainted by self-interest and sectionalism.

These issues were the major ones tackled by evangelical reformers through 1835, but other concerns attracted evangelical attention as well. The Reverend John Mason condemned the extensive use of lotteries in a notable series of essays, and in Pennsylvania the Society for the Suppression of Lotteries was launched in the 1830s.[177] During the War of 1812 evangelicals joined with Unitarians to establish societies for the promotion of pacifism. Most of these disintegrated soon after the war ended, but the peace movement reawakened under the leadership of evangelical lawyer William Ladd when he founded the American Peace Society in 1827. Other key evangelicals who expoused the cause of pacifism at least for a time included Thomas Grimké and Francis Wayland. An important goal of the peace movement during this period was the establishment of a world court for the arbitration of international disputes. A campaign to organize such an institution began in the late 1820s and received widespread support not only in America but also around the world.[178] In another area evangelical groups were formed to help prisoners and persons with disabilities. The Prison Discipline Society worked to improve what can only be called the hellish conditions then prevalent in American prisons, and the Reverend Thomas Galludet pioneered work among the deaf.[179]

Amazingly, despite all these myriad interdenominational efforts, recent scholarship has called into question just how much evangelical cooperation there was during the early nineteenth century in America. Offering a counterpoint to traditional descriptions of evangelical unity during this period, Nathan Hatch highlights the era's often intense rivalry among sects and between ministers within sects. Speaking of what he calls "the splintering of American Protestantism," he reports how "people veered from one church to another. Religious competitors wrangeled unceasingly, traditional clergy and self-appointed preachers foremost in the fray."[180]

Hatch's account provides a useful corrective to past rose-colored descriptions of the Second Great Awakening as a monolithic event that was at once unified and unifying. But Hatch goes too far when he suggests that evangelical differences were so severe that the real dividing line of the period was not between evangelicals and theological liberals but between the educated religious elites of the traditional order (regardless of their specific doctrinal views) and the rising tide of itinerant preachers and enthusiasts who were organizing religion from the bottom up.[181]

Contrary to what Hatch suggests, the theological core that unified evangelicals was far more powerful than any differences they might have had. Evangelicals were all arrayed against theological liberalism and the forces of secularism. Congregationalists, Presbyterians, Episcopalians, Methodists, and Baptists could work together in voluntary associations because, despite vastly differing forms of worship and modes of church organization, they acknowledged that they were devoted to the common cause of salvation through Christ alone. Thus, Lyman Beecher could ultimately reconcile with a revivalist such as Charles Finney but not with universalist and Unitarian opponents.

Hatch's study further exaggerates class as a factor in disputes involving evangelicals. For example, Hatch cites as evidence of his thesis Presbyterian David Rice's condemnation of those who preached the Gospel "relying on their inward call, and neglecting almost every ministerial qualification required in the sacred Scriptures."[182] Yet the major part of Rice's attack focused on the heterodox *doctrines* of those he was examining. In fact, Rice claimed that the enthusiasts he critiqued were closer to deism in their views than to Christianity.[183] Rice was concerned about a lack of adequate training for ministers because of his larger concern with doctrinal heresies. In other words, his "class" concerns were largely subsidiary to his intellectual concerns about doctrine. The same was true for Lyman Beecher. He was critical of ministers without education mostly because he wanted to safeguard church doctrine. When doctrine was not at issue, he did his best to reach out to those who were not part of the established clergy. Perhaps the best example of this is the role he played as peacemaker in the controversies over Charles Finney and his followers. Finney had very little formal theological training, and his "new measures" provoked a great deal of opposition from established ministers. Yet Beecher was the one who brought together the opposing parties to seek a peaceful reconciliation of their views.[184]

There is also some evidence that class distinctions, at least, became less important over time in both the mainline evangelical churches and the voluntary associations. Even though most of the evangelical associations had been started by established clergymen and business leaders, the membership of these associations was becoming noticeably more egalitarian by the end of the 1820s. Revivals provided the impetus for this democratization of the associations. Targeted largely at the working classes, revivals began to draw large numbers of wage earners into the churches, and from the churches it was only a small step to the voluntary associations. Following a series of revivals in Rochester, New York, "hundreds of workingmen were in the churches and participating in middle-class crusades," according to Paul Johnson.[185]

Revivals had an even greater impact on bringing women into evangelical reform. Although "male clerics and reformers led this movement," observes Carroll Smith-Rosenberg, ". . . women were their most zealous adherents. Through sheer numbers, women dominated the Second Great Awakening's revivals and spiraling church membership."[186] As a consequence, women soon began to exercise leadership roles in evangelical associations: "Inspired by revival enthusiasm, they founded national religious organizations, distributed Bibles and tracts, led Sunday schools, and raised money to send missionaries to the Sandwich Islands and to the new urban ghettos. They founded female seminaries. . . . Those more worldly in their orientation followed their millennial enthusiasm into a host of reform movements: Garrisonian abolition, moral reform, temperance. [187]

None of this is to deny that evangelical groups had important (and sometimes severe) differences with each other over church authority, the status of the clergy, and social composition. The differences described by Hatch and others were genuine. But they did not prevent evangelicals from engaging in a host of joint enterprises in the public arena. Ultimately, evangelicals cooperated in efforts to reform society not because of how much they differed but because of how much they shared. Above all, they shared a common vision of the moral and political universe. Even while they disagreed among themselves on the finer points of theology, and even while they sometimes clashed over particular political problems, most evangelicals held in common certain ideas about the nature of man and the proper relationship between religion and civil society.

These ideas, which informed all evangelical efforts, are perhaps best summarized by the following formula: Morality is necessary for republican government; religion is necessary for morality; therefore, religion is necessary for republican government. Evangelicals accepted this formula no less than the Founders but understood it somewhat differently. They disagreed with at least certain Founders about how to define morality and religion and about the precise connection between religion and civil government. Whether these disagreements with the Founders were substantial enough to undermine the Founders' solution to the theological-political problem is a question worth close scrutiny.

## EVANGELICALS AND THE
## THEOLOGICAL-POLITICAL PROBLEM

### Why Republicanism Needs Morality

Evangelicals and the Founders were in perfect accord on one point: They both agreed that morality is necessary for republicanism because "only a virtuous people are capable of freedom."[188] A despot can impose order with a rod of iron, but a republic must depend on self-government—in the broadest sense of the term—to guarantee peace and stability. Citizens of a republic must govern themselves not only by electing their own rulers but also by living self-controlled lives in the wide sphere of freedom that republican society guarantees to them. In other words, republicans must be virtuous enough to use their freedom well. If they are not, the very liberties that make republican society possible will also seal its doom. Citizens will gratify their own passions to such an extent that the whole edifice will collapse. Explained Presbyterian Eliphalet Nott: "The government of our country is a government of opinion, rather than force. More is therefore to be feared from the depravity of ourselves than of our rulers. If *they* become corrupt, the *sovereign people* can displace *them;* but if the sovereign people themselves become corrupt, it is an evil without a remedy."[189]

Baptist divine Francis Wayland amplified this thought, declaring that the success of the American experiment depends on the "moral and intellectual character of the people":

> So long . . . as our people remain virtuous and intelligent, our government will remain stable. While they clearly perceive, and honestly decree justice, our laws will be wholesome, and the principles of our constitution will commend themselves every where to the common sense of man. But should our people become ignorant and vicious; should their decisions become the dictates of passion and venality, rather than of reason and of right, that moment are our liberties at an end; and, glad to escape from the despotism of millions, we shall flee for shelter to the despotism of one. Then will the world's last hope be extinguished, and darkness brood for ages over the whole human race.[190]

Congregationalist Nathanael Emmons argued the same point with an extended analogy. Just as "the natural body is composed of innumerable cords or ligatures, which unite the parts, and strengthen the members to perform their office . . . so the body politic is composed of innumerable moral ties and connections, which, like veins and nerves, give strength and freedom to all its members." Just as sickness decimates the various parts of our natural bodies, said Emmons, vice dissolves society's moral ties and "throw[s] the whole body politic into great and fatal convulsions. . . . Vice, by destroying these moral and social ties, effectually saps the foundation of freedom, and completely prepares a people for the shackles of slavery. For nothing but the rod or arbitrary power is sufficient to restrain and govern a people, who have

lost their virtue, and sunk into vice and corruption. Such a people are neither fit to enjoy, nor able to assert and maintain their liberties. They must be
slaves."[191]

In sum, men cannot live as freemen if they are enslaved to their passions,
and if vice is allowed to triumph, the destruction of a free society will be the
sure result. Hence, individual evils are not only bad in themselves; they also
constitute a threat to civil liberty and republican government. He who would
serve his country best should therefore join efforts to purge the nation of its
vices. "Here is true philanthropy; here is Christian patriotism," declared
Francis Wayland. "And this is one reason why we so often present these
charities to your notice. When, therefore, we ask you to aid us . . . you must
not look unkindly at us; for we plead the cause of our country, of liberty,
and of man."[192]

Thus far most Founders and evangelicals agreed; but a step farther and
the consensus began to break down. If evangelicals and the Founders concurred on why morality is necessary for republicanism, they did not wholly
agree on why religion is necessary for morality. Two points were at issue: the
role of revelation in the acquisition of moral knowledge and the role of
Christianity in the creation of a moral citizenry.

## Revelation and the Acquisition of Moral Knowledge

The Founders steadfastly maintained that morality is knowable by both reason and revelation. Some evangelicals, however, were not so sure. In a lecture titled "Hints on the Insufficiency of the Light of Nature," John Mason
attacked the very notion that "unassisted reason" can know the most important truths about either God or virtue.[193]

In another sermon, this one titled "Nonconformity to the World," Mason
argued that the non-Christian part of society has "its own institutions, statutes, and customs—its own pursuits—its own ethics—its own penal code,
and its own recompenses. It covers the very same ground which is covered by
the law of God; but is, of course, perfectly hostile and contradictory both to
the law and the Lawgiver." According to Mason, the heart of the difference
between Christian morality and worldly morality is the status of one's duty
to God. Worldly morality teaches that doing good to one's fellow men is all
that is required, but Christian morality proclaims as "the first and greatest
commandment, *Thou shalt love the Lord thy God with all thy heart, and*

*with all thy strength, and with all thy mind.*" Mason concluded that there can be no compromise between the two systems. "Obedience to the one infallibly excludes obedience to the other. And it is most idle and ridiculous to attempt their conciliation; the very attempt proves its author to be an enemy to God, and a slave to the usurper."[194]

Mason presented his position with pungent rhetoric, but he did not speak for every American evangelical of the time. Indeed, he spoke for very few of them. Most American evangelicals were more than willing to find an agreement between reason and revelation in the realm of morality. Courses in moral philosophy were staples at evangelical colleges during this era, and the major American texts on the subject were written by such evangelicals as Samuel Stanhope Smith, Francis Wayland, and Jasper Adams. Smith, a Presbyterian, was a staunch Federalist and president of Princeton; Wayland, a Baptist, was a solid Jeffersonian and president of Brown University; and Adams, an Episcopalian from the South, was a defender of slavery and president of the College of Charleston in South Carolina. Despite their differences in theology and politics, all three men firmly agreed with the proposition that morality can be known apart from special divine revelation.[195]

Die-hard Congregationalists such as Timothy Dwight and Nathanael Emmons might have been less sanguine than Smith, Wayland, and Adams about man's capacity to understand morality apart from the Bible, but they, too, acknowledged that man has a natural capacity to understand the principles of morality. In the words of Emmons: "man is capable of holiness. His rational and moral faculties both capacitate and oblige him to be holy. His perception and volition, in connection with his reason and conscience, enable him to discern and feel the right and wrong of actions, and the beauty and deformity of characters. This renders him capable of doing justly, loving mercy, and walking humbly with God."[196] Dwight similarly argued that "all men have consciences," which are "judge[s] of right and wrong," and he condemned adultery and other vices as not only reprehensible to God but also "repugnant to Common sense, and Common good."[197]

Even John Mason—his fiery rhetoric notwithstanding—conceded in a backhanded manner the non-Christian's capacity for knowing civic morality. By stating that the secular world believes men to be virtuous if they "render to every man his due, cultivate the mild and beneficent affections, do good actions, and are free from gross iniquities," Mason all but admitted that non-Christians do come to a knowledge of at least the rudiments of civic morality.[198]

Whatever most evangelicals might have said about reason and revelation agreeing on the moral law, however, they did not believe that reason and revelation constitute equally valid routes to moral truth. Even the staunchest evangelical rationalist knew that reason, like the rest of human nature, is corrupted by sin. Hence, it is at best an inconstant guide. If man tries to ascertain the maxims of morality by his reason alone, he will likely fail because his reason will be perverted by his sin. Evangelicals concluded from this that the only sure foundation for moral education is the Bible. The Bible alone can correct reason's failures vis-à-vis morality because the Bible lays down the fundamental maxims of right and wrong with a clarity and finality that cannot be evaded.[199] Here one sees one of the main springs of action for evangelical Bible societies and Sunday schools: Evangelicals believed that Bible knowledge is needed not only to save Americans in the hereafter but also to show them how to live their lives in the here and now. "There is scarcely a neighbourhood in our country where the Bible is circulated," said Francis Wayland, "in which we cannot point you to a very considerable portion of the population, whom its truths have reclaimed from the practice of vice, and taught the practice of whatsoever things are pure, and honest, and just, and of good report."[200]

One might be tempted to conclude from this belief in biblical primacy that evangelical statements about the harmony between reason and revelation in the moral sphere were only so much window dressing. Evangelicals might have *said* that they believed in a morality sanctioned by both reason and revelation, but they really believed in a morality founded exclusively on special revelation. Early-nineteenth-century evangelicals would reject such an analysis, however, because they saw no radical disjunction between reason and revelation.

In their view to insist that the Bible is the best way to learn about morality is not to divorce morality from reason because revelation itself is reasonable. Like Founder John Witherspoon, they insisted that the Bible is perfectly consistent with the discoveries of human reason. They even granted that if the Bible is not consistent with reason, it should be abandoned. "Without reason there can be no religion," wrote Princeton evangelical Archibald Alexander in *Brief Outline of the Evidences of the Christian Religion*. Indeed, "if a book, claiming to be a divine revelation, is found to contain doctrines which can in no way be reconciled to right reason, it is sure evidence that those claims have no solid foundation, and ought to be rejected." But the Bible is not such a book, according to Alexander. "The reasonings by which it has been attempted to prove, that the doctrines [of the Bible], commonly called orthodox, are contrary to reason, are fallacious."[201] True, some of the Bible's theological doctrines are mysterious and beyond reason; but many other doctrines are not, including the Bible's moral teachings. These most assuredly can be shown to be sanctioned by reason. Even those biblical maxims that fallen reason may not be able to discover on its own (such as the need for humility) can be shown to be agreeable to reason after the fact.[202]

Hence, though evangelicals proclaimed the Bible as their ultimate moral standard, this did not constitute a rejection of reason because evangelicals steadfastly maintained that nothing in the Bible contradicts reason. As a practical matter this position meant that evangelicals were perfectly comfortable arguing public issues with rational appeals—as their campaign against dueling convincingly demonstrated. Even when they did tie their political discussions back to the Bible, however, the "biblical" principles they cited most often coincided with the "natural" principles accepted by freethinkers and deists.

The evangelical use of the idea of human equality is a perfect example. Equality may have formed the bedrock of the political theories of Jefferson and Paine, but that did not prevent evangelicals from proclaiming the same ideal—only they derived their belief in equality not from unassisted reason but from reason in harmony with the Bible. The book of Genesis teaches that Adam and Eve are the parents of all mankind; thus, evangelicals believed that all men are literally part of the same family. In the words of the apostle Paul, God "hath made of one blood all nations of men for to dwell on all the face of the earth."[203] Many evangelicals, taking their cue from a revelation they regarded as inviolable, were far more consistent in applying the equality principle than rationalists such as Jefferson were. Whereas Jefferson might waffle about whether blacks were naturally equal to whites, northern evangelicals such as John Mason, Samuel Stanhope Smith, Nathanael Emmons, and Timothy Dwight had no doubts on the matter.[204] Indeed, Smith went so far as to advocate racial intermarriage between blacks and whites as a way of breaking down the social barriers between the races.[205]

A similar affinity between the evangelicals' biblical principles and the secular principles of reason can be detected in evangelical arguments tying the

American form of government back to the Bible. Lyman Beecher supplied a good example of this type of analysis in his sermon "The Republican Elements of the Old Testament," where he discussed at length how the basic principles of American government could be ascertained from the government of ancient Israel.[206] Beecher may not have realized it, but by seeking to prove that republicanism is Christian, he also ended up guaranteeing that Christianity would be republican. In other words, efforts to interpret American republicanism in terms of the Bible could also be viewed as a reinterpretation of the Bible in terms of American republicanism. As a result, the harmony between reason and revelation was preserved.

Despite this broad common ground between evangelical virtue and a more secular morality, there undoubtedly were areas where the synthesis tore apart. Evangelical beliefs about piety and providence were the chief dividing points. If the Christian God actually existed, the hierarchy of moral duties changed of necessity. Piety *had* to be viewed as the highest expression of morality, and this paved the way for criminalizing offenses such as Sabbath breaking and blasphemy and promoting observances such as public fasts and days of thanksgiving. However, even in these areas the connection between revelation and reason did not completely break down because reasonable pretexts could be found to support these practices by law apart from revelation.

The issue of laws against profanity and blasphemy was discussed previously with reference to John Witherspoon, and the comments made there apply here. Nineteenth-century America was not a society of untrammeled freedom of expression, and once one accepts restrictions on injudicious speech in principle (as nineteenth-century Americans did), a plausible case might be made apart from revelation for some kind of restrictions on blasphemy and profanity. Chief Justice of New York James Kent articulated such a secular justification for blasphemy laws in *People* v. *Ruggles* (1811), where the defendant had been convicted of the offense because he had said that "Jesus Christ was a bastard and his mother must be a whore." Kent made a distinction between the unfettered discussion of religious ideas (which was protected) and the malicious ridicule of religion (which was forbidden): "The free, equal, and undisturbed enjoyment of religious opinion, whatever it may be, and free and decent discussion on any religious subject, is granted and secured; but to revile with malicious and blasphemous contempt . . . is an abuse of that right." Thus, reviling Christ "is not only in a religious point of view, extremely impious, but even in respect of the obligations due to society, in gross violation of decency and good order."[207] This distinction prevailed in American legal theory generally.[208]

Sabbath laws were even more susceptible to secular justifications. Laws closing down all businesses on Sunday effectuate the religious liberty of employees who wish to worship on that day. These laws also encourage religion (regarded as necessary for republican morality) in a way that keeps the state institutionally separate from the church. Thanksgiving and fast days, however, are not nearly so easy to reconcile with religious liberty and a morality based on both reason and revelation. Here the government affirmatively sponsors what are undeniably religious exercises. Unlike most Sabbath-breaking laws (which forbid work on Sunday but do not tell citizens to go to church), prayer day laws affirmatively promote religious devotion. Indeed, their primary—if not their sole—justification is that a God exists who cares about human behavior and who commands national homage. The nation must recognize that all good things come from God and that it cannot survive without his blessing.

One possible way to square such public devotions with a morality derived from reason is to champion the claims of natural religion—that is, a religion discoverable by human reason. During this period of history, Unitarians and evangelicals alike believed that certain attributes of God—such as his existence, his overriding providence, and his supreme goodness—can be known independent of revelation.[209] Hence, it is possible to regard prayer days as consistent with the morality of reason because reason itself can discover that there is a God who should be venerated.

The problem with this solution is that it tends to confuse revelation and reason until there is no longer a clear distinction between the two principles. There is, however, another justification for national days of fasting and thanksgiving, a justification that can be deduced from the Founders' solution to the theological-political problem. James Madison noted that religious adherents could assent to enter civil society only by reserving their ultimate allegiance to God: "Every man who becomes a member of any particular Civil Society, [must] do it with a saving of his allegiance to the Universal Sovereign."[210] Thus, American government claims no right to command duties contrary to the will of God. Instead, it acknowledges that its only *just* authority is derived from a moral order sanctioned by *both* reason and revelation. Days of fasting and thanksgiving serve as an acknowledgment of this critical reservation to the social compact. They constitute a symbolic recognition by the nation that religious adherents do not forfeit the higher claims of religion once they enter civil society. They proclaim that the government exists under the authority of God, not in place of it. The phrase "under God" added to the Pledge of Allegiance in the 1950s fulfills the same function. The allegiance Americans pledge to their government is not unlimited; it is circumscribed by the laws of both God and nature.

What is plausible in theory, of course, may not be tenable in fact. Days of fasting and thanksgiving may in theory pay tribute to the enduring claims of religion; but in fact they can be employed for crassly partisan purposes, which ends up corrupting religion and subjecting it to government control just as surely as in the ancient city. President Adams's proclamation of a national fast, for instance, had supplied Federalist clergy with an opportunity to blatantly boost administration policies.[211]

Blasphemy laws spawn similar difficulties. The distinction between malicious attacks on religion and the legitimate discussion of religious ideas may prove unworkable in practice. Moreover, blasphemy laws may be unequally written and unfairly applied so that they favor only the dominant religion. Witness Justice Kent's comment that reviling religions other than Christianity would not be criminal because "we are a christian people, and the morality of the country is deeply ingrafted upon christianity."[212]

Nevertheless, the recognition that one must supply a secular justification for any protection of religion is a critical one. Once one concedes that blasphemy laws and Sabbath-breaking statutes must be based on the general interests of society rather than on the peculiar dictates of divine revelation, the door is opened to further argument on secular grounds. The stage is then set for abolishing such laws and practices if in fact they do not serve the public interest apart from revelation. This diminishes—though it does not eliminate—the tension between evangelical morality and the morality of autonomous reason.

One can conclude from all this that the evangelical understanding of the relationship among reason, revelation, and morality fits tolerably within the framework laid down by the Founders. When it came to morality and politics, evangelicals for the most part espoused principles common to all rather than peculiar to their own sects. The modern secularist would undoubtedly criticize their heavy reliance on the Bible, but the evangelicals' emphasis on biblical morality was shared with most of the Founders. Thomas Jefferson, no less than John Jay, John Witherspoon, and James Wilson, believed that the moral teachings of Jesus eclipse those of pagan writers and constitute the purest and best expression of morality.[213] The Founders had little problem with those who took their morals from the Bible rather than nature because, like the evangelicals, they saw the Bible's moral teachings as consonant with human reason. If the evangelicals' ideas on how one comes to know morality were ultimately compatible with the Founders' system, their beliefs about the role of Christianity in the creation of a moral citizenry were more problematic.

## Christianity and the Creation of a Moral Citizenry

Evangelicals might concede that morality can be known apart from revelation, but they could never grant that morality can be put into practice without religion. First, they maintained that doctrines such as God's omniscience and mankind's future accountability in the afterlife provide the most powerful incentives to morality in this life.[214] Second, they believed that moral regeneration is intimately tied to spiritual regeneration and that the formation of one's character is ultimately the task of God's Holy Spirit, who works within believers to reclaim their minds and bodies from the enslavement of sin.[215] These beliefs edged perilously close to suggesting that only Christians are capable of being truly moral—and thus only Christians can be good citizens. In practice, most evangelicals did not make such a doctrinaire claim.[216] But if they did not insist that only Christians can be moral, they did imply that Christians are more likely to be so and that on the whole they make the best citizens.[217] Moreover, evangelicals suggested that the reason many atheists and agnostics are moral is because of the beneficial influence of living in a Christian society. Place them in a society without Christianity's influence, said evangelicals, and they will become savages.[218]

This line of argument posed precarious problems for the Founders' solution to the theological-political problem because it once again divided citizens along theological lines. To be sure, this difficulty already arose on a lesser level in the Founders' solution. Most of the Founders divided citizens along theological lines when insisting that a strong connection exists between piety and the inculcation of moral character—thus implicitly agreeing with evangelicals that too many atheists and agnostics may be dangerous to society. But most Founders mitigated this belief by extending the connection between piety and morality to *all* churches—evangelical, Catholic, Unitarian, and Jewish. All teach morality, according to the Founders, and hence all are helpful in promoting good citizenship. Thus, every sect is placed on an equal footing when it comes to morality in the Founders' system. Insofar as the evangelical system undercut this thesis, it pulled against the Founders' solution to the theological-political problem.[219] If Christianity is really needed to make people moral (and morality is necessary for republicanism), then the case for special government protection and support of Christianity is strengthened considerably.

Most of the initial controversies in this area focused on state financial support for churches. As noted previously, the issue of establishments of religion bitterly divided evangelicals. Baptists, Methodists, and many Presbyterians found establishments an offense against their God-given rights of conscience, while New England Congregationalists and Virginian Episcopalians saw establishments as a useful device to secure religion's place in society—and society's prosperity. When disestablishment finally made the discussion moot, most evangelicals who had supported establishments accepted the inevitable, and the more enterprising ones, such as Lyman Beecher, enthusiastically embraced voluntarism as the perfectly republican response to the problem.[220]

But disestablishment, though momentous, did not resolve the larger question of the relationship between the government and Christianity. It merely moved other issues to the forefront. Even after the establishments fell, an elaborate network of blasphemy laws, Sabbath-breaking statutes, public days of prayer, and religious tests for public office remained to protect Christianity's hallowed place in society. As noted earlier, many of these practices could in theory be defended on grounds other than revelation, but in practice they tended to create an uncomfortable link between Christianity and citizenship. It was probably inevitable that as new varieties of religious belief developed in America, support for such practices would disintegrate. The question was whether evangelicals could tolerate the destruction of these last official props of their religious system. For the most part they could—and did.

Religious tests for public office were one of the first restrictions to crumble, receiving a critical blow when the federal Constitution forbade them for federal office. Jedidiah Morse attacked the lack of federal religious tests as impious, but other evangelicals began to see them as less than useless. In

1813 Timothy Dwight told his students that religious tests were impractical because infidels would be the least likely to pay attention to such oaths. They would be perfectly willing to lie about their religious convictions to gain public office.[221]

Sabbath-breaking laws were the next protection to be disregarded. The first response of New England clergy was to press officials for vigorous enforcement.[222] When these efforts ultimately failed on the collapse of the standing order, Lyman Beecher realized that evangelicals had started at the wrong end of the problem. In a democracy laws without social support would never be enforced. Therefore, the evangelicals' first object had to be to convince individual members of society of the need for the Sabbath and to exert social pressure on those merchants and stage owners who continued to abrogate it.[223] Only then would the Sabbath be respected once more, and only then could one hope to enforce Sabbath-breaking laws.

The result of Beecher's proposal, of course, was evangelical moral reform spearheaded by voluntary associations. Urged on by Beecher, evangelicals now concentrated on what they could do as independent actors in society to defend societal morality. Crusades against dueling, drunkenness, prostitution, lotteries, slavery, and other vices followed.

In this new social and political environment, where private action to defend religion began to eclipse government action, some sticky problems remained. The right to vote was one of them. Religious tests for public office might no longer be enforced, but the question naturally arose whether Christians should vote only for fellow Christians as a matter of religious duty. Evangelicals such as Jedidiah Morse and Ezra Stiles Ely argued the affirmative.[224]

Other evangelicals took a broader view. Lyman Beecher stressed general moral character, rather than piety, as the preeminent qualification for office: "Let all Christians and all patriots exercise their rights as electors with an inflexible regard to moral character." But, even Beecher included Sabbath breaking, along with dueling, intemperance, and dishonesty, as a reason to withhold one's vote from a candidate, and he claimed that voters should ask whether a candidate was "an enemy to the Bible, or to the doctrines and institutions of the Gospel."[225] Nevertheless, there is a subtle but important difference between requiring candidates to openly profess Christianity and demanding that they not be "enemies of the Bible."

Even more than John Witherspoon before him, Beecher seemed to leave the door open to quiet skeptics who possessed a good character: "I do not perceive that Christians are forbidden to repose confidence in men, for civil purposes, who do not profess religion, or afford evidence of piety. Men of piety are doubtless to be preferred, and greatly to be desired, other things being equal: but I cannot perceive that the qualifications for civil trust, and for membership in the church, are the same."[226] As long as a candidate did not openly attack Christianity—or the more general idea of an afterlife with rewards and punishments—Beecher saw no problem with Christians voting for them. During a time when virtually no political candidate openly challenged Christianity, such a standard would bar very few candidates from receiving votes because of their private religious convictions.

Evangelical discussions of the right to vote, like evangelical efforts at moral reform, raised the theological-political problem in a new way. Unlike the debate over disestablishment, the paramount question was no longer whether the church should be promoted by the state but how much power religious adherents, acting as citizens, should exercise over the government. Given the evangelical belief that Christians are somehow more intimately connected to morality than unbelievers, sectarian politics became a distinct possibility. Evangelicals waging political war *as evangelicals* raised the specter of a "Christian" party in politics that would pit "believers" against "infidels" to the detriment of both politics and religion. But if the evangelicals' belief in their own moral superiority tended to foster this type of result, another factor worked to forestall it: the legacy of the election of 1800.

## Partisanship Versus the Politics of Morality

The bitter party strife of the early 1800s had exposed the perils of fusing religion with party politics, and evangelical leaders were understandably wary of repeating the same mistake twice. Timothy Dwight, Francis Wayland, and Lyman Beecher all warned of the dangers posed by a Christianity tainted by political partisanship. In his commencement address for 1816, Dwight told students that

> the prejudices, the fervour, and the bitterness, of party spirit are incapable of vindication. I may be permitted to think differently from my neighbour; but I am not permitted to hate him, nor to quarrel with him, merely because he thinks differently from me.

. . . Our countrymen have spent a sufficient time in hostilities against each other. We have entertained as many unkind thoughts, uttered as many bitter speeches, called each other by as many hard names, and indulged as much unkindness and malignity; as might satisfy our worst enemies, and as certainly ought to satisfy us. From all these efforts of ill-will we have not derived the least advantage. . . . Friends and brothers have ceased to be friends and brothers; and professing Christians have dishonoured the religion which they professed.[227]

Beecher similarly complained in an 1826 election sermon that "party spirit prostrates everything within the sphere of its commotion which is venerable and sacred. It directs the attention of the people from their own common interests to the means of gaining objects to which prejudice and passion may direct them."[228] And Francis Wayland, speaking after the deaths of former Presidents Jefferson and Adams, noted how futile past party controversies seemed in light of both men's accomplishments.[229]

Given the inherent dangers of party politics, few evangelicals wished for an explicitly Christian party that would divide political battles along religious lines; they knew that this would merely spread the contagion of partisanship to the churches. But if evangelicals forswore party politics, how could they become effectively involved in politics at all? Evangelical leaders insisted there was a nobler and higher route, one already traveled by the partisans of evangelical moral reform. Christian political action should focus on the moral questions raised by politics. Said Francis Wayland:

Now, whether a Christian may or may not be a politician, I have no question whatever to raise. . . . But this question decided, we beg leave to say, that a Christian has no right, any where, or under any circumstances, to be any thing else than a Christian. He must ask about a political as well as about any other act, the question, Is it right, or is it wrong? and by answer to that question must he be guided. It is just as wicked to lie about politics as to lie about merchandise. It is just as immoral to act without reference to the law of God, at a caucus, as any where else. To prefer our own interests or the interests of party to that of our country, is treason against that country, and sin against God. And it matters not whether that treason be perpetrated with a ballot or a bayonet, at the caucus or in the field.[230]

Embedded in Wayland's statement is an implied limit on evangelical political action. Not every political controversy presents a stark moral choice. The more particular the question is, the greater the difficulty one will have in looking at it purely in moral terms. For instance, determining whether an import tax should be five or seven cents might be a question of fervid interest to those being taxed, but its moral significance will be considerably murkier. One consequence of making morality the overriding standard for political action is that political questions not clearly impinging on morality will be considered unimportant.

In other words, if Christians enter politics as the champions of morality, they will tend to act only on questions where the moral stakes are both significant and clear. Lyman Beecher made this point explicitly in a sermon in 1824:

Christians are not to attempt to control the administration of civil government, in things merely secular.

This is what our Saviour refused to do, when he declined being a king, or ruler, or judge. It would secularize the church, as the same conduct secularized the church of Rome:—and bring upon her, and justly, a vindictive reaction of hatred and opposition. When great questions of national morality are about to be decided, such as the declaration of war; or, as in England, the abolition of the slave trade; or the permission to introduce Christianity into India by Missionaries; it becomes Christians to lift up their voice, and exert their united influence. But, with the annual detail of secular policy, it does not become Christians to intermeddle, beyond the unobtrusive influence of their silent suffrage. They are not to "strive, nor cry, nor lift up their voice in the streets." The injudicious association of religion with politics, in the time of Cromwell, brought upon evangelical doctrine and piety, in England, an odium which has not ceased to this day.[231]

Beecher saw with piercing clarity that if Christians become too avidly involved in ordinary political strife, their activities will damage not only the state but also the church. "No sight is more grievous or humiliating," he wrote, "than to see Christians continually agitated, by all the great and little political disputes of the nation, the state, the city, and town, and village; toiling in the drudgery of ambition; and flowing hither and thither, like waves which have no rest, and cast-up only mire and dirt." Beecher added that "there is no one particular in which it is more important that there should be a reformation."[232]

By focusing evangelical political attention on the great questions of national morality, Beecher found a way to reduce the problem evangelicals posed to the Founders' solution of the theological-political dilemma. If evangelicals entered the political arena only on behalf of these great questions, they would be far less tempted to forge a permanent political association that would make Christianity the litmus test for all political issues. They also might be more likely to forge temporary coalitions with nonevangelicals since arguments in support of the great questions of morality should be accessible to reason as well as revelation. The critical question, of course, is whether most evangelicals adopted Beecher's vision of politics as their own.

Some clearly did not, but their reasons for rejecting Beecher's view differed. Certain evangelical groups opposed Beecher's formulation because they rejected the very idea of organized reform. Perhaps the most vigorous exponents of this view were the followers of Alexander Campbell, who founded the Disciples of Christ. Campbell sought to purge Christianity of anything not specifically commanded by the New Testament. For this reason his followers declined to use musical instruments in worship because no New Testament sanction could be found for the practice; for the same reason they were suspicious of evangelical reform associations such as missionary societies. The New Testament did not command that such groups be organized; therefore, Christians should not organize them, according to Campbell. Campbellites tended to embrace the Jeffersonian separation of church and state with both arms.[233] Baptist John Leland took a similar stand, complaining that those who relied on voluntary associations to spread the Gospel and to reform society were substituting the power of the purse for the power of God's Holy Spirit: "In barbarous times, when men were in the dark, it was believed that the success of the gospel was according to the outpourings of the Holy Spirit, but in the age of light and improvement, it is estimated according to the pourings out of the purse."[234]

This skepticism toward evangelical reform exhibited by populist evangelical leaders such as Campbell and Leland can be tied to the era's more general rebellion against existing hierarchies. As Nathan Hatch has documented, early-nineteenth-century America experienced a widespread democratic revolt against the establishment, a revolt that many populist reli-

gious leaders helped foment.[235] That evangelical reform was being championed by established leaders from business and the churches made it an immediate target of suspicion among evangelical populists. Nevertheless, one
should be careful not to exaggerate support for these criticisms of organized
reform among evangelicals as a whole. Baptist John Leland may have criticized benevolent associations, but many other Baptists actively supported
them. And some early critics of evangelical reform later changed their views
on the matter—Alexander Campbell did.[236]

Evangelical critics of organized reform rejected Beecher's view of religion
and politics because they thought it went too far, embracing worldly means
to achieve spiritual ends. Other evangelicals rejected Beecher's formulation
because they did not think it went far enough. Reformed Presbyterians, for
example, desired a much more explicit connection between church and state
than Beecher was willing to admit. But their peculiar rendering of this doctrine ultimately prevented them from ever endangering the republic. They argued that Christians could participate only in governments that recognized
Christ as king. The U.S. Constitution failed to do this; hence, many Reformed Presbyterians claimed that both holding office and voting were immoral in America under its present system of government.[237] By completely
removing themselves from electoral politics (though not from moral reform
efforts), Reformed Presbyterians virtually guaranteed that their theocratic
agenda could never be achieved.

Perhaps a more serious threat to Beecher's vision from this side came
from evangelical partisans of the Anti-Masonic Party. If any American
party was conceived of largely in religious terms, it was the antimasons. But
the very fact that the Anti-Masonic Party lasted such a short time—and that
it failed to dominate politics even in most of New England—indicates how
unwilling the majority of evangelicals were to tie themselves to a Christian
party.

Only one mainstream evangelical leader talked as if he embraced an intimate connection between the church and politics, and his comments were
misconstrued. In 1827 Presbyterian minister Ezra Stiles Ely precipitated a
storm of protest by actually calling for *"a Christian party in politics."*[238]
Ely's Christian party, however, was in fact no party at all. It was simply a
tacit agreement among Christians to withhold their votes from immoral candidates (such as duelists and the sexually promiscuous) and to bestow their
votes on fellow Christians, irrespective of their party affiliation. The latter

half of Ely's proposal raised problems, but it did not demand that the churches embrace the machinery of party politics. Indeed, Ely was a stalwart supporter of Andrew Jackson, and this proposal was clearly intended to work through the existing party system, not replace it with a new Christian one.[239]

Yet if many evangelicals seemed prepared to follow Beecher's advice and enter politics only when some clear moral principle was at stake, one could scarcely discern this from the rhetoric of the evangelicals' opponents. The more active evangelicals became in reforming society, the more controversy their efforts provoked.

## THE BACKLASH AGAINST EVANGELICAL REFORM

Throughout the 1820s attacks on evangelicals proliferated as both Unitarians and freethinkers castigated the adherents of orthodoxy not only as bigoted but also as politically ambitious and dangerous to free government. Disestablishment had occurred in every state except Massachusetts by 1819, yet cries of "priestcraft" and "union of church and state" seemed to resound even more loudly than before.[240] Now it became wrong not only for religious groups to receive money from the state but also for them to seek voluntary contributions to propagate their ideas about religion and morality.

Scottish-born reformer Frances Wright, whom Lyman Beecher termed "the female apostle of atheistic liberty," was one of the most outspoken critics of evangelicals during this period.[241] Lecturing at packed public meetings around the country, she attacked evangelicalism as "a system of error, which from the earliest date of human tradition, has filled the earth with crime, and deluged its bosom with blood, and which, at this hour, fills your country with discord, and impedes its progress in virtue, by lengthening the term of its ignorance."[242] Wright scoffed not only at evangelical theology but also at the very idea that clergy of any sect were needed to foster societal morality. Far from promoting morality, according to Wright, the clergy actually subverted the principles of freedom by suppressing the truth and free inquiry.

Wright thus attacked the cornerstone of the Founding's consensus on the public role of religion. The Founders had argued that the nation's churches were the bulwark in the battle to inculcate republican virtue; they had to flourish for the republic to survive. Wright, however, turned this proposition on its head: Only if the churches were driven out of business could republicanism truly prosper.[243] Consequently, Wright urged her listeners to withdraw their financial support from evangelical churches and voluntary associations.

"Examine the expenses of your present religious system," she told her audiences. "Calculate all that is spent in multiplying churches and salarying their ministers; in clothing and feeding travelling preachers, who fill your streets and highways with trembling fanatics, and your very forests with frantic men and hysterical women. Estimate all the fruits of honest industry which are engulfed in the treasuries of Bible societies, tract associations, and christian missions. . . . Weigh the expenses of your outlay and outfit, and then examine if this cost and this activity could not be more usefully employed."[244]

In place of the evangelical system, and as a means of thoroughly purging society of the system's evils, Wright proposed taking children away from their parents at age two and sending them off to boarding schools that would supply an education "national, rational, and republican."[245] Wright's friend, socialist Robert Owen, had proposed a similar educational scheme. In addition, as part of his "Declaration of Mental Independence" in 1826 he denounced private property, traditional religion, and even the institution of marriage as "*a TRINITY of the most monstrous evils that could be combined to inflict mental and physical evil upon his whole race.*"[246]

Wright and Owen were radicals on the fringe of society, but evangelicals were under seige from more respectable quarters as well. In Pennsylvania, for example, the state legislature in 1828 refused to grant the American Sunday School Union a charter of incorporation, fearing that it was part of a conspiracy to forge a union between church and state. Opponents circulated a handbill containing quotes from union publications that implied that the union harbored dangerous political ambitions. Senator J. Hare Powell, drawing on the handbill, attacked the union as planning to destroy the freedom of the press and as working to exclude nonevangelicals from political power. Union defenders futilely responded that the quotes were misconstrued and that it was unfair to deny one religious group "the usual corporate privileges . . . which have been granted to all literary, charitable, and religious societies without distinction."[247]

But perhaps the most sustained attacks on evangelical reformers came at the national level. As the 1820s drew to a close, evangelicals plunged headlong into national politics by resurrecting efforts to stop the Sunday mails and by challenging the forced removal of the Cherokee Indians from Georgia. These two protest campaigns constituted the high-water mark in evangelical political activism prior to 1835. They engulfed the nation in bitter controversy, and as we shall see, they epitomized both the peril and the promise of evangelical political action in America.

# THREE

## EVANGELICALS AND THE SUNDAY MAILS

The day was Sunday, April 19, 1829, and the tree-lined streets of Princeton, New Jersey, stood silent and empty. Many inhabitants were likely in church, for Princeton was the citadel of Presbyterianism in America. Site of the staunchly evangelical College of New Jersey, the city remained proud of having provided a home for such giants of the faith as Jonathan Edwards, John Witherspoon, and Samuel Stanhope Smith. Here evangelicalism continued to reign supreme, a fact to which the empty streets bore sublime testimony.

Not that the city's Sabbath tranquillity was solely the product of individual piety: Princeton also legally prohibited commercial traffic on Sundays. The city sat on a major trade route, and regardless of the reverence of its own citizens, wagon drivers liked to pass through the town on Sundays on their way to Trenton. Tired of all the noise and commotion on the Sabbath, residents had petitioned the village council for relief in 1827, and the council had obliged them by enacting the ban. The action had infuriated wagon drivers from other cities, but their lawsuits against the ordinance had proved in vain, and they gradually acquiesced to the obnoxious regulation.

Today, however, a wagoner appeared who either did not know about the ordinance or was determined to flout it. About noon he drove his cart stacked with commercial goods through the city's main thoroughfare, brazenly stopping at a tavern, which just happened to be located next to an alderman's house. The wagon driver then parked and waited, and eventually the alderman materialized. The municipal officer might have detected something peculiar in the situation, given that Princeton's ordinance was notorious by this time and that stopping in front of an alderman's house on Sunday was therefore rather foolish. But peculiar or not, the alderman carried out his duty. He asked the wagoner to store the wagon in the barn for safekeeping until Monday morning, which the wagoner did without protest.

At five o'clock Sunday evening, however, the wagoner made a shocking announcement. He said he carried the U.S. mail on his wagon. Suddenly the stakes of the confrontation rose—precipitously. The conveyance of the mails was within the clear purview of the federal government, and no sane local authority pretended to have the lawful power to stop it.[1] Had the wagoner announced this fact from the start, he would have been allowed to proceed through the town unmolested. Understandably suspicious, the alderman asked to be shown the mailbags, but the wagoner declined to comply with this request and instead walked away. The next morning the wagoner emptied the contents of the mailbags onto the floor of the alderman's barn. When the alderman told the wagoner to take the mail and deliver it, he replied that *"he knew what he was about* and *that he had done as he was directed."*[2]

In other words, the incident had been a frame-up, one apparently concocted by a firm opposed to the city ordinance. Soon unflattering accounts of the Princeton mishap were circulating around the country. *Nile's Weekly Register* reprinted a letter from the firm involved that self-righteously complained: "The driver . . . was forcibly stopped, with the mail bags, by several of the inhabitants, and compelled to remain until Monday morning (all out of piety). The public may be gratified to learn that prosecutions are about to be instituted against the perpetrators, under the post office law of the United States."[3] Princeton officials tried to undo the damage in a letter to the *National Intelligencer,* but it was too late.[4]

The immediate purpose of this manufactured incident was presumably to embarrass Princeton into repealing its ban on Sunday traffic. But there likely was a second objective, one tied to national politics: The nation was then embroiled in a renewed debate over whether to end the Sunday mails. The incident at Princeton effectively tarred evangelical opponents of the mails as subversives who would willingly undermine the Constitution to achieve their ends. It was a difficult smear for evangelical reformers to live down.[5]

The Princeton altercation showed just how rancorous the dispute over the Sunday mails had become by 1829. Three years earlier evangelicals had revived their old petition campaign urging Congress to repeal the Sunday mails. But unlike the evangelical efforts of 1811–1816, which sparked no organized opposition, this new petition campaign struck a raw nerve. Contrary to Arthur Schlesinger's assertion that "few people . . . took the question very seriously," thousands of Americans rallied on both sides of the issue.[6] Congress was soon swamped with petitions, public meetings were held, and newspapers were rife with essays. The time had passed when evangelical reformers could mount a major offensive without drawing significant criticism.

Given the limited statistical evidence available, an accurate depiction of the magnitude of the controversy is difficult to present. But protests were widespread and cut across social and geographic lines. From 1827 through 1830 the House of Representatives alone received 1,077 petitions on the subject, and by the end of February 1830 the signature count for these petitions stood at 66,945.[7] This signature count is at best a partial figure since it does not include petitions sent to the Senate, memorials sent by public meetings without individual subscribers, and petitions that came in after February 1830. Nevertheless, even this incomplete statistic is substantial; the figure would be equivalent to roughly 1.3 million signatures today if adjusted for population differences.[8] More than 80 percent of the petitions during this period and 76 percent of the signatures came from opponents of Sunday mails, though after February 1830 more petitions came in from supporters.[9]

Every region of the country shared in the protest campaign, though all regions did not participate equally. New England was overrepresented when compared to its proportion of the national population, but the region did not provide most of the memorials. Thirty-nine percent of the petitions and 44 percent of the signatures came from mid-Atlantic states, with New York—the most populous state—being the single largest supplier. Another 17 percent of petitions and 15 percent of signatures came from the South. All told, 64 percent of the petitions and 65 percent of the signatures came from outside New England.[10]

The social composition of the anti–Sunday mail movement is more difficult to uncover, but some tentative answers can be gleaned from the more than 100 petitions that supplied the occupations of subscribers. In these petitions farmers appeared most frequently, followed by merchants and mechanics. Physicians, postal workers, clergy, and attorneys also made a respectable showing. Less frequent but still noticeable were manufacturers, judges, and innkeepers.[11] There were also numerous public functionaries, including former governors from Maine, Connecticut, and Vermont, the lieutenant governor of Massachusetts, past mayors of New York City and Albany, the current mayor of Cincinnati, and assorted state legislators, state supreme court justices, and congressmen.[12]

Given the way the Sunday mails controversy mobilized so many people, one might think that the protest would be one of the major topics treated by the era's historians. Instead, it has been mostly ignored by them. Relatively little has been published on either phase of the Sunday mails campaign, and much of what has been published is incredibly one-sided. Those who mention the controversy at all almost uniformly assume that the repeal campaign was an attempt by evangelicals to impose their religious beliefs on the rest of the nation.[13] Admittedly, this is how those who opposed repeal described the Sunday mails controversy. Congressman Richard Johnson, for example, wrote that if Congress should "by the authority of law, sanction the measure recommended, it would constitute a legislative decision of a religious controversy. . . . However suited such a decision may be to an ecclesiastical council, it is incompatible with a republican Legislature, which is purely for political, and not religious purposes."[14] Johnson went on to imply that the petitioners had no right even to raise the Sunday mails issue with Congress.[15]

But Congressman Johnson represented only one-half of the Sunday mails debate. Those who raised the issue vigorously denied that they were asking Congress to decide a religious question. They repeatedly forswore any attempt to link church and state (particularly at the national level). They claimed that all they sought was to guarantee the rights of conscience. In the final analysis these arguments may be unpersuasive, but one gains nothing by ignoring them; indeed, one loses a tremendous opportunity to better understand the pivotal role of religion in America's constitutional system.

The debate over the Sunday mails should pique the interest of both political scientists and constitutional historians because of the larger issues it illuminates. It was the first national controversy to focus significantly on the meaning of the religion clauses of the First Amendment, and it raised fundamental questions about the legitimacy of religious activism in American politics. Although the issue itself may seem obscure today, the principles underlying the clash of arguments continue to be of pressing relevance to those concerned about the relationship between religion and politics over the long term.

## THE CASE AGAINST THE SUNDAY MAILS

Before analyzing the substance of the evangelicals' petitions, one cannot help but note something about their style. The nineteenth century was an age of rough-and-tumble politics, but the rhetoric employed by evangelicals in these petitions was elegant and, for the most part, restrained. The petitioners did not lash out at Congress. They did not accuse the government of being godless. They approached the supreme legislative body of the land "humbly" and "respectfully."[16] They refused to believe that its members were insensible to the evils caused by the Sunday mails or that they were "not duly solicitous to remove them."[17] In sum, the petitioners "confidently appeal[ed] to the piety, the wisdom & the patriotism" of Congress to do what was morally right.[18] The contrast between the civil rhetoric of the mail petitions and the earlier tirades by Federalist ministers such as John Mason and Nathanael Emmons is striking and instructive. Evangelicals had learned that if they wanted to be taken seriously, they had to do more than harangue their opponents.

As far as the substance of the petitions was concerned, evangelicals marshaled five basic arguments. The first was their only outright religious appeal: The Sabbath has been instituted by God; therefore, it must be respected.[19] Many petitions appended to this appeal a threat—namely, that any nation that disregards the Sabbath will bring on itself divine retribution.[20] This line of argument lends most credence to the interpretation that evangelical reformers were simply trying to enforce their religious beliefs by law through the Sabbath mails campaign. Yet one must not place more emphasis on this particular argument than evangelicals themselves did. Evangelicals understandably regarded the divine sanction of the Sabbath as the first in their hierarchy of arguments; as followers of divine revelation, evangelicals were obliged to obey the word of the Lord in everything. But just because they placed revelation first in their lives does not mean that they offered divine sanction as the paramount *political* reason to respect the Sabbath. To the contrary, their declarations about the divine sanction of the Sabbath were invoked almost by rote. Only a few petitions devoted much space to theological exegesis; the vast majority emphasized arguments from reason that were open to evangelicals and nonevangelicals alike.

This can be seen in the second argument that dominated the petitions. Evangelicals contended that apart from its purely spiritual object, the Sabbath is necessary to promote morality, which in turn is necessary for republican government.[21] In this area evangelicals clearly—and forcefully—articulated their common ground with the Founders. In the words of the inhabitants of Castleton, Vermont, "No Republican form of Government, emanating from the People, & reverting to them, can long exist in its original purity, without *virtue & intelligence* in the body politic," and "the principles and practice of the Christian Religion, unshackled by government, are the most effectual means of promoting & preserving that virtue and intelligence."[22] In support of this proposition, the citizenry of Castleton supplied a lengthy paraphrase of Washington's Farewell Address.

Fundamental to this part of the evangelicals' argument was their view of the Sabbath as the efficient cause of "*the moralizing influence of religion.*"[23] Modern scholars may have a difficult time understanding the evangelicals' preoccupation with this point. But their reasoning was really quite commonsensical: Human beings are born neither moral nor pious; therefore, virtuous habits must be instilled if they are to be acquired at all. Evangelicals claimed that the Sabbath supplies the surest method of instilling the habits of virtue. It provides one day each week when men, women, and children can temporarily forget about their daily wants and instead reflect on their timeless duties. Adults who attend worship—and children who attend Sunday school—are perpetually reminded that they are not made for bread and toil alone and that they are morally accountable for their actions.

Of course, secular instruction can also impart moral truths. But the peculiar efficacy of the Sabbath is that it fuses moral education with religion. As noted in the previous chapter, evangelicals insisted—and most of the Founders agreed—that virtuous habits are much more effectively inculcated when backed by the sanctions of revelation. They maintained that a personal devotion to God supplies a much more powerful motive to do good than any textbook on moral philosophy ever can. This motive should not be reduced simply to fear, though this is undoubtedly a component. The nominally pious person growing up in a Christian community may well avoid certain actions simply through an almost superstitious fear of divine retribution. But the converted soul, knowing that God forgives him freely and seeks his good, has another reason to act well. He is driven to do good by his fervent love of God and by his gratitude for God's overwhelming mercy.[24] Thus, although the Sabbath was the bulwark of organized religion in America, evangelicals also believed it to be a necessary institution for the perpetuation of republican government. This secular justification for protecting the Sabbath had been well established by the nineteenth century, and American evangelicals drew on previous theorists on the subject. A petition from a grand jury in Pennsylvania cited English jurist William Blackstone.[25]

Given the prevalence of the forgoing frame of reference, one can understand why the evangelical inhabitants of Hartford, Connecticut, should maintain that "no nation can long possess freedom which does not guard the sacred institutions, and perform the Holy duties of the Sabbath,"[26] or why the citizens of West Springfield, Massachusetts, would regard the Sabbath "as one of the most striking proofs of the divine beneficence, and as the only adequate means for preserving the fear of God, the sanctity of oaths, genuine personal integrity, the public morals, and our civil and political privileges."[27] Even the evangelicals' most virulent opponents perceived the importance of the Sabbath, albeit for wholly different reasons. Recall Thomas Jefferson's bitter complaint to William Short that Americans had given evangelical clergy "stated and privileged days to collect and catechise us, opportunities of delivering their oracles to the people in mass, and of moulding their minds as wax in the hollow of their hands."[28] Jefferson clearly saw the Sabbath as one of the key reasons for evangelicalism's continued success. Thus, evangelicals were not the only ones who believed that their religion would lose "its . . . effects among men, without the unmolested observance of the Sabbath."[29]

The third argument in the evangelicals' petitions centered on the rights of conscience.[30] By the late 1820s the post office employed some 27,000 men, and compelling many of these workers to labor on the Sabbath—or give up their jobs —raised the question of First Amendment rights in a way that few issues could in the early nineteenth century. The Bill of Rights would not be applied to the states for almost a century, and the federal government as yet had limited powers to interfere with the daily lives of citizens. But here the federal government was in the curious position of telling its employees to violate their religious convictions or lose their jobs. In the words of petitioners from Virginia, "Post Masters and their Clerks . . . are in many instances compelled under the present arrangement of the Mails, to do more labour on the Sabbath than on any other day. These men have no cessation from their toils either *Night or Day,* and are debarred the privileges of Christians and Freemen, as they would under the existing Laws of the United States, governing the Post-Office Department, be deprived of their Offices, and suffer disgrace, fine, and penalty, for nonattendance at their respective Office on the Sabbath."[31] That postal employees actually found themselves in an ethical quandary over this issue is attested to by the numerous postmasters who signed petitions against the Sunday mails.[32] Some evangelicals resigned their posts or gave up mail contracts rather than live with the conflict of conscience.[33]

The theoretical context of the evangelicals' free exercise claim was supplied by petitioners from Vermont, who argued that "the uninterrupted enjoyment [of the Sabbath] . . . is as much the equal right of all men, as the enjoyment of life, liberty, or property." The Vermont evangelicals invoked the Declaration of Independence to prove that governments are instituted to secure "certain unalienable rights," and they declared that the Constitution was created to do just that. Among the unalienable rights protected by the Constitution "is the privilege of serving God, obeying his commands, & keeping inviolate the precepts of Christianity." Thus, "any law which requires a portion of the citizens of the United States to violate the fourth commandment, by performing official and secular business on the Sabbath, is prohibiting the free exercise of religion. . . . It is, we believe, inconsistent with the free exercise of religion, for Congress to pass any law requiring duties, in any office, which any citizen cannot perform, without the violation of the Christian Sabbath."[34]

Some petitions analyzed the existing situation by likening it to a religious test. Just as a religious test had the effect of keeping some people out of public office because of their religious beliefs, post office policy had the effect of shutting out evangelicals from postal jobs because of their religious beliefs. Under current regulations no Christian who took the Sabbath seriously could ever work for the Post Office department. A petition from Pennsylvania pointed out what could happen if this principle was extended by Congress to other areas of the government. For instance, what if Congress passed a law requiring every senator and congressman to fulfill his official duties on Sunday? No conscientious evangelical could then run for federal office.[35] The example may have been extreme, but it made a legitimate point. The Sunday mails raised the question of church and state in an acute manner because it forced people to choose between a job and the dictates of conscience.

But the religious liberty arguments offered by evangelicals applied to more than just postal employees. A much more subtle gloss on the theme stressed the fact that the Sabbath was being abrogated by government action. Here the government was not compelling people to observe a religious duty but commanding them to *disregard* one. Evangelicals contended that this meant the government was using its authority to undercut religious religious authority. "Public laws, requiring acts to be done, imply that those acts are morally right; &, therefore those parts of the Post-office laws alluded to, have a direct tendency to influence many to disregard the duties of the Christian Sabbath & the religious rights of others, & to demoralize [the] community."[36] By sponsoring commercial activity on Sunday, the government was undermining the voluntary observance of the Sabbath by using state power to entice citizens into Sabbath breaking.[37]

Federal postal policy was already having a devastating practical effect. Richard John noted that since the post office was the only institution allowed to open on Sundays, it "quickly became a favorite gathering place for anyone venturing out-of-doors. In many cities and towns it was mobbed. . . . [T]he citzenry would flock to the post office 'in multitudes' to collect their letters and newspapers and to hear the latest news. In this way, newspapers came to supplant the pulpit. . . . The Sabbath was fast becoming no different from the rest of the week."[38] Evangelicals were outraged that this assault on their religion originated with their own government.

The fourth argument in the evangelical petitions focused on federalism. States and localities had long possessed the power to enact Sabbath-breaking statutes, most of which were still on the books. The practical effect of the Sunday mails was to carve out a gaping exception to these laws, raising with peculiar vigor the issue of states' rights. "Sabbath profanation by law is a late matter," declared a petition from Pennsylvania. "It is in opposition to the laws of most states in this union, [and] it is therefore an infraction of states rights and we hope the wisdom of Congress will apply the easy remedy."[39] Another petition from the same state supplied a more elaborate discussion of the constitutional principle at stake. Paraphrasing the Tenth Amendment, it argued that the authority to enact Sunday closing laws had never been ceded to the federal government; hence, it remained with the states, and the Sunday mails infringed on this state authority.[40]

The fifth common argument appearing in the petitions was a defensive one. Seeking to disarm opponents, petitioners argued that no public necessity required running the mails on the Sabbath.[41] Several memorials pointed out that London, the greatest commercial city in Europe, survived and flourished without Sunday mails.[42] But even if the discontinuance of the mails on the Sabbath produced some discomfort, petitioners were certain that it would be more than outweighed by the measure's benefits. In the words of a group of merchants from Baltimore, Maryland: "We believe the inconveniences which would result from the regulations prayed for, would be very inconsiderable; and were they greater than we anticipate, we are sure they would be more than counterbalanced by the benefits which would accrue to the community from a due observance of the Sabbath. . . . [A] due and proper observance of the Sabbath greatly tends to promote and strengthen moral habits, and, in a variety of ways, to better the general condition of society."[43]

These five arguments were the ones that appeared most often in the petitions, but they were supplemented by a panoply of others. Some petitions contended that forcing postmen to work on the Sabbath discouraged men who had moral and religious scruples from taking jobs with the post office, thereby promoting corruption in the delivery and transportation of the mails.[44] Other petitions maintained that compelling postal employees to work and mail coaches to run on the Sabbath cruelly deprived both men and beasts of their right to one day of rest per week.[45] It is often easy to forget that the early-nineteenth-century workweek was six days a week, twelve or more hours a day. The plight of those who had to work on the Sabbath in addition to the other six days would be even more horrific.[46] The petitions did not stress this aspect of the controversy as much as they might have, but this theme was strongly articulated in the Sabbath observance literature of the day.[47]

Did evangelicals really believe these secular arguments? Or were they simply being politically astute in their rhetoric? It is, of course, easy to rationalize any position once it has been adopted, and one could argue that evangelicals were forced into making their secular arguments by their political opposition. Richard John supplies evidence for this view by arguing that when evangelicals renewed their petition campaign in the 1820s, they relied on a "new strategy" that downplayed theology and emphasized more general principles of morality and law.[48] "While biblical appeals were by no means ignored," wrote John, "petitioners increasingly framed their appeals in terms derived from republican theory and constitutional law." They argued that "public morality was a necessary precondition for the perpetuation of republican institutions, and that Protestant Christianity was a necessary bulwark of morality," and they also maintained that the Sabbath mails "violated . . . the postmasters' constitutionally guaranteed right to the free exercise of religion."[49]

A careful comparison of the petitions from 1826 to 1830 to those from 1811 to 1816, however, seems to belie John's suggestion that evangelicals secularized their later appeals. For the most part similar arguments were em-

ployed during both phases of the controversy. For example, earlier petitioners likewise argued that disregard for the Sabbath corrupted public morals
and thus undermined the nation's civil institutions.[50] Sabbath observance
"constitutes one of the best foundations of the virtue and happiness of any
people," declared one printed petition signed by citizens from Pennsylvania.[51] Another petition, this one drafted by Congregational ministers from
Massachusetts, argued that "our social & civil institutions cannot be preserved, unless the public manners are formed on the basis of sound morality; that such morality cannot be maintained among a people, without the
active sense of religious obligation; & that neither, can long exist, where the
Sabbath ceases to be regarded as an ordinance of Heaven."[52] The petitioners
of 1811–1816 further claimed that the Sunday mails denied postal workers
the right to worship on the Sabbath and disturbed those who were trying to
worship, that the practice denied both man and beast the day of rest they de-
served, and that this delivery was economically unnecessary, at least during
peacetime.[53]

To be sure, there were a few differences from what would come later. John
was perfectly correct that the *constitutional* rhetoric employed by the later
petitioners was something new. When the petitioners from 1811–1816 talked
about postal workers being denied the rights of the Sabbath, they did not directly articulate it as a broach of the First Amendment's free exercise clause;
similarly, when they mentioned state and local Sabbath laws that the federal
government was violating by the Sunday mails, they did not talk about
states' rights or the reserved powers protected by the Tenth Amendment.[54]
But regardless of such differences of rhetoric, the fact remains that the emphasis on the purely religious aspect of the Sabbath was no greater during
the first phase of the campaign; evangelicals made much of their case on
secular grounds.

This continuity of argument indicates evangelicals had accepted the most
fundamental premise of the Founders' system from the outset of the Sunday
mails campaign: that the morality on which public discourse rests must be
sanctioned by reason as well as revelation. Most evangelicals believed that
revelation itself is reasonable. They did not have to argue solely in terms of
the Bible because they believed that the morality it inculcates is also the morality prescribed by reason. Indeed, by making arguments from reason on
behalf of biblical morality, evangelicals helped validate the trustworthiness
of revelation.

This being the case, the Founders' conceit about the agreement of reason and revelation on moral law naturally appeared in petitions during both phases of the controversy. Evangelicals claimed that their position was sanctioned by both "divine injunction" and "the best interests of the community," by "divine Revelation" and by "general experience," by "the law of the states" as well as "the law of God," and by "considerations temporal" as well as "considerations . . . spiritual."⁵⁵ Evangelicals acknowledged that the Sabbath could be viewed as the result of a "Divine command," but they added that it could also be "viewed as a human institution."⁵⁶ And the "temporal calamities" that will result from disregard of the Sabbath may be "founded on the Word of Inspiration," but they are equally "verified by the Records of profane history."⁵⁷ In sum, the petitioners stoutly maintained that reason and revelation say the same thing when it comes to the civil protection of the Sabbath. "The dictates of a wise policy, as well as a just sense of religious duty, require that the Laws of the United States regulating the Post Office should be . . . amended."⁵⁸ The defenders of the Sunday mails, as might be expected, saw matters rather differently.

## THE CASE FOR THE SUNDAY MAILS

Defenders claimed that Congress would undermine civil and religious liberty if it ordered an end to the Sunday mails.⁵⁹ The argument on this point was a multifaceted one, and its various strands need to be sorted out with some care. Many petitions maintained that by closing the mails on Sunday, Congress would be injecting itself into a religious controversy over what day constitutes the Sabbath.⁶⁰ This was a considerable simplification of the debate; in point of fact, no one was demanding that Congress officially declare Sunday a divine day of rest. The only remedy requested by evangelical reformers was that post offices close on Sundays and that the transport of the mails cease. Although one might argue that such an action would be a *de facto* recognition of Sunday as the Sabbath, the same might be said of the fact that most of the federal government already shut down on Sunday. If closing the post offices on Sunday was unconstitutional because it decided a religious controversy, then by the same logic the closing of the rest of the government on Sunday would be just as unconstitutional.

Few, if any, supporters of the Sunday mails were prepared to go so far, however. Indeed, some of them actually defended shutting down the rest of the government on Sunday. In the words of one petition: "The people of this county, have hitherto believed . . . that the observance of Sunday, in all our national departments was only the proper and respectful deference which . . . [the] law [of the land] paid to the sentiments and feelings of the community over whom it ruled."[61] But it is difficult to see how such deference to the community is different in principle from what the sabbatarian reformers were demanding. Why was shutting down almost the entire government on Sunday mere deference to community views, while the closing of a single part of the government was an impermissible religious declaration? The inconsistency here was palpable.

Another strand of the civil liberty argument stressed that exempting postal employees from work on Sundays would tilt the laws against those Christians and Jews who celebrated their Sabbath on Saturday. This was certainly true, but there was at least a partial solution available: Postal workers who worshiped on Saturday could be exempted from having to engage in their duties on that day. This solution was mentioned in petitions brought by seventh-day Christians, who, even though they supported the Sunday mails, embraced the additional exemption as a fallback position. "Should you deem it expedient to pass a law, exempting postmasters from opening the mail on the first day of the week, we pray that a clause may be added, entitling postmaster, believing the seventh day to be the Sabbath, to the like exemption on the seventh day of the week."[62]

Few petitions favoring the Sunday mails even broached the question of the religious freedom of postal workers who worshiped on Sundays. Those that did dismissed these workers' claims lightly, pointing out that the workers involved could always resign: "The petitioners [against the Sunday mails] object that the present law compels the citizens to violate the Sabbath. If, by this objection, they mean to affirm that there is any legal compulsion in the case, the position is evidently false, inasmuch as all contracts with the Post Office Department are purely voluntary; but if they intend a moral compulsion arising from pecuniary inducements, then, indeed, it has been well answered that their affected piety becomes the mere pretext of mercenary speculation."[63]

This was a rather disconcerting approach for those favoring the Sunday mails to adopt, given their simultaneous protests against the subversion of civil and religious liberty. No matter how loudly they portrayed themselves as the defenders of religious liberty, in the end they defined that liberty extremely narrowly when it came to the rights of employees. They implied that the government was under no obligation whatever to accommodate the religious beliefs of its workers. If government workers could not in good conscience carry out their duties, their only recourse was to find other work.

One likely reason defenders of the mails dismissed the religious liberty claims of their opponents was because they saw a much more frightening threat to religious liberty looming on the horizon. They regarded the campaign against the Sunday mails itself as a dangerous precedent, arguing that the entrance of organized religion into politics would inevitably lead to ecclesiastical tyranny and the unification of church and state.[64] They accused their opponents of a vast conspiracy to subvert republican government. As a consequence, the Sunday mails became a symbol of something much greater than itself, which raised the political stakes considerably. Stopping the mails on Sunday might not seem so terrible on its own, but it had to be resisted because it was only the first step on the road to ecclesiastical domination. "We are under the full impression," declared one petition, "that the petitioners for the abolition of the Sunday Mails, are introducing this measure, in part, for the purpose of ascertaining whether Congress will legislate on the subjects touching religion; and should this object be gained, it will be followed by others of more serious import, which will have a tendency to abridge our religious liberty, and to aggrandize one of the numerous sects of religion, at the expense of others."[65]

"That this measure is intended as . . . an entering wedge—the first step to priestly despotism, there can be no doubt," echoed another memorial.[66] This petition added that once the wedge went in, the nation's doom would be sealed, for it "would be driven by the hands of persecuting bigotry, until this Republic would be as destitute of Liberty and Piety as those Countries where the unhallowed union of Church and State now exists—which we firmly believe is the only aim of the designing few who are the prime movers of this unrighteous and anti-republican measure. That a union of Church and State is their darling and only object is too plain to be questioned." [67]

Many petitioners acknowledged that republican institutions constituted a bulwark against the encroachments of the clergy; but they warned Americans that their country was not invulnerable to clerical subversion. In fact, republics were peculiarly threatened by such schemes because in an "enlightened community," they were much harder to detect:

In an enlightened community, blessed with free and liberal institutions, Religious Despotism can only be established insensibly and by degrees. Every approach to it should be vigilantly guarded against by the Government. Knowing that in all ages, down to the present, the Clergy have been enterprising and ambitious—seizing eagerly upon power, and exercising it without reason and without mercy, it would be arrogance in those of the present age to claim an exemption from similar propensities; and even were they to claim it, their claim would not be credited by careful observers of their conduct.[68]

Taken as a whole, the petitions defending the Sunday mails challenged the idea that religious groups might exercise a salutary influence on the public agenda. These petitions implied that organized religious influence on public issues would lead inevitably to despotism. The paradox created by this line of argument was pointed: In the name of defending civil and religious freedom, the petitioners constricted the scope of religious liberty to the narrowest area possible. In their view religious adherents were free to meet in their own churches and to try persuading others to join them; but they should not join together for political action. Religion was preeminently private, and it should have nothing to do with the political process. The only way religious institutions could legitimately influence politics was indirectly, through the cultivation of general mores—as Tocqueville observed in *Democracy in America*.[69]

Some petitioners begrudged even this role to religion, however. These more radical critics suggested that the whole system of evangelical voluntary associations was dangerous and antirepublican, regardless of whether the associations engaged in politicking:

When we consider the number, talents, and influence of this body of men [the clergy], their zeal and activity, the intimate union that exists among them, and the concert with which all their movements are accomplished, the astonishing credulity of many of their adherents, the support they derive from numerous religious corporations and societies rapidly increasing in numbers and in wealth, the almost unlimited control which they exercise over colleges and other literary institutions, with no power but the laws, which they are ambitious to control, to watch or check them, we see reason to dread even their unassisted efforts to deprive us of our liberties.[70]

The fiery rhetoric of the Sunday mail supporters cooled a bit when they turned from church and state to the economic reasons for an everyday mail establishment. They contended that dispatch in communications was critical in a commercial republic such as America and that stopping the mails on Sunday would have a baleful influence on the American economy.[71] One might argue that business interests such as these were the real reason behind much of the opposition to shutting down the Sunday mails. This may well be the case, but the interesting point is that commerce was not the main reason offered as the justfication for opposing the evangelical reformers. Defenders of the Sunday mails devoted considerably more space in their petitions to describing the harmful effects that would result to religious and civil liberties should the evangelical reformers succeed; these petitioners sought to portray the conflict as a battle between church and state, a fight pitting freemen against religious tyrants. Nineteenth-century America may have been a commercial republic par excellence, but the interests of commerce were raised in this debate only after the more fundamental concerns of civil and religious liberty had been dealt with.

Perhaps one reason for this ordering was the composition of the coalition that supported the Sunday mails. The coalition included many who were concerned about the issue precisely because of its religious ramifications. These included freethinkers who wanted to destroy evangelicalism, such as Robert Owen and Frances Wright, but also more traditional religious adherents. Despite the virulent antireligious rhetoric of many who defended the Sunday mails, some of the most potent sources of support for the Sunday mails came from *within* evangelicalism, from dissenters who had never fully accepted the active public role of religion championed by the leaders of the evangelical reform movement. Petitions on behalf of the mails from Baptist groups and from others professing to be Christians underscored this fact, as did petitions that defended the voluntary observance of the Sabbath even while attacking those who would stop the Sunday mails.[72]

As pointed out in Chapter 2, perhaps the most substantial evangelical critics of the evangelical reform movement were the followers of Alexander Campbell. Still other evangelical dissenters (particularly among the Baptists) joined the Campbellites in their suspicion of mixing religion and politics but did not share the total rejection of evangelical reform. These dissenters might support Bible societies and missionary efforts (and even government support for missionary efforts), but they clung to their doubts about the wisdom of having churches and benevolent societies organize political movements.[73] Establishments of religion had not disappeared so long ago in many states that their deleterious effects could be easily forgotten by sects that had suffered under them. As the Alabama Baptist Association pointedly reminded Congress in an attack on those opposed to the Sunday mails: "We . . . have not yet forgotten our whipping Posts, Prisons, Fines, Lawsuits, and costs that we suffered in the States of Virginia, and Massachusetts. . . . Our object is, to avoid the like consequences, by rejecting the principle [of establishments of religion]. For persecution follows in the train with law established Religion."[74] These evangelical undercurrents against mixing religion and politics found a ready spokesman in Colonel Richard Johnson, an influential U.S. senator from Kentucky who was later elected vice president.

## COLONEL JOHNSON AND THE CONGRESSIONAL RESPONSE

A vigorous partisan of Andrew Jackson,[75] Johnson chaired the Senate Committee on the Post Office in 1829, and he quickly became the nation's most vehement defender of the Sunday mails—and one of the most outspoken critics of mixing religion and politics. This latter stance was a little curious given some of Johnson's own activities and family connections. His father and brothers were heavily involved in Baptist missionary work, and he himself promoted missions among the Indians, obtaining federal money for such efforts.[76] He also assisted the temperance movement by securing the hall of the House of Representative for a temperance meeting.[77] Johnson was probably more of a fellow traveler than a true believer in evangelical moral reform, however. He was not exactly known for his personal piety, at least once being called to account by his Baptist church for a lack of attendance at meetings.[78] He also challenged another man to a duel, and despite Johnson's courtesy to the temperance movement, he owned and operated a tavern.[79]

Johnson catapulted himself to the forefront of the Sunday mails controversy by producing two committee reports on the issue, one in 1829 and the other in 1830 after he was elected to the House of Representatives. Baptist minister Obadiah Brown, who also happened to be a postal clerk, apparently ghostwrote both reports for Johnson. Almost immediately they were reprinted for public consumption as pamphlets; according to one estimate, 3 million copies of the first report were put in circulation.[80] One measure of the first report's effectiveness is the fact that most petitions in support of the Sunday mails came in after it was released, and many petitions cited the report with approbation and appropriated its arguments.[81]

Johnson began his first report by acknowledging that "some respite is required from the ordinary vocations of life" and that "in conformity with the wishes of the great majority of citizen of this country, the first day of the week, commonly called Sunday, has been set apart to that object." He further admitted that the principle of setting aside Sunday for rest "has received the sanction of the national legislature, so far as to admit a suspension of all public business on that day, except in cases of absolute necessity, or of great public utility." Far from wishing to abolish this implicit sanction of Sunday rest, the postal committee, Johnson claimed, wanted to preserve it. "This principle the committee would not wish to disturb. If kept within its legitimate sphere of action, no injury can result from its observance."[82]

But Johnson argued that to apply this principle to the post office would inevitably involve the government in deciding whether Sunday was the true Sabbath appointed by God, and this would put the government in the position of resolving by fiat a theological contention among several sects. How Johnson arrived at this assessment of the situation is obscure. The petitioners did not ask Congress for any sort of theological declaration; neither did they justify their position primarily on religious grounds. They did, however, state their own belief that Sunday was the Sabbath and that to work on that day was to violate the law of God. Johnson seems to have determined that this was enough to taint the rest of their request. That they had an underlying motivation that was religious, even though they framed their arguments primarily in secular terms, disqualified their petition from being heard on its merits.

Johnson added that organized religious influence on public questions was unhealthy in a republic:

Extensive religious combinations to effect a political object are, in the opinion of the committee, always dangerous. This first effort of the kind calls for the establishment of a principle which, in the opinion of the committee, would lay the foundation for dangerous innovations upon the spirit of the Constitution and upon the religious rights of the citizens. If admitted, it may be justly apprehended that the future measure of the government will be strongly marked, if not eventually controlled, by the same influence. All religious despotism commences by combination and influence; and when that influence begins to operate upon the political institutions of a country, the civil power soon bends under it; and the catastrophe of other nations furnishes an awful warning.

Note that Johnson claimed that this was the "first effort" in America to employ "extensive religious combinations to effect a political object." But this claim was simply wrong. A decade previously similar efforts had been conducted to end the Sunday mails—and had won the respect of Congress. Earlier still ministers had lobbied for laws against dueling. And during the elections of 1796 and 1800, Federalist clergy had campaigned against Jefferson. Even during the Revolutionary War, Patriot ministers had exhorted their followers to support the separation from Great Britain. Johnson's vision of America as a place where religion had always been kept in pristine isolation from politics was an America that had never actually existed.

Indeed, Johnson's own efforts to support temperance and to secure federal funding for Baptist missions undercut his strident rhetoric. He hardly could have intended to condemn all evangelical reform movements or even all financial connections between church and state. As if to intimate this fact, Johnson relented at the end of his report and praised the moral function of religion; but he steadfastly maintained that it is purely private in character. "Let the professors of Christianity recommend their religion by deeds of benevolence, by Christian meekness, by lives of temperance and holiness. . . . Their moral influence will then do infinitely more to advance the true interests of religion than any measure which they may call on Congress to enact."[83]

Of course, the evangelical reformers claimed that they were not asking the federal government to advance the interests of religion; they merely wanted the government to stop interfering with religion. In their view the government was the one that undercut the voluntary observance of religion by siding with those who opposed a strict observance of the Sabbath; the government likewise diminished the religious liberties of its employees by compelling postal workers to engage in secular labor against their religious beliefs. Johnson did not try to grapple with the first argument; as to the second, he noted in passing that postal workers entered into their jobs voluntarily. In other words, they could resign if they did not like their Sunday duties.

By disregarding the arguments petitioners made about religious liberty and the connection between the Sabbath and civic morality, Johnson tried to recast the framework in which the Sunday mails controversy would be argued. He sought to transform the debate from a discussion of the civic role of religion to an attack on the motivations and affiliations of those bringing the petitions. According to Johnson, the fact that those against the Sunday mails believed Sabbath breaking to be against the divine law was enough to disqualify their secular arguments from being heard. This being decided, the only question for Congress to consider was one of expediency, which dictated that the mails continue. "The various departments of Government require, frequently in peace, always in war, the speediest intercourse with the remotest parts of the country; and one important object of the mail establishment is, to furnish the greatest and most economical facilities for such intercourse."[84]

Not everyone in Congress was willing to accept Johnson's formulation of the controversy. Congressman Samuel McKean, chair of the House Committee on the Post Office, attempted to stake out a middle position between Johnson and the evangelical reformers. In February 1829 McKean issued his own report on the controversy. Unlike Johnson, McKean accepted the framework presented by the petitioners opposed to the Sunday mails. He and his committee agreed with them "that a proper observance of the Sabbath is calculated to elevate the moral condition of society," and he further granted that the policies they requested would not tend toward "the justly odious combination of church and state."[85] Nevertheless, McKean could not sanction a complete end to the transportation of the mails on Sunday because—like Johnson—he disagreed with the petitioners about the importance of expeditious mails to the functioning of the republic.

McKean argued that "[a] well-regulated mail establishment is an indispensable requisite to a free Government, and to the commercial agricultural, and manufacturing interest of an enterprising and growing people."[86] Hence, it was unreasonable to stop the mail coaches on the major postal routes on Sundays. But McKean then met the evangelical reformers halfway.

Acknowledging that no similar necessity existed for the opening of post offices on Sundays for the delivery of letters to customers, he and the House postal committee subsequently recommended that Congress repeal the part of the post office law requiring postmasters to deliver mail to customers on the Sabbath.

McKean's proposal conceivably would have satisfied many petitioners. Although the petitions against the mails sought an end to all postal business on Sundays, the mandatory opening of the post offices was undeniably what had spurred initial protests over this issue back in 1811. In fact, several petitions during this earlier period were silent on the transport of the mails and directed their comments solely against the opening of post offices.[87] In addition, evangelical reformers were not completely inflexible on Sabbath observance; they acknowledged that works of mercy and necessity did not desecrate the day. This being the case, McKean's argument about the indispensability of daily mail conveyance was well calculated to defuse the opposition.

Given the mixed signals sent by the Johnson and McKean reports, it was inevitable that petitions would keep pouring into Congress on both sides of the issue. They did, and political passions continued to rise, especially among those defending the mails. Efforts promoting the mails soon exhibited all the trappings of a malevolent party campaign, including the obligatory mudslinging and dirty tricks. Public meetings were held around the country to denounce religious zealots for trying to undermine America's republican government.[88] In April defenders of the mails seized on the manufactured incident at Princeton to smear their opponents as lawbreakers. In December a meeting held at Tammany Hall in New York accused Sunday mail petitioners of padding their petitions by collecting signatures from children who attended the city's Sunday schools.[89] In January a meeting in Poughkeepsie, New York, darkly prophesied that "if the present combination of professedly religious individuals be persevered in for the discontinuance of the Mails . . . it will produce discord and disunion among the people, lead to a civil war, deluge our country in blood, and finally overthrow our republican institutions."[90]

But perhaps the most vivid piece of rhetoric was Richard Johnson's second report on the mails, issued on March 4, 1830, after he had been elected to the House and assumed the chairmanship of the House Committee on the Post Office.[91] In the new report Johnson at first claimed that he and others on the postal committee did "not feel disposed to impugn . . . [the] motives" of those who opposed the Sunday mails.[92] He then spent the rest of his report doing almost nothing else.

As before, Johnson charged that opponents of the Sunday mails wanted Congress to decide a religious controversy and determine what particular day God had appointed as the Sabbath. This contention was somewhat plausible if one meant that shutting down the mails on Sunday implicitly acknowledged that day as the Sabbath. But Johnson now accused opponents of the Sunday mails of a conscious effort to exert coercion on those who celebrated their Sabbath on Saturday. According to Johnson, the real object of the campaign against the Sunday mails was to compel those who worshiped on Saturday to recognize Sunday as the true Sabbath. "As argument has failed, the Government has been called upon to interpose its authority to settle the controversy" over what day is the true Sabbath. This was demagoguery on Johnson's part. The goal of evangelical reformers had nothing to do with coercing those who worshiped on Saturday. The object was to secure the rights of those who already chose to worship on Sunday; and the reason they had to seek legal recourse was because postmasters and clerks currently had no choice in the matter. Federal law compelled post offices to open every day of the week, regardless of the wishes of the postmasters involved. Thus, federal law effectively nullified the right of postal workers to follow their individual scruples; the only way this could be corrected was by a change in the laws.

The rest of Johnson's report was even more biting. Johnson implied that evangelicals had no right to bring the subject of the Sunday mails before Congress, and he proceeded to compare the evangelical reformers with a pantheon of traitors and tyrants from the days of yore:

> With these facts before us, it must be a subject of deep regret that a question should be brought before Congress which involves the dearest privileges of the constitution, and even by those who enjoy its choicest blessings. We should all recollect that Catiline, a professed patriot, was a traitor to Rome; Arnold, a professed whig, was a traitor to America; and Judas, a professed disciple, was a traitor to his Divine Master. . . .
>
> It was with a kiss that Judas betrayed his Divine Master; and we should all be admonished—no matter what our faith may be—that the

rights of conscience cannot be so successfully assailed as under the pretext of holiness.[93]

Johnson then went on to impugn the religious liberty claims of the petitioners: "Do the petitioners allege that they cannot conscientiously participate in the profits of the mail contracts and post offices, because the mail is carried on Sunday? If this be their motive, then it is wordly gain which stimulates to action, and not virtue or religion. Do they complain that men less conscientious in relation to the Sabbath obtain advantages over them by receiving their letters and attending to their contents? Still their motive is worldly and selfish." Finally, Johnson mockingly urged the petitioners to show their true colors and seek state laws that would forbid people from writing letters on the Sabbath and would compel their attendance at public worship.[94]

Dissenting from Johnson's harangue, Congressman William McCreery filed a minority report that attempted to rescue the evangelical reformers' arguments from complete misconstruction. McCreery pointed out that, contrary to Johnson's claims, the petitioners "ask not Congress to meddle with theological controversies, much less to interfere with the rights of the Jew or the Sabbatarian . . . but they do ask that the agents of Government, employed in the Post Office Department, may be permitted to enjoy the same opportunities of attending to moral and religious instruction or intellectual improvement on that day which is enjoyed by the rest of their fellow-citizens."[95] McCreery added that he thought the petitioners' request should be granted because the only real arguments in support of the Sunday mails were based on "commercial convenience," and these, of course, had to give way to the dictates of moral principle.

The unsparing onslaught by Johnson and his supporters had a discernible effect on opponents of the Sunday mails. It did not change the substance of their major arguments, but it did make them reformulate their reasons in explicitly constitutional language—which helped them counter charges that they were acting unconstitutionally. This onslaught further inspired opponents to aggressively defend their right to participate in the political process. They were being accused of being traitors to republicanism, and they were not about to let the charge go unrebutted.

Seizing on the right of petition guaranteed by the First Amendment, evangelical reformers contended that their political activities were perfectly con-

sistent with American liberties. As a pamphlet published after Johnson's
first report declared: "Have not religious persons the same right as others to
petition Congress? And when they have done so, are they to be denounced
before the nation as a treasonable combination to change the government—
as taking the first step, and entering the opening wedge of revolution?"[96]

The same pamphlet went on to acknowledge, however, that Christians—as
Christians—should not enter politics for light and transient causes. Adopting Lyman Beecher's formulation of Christian political action (and it is possible that Beecher wrote the pamphlet), the author continued:

> We admit that Christians, as such, ought not to attempt to influence the
> administration in things merely secular, beyond the unobtrusive influ-
> ence of their silent suffrage; and ought not to become political parti-
> sans, heated and agitated by all the little and great disputes which must
> ever attend popular governments; and ought never to attempt, or be
> permitted, to make the government a religious instead of a civil institu-
> tion. But it is not a civil, but a moral effect for which the petitioners
> ask, and one in their view indispensable to the perpetuity of our repub-
> lican institutions.[97]

Another writer snapped that if Colonel Johnson wanted to abolish religious
combinations for political objects, he ought to take care "that no legislative
sanction be given to political objects *which violate the moral feelings of the
community.* Then he will be sure to have no religious combinations."[98]

The evangelical reformers further protested that their opponents had distorted what they were requesting Congress to do. One pamphleteer with a
dry wit noted:

> The petitioners . . . are gravely told that Congress cannot expound the
> ten commands, cannot settle theological disputes, cannot invade the
> conscience of the Jew, cannot introduce religious observances into our
> institutions, cannot coerce the observance of the Sabbath, cannot pre-
> clude the discretion of the people to think for themselves, cannot sanc-
> tion a principle of persecution which has stained almost every page of
> history; and they might have added with just as much relevancy, and
> with as little insult to the petitioners, cannot sustain a crusade to rescue
> the holy sepulchre from infidels, or make a pilgrimage to Mecca in

honor of Mahomet, or send an embassy to explore the concavity of the North Pole. [99]

According to this author, petitioners had never pretended to ask the national legislature "to compel the people of the United States, by law, to observe the first of the week."[100] In fact, they agreed with their opponents "that it is not the business of the national government to sustain by positive legislation, either the religion or the morals of the nation."[101] What petitioners found offensive was not that the federal government did not actively encourage the Sabbath but that it was actively subverting the Sabbath. By authorizing agents to break the Sabbath in hundreds of communities across the nation, the government had in effect placed its official stamp of approval on Sabbath breaking.[102] The case would be different if private individuals were breaking the Sabbath on their own, "for that is not the fault of the government, and does not expose the people to punishment on their account."[103] But here *government* action was involved. The situation was aggravated by the fact that not all government agents were acting willingly; many had been forced to choose between their consciences and their jobs. According to the petitioners, then, all they desired was that the government end its interference with the Sabbath so they could promote its observance free of government.

Yet petitioner disavowals of government coercion were not entirely persuasive. First, although evangelical reformers disclaimed any attempt to make Congress enforce Sabbath observance, many of them continued to embrace the use of state and local laws to do the same thing. In other words, they wished federal government out of the way so that they might employ state coercion.[104] Even more troublesome, some evangelicals coupled their arguments about religious liberty with proclamations that America was a Christian country where offenses such as blasphemy ought to be punished by laws.[105] The evangelical reformers may have prized religious liberty when applying it to themselves, but they seemed far less charitable when applying it to others. This meant that Colonel Johnson was not completely unjust in accusing the Sabbath observance movement of wanting to employ government power in support of the Sabbath. Some in the movement did want this, though not at the federal level.

Nevertheless, this coercive element should not be overdramatized. For one thing, given the context of the times, Sabbath-breaking laws could be as eas-

ily justified on grounds of religious liberty as on the theory that the government had the power to promote religion. Early-nineteenth-century America
had nothing equivalent to the modern administrative state, and the legal op-
tions of those seeking to protect their right to observe the Sabbath were decidedly few. Today the government might protect a person's right to worship
(as well as his right to rest from work) by regulating the workweek or by providing a legal right to a day of rest on his Sabbath. In the nineteenth century,
however, such intrusive regulations enforced on private businesses were untenable. The only recognized way for the government to safeguard a person's
right to observe the Sabbath was by shutting down *all* businesses on the
same day. This was admittedly an imperfect solution because it ignored the
rights of those workers who celebrated their Sabbath on a different day than
the one protected by the state. But a Sabbath-breaking law did effectively
protect the rights of the vast majority of the citizens who could not in good
conscience work on their appointed day of worship.

More to the point, the Sunday mails crusade was part of the larger Sabbath reform movement that had been reborn in the mid-1820s, and this
movement—contrary to the assertions of Congressman Johnson—did not
see laws as the solution to the problem of Sabbath breaking. Indeed, the
General Union for Promoting the Observance of the Christian Sabbath, the
major evangelical organization in this area, officially disclaimed legal efforts to enforce the Sabbath in its constitution: "As the weapons of the
christian warfare are not carnal, but spiritual, the means employed by this
Society for effecting their design, shall be, exclusively, the influence of personal example, of moral suasion, with argument drawn from the oracles of
God, from the existing laws of our country, and appeals to the consciences
and hearts of men."[106]

Although the General Union did not advocate laws to protect the Sabbath, it did encourage individuals to boycott businesses that were open on
the Sabbath. Operating on the precept that Christians could not in good
conscience assist others in breaking God's law, union members believed that
they had an obligation to spend their money only on those businesses that
respected the Sabbath.[107] This emphasis on individual action helped keep the
disparate elements of the Sabbath reform coalition together, and it likely ac-
counted for the fact that the General Union attracted prominent Methodists
and Baptists as officers, in addition to Congregationalists and Presbyterians.[108] (Critics of Sabbath reform found such economic boycotts equally un-

republican, terming them an "arbitrary instrument of religious despot-ism."[109])

In the end, then, Johnson's charges had elements of truth to them, but they were overblown. This fact did not keep them from being politically powerful, however, as the swell of petitions echoing Johnson's complaints attested. Johnson clearly put the evangelicals on the defensive, and evangeli-cal reformers were still scrambling to recoup from Johnson's second report when the Sunday mails issue finally came to a head in Congress.

Six days after Johnson's new report came out, Theodore Frelinghuysen of New Jersey introduced legislation in the U.S. Senate to curb the Sunday mails. Frelinghuysen was the nation's preeminent evangelical statesman, heavily involved in evangelical reform, and respected by even his political opponents for his rigid personal integrity.[110] Before being appointed to the Senate, Frelinghuysen had served as New Jersey's attorney general, a post also filled by the state legislature. Notably, the legislature that had chosen him as attorney general had been dominated by a political party different from his own.[111] Throughout his public career Frelinghuysen made clear that he valued piety more than politics. While serving in the Senate, he frequently remarked that his occupation as a Sunday school teacher was more honor-able than his political employment, and he spared no efforts trying to spread the gospel, even attempting to convert political friends such as Henry Clay.[112] If the religious appeals had come from any other politician, perhaps they would have been found offensive, but coming from Frelinghuysen, they only inspired greater respect. On leaving the Senate, Frelinghuysen became chancellor of the University of the City of New York and then president of Rutgers College.[113] In 1844 he was selected as the Whigs' vice-presidential candidate in Clay's doomed bid for the presidency.[114]

Frelinghuysen vigorously supported the evangelical effort to stop the Sun-day mails, but he had been uncertain about whether the time was right to bring the subject before Congress. By early 1830 Richard Johnson's first re-port had brought in so many counterpetitions on the subject that emotions were running high, and Frelinghuysen feared that a congressional debate now might do more harm than good. Undecided about what course to take, he turned for counsel to Jeremiah Evarts of the American Board of Com-missioners for Foreign Missions. Evarts was deeply involved in evangelical reform and was helping coordinate the petition campaign. On Feburary 1 Frelinghuysen wrote him asking his advice:

I had almost determined to ask leave to bring in a Bill, as I found the committee would not act. . . . But my friend Jacob Burnet is strongly of opinion, that we should suffer the subject to rest, until the public mind becomes calm again—that the majority is now very strong & a defeat would only strengthen the opposition—great excietment prevails in the western count[r]y—the Baptists oppose us in a body—even their ecclesiastical conventions have sent their remonstrances—Now my dear friend, do not mistake me. I trust my sole desire is to act as God shall approve—I hope I am not afraid or ashamed to meet all questions, connected with the glory of His Kingdom and the best good of my country. But I wish your deliberate judgment as to the better course to be pursued.[115]

Evarts apparently recommended that Frelinghuysen go ahead and introduce a bill, for Frelinghuysen in his next letter said he had "been anxiously considering [the Sabbath question] since you wrote to me on that subject" and that he had "drawn a resolution to try the sense of the Senate." Frelinghuysen also reported that he had been informed that Johnson would "make a tremendous Report against us" that would "assail our motives."[116] Johnson released the report on March 4–5, and less than a week later Frelinghuysen introduced his bill. Two months later, on May 8, a Senate floor debate over the proposal ensued, with Frelinghuysen squaring off against Senator Edward Livingston of Louisiana.

Frelinghuysen recapitulated the Sunday mail petitioners' major arguments about religious liberty and the need for the Sabbath to promote morality.[117] He also defended evangelical reformers from "the absurd imputation of a design to tyrannize over the consciences and rights of men." Frelinghuysen wryly noted that if the evangelical reformers really sought to impose a tyranny, their methods were "a strange engine of oppression. In all past time, to hold men in bondage it was found necessary to keep them in ignorance: but here is 'a dangerous party,' which some affect to fear, that none but tyrannts have ever dreaded before. A party whose labors are spreading the means of general information; whose philanthropy is engaged in enlightening the ignorant and reclaiming the deluded, whose charities have penetrated the abodes of the convict and opened a ray of hope even to *him;* and such men are assailed and summoned to a defence of such conduct."[118]

For Frelinghuysen the question before Congress had turned into a referendum on the Sabbath, and he was perfectly prepared to argue it on those grounds. His summary of the cardinal importance of the Sabbath in America's scheme of government was among the best offered during the controversy.[119] Frelinghuysen wanted to turn the controversy into a debate over the nature of human beings and the ends of human life. Are all men rational beings capable of reflection and choice, or are some fit only to work as unthinking drudges? Is man's highest end material gratification, or does he exist for purposes more noble and sublime? For Frelinghuysen, the vindication of the Sabbath was a vindication of idealism over self-interest, of human reason over human passions. The nation that consecrated one day a week for reflection and worship proclaimed that acquisitiveness and sensual gratification had to be subordinated to man's rational and eternal ends.

Here was a defense of the Sabbath that could be appreciated even by non-evangelicals, and had Frelinghuysen stuck to this line of attack, he might have been thoroughly convincing. As it was, however, he ended up supplying his opponents with more ammunition. At one point he discussed coercive state laws that not only punished Sabbath breaking but also recognized its religious authority. Ostensibly this was to show that if such stringent measures could stay on the books without a general outcry, it was ludicrous to claim that the mere suspension of mail delivery on the Sabbath was unduly coercive. The difficulty was that Frelinghuysen actually seemed to agree with the laws in question.[120] Given that Frelinghuysen was one of the directors of the General Union for Promoting the Observance of the Christian Sabbath, such opinions were embarrassing at best.[121]

Evangelical reformers nevertheless thought highly of Frelinghuysen's performance, and his speech was printed up as a pamphlet. Jeremiah Evarts, who was in Washington at the time, jotted down in his journal that a spectator told him that Frelinghuysen "spoke an hour and a half, or more, and very much to the purpose. Mr. Livingston replied, in a speech of three quarters of an hour, in which he gained no credit. It was a low piece of bar-room talk about church and state, the blue laws of Connecticut, hanging witches at Salem, &c.&c. Mr. F., in a short reply, made Mr. L. rather ashamed of his tirade."[122] An aged former senator from New England remarked that Frelinghuysen's speech "would console all the pious people of the country, who had been compared to Cataline, Arnold, and Judas."[123] Console them it might, but for the moment it did little else. At the end of the debate, Frelinghuysen's proposal was tabled, and the issue never saw the light of day during that session of Congress. "In fact, the whole Sunday-mail contro-versy evaporated with great rapidity," writes Arthur Schlesinger.[124]

Actually, the respite from controversy was only temporary, and the Sun-day mails issue persisted tenaciously for almost another century. Perhaps most important, evangelical reformers eventually achieved much of their agenda. Advances in communications and transportation technology gradu-ally made the Sunday mails less profitable, which in turn made evangelical demands easier to grant, and by the 1840s thousands of miles of Sunday mail routes had been eliminated.[125] By 1863 evangelical Talcot Chambers could boast that evangelical efforts had "caused a reduction of Sunday-mail service to an amount scarcely one fourth of what it was when the question was first mooted."[126] Post offices were also gradually closed, the last of them in 1912, when "an alliance of ministers and postal clerks convinced Con-gress to close down all of those offices still open on the Sabbath for good."[127]

## THE LEGACY OF THE SUNDAY MAILS CRUSADE

The Sunday mails debate remains an important episode in American history because it raised the sticky question of what to do when religious and civil authority collide. The Founders tried to preempt this problem by separating church and state and by pledging that government decisions would be made according to a moral standard acceptable to both reason and revelation. But there were bound to be cases that fell through the cracks, and this was one of them. Evangelical religion demanded that the Sabbath be free from secular labor. The federal government violated this command by running the postal service on Sunday—deciding, in effect, that the Sabbath need not be re-spected by the government. The prestige and authority of the general gov-ernment were thus placed on the side of the Sabbath breaker, and evangeli-cals were offended because they thought the government had taken sides against them.

Of course, defenders of the mails claimed that if the government did stop the mails on Sunday, it would be dismissing the beliefs of those who wor-shiped on Saturday or on no day at all. In other words, the government seemed to take sides however it acted. If it continued the mails on Sunday, it denied that Sunday should be kept as the Sabbath; if it stopped the mails on

Sunday, it decided that Sunday *was* the Sabbath and thus disapproved of those who held Saturday sacred. Actually, the two cases were not quite analagous because government inaction is not nearly so intrusive as government action. When the government acts, it inevitably sends the message that the action is permissible; when the government refrains from acting, however, it may do so without passing judgment on whether the action is good, indifferent, or vile. In this case the government might stop the mails on Sunday out of respect for the "moral feelings of the community," not because it wanted to decide the theological controversy of which day, if any, constituted the true Sabbath. Defenders of the mails themselves conceded this principle when discussing the practice of shutting down the rest of the federal government on Sunday.

This is not to say that shutting down the mails on Sunday posed no problems with respect to those who worshiped on other days. Proponents of the Sunday mails properly pointed out that stopping the mail only on Sundays undeniably showed favoritism toward those who held the Sunday as the Sabbath. If government violations of the Sabbath really were an infringement of religious liberty, then the government should stop the mails on every day held to be the Sabbath by some citizen. "If the Mails are stopped, and the Post Offices closed on the first day of the week to gratify some religious sects, it would be no more than equal justice, that the same course should be adopted on the seventh day of the week, to gratify others who are equaly entitled to favor and respect."[128] But this led to an untenable result. Once one adopted the principle that the government should not violate religious duties, there would be no end to the practical difficulties. As Richard Johnson pointed out with regard to Sabbath observance: "The committee [cannot] discover where the system could consistently end. If the observance of a holiday becomes incorporated into our institutions, shall we not forbid the movement of an army, prohibit an assault in time of war, and lay and injunction upon our naval officers to lie in the wind while upon the ocean, on that day?"[129]

Those who led the Sunday mails campaign were aware of these difficulties with their theory of religious liberty, and they carefully tried to avoid the absurdities pointed out by Johnson. For instance, they acknowledged the practical difficulties of stopping government work on the Sabbath of every religious group no matter how small, and they responded that the government simply ought to do the best it could for the vast majority of religious adherents. The world was not a perfect place, and protecting the religious rights of as many people as possible to the fullest extent was better than protecting the religious rights of everyone to a very limited extent. In the present case the vast majority of people celebrated their Sabbath on Sundays, so this was the day that ought to be protected.[130] True, this meant that seventh-day Christians, Jews, and anyone else who did not celebrate Sunday as their Sabbath were not equally protected by the laws. But neither were they placed at an added disadvantage.[131] Under existing laws the post office already operated on Saturdays, and any postal worker who was a Jew or a seventh-day Christian had to work on that day. Shutting down the post office on Sundays did not increase this burden; doing so merely did nothing to alleviate it. At the same time, it did alleviate the burden on the vast majority of workers. In the mind of the evangelical reformers, that the government could not provide the same protection for everyone did not mean that it should not protect as many people as possible.

As far as Johnson's assertion that the government would be seriously impeded in the use of the army or other vital resources if it accepted evangelical arguments, the petitioners acknowledged that even their own claims on the government had limits. Contrary to Johnson's intimations, evangelical reformers never claimed an unqualified right to stop the government from sponsoring work on the Sabbath. They invariably acknowledged that if the Sunday mails were shown to be *necessary*, the government might continue them.[132] Reformers likewise acknowledged that other government work on the Sabbath could be countenanced when shown to be necessary. Noted one reformer: "If the jailer . . . were to suspend the exercise of his duty on Sunday, his prisoners would all escape; so that there is an absolute necessity for his continuing it. If the commander of an army were to suspend the exercise of his functions every seventh day, his adversary might, under certain critical circumstances, obtain such an advantage over him, as would decide the fate of a campaign—perhaps the political situation of the country. Here the inconvenience of observing the rule is so great as to produce a moral necessity of violating it."[133]

In effect, evangelicals espoused a compelling state interest standard. The government should not abridge religious duties (and thus violate religious liberty and send a message of disapproval to pious citizens) unless there is some compelling reason to do so. Under this formulation of the problem, it is perfectly clear why the government would not have to accede to every request from every religious group seeking a suspension of government activities. But the government should not reject the requests arbitrarily; it must justify its actions.

Defenders of the Sunday mails articulated a substantially different vision of civil and religious liberty. Their line of argument implied that the government could routinely pursue policies that undermined the tenets of a religious group without raising free exercise objections; the government could also burden the religious beliefs of individual citizens so long as the citizens were not absolutely compelled to engage in the offensive behavior. In this case government employees could be required to work on Sunday because they could always resign their jobs if they disagreed. By adopting this narrow view of religious liberty, the Sunday mail defenders made the compelling interest standard expendable. The Sunday mails did not even burden the rights of conscience as they understood them; hence, it did not matter if Sunday mails were necessary or unnecessary. They could be justified on grounds of expediency alone.[134] Many petitions nevertheless argued that the Sunday mails *were* necessary to a commercial republic; but these arguments were peripheral once the religious liberty question had been decided.

Thus, the Sunday mails debate spawned two radically different conceptions of religious liberty in America. One was a broad view, which recognized that government coercion involved far more than absolute demands for certain kinds of behavior. Proponents of this view believed that the government could discourage religious belief and practice by its own example; hence, it should avoid offending religious sensibilities by its own behavior whenever possible. The other conception of religious liberty was far narrower. According to this interpretation, only the most direct forms of coercion interfered with the free exercise of religion. Both views continue to exert a striking influence in debates over church and state in America.

Contrary interpretations of religious liberty were not the only legacies bequeathed by the Sunday mails controversy, however. The debate generated a similar division over the public role of religion. Those who attacked the Sunday mails championed an aggressive public role for religious groups. Like most of the Founders, these evangelical reformers regarded civic morality as the lifeblood of republicanism, and they viewed religion as the necessary cultivator of that morality. Their support of the Sabbath was clearly articulated within this framework, and so was their justification of their own involvement in politics. They contended that the Sabbath must not be disparaged because it is the cornerstone of religious efforts to inculcate civic virtue and industrious habits among the citizenry; and they claimed that they had a right to be involved in politics to uphold the principles of morality. This active political role for religion had not been explicitly appreciated by all of the Founders, but it had been anticipated by several of them, most notably Franklin, Witherspoon, and Adams.[135]

Those who chastised the evangelical reformers on this point were the innovaters of the American political tradition. When they intimated that religion has no public role and that religious groups should not speak out on public issues, they undermined the Founding idea that religion has a special role in creating and defending civic morality. The most radical critics of evangelical reform understood this perfectly, but many cobelligerents probably did not.

Part of the difficulty was that the Sunday mails campaign, whatever its secular justification, still smacked of state-sponsored religion. The Sabbath might promote civic morality, but its cardinal purpose was still spiritual, not temporal. It was difficult to separate these two objects in the public mind, and one can understand why some people viewed evangelical activism on this matter with suspicion. What evangelical crusaders needed to make their point was a moral issue divorced from theological controversy. Then they might make the case for religion in politics without raising justifiable fears about illicit motives. They did not have long to wait.

In the heat of the Sunday mails flap, Congress and the Jackson administration embarked on a policy to expel the Cherokee Indians from their ancestral home in Georgia and remove them to the western hinterlands. Evangelical missionaries had been working among the Cherokees for years, teaching them the arts of Western civilization as well as the doctrines of Christianity. Now their Indian brethren appealed to them for help, and many evangelicals decided to take a stand.

# FOUR

## EVANGELICALS AND CHEROKEE REMOVAL

Samuel Worcester was anguished but determined. "I cannot remove," he wrote the American Board of Commissioners for Foreign Missions on May 31, 1831. "If all my brethren forsake me, I am willing to bear the burden alone. Only let not *God* forsake me."[1] Born and raised in New England, the lanky Worcester now lived as a missionary among the Cherokees on their lands within Georgia. Thirty-three years old, he had worked among the Cherokees since his ordination as a minister in 1825, and he had already begun to translate the New Testament into their native tongue.[2] But now he was being pressured to abandon his post, and he balked.

Georgia wanted to confiscate Cherokee lands, and missionaries like Worcester were regarded as a stumbling block to the scheme because they supported the Cherokees' treaty rights. Wishing to be rid of the meddlesome clerics, Georgia decided to expel the missionaries, and it passed a law forbidding white men from living among the Indians unless they swore an oath of allegiance to Georgia and procured a state license. The penalty for breaking the law was imprisonment for not less than four years at hard labor.[3]

Not easily cowed, Worcester and his colleagues at first spurned Georgia's threats, arguing that the state had no authority over them because it had no jurisdiction over Indian lands. Their legal analysis may have been impeccable, but Georgia had an army to enforce its view, rendering the missionaries' argument moot. Already Worcester and other missionaries had been arrested and harassed by units of the Georgia Guard. The missionaries had escaped prosecution after their first arrest only on a technicality. The judge had ruled that the restriction could not apply to them because they were all agents of the federal government: Worcester especially because he was postmaster at New Echota in Cherokee Territory and the missionaries generally because they helped distribute federal funds earmarked for civilizing the Indians. The missionaries' status as federal agents raised a thorny jurisdictional question that even Georgia did not want to confront alone, and it quickly consulted its allies in the Jackson administration.[4]

The administration disposed of the question by stripping Worcester of his office as postmaster and by disavowing any connection with the missionaries. This was good enough for Georgia, and on May 31 Worcester received a letter warning him that if he did not leave his home within ten days, he would be subject to arrest and punishment.[5] Worcester told the ABCFM that he would not remove unless the board ordered him to do so. He *wanted* Georgia to prosecute him. The reason was a Supreme Court decision issued a few weeks earlier.[6] The Cherokees had applied to the Court for protection of their treaty rights, but the Court had dismissed the case, claiming it could not exercise its original jurisdiction because the Cherokees were neither citizens nor members of a foreign nation.[7] Yet the Court had been apologetic. Two justices dissented from the decision, and Chief Justice Marshall, who did not, began his opinion by noting that "if courts were permitted to indulge their sympathies, a case better calculated to excite them can scarcely be imagined."[8]

Worcester wanted to supply the Court with a second opportunity to rule on the rights of the Cherokees, and he believed he had found the way to do so. If he was convicted of living among the Cherokees, he could claim in court that Georgia's prohibition was unconstitutional because under federal treaties the state had no jursidiction over Cherokee treaty lands. Because Worcester was an American citizen, the federal courts would clearly have jurisdiction. To uphold Worcester's rights and release him from jail, the Supreme Court would have to declare that Georgia had no jurisdiction over Cherokee territory. Thus, by upholding the rights of Worcester, the Court would simultaneously uphold the rights of the Cherokees.

Nevertheless, Worcester had few illusions about the ultimate effect of his legal ploy. Although certain in his own mind that the Supreme Court would support him, he feared that the Court's decision would achieve nothing in the end. But a great injustice was about to be perpetrated on the Cherokees, and Worcester believed he was morally bound to pursue every opportunity to save them. "I apprehend there is a danger of my having to suffer the full penalty of the unrighteous law," he admitted, "but still it appears to me that the effort ought to be made, though it ends in defeat."[9]

Those were words of despair, but they were understandable. For three years the missionaries and their friends had been fighting to secure the Cherokees' legal rights. For three years they had failed. As Worcester looked toward the future, he might have wondered why the situation had gone wrong. It was a difficult question to answer.

## THE ORIGINS OF THE REMOVAL CRISIS

The controversy over Indian lands had been brewing for decades, and the specific dispute between Georgia and the Cherokees could be traced back at least to 1802. That year the federal government promised it would purchase remaining Cherokee lands and transfer their title to Georgia.[10] There was only one difficulty: The federal government had already entered into treaties with the Cherokees that guaranteed them their lands in perpetuity.[11] As long as the Cherokees continued to sell their lands to the federal government, this potential problem never became an actual one. But in 1819 the Cherokee Nation decided it would cede no more territory, and the crisis began to unfold.[12]

Georgia cried foul, claiming that the federal government had an obligation under the compact of 1802 to remove the Cherokees.[13] But the Cherokees obstinately refused to move. In 1827 they adopted a written constitution, making even more manifest their desire to stay where they were and govern themselves.[14] This action infuriated the Georgians, but it also provided a telling indication of why the Cherokees refused to sell out. They were rapidly becoming a nation of agrarian republicans with farms, schools, stores, and settlements.[15] Like the white men, they had attached themselves to their land by improving it, and they were not about to give up what they had worked so hard to secure.

Cherokees such as Elias Boudinot tried to bring this message to the American public. Educated by the missionaries, Boudinot founded the tribe's first newspaper, the *Cherokee Phoenix,* and he soon became one of the most eloquent champions of Cherokee progress and independence. In 1826 he trumpeted the transformation of Cherokee society before the First Presbyterian Church of Philadelphia. He told his audience about the invention of a written alphabet for the Cherokee language, the establishment of a republican form of government, and the gradual transmission of Christianity among tribe members.[16] As further proof of advancement, he touted the Cherokees' ownership of "762 looms; 2488 spinning wheels; 172 waggons; 2,943 ploughs; 10 saw-mills; 31 grist-mills; 62 Blacksmith-shops; 8 cotton machines; 18 schools; 18 ferries; and a number of public roads."[17] Boudinot's account was optimistic but not untruthful. He did not claim that every Cherokee had become literate or pious; he merely declared that a promising start had been made and that further progress should be encouraged by whites.

The rise of educated Cherokees posed an acute problem for the federal government. Steeped in the republicanism imparted by their missionary teachers, educated Cherokees were more than willing to press for their rights, creating major frustrations for a president such as John Quincy Adams. Adams wanted the Cherokees to emigrate, and he tried his best to persuade them to do so, employing subterfuge when necessary.[18] But Adams would not compel the Indians to remove, and when pressed, he acknowledged that the federal government had an obligation to uphold treaty obligations. In the words of historian William McLoughlin, "Adams was willing to give the Indians a choice and to protect their treaty rights while at the same time exerting every possible inducement and pressure to negotiate a removal treaty."[19] Hampered by his own scruples, Adams in the end accomplished very little.

Adams's successor, Andrew Jackson, was less troubled by the pangs of conscience. Regarding federal treaties with the Indians as mere parchment barriers, he came up with a plan for removing the Cherokees that was both simple and barbaric: Leave them at the mercy of Georgia, and encourage Georgia to be merciless. As Jackson instructed one congressman from Georgia, "Build a fire under them. When it gets hot enough, they'll move."[20] Shortly after Jackson's election Georgia followed the incoming president's advice and passed a law stripping the Cherokees of their civil rights and placing all of Cherokee Territory under the state's jurisdiction. Georgians seemed well on their way to disposing of the Cherokee problem both quickly and easily.

They did not succeed. The Cherokee problem dragged on for nearly a decade longer. That it did so was largely a testimony to one man—Jeremiah Evarts, corresponding secretary for the ABCFM. Highly respected by all who knew him, Evarts had a long acquaintance with the Cherokees through his missions work, and he had traveled extensively throughout Cherokee Territory in 1826.[21] Evarts loved the Cherokees as his brothers and decided to do what he could to prevent their forced removal from Georgia. In the process he demonstrated how evangelicals could play a vital positive role in American politics.

## JEREMIAH EVARTS AND THE CAMPAIGN TO
## DEFEND CHEROKEE RIGHTS

Immersed in evangelical reform ever since his days as editor of the *Panoplist,* Evarts rivaled Lyman Beecher as evangelicalism's most astute political strategist.[22] He was the epitome of the Christian gentlemen—in public, principled and resolute; in private, balancing his passion for justice with humility. Generally refraining from personal attacks on his opponents, Evarts was forever questioning the purity of his own motives. He prayed daily that he might "be preserved from rash and imprudent speeches in regard to the government, the opposers of missions, or any other subject" and that he might "cultivate a temper universally mild and amiable towards all men."[23] He also pleaded for divine assistance in avoiding self-righteousness: "Whenever I hear of sinful actions, before I say a word by way of censure, [let me] remember how much I find to blame in myself, though under so great advantages."[24]

Evarts had been lobbying Congress on behalf of Cherokee rights since 1828, and he became determined to bring the plight of the Indians before the American public. To this end he wrote a series of twenty-four essays in the *National Intelligencer,* writing under the nom de plume "William Penn," in reference to the Quaker founder of Pennsylvania who had treated the Indians as his brothers. The "William Penn" essays commenced with a prefatory letter on August 1 and continued through December 19, and the articles soon became the most celebrated piece of political journalism since *The Federalist.*[25] The series was subsequently republished in journals around the country; estimates of the number of papers reprinting the articles range from 40 to more than 100.[26] The series was subsequently published as a pamphlet in both Boston and Philadelphia.[27] Chief Justice John Marshall called the essays the "most conclusive argument that he ever read on any subject whatever."[28] At the very least, they were a tour de force of law, logic, and morality.

In the inaugural essay Evarts outlined what he thought was at stake. In his view the controversy over Cherokee removal was nothing less than a momentous issue of public morality, and hanging in the balance were the honor and reputation of the United States.[29] The eyes of the world rested on America to see what it would do. If Americans treated Indians with fairness and benevolence, they would earn the "decided approbation of intelligent men, not only in the present age, but in all succeeding times."[30] But if Americans should act otherwise, they would become an object of international infamy.[31] Evarts concluded his gloomy picture with an appeal to the story of Naboth in the Bible. After Naboth refused to sell his ancestral lands to King Ahab, Queen Jezebel had Naboth put to death, and his lands were confiscated by the king anyway. "If the people of the United States will imitate the ruler who coveted Naboth's vineyard," wrote Evarts darkly, "the world will assuredly place them by the side of Naboth's oppressor."[32]

But Evarts did not merely argue from abstract notions of national honor. To those who might listen only to an appeal to utility, Evarts added that fair dealing is the surest road to national prosperity. Other nations would never trust a country that proves itself faithless in its agreements, especially during peacetime.[33] Thus, according to Evarts, virtuous national conduct naturally leads to temporal blessings. To be sure, virtue is its own reward, but it brings other good things along with it. Good people—and nations—do prosper, at least in the long term.

Up to this part of his argument, Evarts relied on the principles of natural reason as opposed to revelation. Yet his steadfast conviction that good nations prosper in the end seems to presume more certainty than natural reason can supply. In short, it suggests the existence of some superintending power that will guarantee the results of history. That this is precisely what Evarts was implying becomes clear in his next paragraph, where he suddenly shifted the grounds of argument from reason to revelation. Insisting that divine judgment is the highest consideration vis-à-vis national conduct, Evarts declared, "The Great Arbiter of Nations never fails to take cognizance of national delinquencies."[34] Evarts continued that his appeal to God the judge was not mere "rhetorical embellishment" on his part. "In my deliberate opinion, it is more important, and should be more heeded, than all other considerations relating to the subject."[35]

Thus, Evarts supplemented his arguments from reason with an equally charged appeal to revelation. The Founding truism that reason and revelation agree about morality reappeared once more. With regard to the Cherokees, reason and revelation spoke with one thundering voice, according to Evarts: Any reasonable conception of morality and honor forbade treating the Cherokees unfairly; and anyone who believed in divine providence had to realize that acting in bad faith in this matter would bring down divine wrath on the country.

Evarts concluded his first essay by summarizing the Jackson administration's position toward the Cherokees. According to Evarts, the administration maintained that Great Britain had claimed sovereignty over Indian lands and that this sovereignty had transferred to the states on American independence. The Cherokees subsequently had no rights to their ancestral lands whatever. They were permitted to occupy them solely at the pleasure of the states wherein they resided, and the federal government had no authority to block the laws those states chose to inflict on the Indians.[36]

Evarts launched his rebuttal to this view in his second essay, where he once again returned to the domain of nature, drawing on those rights and duties that could be accessed apart from revelation. In language reminiscent of the Declaration of Independence, he observed that "the Cherokees are human beings, endowed by their Creator with the same natural rights as other men." One of those natural rights is the right to property, and this ultimately was why the Cherokees had title to their ancestral lands. "They are in peaceable possession of a territory which they have always regarded as their own. This territory was in possession of their ancestors, through an unknown series of generations, and has come down to them with a title absolute unincumbered in every respect."[37]

But here Evarts was forced to meet an objection. Some critics of the Cherokees, drawing on the very natural law tradition invoked by Evarts, claimed that "the savage of the wilderness can acquire no title to the forests, through which he pursues his game"; to possess land, people had to cultivate and settle it. Without granting the merit of this objection, Evarts said that it could supply no valid argument against the Cherokees because "at the earliest period of our being acquainted with their condition, they had fixed habitations, and were in undisputed possession of a widely extended country. They were then in the habit of cultivating some land near their houses, where they planted Indian corn, and other vegetables."[38] In more recent times, moreover, the Cherokees had adopted all the requisites of civilization, including schools, churches, civil government, farms, and looms to make fabric. The Cherokees had lived on and worked their lands just as surely as the whites had theirs; being equally human with the whites, their natural right to their property could not be justly abridged without their consent.

Evarts next sought to prove that the Cherokees' natural rights had become conventional through the adoption of treaties. Over the next twelve essays he proceeded provision by provision through every treaty and compact that the federal government had concluded with the Cherokees, and he demonstrated that the government had repeatedly treated the Cherokees as a sovereign people whose lands had to be acquired by voluntary purchase or not at all. In the Treaty of Holston (1791), for example, the United States obliged itself to "solemnly guaranty to the Cherokee nation all their lands not hereby ceded."[39] By the same treaty no persons who were not Indians could settle on Cherokee lands, and if they tried, they forfeited the protection of the United States and the Cherokees could punish them accordingly. The treaty further stipulated that any suspected criminals residing among the Cherokees would have to be given up by the Cherokee Nation; that is, no power was granted to the United States to pursue the criminals into Cherokee Territory.[40] Finally, the fourteenth article of the treaty looked to the future of the Cherokees, providing that the United States would encourage "the Cherokee Nation [to] . . . be led to a greater degree of civilization, and to become herdsmen and cultivators, instead of remaining in a state of hunters."[41] In other words, the federal government actually promoted the idea that the Cherokees would permanently settle their remaining lands.

No subsequent treaty or compact with the Cherokees ever annulled any of the provisions of the Treaty of Holston, except for modifying the boundary lines of Cherokee Territory whenever the tribe sold more land to the federal government. If anything, subsequent treaties made federal promises to the Cherokees more emphatic. In the Treaty of Tellico (1798), wrote Evarts, the United States promised that it would "*continue the* GUARANTY OF THE RE-MAINDER OF THEIR [Cherokee] COUNTRY FOREVER, *as made and contained in former treaties.*"[42]

Evarts noted that according to Article 6 of the U.S. Constitution, these treaties with the Cherokees were now part of "the supreme law of the land," and the judges of every state were bound to follow them. "The question of jurisdiction is, therefore, easily settled," he concluded.[43] It was easily settled because Georgia *had* no jurisdiction when it came to the Cherokees. The Cherokees existed in their own protected enclave, their lands and their rights secured by federal treaty forever.

Georgians, of course, fiercely maintained otherwise, and in the fifteenth installment of his series Evarts finally began to meet their claims head-on. Evarts turned part of essay fifteen into an imaginary dialogue between Georgians and Cherokees, each advancing their respective claims. During the dialogue Evarts stood typical anti-Indian stereotypes on their heads. He depicted the Cherokees as the true Christians (they even invoked the Bible) and implied that the Georgians were the true heathens, impervious to the claims of revelation. In a similar manner he depicted the Cherokees as the ones who were truly civilized ("We have a legislature and a judiciary") and placed the Georgians in the position of savages, whose uncivil demands for the property of their "neighbors" were rightly chastised by the Cherokees as displaying "neither great modesty nor benevolence."[44]

The point of all this was to undermine Georgia's appeal to the law of nations. Defenders of Georgia had cited German legal theorist Emmerich de Vattel to justify their argument that nomads who lived by hunting could be rightly dispossessed of their hunting grounds by another nation "whose inhabitants live[d] by agriculture." Even if this argument happened to be correct, said Evarts, it could not apply to the Cherokees because they were no longer either nomads or hunters. Evarts added that Vattel applied his analysis to populous nations that actually needed more land. But "Georgia is not populous. She has many millions of acres of unoccupied land. . . . When Georgia shall have a hundred souls to the square mile; (and her soil is capable of sustaining a larger number than that;) the Cherokees may have four times as many to the square mile as Georgia now contains."[45]

Having disposed of Georgia's appeal to the law of nations, Evarts next turned to Georgia's assertion that it held Indian lands by virtue of the state's British charter. He first noted the irony that "there are some people, even in our republican country, who appear to suppose that there is a wonderful virtue in the grant of a king."[46] This was a nice slap at the Jacksonians, who touted themselves as the defenders of republican government against the aristocracy. For Jacksonians to claim monarchical grants as the ultimate basis of their authority was indeed curious. Evarts, for one, thought the notion ridiculous: "Is it not manifest, on the bare statement of this subject, that not even a king can grant what he does not possess? And how is it possible, that he should possess vast tracts of country, which neither he, nor any European, had ever seen; but which were in fact inhabited by numerous independent nations, of whose character, rights, or even existence, he knew nothing[?]"[47]

Even if one accepted British charters as authoritative, however, there was an insuperable difficulty in trying to use them to establish Georgia's claims against the Cherokees: namely, the British Crown itself had recognized the Indians' title to their lands and had insisted that Indian lands be acquired by treaty.[48] Even more damning, colonial Georgia had entered into treaties on behalf of the Crown that guaranteed the lands of the Creeks and Cherokees.[49] Thus, it was completely disingenuous for Georgia to try to make a case by appealing to British land grants.

One final point in Georgia's case was left for Evarts to consider. Georgia based much of its claim on the 1802 statute, in which the federal government agreed to purchase and then cede to Georgia any remaining Cherokee lands within Georgia's chartered limits. Evarts pointed out that Georgia conveniently ignored the important qualification that had come attached to this promise: The United States agreed to purchase remaining Cherokee lands only *"as early as the same can be peaceably obtained, on reasonable terms."*[50] In other words, the federal government would not compel the Indians to sell their lands; it would only encourage them to continue further cessions of their territory. This qualified pledge the United States had faithfully sought to fulfill, said Evarts: "The Indian title to three quarters of the lands, which belonged to the Indians in 1802, within the intended limits, has been extinguished by the United States, in the manner prescribed; and Georgia is now in actual possession. The remaining quarter has been repeatedly applied for; and the United States have always stood ready to purchase it of the rightful owners, 'on reasonable terms.' At least, this had been repeatedly and officially declared to be the fact, by public functionaries of the United States."[51]

This was all the federal government legitimately could be asked to do in the matter, said Evarts. It certainly could not be requested to compel the Cherokees to leave. Evarts noted that even if the federal government had pledged to take away Cherokee lands by force (which it had not), such a pledge to Georgia would have been "absolutely void. . . . First, it would be palpably and monstrously unjust. Secondly, it would be in opposition to previously existing treaties, between the United States and the Indians, which treaties were the supreme law of the land. Thirdly, it would be in opposition to treaties between Georgia and the Indians,—treaties never abrogated nor annulled,—and therefore Georgia could not insist upon its execution."[52]

It may be true, continued Evarts, that Georgia had *"expected"* the United States "to have long since extinguished the title to all the Indian lands."[53] But this fact was irrelevant—one person's rights cannot be nullified on the basis of someone else's disappointment. "The history of every man, and of every community, is full of disappointed expectations."[54] Georgia might not like the outcome of the agreement it had concluded in 1802, but the state had already bound itself to the contract's terms. As the Georgia legislature itself had declared at the time, the compact was "binding and conclusive on the said State, her government and citizens, forever."[55]

In his final three essays Evarts again considered the broader moral context of the Indian question. In essay twenty-two he attacked the methods by which Georgia was attempting to remove the Cherokees as an unconscionable deprivation of their rights as human beings. In December 1828 Georgia had enacted a law obviously designed to prod the Cherokees into removing "voluntarily." The law extended Georgia's jurisdiction over Indian lands, and it nullified "all laws, usages, and customs, made, established, and in force" by the Cherokees as of June 1830. It also declared that no Indian (or descendant of Indians) "shall be deemed a competent witness, or a party to any suit . . . to which a white man may be a party."[56] According to Evarts, the effect of such strictures was to present the Cherokees with a choice between exile and slavery.[57] Actually, the Cherokees' fate if they stayed within Georgia would actually be worse than slavery because "even the slaves of his new neighbors are defended by the self-interest of their masters. But he has not even this consolation. He is exposed to the greatest evils of slavery, without any of its alleviations. . . . How could a Cherokee live under such treatment as this?"[58]

The answer, of course, was that he could not. "Accustomed from his birth to feelings of entire equality and independence, he would find himself, at a single stroke, smitten to the earth, and there held till manacles of a most degrading vassalage were fastened upon him." Here was the crux of the question as far as Evarts was concerned: The Cherokees were human beings, and so the obligations of equity and justice applied to them just as surely as to whites. The rights and duties of God and nature knew no racial barriers. They applied to all men.

According to Evarts, however, the equality possessed by the Cherokees was more than a mere equality of rights. It was an equality of character. The Cherokees had embraced civilization and had become "practical republicans," with a republican government, schools, and a written language. Many had also become Christians.[59] Thus, according to both revelation and reason, the Cherokees were the equals of white Americans. According to reason, they were equals because they had embraced civilization and republicanism; according to the Bible, they were brothers and sisters because they had become "*fellow-citizens with the saints and of the household of God.*"[60] Thus, the Cherokees' natural rights were reinforced by the claims of civilization and religion. Even if Americans refused to treat Cherokees as equals because they were fellow human beings, Americans were obliged to treat them fairly because they were republicans and Christians.

Yet the fact remained that many Americans were not prepared to treat the Cherokees as equals. In Evarts's mind this raised a terrible question about America's identity. In the end what defined America—a common racial ancestry or devotion to a common idea? Evarts had no doubts about the answer: "Who are the men, that impose so fearful an alternative [on the Cherokees]? and what is the government, that hesitates to redeem its pledge? Is it some rotten Asiatic despotism, sinking under the crimes and corruptions of by-gone centuries, feeling no responsiblity, and regarding no law of morality or religion? Not so. It is a government, which sprung into existence with the declaration 'that all men are created equal; that they are endowed by their Creator with certain unalienable rights; that among these are life, liberty, and the pursuit of happiness.' "[61]

Evarts played the ultimate trump card. The battle over Cherokee removal was not merely about national honor; it was about the nation's soul. It raised the question of whether America truly was a nation dedicated to the proposition "that *all men* are created equal . . . [and] endowed by their Creator with certain unalienable rights." The Cherokees had embraced this creed, and now they demanded to know whether their American brothers still adhered to it.

Evarts feared the answer to that question. The problem was not merely that some rejected the idea that all men are created equal; it was that many seemed to disregard the notion of rights and duties that are unalienable. For Evarts the root of the problem was this latter belief. Those supporting Georgia believed that self-interest, rather than morality, should be the guiding light of politics. Thus, whenever morality stood in the way of self-interest, it had to be sacrificed. Under this view of matters, right became synonomous with power; that is, the side with the most power was always right. This was not an unfair characterization of Georgia's reasoning, given a legislative report adopted by Georgia's senate in 1827. In that document the state acknowledged that the European land claims on which it based its own rights might be said to have been founded more on *"force"* than *"justice,"* "but they are claims, which have been recognized and admitted, by the whole civilized world; and it is unquestionably true, that, under such circumstances, *force* becomes *right*."[62] In other words, land claims based on force rather than justice became right because the claims had been recognized by the very European nations making the claims to begin with. The only morality is the morality of the strongest.

Evarts launched a full-scale attack on this proposition in essay twenty-three, where he argued that "the great principles of morality," rather than self-interest, should guide all our political decisions and that these "principles . . . are immutable."[63] In the words of New York jurist James Kent, "We ought not . . . to separate the science of public law from that of ethics, nor encourage the dangerous suggestion, that governments are not as strictly bound by the obligations of truth, justice, and humanity, in relation to other powers, as they are in the management of their own local concerns."[64] These moral obligations are drawn both from "the law of nations . . . so far as it is founded on principles of natural law" and from the moral precepts of Christianity. In other words, the standard of morality used to judge political actions is sanctioned by reason as well as revelation.

Concluding his discussion of the relationship between morality and politics, Evarts turned in his final essay to the likely consequences of removal on the Indians. In his view the result would be wanton suffering. This outcome was inevitable given the poor quality of the lands to which the Indians were to remove, the difficulties of the forced migration of such large numbers of people, and the chaos that would be produced by throwing together "Indians of different tribes, speaking different languages, in a different states of civilization . . . under one government."[65] In addition, removal could be but a temporary solution to the problem. When white settlements encroached on the new Indian lands, the cry for removal would again sound loud and clear. Were the Indians to be transformed into a nation of vagrants without any permanent home?[66]

As Evarts drew his series to a conclusion, he issued another joint appeal to the dictates of revelation and the principles of reason. He again spoke of the possibility of God's judgment, this time recalling a famous passage from the Old Testament in which Moses exhorted the people of Israel to obey God's law or be cursed.[67] Evarts then shifted to the principles of natural justice while connecting them with the morality of revelation. Expanding on the biblical injunction against the removal of landmarks, Evarts said that "it is now proposed *to remove the landmarks* in every sense."[68] Turning the biblical injunction into a metaphor, Evarts argued that to "remove landmarks" means

> to disregard territorial boundaries, definitely fixed, and for many years respected;—to disregard a most obvious principle of natural justice, in accordance which the possessor of property is to hold it, till some one claims it, who has a better right;—to forget the doctrine of the law of nations, that engagements with dependent allies are as rigidly to be observed, as stipulations between communities of equal power and sovereignty;—to shut our ears to the voice of our own sages of the law, who say, that Indians have a right *to retain possession of their land and to use it according to their discretion,* antecedently to any positive compacts; and, finally, to dishonor Washington, the Father of his country,—to stultify the Senate of the United States during a period of thirty-seven years, to burn 150 documents, as yet preserved in the archives of State, under the denomination of treaties with Indians, and to tear out sheets from every volume of our national statute-book and scatter them to the winds.[69]

Thus, according to Evarts, the commands of the Bible were informed by the principles of natural justice, the law of nations, and the desire for national honor. This theme underlay his whole series, which used the moral principles of the Bible as a springboard for discussing the natural right to property, the inviolability of contracts, and the equal rights of all human beings. Here was a perfect example of what James Wilson might have been speaking of when he said that "religion and law are twin sisters, friends, and mutual assistants. Indeed, these two sciences run into each other. The divine law, as discovered by reason and the moral sense, forms an essential part of both."[70] This was evangelical rationalism at its best.[71]

An estimated half a million people read Evarts's essays on the Cherokees, and the articles played a crucial role in galvanizing opposition to the government's Indian removal policy.[72] First, they established the terms of the debate over removal in both the public mind and in Congress. Second, they prepared the way for a citizens' campaign on behalf of the Cherokees.

Taking a page from the Sunday mails crusade (which even now was taking place), Evarts moved to instigate a similar petition campaign on the Indian issue.[73] Congress was in recess until its second session began in December, and during this period petitions on Indian removal started to stream in. The petitions, some of which were written by Evarts, echoed the themes found in the William Penn essays. They argued that Cherokee rights were dictated both by natural justice and by written treaties. They maintained that American policy toward the Cherokees had to be guided by humanity and justice rather than self-interest. And they declared that America risked both its reputation and its prosperity by dealing with the Cherokees in bad faith. America's reputation would be sullied in the sight of other nations, and the country's prosperity would be annihilated by the wrath of an angry God.[74] The latter theme of divine judgment was the main religious argument stressed in the petitions, but usually it was not dwelt on at much length.

From the start the citizens' campaign for Cherokee rights was almost wholly driven by partisans of evangelical reform. Indeed, in some cities the Cherokee crusade was conducted hand in hand with efforts against the Sunday mails.[75] The campaign's evangelical origins were further indicated by the number of petitions sent in by women, who were important backers of evangelical missions.[76] The memorial from the women of Hallowell, Maine, made the connection between missions and Cherokee rights explicit, arguing that removal would frustate efforts to "enlighten and christianize" the Indians:

These efforts have been sustained chiefly by the charity of our own sex—by the two mites of the widow and the penny of the poor. We are unwilling that these truly benevolent exertions should, by the strong arm of the government, be prostrated at a blow. We are unwilling that the church, the schools, and the domestic altar should be thrown down before the avaricious god of power, and those groves dear to the heart of the Indian, and which now echo the hymns of Jehovah, should be again the resort of the hunter, the wildman, and the savage.[77]

Precisely how many petitions against removal were received by Congress remains unclear. If one goes by the number of petitions filed at the National Archives, only fifty-four memorials were received by the end of the twenty-first Congress in May 1830.[78] But these may be only a portion of the total number. Many other petitions probably were never preserved because proponents of removal tried to prevent them from being referred to committee.[79] Wilson Lumpkin, then a congressman from Georgia, provided a much more extravagant estimate in his memoirs, where he bitterly recalled that "during the recess . . . the Northern fanatics, male and female, had gone to work and gotten up thousands of petitions, signed by more than a million, of men, women and children, protesting against the removal of the poor dear Indians."[80] Since Lumpkin tried to downplay popular opposition to removal, he likely did not consciously inflate these figures.[81] Nevertheless, the figures do seem exaggerated.

Whatever the actual number of petitions, there were more than enough to infuriate supporters of removal. During the debates on removal in 1830, Lumpkin complained about being "inundated with memorials, pamphlets, and speeches made at society and town meetings."[82] The petitioners had made their point.

Efforts on behalf of the Cherokees had been well timed. As soon as Congress's second session opened, President Jackson requested authority to pursue his policy of removal, and both chambers' committees on Indian affairs began to draw up appropriate legislation shortly thereafter. Passions on both sides of the issue waxed hot, and by January 1830 the mood was fast becoming acrid.

## THE REMOVAL BATTLE IN CONGRESS

On February 24 the House of Representatives reported its removal bill out of committee. But instead of proceeding to debate the bill, members became embroiled in political dogfights. Congressman (later President) James Buchanan provoked the first uproar when he proposed printing 10,000 copies of the report on removal prepared by the House Committee on Indian Affairs. The request was unusual both because of the large number of copies sought and because general House members had not even had the opportunity to read the report. In other words, Buchanan was asking the House to print up extra copies for public distribution sight unseen. Opponents of removal smelled a rat and challenged the request. When they failed to block the printing, they proposed appending to the report a copy of the laws Georgia had enacted to subjugate the Cherokees. They also pressed for the printing of a Quaker memorial against removal. Entangled in such disputes through early March, the House did not resume discussion on the bill itself until May 13.

While House members brawled, the Senate moved to consider the removal issue on its own. Senator Hugh White from Tennessee, chair of the Senate Committee on Indian Affairs, reported out a removal bill on April 6. Like the politicians from Georgia, White ultimately founded Georgia's claim to Cherokee Territory on its original charter from Great Britain. Because of the British charter, the federal government had no authority to guarantee Cherokee lands; thus, all treaties that sought to protect Cherokee lands were void. Evarts, who listened to White's address in the gallery, found it lackluster but moderate. "There was nothing bitter, or provoking, or ungentlemanly, in his speech," Evarts noted in his journal. "Nor was there anything striking or forcible."[83]

Theodore Frelinghuysen from New Jersey provided the opening blast from the opposition. On April 7 he commenced a three-day oration, speaking roughly two hours each day. Unveiling the strategy of the opposition, Frelinghuysen proposed an amendment to the bill that would protect the Indians' "rights of territory and government . . . from all interruptions and encroachments" until the Indians decided to remove.[84] The amendment would transform the removal bill into an Indian protection act.

Although heavily involved in evangelical reform, Frelinghuysen issued an appeal that was even more secular than Evarts's. He only fleetingly mentioned the possibility of God's judgment and the fact that many Cherokees had become Christians. He placed most stress on the law of nature and the rights that it bestowed on all human beings, regardless of race. Following the argument already set out in the William Penn essays, Frelinghuysen contended that the Cherokees had a natural right to their lands by vitue of "immemorial possession, as the original tenants of the soil." God had "planted these tribes on this western continent, for aught that we know, before Great Britain herself had a political existence," and the Indians, as human beings, were "justly entitled to a share in common bounties of a benignant Providence."

According to Frelinghuysen, it did not matter if the Indians had originally used their lands for hunting. Writers who argued otherwise pursued "a system of artificial reasoning" intent on excusing after the fact the appropriation of Indian lands. "In the light of natural law, can a reason for a distinction exist from the mode of enjoying that which is my own? If I use land for hunting, may another take it because he needs it for agriculture?" Frelinghuysen answered that only "the increase of the population and the wants of mankind" could create a "right" to acquire someone else's hunting ground for agriculture. But even then the lands had to be "obtained by fair contract," and although the owners might have a duty to sell in such as case, "we cannot rightfully compel the cession of his lands, or take them by violence if his consent be withheld."[85] This meant that even apart from any treaties, the Cherokees had an inviolable natural right to their territory.

Frelinghuysen then hinted that race was the real reason some were willing to deny the Cherokees their natural rights. "Do the obligations of justice change with the color of the skin?" he asked pointedly. "Is it one of the prerogatives of the white man, that he may disregard the dictates of moral principle, when an Indian shall be concerned?" His answer was clearly no, and he added that his listeners should consider their feelings if the roles in this drama were reversed: "If the contending parties were to exchange positions; place the white man where the Indian stands; load *him* with all these wrongs,—and what path would his outraged feelings strike out for his career?"

Reaching the climax of this portion of his oration, Frelinghuysen recalled the American Revolution and warned his fellow citizens not to turn traitor to their heritage of freedom. The Indians were fighting for their right of self-government and independence. Of all people in the world, how could Americans spurn their demands? Observed Frelinghuysen:

We successfully and triumphantly contended for the very rights and privileges, that our Indian neighbors now implore us to protect and preserve to them. Sir, this thought invests the subject under debate with most singular and momentous interest. We, whom God has exalted to the very summit of prosperity—whose brief career forms the brightest page in history; the wonder and praise of the world; Freedom's hope, and her consolation; we, about to turn traitors to our principles and our fame—about to become the oppressors of the feeble, and to cast away our birthright![86]

In the final portion of his address, Frelinghuysen showed how America had previously confirmed the Cherokees' natural right to their property through numerous treaties.[87] Thus, even if some Americans were willing to deny the Cherokees' natural rights, they must also consider the positive enactments confirming those rights. Americans had already promised the Cherokees their land, and they would be breaking their word and violating the national faith should they disregard previously negotiated guarantees. Frelinghuysen's oration won him the accolade of "Christian Statesman," and his conduct on behalf of the Indians was eulogized around the country.[88] William Lloyd Garrison even dedicated a poem to Frelinghuysen, announcing that the senator merited "loftier praise than language can supply."[89]

Frelinghuysen's opponents in Congress were less complimentary. Senator John Forsyth of Georgia, who came next in the debate, implied that Frelinghuysen had deserted his race. He accused his colleague of "display[ing] . . . little sympathy for the whites" and of having no compunction about "shedding the blood of white men . . . in favor of Indian rights." But this was to be expected, added Forsyth, for "having exhausted all his sympathy upon the red men, none for the whites could be reasonably looked for from him."[90]

Forsyth also tried to focus attention on those organizing the protests against removal. Picking up the cudgel that had already been put to good use by Congressman Richard Johnson against the Sunday mail petitioners, Forsyth spoke of the "Christian party in politics" that was seeking to convince people to petition Congress on behalf of the Indians.[91] He implied that women and the elderly had been duped into signing petitions by designing missionaries, who were intent on protecting their "comfortable settlements on the land occupied by the Cherokees."[92]

The core of Forsyth's argument, however, was his theory of territorial acquisition. How does a people obtain territory on which to settle? Forsyth's answer could have come straight from Machiavelli: The origin of regimes lies in conquest or deceit.[93] Going back to the days of European colonization, Forsyth first maintained that Europeans had always asserted an absolute right to everything they discovered on unknown lands, "including the human inhabitants."[94] In this view the original inhabitants remained on their lands only at the pleasure of the discoverer. According to Forsyth, this theory of acquisition formed the basis of European colonies in the New World, including those founded by the British. The only reason American colonists obtained many Indian lands by treaties, rather than conquest, was convenience. Treaties were a cheaper way to take over Indian land than by force. Morality had nothing to do with the agreements.[95]

To prove his case, Forsyth recited how other American states had dealt with Indians both before and after the Revolution.[96] It was the most potent part of his address and surely the most discomfiting for his northern opponents. Here Forsyth sought to supply the "real" account of how northern whites had dealt with Indians. Regardless of what treaties said, what had whites actually done? He claimed that even the exalted William Penn had had dirty hands, for he had countenanced a fraudulent purchase of Indian lands.[97] Forsyth further alleged that other states had passed laws exerting their jurisdiction over Indian Territory.[98] Forsyth's message was clear: Critics from other states who so indignantly attacked Georgia's conduct were either hypocrites or ignorant of their own history. "Let him without sin cast the first stone."[99]

Forsyth's brutal recital of American history was distorted and inaccurate.[100] But there was enough truth in it to raise a critical point, one that exposed the fundamental disagreement underlying the whole debate over Indian removal. Relations between whites and Indians in America had never been untroubled. American whites may have acquired Indian lands primarily by treaties, but the treaties themselves were not always voluntary; and their exalted provisions were often disregarded. On paper whites had respected Indian rights; in practice they had often trampled on them. The two sides of the removal controversy drew different lessons from these contradictions of history. Opponents of removal trumpeted the ideals proclaimed in past treaties, even though those ideals had been frequently disregarded in practice. Georgia appealed to the sordid reality underneath the idealistic rhetoric.

In the most fundamental sense, then, the debate over removal became precisely what Jeremiah Evarts had said it would become: a question of whether morality had any connection to politics. Is political action to be guided by self-interest or by the moral law? For Evarts and fellow evangelicals, the answer was unmistakable: The moral law, sanctioned by God, is the only guide. Private morality is also public morality, and public men have an "obligation to bring their measures of state within the rules of private morality."[101] Thus, past crimes did not justify present iniquities. Whatever the previous injustices of American treatment of Indians, these actions provided no excuse for further wrongs.

For the partisans of Georgia, however, past practices clearly sanctioned present policy. The logical conclusion of their position was that any treaty guaranteeing Cherokee rights was not worth the paper it was written on and therefore could be disregarded. Cherokees resided on their present lands solely at the pleasure of the government. To those who might respond that the Constitution's supremacy clause regarded treaties rather differently, Forsyth had a ready, if astonishing, reply: The supremacy clause did not apply because treaties with Indians really were not treaties at all. "How . . . can a contract made with a completely dependent tribe of half starved Indians be dignified with the name, and claim the imposing character of, a treaty?"[102] This was an incredible assertion, and it showed the lengths to which Georgia was willing to go to justify itself.

Debate in the Senate continued until Saturday, April 24, when the removal bill came up for a final vote. Frelinghuysen and his supporters again tried to offer amendments, but they were rejected, and the bill finally passed 28-19. Now attention shifted to the final battleground, the House of Representatives.

Congressman Henry R. Storrs of New York supplied the opening for the opposition. Storrs acknowledged the past crimes of whites against Indians but argued that past wrongs did not change the requirements of moral law. He regarded America as a Christian nation, and for him that meant above all that America is "bound by that code of universal morality, which is confessed by every government, which feels it to be honorable to stand within the pale of Christian nations."[103] This moral code is the morality of conscience, nature, and reason as well as that of revelation. It is morality informed by "humanity" and "the sounder principles of justice."[104] It teaches that men have a natural right to their property and that treaties must be respected. Nations that disregard these precepts, said Storrs, risked judgment not only from God but also from posterity.[105] If American legislators broke faith with the Indians, reason and revelation would join to condemn these legislators in the minds of future generations. "Your history, your treaties, and your statues, will confront you," he declared. "The human heart will be consulted—the moral sense of all mankind will speak out fearlessly, and you will stand condemned by the law of God, as well as the sentence of your fellow men. You may not live to hear it, but there will be no refuge for you in the grave. You will yet live in history."

That opponents of removal had staked out the moral high ground galled the delegation from Georgia, which sought to undermine its opponents' moralistic message by smearing the messenger. Senator Forsyth had broached this line of attack with his criticism of the Christian party in politics, and now fellow Georgian Wilson Lumpkin set out to finish the job. Like Richard Johnson, Lumpkin was a supporter of Christian benevolence (in fact, he served as a vice president of the American Sunday School Union).[106] But Lumpkin decried those Christians who left their proper realm and sought to involve themselves in politics as "canting fanatics."[107] He said he had no quarrel with "pure religion" (that is, religion that steered clear of politics), "but the undefiled religion of the Cross is a separate and distinct thing in its nature and principles from the noisy cant of the pretenders who have cost this Government, since the commencement of the present session of Congress, considerably upwards of $100,000 by their various intermeddlings with the political concerns of the country."[108]

Lumpkin claimed that the majority of the religious community stood on his side, but he also observed that the "religious party in politics" had drawn "recruits from many, if not all the different sects of the country."[109] This army of fanatics was led by "philanthropists who are going up and down in the land seeking whom they may devour."[110] These meddlers "condemn all their brethren who will not unite with them in all their machinery of societies and schemes for governing public opinion in this land of freedom."[111] Far from being true Christians, these political Christians were actually children of the Devil,[112] and they were the real reason the Cherokees refused to remove. In short, the poor Indians had become the dupes of these "designing men, veiled in the garb of philanthropy and Christian benevolence."[113]

Lumpkin expressed particular disgust with Jeremiah Evarts, though not by name. Lumpkin observed that, although the essays of William Penn were "said to be written by a very pious man, deeply merged in missionary efforts, they evidently have much more of the character of the politician and lawyer than that of the humble missionary."[114] Note Lumpkin's disjunction between the "humble missionary" and the "politician and lawyer." Apparently one could not be both. True Christians were meek and mild; they stayed out of temporal affairs. Those who did not should forfeit the protection of religion, said Lumpkin, and he asked the rest of the religious community to disown the evangelical activists as criminals: "These intermeddlers and disturbers of the peace and harmony of society have no just claims to the protection of that impenetrable fortress in which they have hitherto found refuge and protection. I rely with entire confidence upon those who carry the keys of this fortress; they will deliver up the guilty to be dealt with according to law and justice. 'By their fruit ye shall know them.'"[115] Lumpkin's speech was incongruous, if not disingenuous. At the same time he criticized evangelicals opposed to removal for meddling in politics, he

praised missionaries such as Baptist Isaac McCoy who had spearheaded efforts in support of removal.[116] Lumpkin's contempt for religion in politics
was decidedly one-sided.

Congressman George Evans from Maine capitalized on this hypocrisy in
his response to Lumpkin the next day. Evans noted that, if Lumpkin were
truly concerned about the dangers of mixing religion and politics, he should
have been outraged by the Indian Board in New York City, a religious group
organized to lobby in favor of removal.[117] The Indian Board had been
dreamed up by Thomas McKenney, head of the War Department's Indian
Office.[118] But nary a word of complaint had come from Lumpkin about this
political manipulation of religion by the executive branch. Commented
Evans:

> The gentleman regards it perfectly proper and correct to form religious
> associations, and issue pamphlets even in the northern States, when the
> object is in aid of his designs. But when a sense of right and justice and
> humanity leads to a different conclusion, then the gentleman can
> hardly find terms strong enough to express his abhorrence of intermin-
> gling religious considerations with political movements. Sir, I wish gen-
> tlemen would fairly meet and answer the arguments which have been
> addressed to us, and not content themselves with the . . . imputation of
> base motives.

Evans also defended Jeremiah Evarts, who had come under attack by others
besides Lumpkin. "I know him," said Evans, ". . . as possessing a reputation for intelligence, philanthropy, benevolence, and untiring zeal in the promotion of human happiness, which any one upon this floor might be proud
to possess." As to whether Evarts was an "intermeddler," Evans asked in-
credulously: "Do gentlemen forget in what age and in what country we live?
. . . Have the free citizens of this nation no right to investigate subjects so
highly interesting to our national prosperity and character, and to form
opinions, except in accordance with the views of the Government?"[119]

This defense must have been appreciated by Evarts, who sat in the House
gallery listening. But words of kindness could do nothing to salve his fears.
The campaign against removal was faltering, and Evarts had to try hard to
stave off despair. On Sunday, May 16, Evarts wrote in his journal that he
had only one "ground of hope left, that God will not leave us as a people to

such guilt and infatuation as would be involved in the success of the bill from the Senate. On any calculation of numbers and probabilities, made without reference to what God will do, I cannot sustain a hope that the bill will be defeated."[120]

Evarts was particularly distressed by the likelihood that many congressmen would not vote their consciences. Despite the brave front put up by Georgia, even some southern representatives acknowledged in private the justice of the Cherokees' demands. One congressman from Alabama indicated that he had found a speech against removal convincing, but he declined to change his vote because of political cowardice. He told the Cherokee delegation then visiting Washington, "I must vote against you, or I shall be scalped when I go home."[121] Besides fearing the electorate, legislators were intimidated by the administration. The president had turned the Indian bill into a test of party loyalty, and congressmen were warned not to stray from the administration line. One congressman from Tennessee who had been a friend and supporter of Jackson in the past later recalled:

It was expected of me that I was to bow to the name of Andrew Jackson, and follow him in all his motions, and mindings, and turnings, even at the expense of my conscience and judgment. . . . His famous, or rather I should say his in-*famous,* Indian bill was brought forward, and I opposed it from the purest motives in the world. Several of my colleagues got around me, and told me how well they loved me, and that I was ruining my self. They said this was a favourite measure of the president, and I ought to go for it. I told them I believed it was a wicked, unjust measure, and that I should go against, it, let the cost to myself be what it might.[122]

This recalcitrant congressman lost his seat in the next election. Yet he remained proud of his role in opposing the bill. "I gave a good honest vote," he wrote later, "one that I believe will not make me ashamed in the day of judgment."[123] The congressman was Davy Crockett. It was his finest hour.

By the week of Monday, May 17, the tactics of the bill's supporters had become glaringly apparent. They wanted to ram the legislation through the House as quickly as possible. Toward that end they forced a marathon twelve-hour session on Tuesday, refusing to adjourn until a majority agreed to rise from the Committee of the Whole, which cut off the possibility of further amendments.[124]

Another grueling session came on Wednesday. Under consideration was the lone amendment adopted while the House had sat in committee. Proposed by Congressman William Ramsey from Pennsylvania, the amendment provided that "nothing in this act . . . shall be construed as authorizing or directing the violation of any existing treaty between the United States and any of the Indian tribes."[125] The proposal handed a sop to opponents of removal but had little practical value. Opponents worked to strengthen it. In the meantime the hours fleeted by with no adjournment in sight. Supporters of the bill had resorted to their tactics of the previous day. They refused to vote to adjourn unless the House passed the bill to a third reading, thereby killing Ramsey's amendment and clearing the way for the final vote on the bill.

Edward Everett, the thirty-six-year-old Unitarian minister and classical scholar from Massachusetts, took the floor and denounced the tactics of the other side. "You have given us less time to discuss this all important measure than you devoted to the subject of a draughtsman for the House," he complained. He then attacked the marathon sessions: "For the purpose of pushing forward this measure, the sessions of the House have been protracted to a point beyond the power of the human constitution to bear; and the little strength which I brought with me five hours ago to the House, has failed in the long waiting for an opportunity to address the House."[126] Perhaps Everett embarrassed the other side sufficiently, for the bullying tactics failed this time. At 10:15 P.M. the motion for adjournment finally carried without any vote on the bill. The debate would continue.

Evarts hopes now began to rise. "If we could only have a respite," he wrote the next day, "all our friends here think we could defeat the measure." But there was the rub. Supporters of the bill were not about to let debate continue any longer than they could help it. The question was whether they had enough votes to get their way. Evarts was uncertain, but so were the Georgians. "I am afraid to hope," he wrote on Friday, "lest I experience a cruel disappointment. The countenances of our friends, however, are brightening with hope; while the Georgians are obviously and greaty alarmed for the fate of the bill."[127] The chief reason for Evarts's new optimism was Congressman Joseph Hemphill from Pennsylvania, who planned to offer a substitute for the removal bill; it was rumored that all except one member of the

Pennsylvania delegation would support it.[128] The only problem was that debate had to continue long enough for Hemphill's substitute to come up for a vote.

When debate resumed the following Monday, Ramsey's amendment was enacted as submitted,[129] and Hemphill then offered his substitute. It would appoint a commission to ascertain the views of the Indian tribes toward removal and to investigate "the country west of the Mississippi, and ascertain the quality and extent of the country which could be offered to the Indians in exchange for their lands east of the river."[130] When supporters of the bill failed in their bid to call the previous question, which would have moved the bill to its third reading without a vote on Hemphill's substitute, the prospects of passage dimmed. Even Congressman Wilson Lumpkin began to have doubts about the bill's prospects, telling colleague Henry Storrs that it would be defeated. Throughout the day tensions rose. The first three times the previous question was moved, it was rejected because a majority refused to second the motion. The fourth time the vote was so close that it had to be retaken thirteen times. It was finally determined that the House had deadlocked 98-98, allowing the Speaker of the House to break the tie and force the vote on the third reading.[131]

Two minutes later Congressman John Dickinson arrived. An opponent of removal, he had been sick in bed. Had he arrived sooner, he could have prevented the vote, and the debate on Hemphill's substitute would have continued. Had Hemphill's proposal come to a vote, it likely would have passed by a margin of 101-98. But Dickinson had come too late, and the vote on the third reading took place at 10 P.M. The motion for the bill passed because four members who had pledged to vote for Hemphill's amendment switched sides. The margin was thin, 102-97, but decisive.[132]

Passage of the legislation now seemed assured. The next day, however, Congressman Hemphill made one last attempt to change the bill. He moved that the House return to the Committee of the Whole so that his substitute could be offered as an amendment. Supporters tried to circumvent this move by calling for the previous question, which now would force the final vote on the bill. They finally succeeded on Wednesday, May 26, and shortly after one o'clock the bill passed the House, the vote again being 102-97. The Senate concurred two hours later.[133]

After having come so close to victory, the defeat was heartbreaking. But Evarts looked to God for help. Coming to the capitol building before the final vote he and a friend found a vacant room in which to pray. After the vote, he commented, "My comfort is that God governs the word," and he again resorted to prayer.[134] His faith remained, but it had been sorely tested.

It was tested again the next day when President Jackson returned an internal improvements bill to Congress with his veto. This was the last possible day Jackson could return the bill without it becoming law. Now the reason the removal bill had been rammed through Congress became painfully clear. Had Jackson's veto been known prior to the vote on removal, the removal bill never would have passed. The veto alienated many of Jackson's supporters, and they no longer would have felt compelled to vote for the administration's Indian policy. "Several who voted for the Indian bill, now say that they would vote against it," wrote Evarts on May 27. "But it is too late."[135]

Evarts struggled to understand why God would allow the defenders of the Indians to come so close and then be defeated. "At times I am exceedingly cast down as to the result," he wrote in his journal. "It seems a most remarkable Providence, that the bill should pass, when a majority present shewed themselves to be really and obstinately opposed to it; and that it passed by a majority of five, when the very next day . . . no one doubts that it would have been rejected. This strange state of things should make us stand astonished at the ways of Providence."[136]

Despite the crushing setback, Evarts vowed to continue the battle, and over the next two years more than 200 additional petitions were sent to Congress opposing removal.[137] Supporters of the Indians also looked to other avenues of protest. In 1831 they helped the Cherokees seek an injunction from the Supreme Court to prevent Georgia from enforcing its laws on Cherokee land. But their hopes were again dashed. A majority of the justices did acknowledge the validity of the Cherokees' treaty rights, but the Court also decided 4–2 that the Cherokee Nation was not a foreign state within the meaning of the Constitution. Thus, the Cherokees had no standing to invoke the Court's original jurisdiction.[138]

The situation rapidly deteriorated from then on. Less than two months after the Court's ruling, Jeremiah Evarts died, depriving the Cherokees of their most effective champion among whites.[139] Evarts had been in poor health for some time, and his exhaustive efforts on the Cherokees' behalf had proved too much. At the same time, support for the removal policy had solidified. Congress was unwilling to repeal the removal act, the Jackson adminstration was in no mood to reverse course, and Georgia was not about to back down. The situation, in short, was dire. Only one card remained to be played. Down in Georgia Samuel Worcester prayed that he would have courage enough to use it.

## WORCESTER V. GEORGIA

By mid-1831 Worcester had become convinced that a new Supreme Court case was the Cherokees' last hope. But he also knew that the cost of bringing the case would be high. If convicted, he faced four years of hard labor at the hands of Georgian authorities. And he risked alienating his colleagues, some of whom were already questioning whether opposition to removal had gone too far.

The Reverend Daniel Butrick, for example, had written the ABCFM a lengthy letter advocating noninvolvement. Butrick argued that "as missionaries of Christ we have gone to the extent of our authority in defending the temporal and political rights of the Cherokees." Now that legal routes of protest had been closed off, the missionaries had to submit to the government of Georgia. Butrick did not wholly deny Christians the right to engage in civil disobedience, but he argued that such resistance could be offered only in defense of the Christian faith itself. "Though we are to obey God rather than man," he wrote, "yet obedience to Him will not admit of our resisting the civil authority for the purpose of supporting schools, or preserving property, or securing the temporal interests or rights of others, or of promoting our own influence or usefulness, or of avoiding afflictions, poverty, reproach & hardships."

Actually, Butrick's objection to the use of civil disobedience was only part of his difficulty with the effort to defend Cherokee rights. Although he did not overtly fault previous efforts to stand up for the Cherokees, he criticized them implicitly by attacking any political activities on the part of Christian missionaries. In his view missionaries had virtually no duties as citizens of the present world. They were citizens of the heavenly kingdom, and their sole duty was to promote its interests. Butrick granted that others disagreed with his view, but he found their critique unconvincing:

Some may be ready to say that as citizens of the United States we are bound to bear a part in the political struggle of the day, and do all in our power to put down those rulers who do not act according to our views of justice; and that therefore we are justified in decrying them and using the most direct methods to bring their characters into public contempt. So they may think and so they may act; but I must confess that I have not so learned my duty. As a missionary among the heathen, I feel that I have a right to be dead to the political world, and that I have no call from the example of Christ or his apostles to engage in political contests, or to speak evil of dignities.[140]

According to Butrick, the missionaries could bless the Cherokees and pray for a miracle but could not lift a finger to help them. "Let missionaries be more dead to the world and all its interests and concerns and alive only to the great concerns of eternity," wrote Butrick on June 9. "Let God govern the world."[141]

Butrick's view of the matter was reinforced by his concern for the feelings of white Christians in Georgia. Butrick thought Georgians had been hurt enough by the controversy, and he was loathe to offend them.[142] Butrick apparently harbored no similar fears about offending Cherokee Christians. His advice to them was to prepare to suffer: "Our blessed Lord does not promise to preserve his people from oppression & violence. He does not promise to preserve to them their temporal rights & privileges."[143]

Worcester found Butrick's narrow conception of the gospel unacceptable. For him the law of God encompasses the laws of morality, and thus gross violations of public morality *had* to concern the missionaries. They had a duty to prevent the law of God from being trampled on, and this was the manner in which the whole controversy should be argued. Worcester noted that defenders of Georgia ignored this aspect of the uproar. In Gwinnett County he could find no one "who dared undertake to defend the right of Georgia, considered in immediate reference to the law of God." The problem, he said, was that most people continued to view the Cherokee problem as a "political question" rather than a moral one. He urged the ABCFM to draw up and circulate among southern Christians a memorial that would make the moral aspects of the controversy manifest. Worcester hoped to disarm Georgia by dividing it; if enough Georgian Christians could be persuaded of the moral principle at stake, they might be able to prevent the state from using force against Cherokees.

Looking toward the presidential election of 1832, Worcester also called on the board to remind Christians of their duty to vote. "Have not ministers and private christians felt so much that politics belonged not to them," he complained, "as to withhold their votes when they ought to have been given [?]" Worcester added that he was "not and would not be a politician, but it does appear to me that in such a case, when the question was whether the nation shall trample divine authority under feet and contract most glaring and enormous guilt, if my vote or my influence could do anything to prevent the evil, and I neglected it, I should be a partaker in the guilt."

Worcester said his Jacksonian friends had all cautioned him "to be prudent" and warned him that he would destroy his "influence and injure the Institution with which I am connected" by continuing on his avowed course. Worcester agreed that he ought to be prudent, but he defined the virtue rather differently: "I feel sensible that great wisdom and prudence are necessary on the part of the friends of the Indians here, in order to succeed in our object—but not the prudence of the world, or that cowardliness which shirks from duty."[144]

The board sided with Worcester, agreeing that additional effort had to be made to save the Cherokees. The decision having been made, the missionaries waited to be arrested again, knowing that each day they remained free might be their last. On the evening of Thursday, July 7, a group of the Georgia Guard finally approached Worcester's residence in New Echota and placed him under arrest by four officers under the direction of Sargeant Brooks. Worcester was sick with fever at the time, and his friends supposed that he would be granted a temporary reprieve. "But we were mistaken," wrote Cherokee Elias Boudinot to the ABCFM. "We overrated the humanity of these law officers of Georgia."[145] That would turn out to be an understatement.

On Friday morning Brooks took Worcester ten miles by horseback to the main detachment of troops under Colonel Charles Nelson. There Worcester met the Reverend James Trott, a Methodist missionary with a Cherokee family, and Proctor, a Cherokee who had been arrested for digging for gold on Cherokee lands. The day before Trott and Proctor had been marched twenty-two miles on foot, with Proctor "chained by the neck to the wagon."[146] On Worcester's arrival, all three men were marched back to the place that Trott and Proctor had come from the day before.

Along the way two Methodist circuit riders, Dickson McLeod and Martin Wells, met them and rode alongside. Neither of the men resided within Cherokee Territory, so they were not in violation of the residency law. But that did not quell their outrage at the treatment of their Christian brothers.

McLeod asked Trott whether he had been chained the night before. When Trott replied that he had, McLeod asked whether it was lawful to chain a man who showed no intention of escaping. Trott said that he thought not but that the guards were merely following orders.

"It seems they proceed more by orders than by law," McLeod then responded. This barb offended members of the guard. Words were exchanged, and Colonel Nelson came back to determine what was going on. When Nelson heard about McLeod's comment, he told him to "flank off."

"I will, sir, if it is your command," replied McLeod, but he added, "You will hear from me again."

Nelson then arrested McLeod, took away his horse, and forced him to walk with the others. MacLeod was compelled at bayonet point to slog through the mire and puddles in the middle of the road. At the same time, Brooks and other officers openly ridiculed the missionaries.

While all this was taking place, the second circuit rider, Martin Wells, had resumed his journey in the opposite direction. He soon met with another detachment of soldiers, this one having as its prisoner another missionary of the ABCFM, the Reverend John Thompson. Wells decided to accompany them in hopes of discovering what would become of MacLeod. When this new group caught up with the larger contingent ahead of them, Nelson became livid at Wells's return and ordered him out of sight. When Wells fell back but continued to follow the group, Nelson rode back and brutally beat him in the head with a stick. Hurt but unfazed, Wells replied that he had a right to travel the public road and that he would continue to do so.

When the prisoners were finally allowed to rest for the night, they were chained at the ankle in pairs. At midnight a third detachment of soldiers stumbled into camp with yet another missionary taken prisoner, Dr. Elizur Butler of the ABCFM. For much of his trip Butler had been chained by the neck to a horse and forced to keep a quick pace or be dragged by the neck and strangled.

The next day the prisoners journeyed thirty-five miles more. "When we had travelled a considerable distance," wrote Worcester later, "four of the soldiers were so kind as to walk four or five miles, and allow the prisoners to ride; for which we were told they were afterwards abused by Brooks, who now had the command of the detachment." On Sunday the prisoners were compelled to travel twenty-two miles. This was a blatant violation of the Sabbath, but the missionaries chose not to protest. They knew it would be futile. When they finally reached the jail, Brooks got in one last swipe. He told the missionaries that "there is where all the enemies of Georgia have to land—there and in hell."

On September 15 the prisoners were tried and found guilty of illegally residing among the Cherokees. The next day the men were sentenced to four years at hard labor at the state penitentiary in Midgeville, Georgia. Once at the penitentiary, the convicts were offered pardons if they pledged to leave the state. All but Worcester and Butler accepted the offer. They were berated for hours to change their minds, but they refused.[147] Worcester had received what he wanted, a chance to raise the issue in federal court, and he was not about to throw it away.

Outraged at the conduct of Georgia, the public rallied around the missionaries, and the Supreme Court subsequently upheld the rights of both the missionaries and the Cherokees.[148] But as Worcester had feared, he and Butler won the battle only to lose the war. Georgia ignored the Court's decision. Not only did the state refuse to uphold the rights of the Cherokees; it also refused to release Worcester and Butler until they acknowledged their crime. As for President Jackson, he reportedly sniped, "John Marshall has made his decision; let him enforce it now if he can."[149]

In response, the two missionaries asked the Supreme Court for a writ commanding Georgia to release them. While they waited for the Court to act, however, political events caused them to reconsider their course. In the fall Andrew Jackson was reelected by an overwhelming margin, and so a change in Indian policy at the federal level now seemed unthinkable. In South Carolina the nullification crisis was threatening a civil war, and many were pressuring Worcester and Butler to give up their fight so that Georgia would support the federal government. And in Georgia itself the state legislature repealed the obnoxious law under which Worcester and Butler had been prosecuted. In view of the changing circumstances, the missionaries hinted to the ABCFM that they should abandon their appeal. The board agreed, and by January both men were free and back in Cherokee Territory.[150]

## THE LESSONS OF THE REMOVAL CAMPAIGN

The release of the missionaries effectively ended the mass protests against removal, and the missions establishment now generally acquiesced to removal as the lesser of two evils. Even Worcester counseled Indians to accept the inevitable, and Cherokee Christians such as John Ridge and Elias Boudinot eventually agreed. In 1835 a small number of Cherokee leaders concluded a treaty with the government agreeing to removal.[151] Most Cherokees did not support the treaty and resisted removal; a handful of missionaries supported them, including Worcester's old cellmate Elizur Butler and—ironically—Daniel Butrick.[152] The latter had been the most vociferous opponent of Worcester and Butler's previous efforts on behalf of Cherokee rights. But when actually confronted with the impending horrors of forced removal, Butrick admirably changed course.[153]

When recalcitrant tribe members were finally compelled to remove, the results were tragic. In 1838 more than 12,000 Cherokees were rounded up by soldiers and corralled into detention camps.[154] From 300 to 2,000 persons died there because of the unsanitary conditions. Another 500–2,000 people perished en route to Oklahoma on the "trail of tears."[155] But these were perhaps the kindest consequences of removal. Once in Oklahoma a bloody civil war within the tribe ensued, and John Ridge, his father, and Elias Boudinot were brutally murdered because of their role in securing the treaty of 1835.[156]

The removal of the Cherokees remains a sorry, criminal episode in American history. Yet as Francis Paul Prucha points out, the results could have been much worse. "However tragic the removal of the southern tribes was, the tribes moved west under treaties that recognized the nation status of the tribes, that granted them lands in the West in fee simple, and that guaranteed to the tribes the jurisdiction and government of all persons and property within their western limits."[157] And those Cherokees who removed prior to the trail of tears apparently found their new home a land of bounty and opportunity. In 1838 John Ridge wrote his old nemesis Wilson Lumpkin that "the streams here of all sizes, from the rivers to the brooks, run swiftly over clean stones and pebbles, and the water is clear as crystal, in which excellent fish abound in vast numbers. The soil is diversified from the best prairie lands to the best bottom lands, in vast tracts. Never did I see a better location for settlements and better springs in the world. God has thrown His favors here with a broad cast."[158]

Lumpkin seized on such statements to justify Georgia's appropriation of Indian lands. In his view the fact that some Cherokees now prospered in their new territory vindicated the policies he had pursued so ruthlessly. "In magnanimity and liberalty [sic] towards the Indians, no man has surpassed me," he later maintained.[159] If Lumpkin had pangs of conscience about his role in removal, he never showed them. He did regret the later murders of both the Ridges and Elias Boudinot; but here he conveniently disclaimed responsibility, arguing that the federal government should have prevented John Ross, leader of the Cherokee resisters, from emigrating to the new territory and stirring up trouble.[160] Given what transpired, Lumpkin was probably right. But his protestations of innocence were self-serving. Ross became a problem only because of forced removal. The civil chaos in Indian Territory was an inevitable result of Lumpkin's own policies.

Whatever the results of the protests on the Cherokees, the removal controversy left an important legacy to evangelical reform. First, the crisis forced evangelicals to confront the limitations of politics. Moral right does not always equal political might, and Cherokee removal compelled evangelicals to reconcile their idealism with the exigencies of the time. After four years of failure evangelicals had to ask themselves whether they should continue their protests. Most decided that removal was now inevitable and decided to capitulate. Why they did so indicates something of the realism that undergirded their moral idealism.

Historian William McLoughlin confused matters when he concluded that the missionaries gave up their fight because "blood was thicker than water; ethnocentrism was stronger than righteousness."[161] In fact, ethnocentrism had little to do with it. The nullification crisis did foster a tension between support for Cherokee rights and support for Jackson's efforts to save the Union; but this was not the decisive factor in the evangelicals' abandonment of their crusade. Their most important reason was that further protests would have been futile or even counterproductive. As Samuel Worcester explained to someone who had continued to support the appeal for a writ from the Supreme Court:

That we could not benefit the *Cherokees* by further perseverance appeared to me perfectly certain. On the other hand, I was apprehensive that our perseverance was becoming an injury to them, by cherishing a vain and delusive hope of protection, when the decision in our favor should be executed, and thus strengthening them in measures contrary to their interests. For I have been for a good while decidedly of the opinion, that the Cherokees would do well to form a treaty and remove in a body to the west. As long as there was the least hope of their obtaining that protection, which is their due, from the robbery and intolerable oppression which afflict them, I was for having them stand fast; but that hope is, in my mind, utterly extinct.[162]

Worcester had come to realize that what is best in an absolute sense may not be best under the circumstances. Idealism does not exclude the need for a prudent realism. Saving Cherokee lands might have been the right thing to do, but when this became impossible, one had to salvage the situation. If the Cherokees had to remove, it would be better if they did so voluntarily and on as generous terms as possible.[163]

Not all evangelicals accepted such reasoning. As noted earlier, though the majority of evangelical reformers urged the Cherokees to accept a treaty, several continued to support their resistance. Some of these undoubtedly accepted the idea of prudence in politics while rejecting its particular application. Reasonable people might differ about the nature of the circumstances and hence the dictates of prudence in a given situation. Others likely saw only the unrighteousness of removal and knew they had to oppose it. These differences over the role of prudence during Cherokee removal proved prophetic, foreshadowing the divisions that were already forming in the debate over abolition.

But if the campaign against removal foreshadowed things to come, it also epitomized the culmination of things past. In the broadest terms the antiremoval campaign represented the working out of the Founders' solution to the theological-political problem. The Founders had claimed that morality was connected to religion, and the removal controversy vindicated the political promise inherent in that proposition. To be specific, it showed the peculiar strength of religious groups in pressing moral claims in politics, for political opposition to removal would not have existed without the missonaries and the churches. Religious idealism alone had shown itself firm enough to defend the Cherokees' rights, which suggested that the Founders had been correct in claiming that religion would be the guarantor of morality in America.

The antiremoval crusade also displayed the promise of religion in politics while avoiding most of the perils. Evangelicals had successfully championed a cause without dividing the nation along sectarian lines. This point was an especially critical one, for the Sunday mails campaign (as well as growing anti-Catholicism) had raised doubts on the subject. The crusade for the

Cherokees showed that evangelicals could act on behalf of the rights of others rather than appearing to claim special privileges for themselves. It demonstrated that evangelicals were capable of operating in a political order grounded in reason as well as revelation. Because of this, no one dared attack the Cherokees' defenders for trying to enforce their religious beliefs by law.

However, some supporters of Cherokee removal did denounce evangelical reformers for dangerously mixing religion and politics. But this merely demonstrated how elastic the attack on political religion had become. Just as some evangelical reformers recklessly tagged all their opponents as atheists and infidels, some critics of evangelical reform uncritically applied the epithet "priestcraft" without much regard for particular circumstances. In the case of Cherokee removal, no one even pretended that evangelicals were seeking government sanction of their religious doctrines by defending the Cherokees. Yet evangelicals were still accused of being part of a theocratic cabal. That they had organized as citizens to engage in politics made them subversives.

Defenders of the Cherokees rightly exposed the absurdity of this charge, but some of their critics really did not care whether the charge was absurd in the present instance. They certainly did not care if they were inconsistent. Wilson Lumpkin condemned religion in politics even while praising clergy who advocated removal. In the end the hue and cry against priestcraft in the Cherokee removal controversy was more a rhetorical ploy than anything else. It had become a convenient way of delegitimizing opponents without answering their arguments.

The harangues about religion in politics did not noticeably detract from the evangelicals' efforts, however. The campaign to defend Cherokee rights was the crowning achievement of the politics of revelation and reason up to 1835, and it showed the salutary influence that could be exercised by evangelicals during the debate of a great question of national morality.

# EPILOGUE
## THE ENDURING LEGACY OF THE
## POLITICS OF REVELATION AND
## REASON

On November 25, 1992, Samuel Worcester finally received his vindication from the State of Georgia. More than 160 years after having been imprisoned for defending the rights of the Cherokees, Worcester and fellow prisoner Elihu Butler were officially absolved of wrongdoing by the Board of Pardons and Paroles, which acknowledged that the two missionaries' convictions were "a stain on the history of criminal justice in Georgia."[1]

The story was carried by newspapers around the country, including the *New York Times,* but most Americans probably had only a dim notion of what it was all about. Unlike some episodes in American history, the controversy over Cherokee removal has not been deeply etched into the popular mind. The same can be said about the evangelical reform movement of which the removal controversy was a part. Evangelical political activism during the early 1800s has been all but forgotten today, overshadowed by later high-profile crusades over slavery and prohibition.

This cultural amnesia is understandable. History is often forgetful of losers, and by the mid-1830s the evangelicals' two major national crusades— the Sunday mails and Cherokee removal—had both ended in defeat. Yet these two failures were not the whole story. Despite setbacks, evangelical reformers had made a major impact on society. They had forged a public consensus against dueling, which produced new state laws outlawing duelists from public office. They had schooled hundreds of thousands of children in reading, writing, and morality through the institution of Sunday schools. They had reduced alcohol consumption, and they had improved the living conditions of prisoners and the handicapped. If evangelicals' early efforts had not created an American utopia, wiser heads among them probably had not expected that such actions would. As Lyman Beecher had cautioned his fellow reformers in 1803, "We are not angels, but men. If we can gradually improve ourselves, and improve the society in which we live, though in a small degree, it is an object not to be despised."[2]

Not all evangelical initiatives were quite so admirable, of course. Evangelical anti-Catholicism, though ostensibly grounded in a concern for religious liberty, verged on hysteria; and demands by certain evangelicals that Christians vote only for fellow believers confused Christian piety with good citizenship. Such continuing examples of intolerance made evangelical reform a two-edged sword, which nineteenth-century author Nathaniel Hawthorne seemed to understand in some of his writings. Hawthorne was not a political theorist, but his short stories about the American Puritans presented a lucid portrait of both the perils and promise of evangelical reform.

Hawthorne criticized the Puritans chiefly for their religious intolerance. He depicted them as so convinced of their own righteousness that they cut themselves off from their fellow men. In "Young Goodman Brown," for example, the title character thinks he is the only one to resist the temptations of Satan; thus, he shrinks from fellowship with anyone else, including his wife (appropriately named "Faith").[3] Yet according to Hawthorne, the same rigid idealism that spawned the Puritans' religious bigotry also produced a powerful commitment to moral principle that made them resist political tyranny. This message surfaces most vividly in the short story "The Gray Champion," where a first-generation Puritan mysteriously returns to Boston in 1689 to thwart the subjugation of the colonies by King James II. Like a fiery Old Testament prophet, the old Puritan—the "Gray Champion" of the story's title—denounces the usurpations of royal governor Sir Edmund Andros and urges the people to resistance.[4]

The character of the Gray Champion symbolized the Puritans' rigid moral idealism, which typified evangelicalism in general. In Hawthorne's view this rock-solid idealism might turn out to be the republic's saving grace during times of crisis. Indeed, it is during the "hour . . . of darkness, and adversity, and peril" that the spirit of the Gray Champion comes into its own. "Should domestic tyranny oppress us, or the invader's step pollute our soil, still may the Gray Champion come," wrote Hawthorne, "for he is the type of New England's hereditary spirit; and his shadowy march, on the eve of danger, must ever be the pledge, that New England's sons will vindicate their ancestry."[5]

In a crisis, then, evangelicalism's intolerant commitment to principle might be the very thing that can save the nation from a great evil. For example, during the Cherokee removal controversy evangelicals alone made the violation of Indian rights a pressing public issue. They did not succeed in their efforts, but they were the one group in society that made the attempt to defend national honor. Hence the ultimate paradox of evangelical Christianity: Its religious intolerance may destroy republican government, but its rigorous attachment to moral principle may be needed to preserve that same government.

Perhaps the most notable fact about evangelical reform through 1835 was that it largely fulfilled Hawthorne's hopes without realizing his fears. For the most part American evangelicals entered politics in the new nation in order to defend moral principle rather than impose evangelical theology. Their political and social efforts focused on issues such as dueling, temperance, prostitution, war, lotteries, slavery, and Cherokee removal. That these issues could be argued with reference to a shared morality diminished their theological divisiveness and opened the door for evangelicals to form coalitions with nonevangelicals to achieve common ends. Thus, during Cherokee removal evangelicals were able to enlist the support of prominent Unitarians such as William Ellery Channing and Edward Everett.

Moreover, when evangelicals did broach theology in the political arena, they often argued their case within the framework of religious liberty. They claimed that the Sunday mails subverted the religious rights of postal workers, and they maintained that Catholicism was dangerous because it propagated doctrines inimical to religious freedom. The former argument made sense; the latter contention was overblown. But the very manner in which evangelicals argued both issues demonstrated the moderating influence that American republicanism exerted on their theory of politics.

To be sure, there were exceptions and ambiguities. One can argue that those evangelicals who joined the Anti-Masonic Party came close to forming a Christian party in politics. As mentioned earlier, certain evangelical leaders—Jedidiah Morse and Ezra Stiles Ely, to name two—wished to turn elections into referendums on Christian orthodoxy. Some evangelicals also continued to support blasphemy laws. However, most of these practices and beliefs turned out to be less divisive in reality than they might have initially seemed. As far as antimasonry was concerned, the Anti-Masonic Party never really became an exclusively evangelical political party because it drew support from universalists and prominent Unitarians such as Edward Everett and John Quincy Adams.[6] In addition, most of the party's agenda focused not on the inculcation of religious orthodoxy but on moral issues that could be justified by reason apart from revelation, such as the abolition of slavery.[7]

Other potential problems were reduced in practice because evangelicals did not speak with one voice. Ezra Stiles Ely fostered tensions when he argued that Christians could vote only for fellow Christians, but he received little support for his position from other evangelicals.[8] Similarly, when Abner Kneeland was prosecuted for blasphemy in Massachusetts in the 1830s, orthodox Congregationalists supported the prosecution, but Baptists joined in a petition asking that Kneeland be pardoned.[9] Moreover, Kneeland's defense attorney was able to appeal for support to a grand jury charge delivered by prominent evangelical reformer (and New York judge) William Jay. Jay had declared that "infidels and Christians, and politicians of every name and character, have an equal and undoubted right to publish their sentiments, and to endeavor to make converts to them." He likewise maintained that "this guaranty of freedom of discussion . . . extends equally to religious and political topics."[10]

The most significant challenges to evangelical political moderation came after 1835: the rise of political nativism, the fight over religion in public education, and the crusade to amend the Constitution to recognize the authority of Christ.[11] How involvement in these later issues may have compromised the evangelicals' commitment to the Founders' framework is a question that merits a study of its own. But during the period examined here—the formative years of evangelical reform—most evangelical reformers limited their political activities to what Beecher liked to call the "great questions of national morality."[12]

This moderation on the part of most evangelical reformers was made possible by the Founders' solution to the theological-political problem. Evangelicals could limit their political claims precisely because the Founders had created a framework where allegiance to government need not contradict obedience to God. The Founders' framework guaranteed this result in two ways. First, political authority would be limited to those areas where autonomous reason and divine revelation agree, so that government actions could be accepted as legitimate by believers and unbelievers alike. Second, religious liberty would be scrupulously protected to preserve the mutual supremacy of church and state, each in its respective sphere. Together these two guarantees made possible a positive role for religion in politics. Because government authority would be kept separate from ecclesiastical authority, churches now could be trusted to create—and defend—civic morality. Stripped of any pretensions that might have made them dangerous to republicanism, churches were free to reform society according to the moral law held in common by both revelation and reason.

This is not to say that the Founders' system was self-enforcing. It was not. Ultimately, it had to be sustained in the court of public opinion. Americans themselves had to ensure that neither religion nor government would step outside its appointed sphere by censuring any violation from the Founders' principles. In the words of one perceptive observer: "No denomination of Christians, and no class of politicians, are so good as to justify implicit confidence, or supersede the necessity of being watched. Responsibility to an enlightened public sentiment is the only effective guarantee of unperverted liberty and political prosperity."[13] The author of that warning was Lyman Beecher, who was directing his comments toward Catholics. But the warning applied equally to American evangelicals. Freedom of action did not guarantee freedom from censure; and if evangelicals wanted to prevail in their political efforts, they would have to justify their efforts before the bar of public opinion.

This fact makes manifest the positive role played by opponents of evangelical reform. These critics continued to condemn evangelical efforts as "dangerous" and "unrepublican," even as evangelicals were leaving behind the trappings of state sponsorship. During both the Sunday mails campaign and Cherokee removal, critics argued that religious motivations should disqualify evangelical arguments from even being heard by Congress. They claimed that religious groups had no business meddling in civic affairs. The more radical critics even denied the connection between religion and public morality, which placed them in direct opposition to the Founders. But as erroneous and demagogic as many of these charges were, they served a useful purpose. By tarring evangelical efforts with such epithets as "priestcraft" and "union of church and state," critics helped delineate the proper bounds within which evangelicals could legitimately operate.

If only to disprove the attacks, evangelicals were encouraged to confine their efforts within the Founders' solution to the theological-political problem. They were prodded to defend themselves on the grounds of their equal rights as citizens, instead of appealing to special privileges as Christians. And that is precisely what they did. Seizing the constitutional high ground, they accused their critics of fanning the flames of intolerance with all their cries of priestcraft and persecution.

The Reverend F. Freeman, for example, declared that "this cry of persecution is itself the bitterest persecution. This charge of intolerance is the very hand of intolerance itself, stretched forth with unrelenting grasp."[14] Religious liberty encompasses the freedom to speak as well as the freedom to think, said Freeman, and no person has the right to hinder another person from candidly expressing his views. That nation is not free where one group of people cannot express their views about God and morality without subjecting themselves "not only to the jeers and revilings of the debased, but to every unamiable feeling shewn by those who profess respectability and would fain be considered liberal."[15] In Freeman's view true religious liberty implies not only the absence of government coercion but also the maintenance of civility between those who differ in religion:

We are authorized to maltreat no one for the honest expression of his views. He is none the less our fellow-citizen and neighbour, possessing equal rights with ourselves and entitled to the same urbane and respectful treatment, whether he be a Christian or a Jew, a Turk or a Pagan—whether a Catholic, an Episcopalian, a Baptist, a Methodist, an Universalist, a Presbyterian, an Independent, or Unitarian, or Nothingarian. And all disrespectful treatment arising from such a cause, whatever that treatment be, whether simply hard looks, or public or private slights, menaces, scoffs, ridicule, misrepresentation, impeachment of motives without cause, or whatever else that is discourteous, is the expression of a feeling which is diametrically opposed to true religious liberty, and is the offspring of a little, a very contracted mind.[16]

Other evangelicals tried to show that evangelical reform did not threaten a union between church and state. In an address titled "On the Misrepresentation of Benevolent Actions," the Reverend David Ogden pointed out that evangelical reform was spearheaded by all major evangelical denominations, and he contended that it was ludicrous to think that these different denominations (each with its own peculiar doctrines and form of worship) would join together on behalf of church-state union. This was true however such a union was defined. Evangelical reformers could not be working toward the establishment of one denomination over the rest because they could never agree which denomination to establish. They could not even be working together for nonpreferential aid to all sects because "some large [evangelical] sects as a body, and individuals in all [evangelical] sects believe that this is an unchristian way of supporting religion. And then there are innumerable small sects, besides a multitude of infidels and men indifferent to all religion, who would join together on this subject, and defeat such a plan."[17]

In other words, the sheer multiplicity of sects in America discouraged evangelical union on any other grounds than the common good. According to Ogden, this was precisely the motive that had spurred Methodists, Episcopalians, Baptists, and Presbyterians to join together for evangelical reform. They sought to promote the "moral welfare of their species" by distributing the Bible to those who could not afford it, by educating children so they would not become delinquents, and by promoting "respect for the Sabbath which they believe to be essential to our political prosperity."[18]

Ogden did not invoke James Madison in this discourse, but Ogden's analysis rested squarely on Madisonian principles. In effect Ogden claimed that the theoretical position staked out by Madison in *Federalist* no. 10 had been vindicated in practice. America had such a variety of sects, evangelical and otherwise, that the only successful religious combinations would be those based on the "principles . . . of justice and the general good."[19] In other words, these combinations would be based on principles shared by reason as well as revelation. In this view joint religious efforts on behalf of common ends became a help, rather than a threat, to American politics.

By vindicating this proposition, evangelical reformers in the early nineteenth century showed that the Founders' solution to the theological-political problem could work in the real world. But they also demonstrated that the Founders' solution is not inevitable. The long-term success of the Founders' solution depends on continuing concessions from people of faith and from secularists. Both have to limit their political claims to proposals articulated in terms of the common moral ground shared by reason *and* revelation. People of faith have to be careful that they do not demand government support for their specific doctrinal beliefs; and those who think religion should stay out of politics (either for secular or religious reasons) have to refrain from advocating government policies that flatly contradict the deeply held religious beliefs of other citizens.

Such concessions were difficult enough to achieve in the early 1800s. They are considerably more difficult to obtain today. In the nineteenth century most Americans at least could agree on the basic moral code for society, which reduced the areas of outright disagreement between religious adherents and secularists. Moreover, the scope of government itself was limited, which meant that the areas where government and faith could conceivably come into conflict were few and far between.

During the past several decades, however, both the moral consensus and limited government have been sorely tested. The old idea that reason and revelation can come to a common agreement on moral truth has eroded, sparking what sociologist James Davison Hunter has aptly termed "culture wars."[20] One cannot limit political activities to the common moral ground if no common ground exists. Nor can one ensure that government action will not encroach on religious beliefs when government itself is no longer limited. American government at all levels increasingly handles matters that were once the domain of individuals, families, and private associations. This expansion of government power may have been necessary, but it inevitably aggravates the theological-political problem by decreasing the sphere of government neutrality. The more the government seeks to intervene, the more it must promulgate definitive policies, and the more it does promulgate policies, the more conflicts will inevitably arise between the government and those religious adherents who disagree with those policies. This is especially the case in a society where the moral code is no longer shared by reason and revelation.

All of these developments bring into question the adequacy of the Founders' solution for twentieth-century America. No political system can long endure once its fundamental premises have been abandoned by society. Without the existence of a moral common ground that justifies as well as limits the role of government, the possibility for explicit hostilities between theology and politics increases substantially.

"There is a *religious* war going on in our country for the soul of America!" declared one prominent politician during the 1992 presidential campaign.[21] If the Founders' solution to the challenge of religion and politics cannot be successfully defended in our own day, that cry may turn out to be a preview of things to come.

# NOTES

## INTRODUCTION

1. Alexis de Tocqueville, *Democracy in America,* trans. George Lawrence, ed. J.P. Mayer (Garden City, N.Y.: Anchor Books, 1969), 448.

2. Ibid., 291.

3. See citations of Tocqueville in Charles W. Dunn, "The Dynamics of Democratic Tension: Religion in American Politics," in *Religion in American Politics,* ed. Charles W. Dunn (Washington, D.C.: CQ Press, 1989), xvi; Richard P. McBrien, *Caesar's Coin: Religion and Politics in America* (New York: Macmillan, 1987), 37; Mark A. Noll, Introduction to *Religion and American Politics from the Colonial Period to the 1980s,* ed. Mark A. Noll (New York: Oxford University Press, 1990), 12; Robert S. Alley, *So Help Me God: Religion and the Presidency, Wilson to Nixon* (Richmond, Va.: John Knox Press, 1972), 21; Ernest Fortin, "Did the Separation of Church and State Benefit Religion? The Pros and Cons of Disestablishment" (Paper presented at the American Political Science Association Annual Convention, San Francisco, Calif., August 1990), 4; Timothy L. Smith, *Revivalism and Social Reform in Mid-Nineteenth-Century America* (New York: Abingdon Press, 1957), 35. See also Alexis de Tocqueville, "Principal Causes which Render Religion Powerful in America," reprinted in *Politics of Religion in America,* ed. Fred Krinsky (Beverly Hills, Calif.: Glencoe Press, 1968), 35–41. Occasionally a scholar will raise doubts about Tocqueville's analysis, as George Armstrong Kelly did rather timidly in *Politics and Religious Consciousness in America* (New Brunswick, N.J.: Transaction Books, 1984), 45–46. Kelly cited Tocqueville's comment about American clergy staying out of politics but added, "Perhaps it was a bit of an exaggeration" (46).

4. Wilson Lumpkin, *The Removal of the Cherokee Indians from Georgia* (New York: Dodd, Mead, 1907), 47, 73.

5. *Cherokee Nation* v. *State of Georgia* 5 Peters 1 (1831); Richard Peters, *The Case of the Cherokee Nation against the State of Georgia* (Philadelphia: John Grigg, 1831); *Worcester* v. *State of Georgia* 6 Peters 515 (1832); Leonard W. Levy, "Cherokee Indian Cases," in *Encyclopedia of the American Constitution,* ed. Leonard W. Levy, Kenneth L. Karst, and Dennis J. Mahoney (New York: Macmillan, 1986), 1:241.

6. Tocqueville, *Democracy in America,* 334–39.

7. Anson Phelps Stokes, *Church and State in the United States* (New York: Harper and Brothers, 1950), 2:13–14; *An Account of Memorials Presented to Congress During the last Session, By Numerous Friends of Their Country and Its Institu-*

*tions; Praying That the Mails May Not Be Transported, nor Post-Offices Kept Open, On the Sabbath* (New York: T. R. Marvin, 1829), 4-7, 25-29.

8. See, for example, the petition of citizens of Windham County, Vermont (January 12, 1831), in *American State Papers,* Class 7: Post Office Department (Washington, D.C.: Gales and Seaton, 1834), 1:263.

9. For an overview of religious activism in politics during this period see Stokes, *Church and State,* 2:3-84.

10. See Robert Wuthnow, "The Political Rebirth of American Evangelicals," in *The New Christian Right: Mobilization and Legitimation,* ed. Robert C. Liebman and Robert Wuthnow (New York: Aldine, 1983), 149-60.

11. "Those of the present New Right conscience constituency differ from the liberals of the '60s in that they take religion as *content* in public issues, whereas the liberals took religion as a motivating *source.* This is the kind of attitude which in previous eras led to holy wars" (James M. Wall, "Bringing Back the Conscience Vote," *Christian Century* 97 [December 17, 1980]: 1235). For similarly harsh assessments of the Christian Right by mainline Protestants, see James Wall, "The New Right Exploits Abortion," *Christian Century* 97 (July 30-August 6, 1980): 747-48; John Scanzoni, "Resurgent Fundamentalism: Marching Backward into the '80s?" *Christian Century* 97 (September 10-17, 1980): 847-84; "What's Wrong with Born-Again Politics? A Symposium," *Christian Century* 97 (October 22, 1980): 1002-4; "Countering the Christian Right," *Christian Century* 97 (October 29, 1980): 1031; Allan J. Lichtman, "The New Prohibitionism," *Christian Century* 97 (October 29, 1980): 1029-30. More temperate reactions from mainline Christians can be found in Robert Zwier and Richard Smith, "Christian Politics and the New Right," *Christian Century* 97 (October 8, 1980): 937-41; Peggy Schriver, *The Bible Vote: Religion and the Right* (New York: Pilgrim Press, 1981); James M. Wall, "A Changing Political Climate," *Christian Century* 97 (September 24, 1980): 867-68. Wall, who excoriated the Religious Right in the two other cited articles, here argued that liberals helped create the Religious Right by "an insensitivity to what cultural changes were doing to traditional values" (867).

12. See James Davison Hunter, "The Liberal Reaction," in *The New Christian Right,* ed. Liebman and Wuthnow, 149-60.

13. "I am beginning to fear that we could have an Ayatollah Khomeini in this country, but that he will not have a beard, but he will have a television program" (Patricia Roberts Harris, "Religion and Politics: A Commitment to a Pluralistic Society," *Vital Speeches* 47 [November 1, 1980]: 50-53).

14. See Benedict de Spinoza, "A Theological Political Treatise" in *The Chief Works of Benedict de Spinoza,* trans. R. H. M. Elwes [New York: Dover, 1951]), vol. 1; Leo Strauss, "Preface to Hobbes *Politische Wissenschaft,* " *Interpretation* 8 (January 1979): 1; Harry Jaffa, "Seven Answers for Professor Anastaplo," *University of Puget Sound Law Review* 13 (Winter 1990): 392; Harry Jaffa, "Crisis of the Strauss Divided" (unpublished paper, April 22, 1987), 17.

15. Harry Jaffa, *The American Founding as the Best Regime: The Bonding of Civil and Religious Liberty* (Montclair, Calif.: Claremont Institute for the Study of

Political Philosophy and Statesmanship, 1990), 19–22; Numa Denis Fustel de Coulanges, *The Ancient City: A Study on the Religion, Laws, and Institutions of Greece and Rome* (Baltimore: Johns Hopkins University Press, 1980), 143–44, 146–47, 383–84; Leo Pfeffer, *Church, State, and Freedom,* rev. ed. (Boston: Beacon Press, 1967), 8–11.

16. Fustel de Coulanges, *The Ancient City,* 147–68.

17. Niccolò Machiavelli, *The Discourses,* translated by Leslie J. Walker, ed. Bernard Crick (Harmondsworth, Eng.: Penguin, 1983), 139–52; see also Pfeffer, *Church, State, and Freedom,* 3–4, 8–11. Judaism constitutes a partial exception to this description of ancient religion; it maintained a recurring conflict between religion and politics in the form of prophets who criticized political rulers for disobeying the law of God. See 1 Samuel 10:8, 13:8–14, 15:12–34; 2 Samuel 12:1–14; 1 Kings 14:2–11, 13:1–8; 1 Kings 21:17–26, 22:13–28; Jeremiah 21:1–14, 26:1–24, 27:1–22 (RSV).

18. Galatians 3:26, 28 (RSV); see also discussion by Fustel de Coulanges, *The Ancient City,* 383–85. But note the anticipation of this theme in such Old Testament passages as Isaiah 2:1–3 and Zephaniah 3:9.

19. Fustel de Coulanges, *The Ancient City,* 385–86; Philip Schaff, *History of the Christian Church,* 5th ed. (Grand Rapids, Mich.: Eerdmans, 1910), 2:11.

20. Schaff, *History,* 2:9–10.

21. Philippians 3:20 (NIV); the Greek word translated here as "citizenship" is *politeuma.* Also relevant is Colossians 3:2 (RSV): "Set your minds on things that are above, not on things that are on earth."

22. Machiavelli, *The Discourses,* 277–78; Schaff, *History,* 2:334–86.

23. Schaff, *History,* 2:43.

24. Jaffa, *The American Founding,* 22.

25. Ibid.; Pfeffer, *Church, State, and Freedom,* 9.

26. Jaffa, *The American Founding,* 22–23.

27. Ibid., 23.

28. Pfeffer, *Church, State, and Freedom,* 14–30; Schaff, *History,* 3:125–46, 4:250–303, 386–96, 5:1–307, 458–533, 6:1–114, 400–554, 7:50–86, 262–340, 375–99, 440–49, 8:165–201, 461–523.

29. Samuel Elliot Morison, *The Oxford History of the American People* (New York: Oxford University Press, 1965), 61–69; William Bradford, "History of Plimoth Plantation," in *The Puritans: A Sourcebook of Their Writings,* ed. Perry Miller and Thomas H. Johnson, rev. ed. (New York: Harper and Row, 1963), 1:91–117.

30. Leonard W. Levy, *The Establishment Clause: Religion and the First Amendment* (New York: Macmillan, 1986), 1–24.

31. James Madison, Letter to William Bradford (January 24, 1774), in *Papers of James Madison,* ed. William T. Hutchinson and William M. Frachal (Chicago: University of Chicago Press, 1962–), 1:106; see also Pfeffer, *Church, State, and Freedom,* 71–90, 91–93.

32. Previous studies that deal significantly with the Founders and religion include James O'Neill, *Religion and Education under the Constitution* (New York: Harper

and Brothers, 1949); Stokes, *Church and State;* Pfeffer, *Church, State and Freedom;* Walter Berns, *The First Amendment and the Future of American Democracy* (New York: Basic Book, 1976), 1–32; Michael Malbin, *Religion and Politics: The Intentions of the Authors of the First Amendment* (Washington, D.C.: American Enterprise Institute, 1978); James McClellan, "The Making and Unmaking of the Establishment Clause," in *A Blueprint for Judicial Reform,* ed. Patrick McGuigan and Randall Rader (Washington, D.C.: Free Congress Research and Education Foundation, 1981), 295–325; Robert Cord, *Separation of Church and State: Historical Fact and Current Fiction* (New York: Lambeth Press, 1982); Levy, *The Establishment Clause;* Thomas J. Curry, *The First Freedoms: Church and State in America to the Passage of the First Amendment* (New York: Oxford University Press, 1986); Daniel Dreisbach, *Real Threat and Mere Shadow: Religious Liberty and the First Amendment* (Westchester, Ill.: Crossway Books, 1987); John Eidsmoe, *Christianity and the Constitution: The Faith of Our Founding Fathers* (Grand Rapids, Mich.: Baker Book House, 1987); Edwin S. Gaustad, *Faith of Our Fathers: Religion and the New Nation* (San Francisco: Harper and Row, 1987); Robert Goldwin and Art Kaufman, eds., *How Does the Constitution Protect Religious Freedom?* (Washington, D.C.: American Enterprise Institute, 1987); McBrien, *Caesar's Coin;* Jaffa, "Crisis of the Strauss Divided" and *The American Founding;* Michael W. McConnell, "The Origins and Historical Understanding of the Free Exercise of Religion," *Harvard Law Review* 103 (1990): 1409–1517.

33. General studies that have been done on evangelicals and politics during this era include John R. Bodo, *The Protestant Clergy and Public Issues* (Princeton: Princeton University Press, 1954); Charles C. Cole Jr., *The Social Ideas of Northern Evangelists, 1826–1860* (New York: Columbia University Press, 1954); Charles I. Foster, *An Errand of Mercy: The Evangelical United Front, 1790–1837* (Chapel Hill: University of North Carolina Press, 1960); Clifford Griffin, *Their Brothers' Keepers: Moral Stewardship in the United States, 1800–1865* (New Brunswick, N.J.: Rutgers University Press, 1960); Mark Hanley, *Beyond a Christian Commonwealth* (Chapel Hill: University of North Carolina Press, 1994); Robert Abzug, *Cosmos Crumbling: American Reform and the Religious Imagination* (New York: Oxford University Press, 1994).

34. Major denominations generally classified as evangelical during this period included Episcopalians, Congregationalists, Baptists, Presbyterians, Methodists, Moravians, Lutherans, German Reformed, Reformed Dutch Church, Cumberland Presbyterians, Protestant or Reformed Methodists, Reformed Presbyterians or Covenanters, Associate Church, Associate Reformed, and Quakers. See comprehensive listing and discussion in Robert Baird, *Religion in America; or an Account of the Origin, Relation to the State, and Present Condition of the Evangelical Churches in the United States with Notices of the Unevangelical Denominations* (New York: Harper and Brothers, 1856), 438–539, 665. After the advent of theological liberalism within the major Protestant denominations in the late nineteenth and early twentieth centuries, the task of identifying evangelicals became more complex. Additional ambiguity was created by the introduction of the term *fundamentalist* to describe some

evangelicals. See N. H. Maring, "Evangelical" and "Evangelicalism," in *Encyclopediac Dictionary of Religion* (Philadelphia: Sisters of St. Joseph of Philadelphia, 1979), 1268, 1270–71; B. L. Shelley, "Evangelicalism," in *Dictionary of Christianity in America* (Downers Grove, Ill.: Intervarsity Christian Fellowship, 1990), 413–16.

35. For a good summary of the theological common ground shared by evangelicals during the period, see Lyman Beecher, *The Faith Once Delivered to the Saints,* 2d ed. (Boston: Crocker and Brewster, 1824), 2:243–300; Baird, *Religion in America,* 665.

36. For a general discussion of evangelicals in politics from 1840 to 1861, see Richard Carwardine, *Evangelicals and Politics in Antebellum America* (New Haven: Yale University Press, 1993).

37. As William G. McGloughlin noted in his massive, definitive study of the Baptists in Massachusetts: "Historians have rightly given most of their attention to evangelical Congregationalists like Jedidiah Morse, Lyman Beecher, Timothy Dwight, Jeremiah Evarts, and Leonard Woods rather than to the less effective and less influential Baptists who were doing the same things during this time. Except for Luther Rice and Adoniram Judson, two Congregational missionaries who became Baptists in 1812 after embarking for India, the Baptists produced no popular figures before [Francis] Wayland to compare with Congregational leaders" (*New England Dissent, 1630–1883: The Baptists and the Separation of Church and State* [Cambridge, Mass.: Harvard University Press, 1971], 1113–14.]

38. H. Richard Niebuhr, *The Social Sources of American Denominationalism* (New York: New American Library, 1957).

39. C. S. Lewis, *The Abolition of Man* (New York: Macmillan, 1947), 91.

40. H. Richard Niebuhr, *The Kingdom of God in America* (New York: Harper Torchbooks, 1959), ix–x.


## CHAPTER I. RELIGION AND THE AMERICAN FOUNDING REVISITED

1. William Pierce, "Character Sketches of Delegates to the Federal Convention," in *Records of the Federal Convention of 1787,* rev. ed., ed. Max Farrand (New Haven: Yale University Press, 1966), 3:91.

2. Franklin, quoted in letter from William Steele to Jonathan D. Steele (September 1825), *Records,* 3:471.

3. Dayton, quoted in ibid., 471–72.

4. Ibid., 467, n. 1.

5. See Acts 10.

6. Thomas S. Grimké, *Oration on the Principal Duties of Americans* (Charleston, S. C.: William Estill, 1833), 15.

7. James Madison to Thomas S. Grimké (January 6, 1834), *Records,* 3:531.

8. Madison to Grimké (January 6, 1834), ibid., 531; Franklin, speech to the

Constitutional Convention on June 28, 1787, in James Madison, *Notes of Debates in the Federal Convention of 1787* (New York: Norton Company, 1987), 209–10. The *National Intelligencer* account garbled other facts as well. The compromise proposal for equal state representation in the Senate came about well after Franklin's speech, and the adjournment referred to took place at a different time altogether and was not proposed by Franklin.

9. See Paul F. Boller, *George Washington and Religion* (Dallas: Southern Methodist University Press, 1963), 15–16.

10. Wright, quoted in ibid., 15. Even in some evangelical pulpits Washington's orthodoxy came under suspicion; in Albany, Episcopal divine Bird Wilson lamented that Washington "was a great and good man, but he was not a professor of religion" (quoted in ibid., 15).

11. E. C. McGuire, *The Religious Opinions and Character of Washington* (New York: Harper and Brothers, 1836).

12. William J. Johnson, *George Washington the Christian* (New York: Abingdon Press, 1919); John Eidsmoe, *Christianity and the Constitution: The Faith of Our Founding Fathers* (Grand Rapids, Mich.: Baker Book House, 1987); Edwin S. Gaustad, *Faith of Our Fathers: Religion and the New Nation* (San Francisco: Harper and Brothers, 1987); and Boller, *George Washington*. See also Norman Cousins, ed., *"In God We Trust": The Religious Beliefs and Ideas of the American Founding Fathers* (New York: Harper and Brothers, 1958).

13. John W. Whitehead, *The Second American Revolution* (Elgin, Ill.: David C. Cook, 1982), 190. This is a version of what has been called "the Christian America" thesis, the idea that America was founded as a peculiarly Christian nation. This interpretation, with its multitude of variations, has long roots in America (see John G. West, Jr., "The Politics of Revelation and Reason" [Ph.D. dissertation: Claremont, California, 1992], 17–20, 22–23).

For nineteenth-century expounders of the Christian America thesis, see Jasper Adams, *The Relation of Christianity to Civil Government in the United States,* 2d ed. (Charleston, S.C.: Miller, 1833), and Theodore Frelinghuysen, *An Inquiry into the Moral and Religious Character of the American Government* (New York: Wiley and Putnam, 1838); Gilbert McMaster, *The Moral Character of Civil Government, Considered with Reference to the Political Institutions of the United States* (Albany: Little, 1832; Robert Baird, *Religion in America* (New York: Harper Brothers, 1856), 240–61. For more recent defenders of this view (besides Whitehead), see Peter Marshall and David Manuel, *The Light and the Glory* (Old Tappan, N.J.: Fleming H. Revell, 1977); Francis A. Schaeffer, *A Christian Manifesto* (Westchester, Ill.: Crossway Books, 1981); and Peter Marshall and David Manuel, *From Sea to Shining Sea* (Old Tappan, N.J.: Fleming H. Revell, 1986).

14. Walter Berns, *The First Amendment and the Future of American Democracy* (New York: Basic Books, 1976), 26. More generally, see ibid., 1–32; Walter Berns and Edward R. Norman, "Christians, Politics, and the Modern State (with a comment by Walter Berns)," *This World* (Fall 1983): 97–98; Walter Berns and Harry Jaffa, "Were the Founding Fathers Christian?" *This World* (Spring–Summer 1984):

7; and Walter Berns, "Religion and the Founding Principle," in Robert H. Horowitz, ed., *The Moral Foundations of the American Republic,* 3d ed. (Charlottesville: University Press of Virginia, 1986), 223. A somewhat similar, if more nuanced version of this approach can be found in Thomas Pangle, *The Spirit of Modern Republicanism: The Moral Vision of the American Founders and the Philosophy of Locke* (Chicago: University of Chicago Press, 1988), 17–21, 82–85. Also see discussion of Berns and Pangle in West, "The Politics of Revelation and Reason," 11–17, 21–22.

15. Harry V. Jaffa, *The American Founding as the Best Regime* (Claremont, Calif.: Claremont Institute for the Study of Political Philosophy and Statesmanship, 1990), 15. Also see discussion in West, "The Politics of Revelation and Reason," 20–21, 23–24.

16. See, for example, *Reynolds* v. *United States* 98 U.S. 145 (1878) at 163–64 (C. J. Waite, opinion of the Court); *Everson* v. *Board of Education* 330 U.S. 1 (1947) at 11–13 (J. Black, opinion of the Court), 31, 33–46, 51–53, 57, 63–72 (J. Rutledge, dissenting); *McCollum* v. *Board of Education* 333 U.S. 203 (1948) at 214, 216, 231 (J. Frankfurter), at 238 (J. Jackson, concurring), at 245–48 (J. Reed, dissenting); *Engel* v. *Vitale* 370 U.S. 421 (1962) at 428, 436 (J. Black, opinion of the Court), at 444 (J. Douglas, concurring), at 447, n. 3 (J. Stewart, dissenting); *Abington School District* v. *Schempp* 374 U.S. 203 (1963) at 213–14, 225 (J. Clark, opinion of the Court), at 233–36, 281, n. 57 (J. Brennan, concurring); *Wallace* v. *Jaffree* 472 U.S. 38 (1985) at 91–100, 103 (J. Rehnquist, dissenting); *O'Lone* v. *Estate of Shabazz* 482 U.S. 342 (1987) at 356 (J. Brennan, dissenting).

17. This term can be found in Franklin, "Proposals Relating to the Education of Youth in Pennsylvania" (1749), in *The Papers of Benjamin Franklin,* ed. Leonard W. Labcree (New Haven: Yale University Press, 1959–), 3:413.

18. See Herbert Storing, *What the Anti-Federalists Were For* (Chicago: University of Chicago Press, 1981), 22–23.

19. See Alfred Owen Aldridge, *Man of Reason: The Life of Thomas Paine* (Philadelphia: Lippincott, 1959), 273–77, 282–83, 291–92, 312, 315.

20. Franklin, "Autobiography," in *Benjamin Franklin's Autobiography and Selected Writings* (New York: Holt, Rinehart and Winston, 1959), 14.

21. Ibid., 14–15; also see 87–88.

22. Franklin to Sarah Franklin (November 8, 1764), *Papers,* 11:449.

23. Franklin, "Autobiography," 104.

24. Franklin to Ezra Stiles (March 9, 1790), *Works of Benjamin Franklin,* ed. Jared Sparks (Philadelphia: Childs and Peterson, 1840), 10:425.

25. Franklin, "Poor Richard Improved" (1758), *Papers,* 7:341, 342.

26. Franklin, "Autobiography," 76–77.

27. Franklin, "Proposals Relating to the Education of Youth in Pennsylvania," *Papers,* 3:413.

28. Franklin, "Autobiography," 76–77.

29. Franklin wrote Reverend Ezra Stiles that he believed "in one God, the creator of the universe. That he governs it by his Providence. That he ought to be worshipped. That the most acceptable service we render to him is doing good to his other

children. That the soul of man is immortal, and will be treated with justice in another life respecting its conduct in this" (Franklin to Ezra Stiles [March 9, 1790], *Works,* 10: 423). On the other hand, in his "Articles and Belief and Acts of Religion" prepared for his own use in 1728, Franklin proclaimed that the God and Creator of our own solar system was but one of "many beings or Gods" created by a single most perfect being, the "Author and Father of the Gods themselves," who is so perfect that he is "INFINITELY ABOVE" praise or worship (Franklin, *Papers,* 1:102–3).

30. Pangle, *The Spirit of Modern Republicanism,* 80.

31. Franklin, speech to the Constitutional Convention on June 28, 1787, 209–10.

32. Ibid., 209.

33. For relevant examples of the terms "reproach" and "byword" in the Bible, see Deut. 28:37; Job 17:6, 30:9; Ps. 44:13–14, 79:4; 1 Kings 9:7; 2 Chron. 7:20; Jer. 24:9, 29:18, 44:8, 44:12; Ezek. 5:14, 5:15, 22.4; Dan. 9:16; Joel 2:19.

34. Even in the convention speech, one finds Franklin undercutting his own religious appeal. To be sure, he begins by deprecating human reason and advocating a reliance on divine wisdom, but he ends his speech by arguing that if the convention fails, "mankind may hereafter from this unfortunate instance, despair of establishing Governments *by Human wisdom* and leave it to chance, war and conquest" (emphasis added). What began therefore as a choice between human wisdom and divine wisdom is reduced to a stark choice between human wisdom and "chance, war and conquest" (see Pangle, *The Spirit of Modern Republicanism,* 80–81). The end of Franklin's speech anticipates Hamilton's opening in *Federalist* no. 1 (see Alexander Hamilton, James Madison, and John Jay, *The Federalist Papers* [New York: New American Library, 1961], 33).

35. Franklin, "Autobiography," 76.

36. Franklin to Madame Brillon, "The Ephemera" (September 20, 1778), *Papers,* 27:433–35.

37. Ibid., 433.

38. Ibid., 434–35; emphasis added.

39. Ibid., 435.

40. Franklin, "The Levee" (1779), *Works,* 2:164–66.

41. Ibid., 164.

42. Ibid., 165–66.

43. See also Franklin's attack on New England's strict observance of the Sabbath (Franklin to Jared Ingersoll, December 11, 1762 in Benjamin Franklin, *Writings* [New York: Library of America, 1987], 796). Four years after writing "The Ephemera," with all of its hints of agnosticism, Franklin wrote to James Hutton from Paris that he indeed believed in the existence of an afterlife, but Franklin's reasoning in the letter reads more like wish fulfillment than anything else: "The more I see the Impossibility, from the number & extent of his Crimes, of giving equivalent Punishment to a wicked Man in this Life, the more I am convinc'd of a future State, in which all that here appears to be wrong shall be set right, all that is crooked made straight. In this Faith let you & I, my dear Friend, comfort ourselves; it is the only

Comfort, in the present dark Scene of Things, that is allow'd us" (Franklin to James Hutton [July 7, 1782], *Writings* [Library of America ed.], 1052).

44. Franklin to Messrs. The Abbe's Chalut and Arnaud (April 17, 1787), *Writings of Benjamin Franklin,* ed. Albert Henry Smyth (New York: Macmillan, 1905–1907), 9:569.

45. Franklin, "Autobiography," 76–77, 100–102, 107.

46. Ibid., 53.

47. Ibid., 53–54.

48. Pangle, *The Spirit of Modern Republicanism,* 20.

49. Franklin, "Autobiography," 77–78.

50. Ibid., 78.

51. Ibid., 80–81.

52. Ibid., 85.

53. Matt. 22:37–39; Deut. 6:5; Lev. 19:18.

54. Franklin, "Autobiography," 77.

55. Ibid., 76.

56. Franklin to Samuel Mather (July 7, 1773), *Writings* (Library of America ed.), 880.

57. Franklin, "Autobiography," 76.

58. See John Locke, *The Reasonableness of Christianity, as Delivered in the Scriptures,* ed. George W. Ewing (Washington, D.C.: Regnery Gateway, 1965), 169–81, paras. 241–43; for a similar argument see Thomas Aquinas, *Treatise on Law* (Chicago: Regnery Gateway, n.d.), Q. 91, Art. 4, 21.

59. Franklin to ? (December 13, 1757), *Writings* (Library of America ed.), 748–49.

60. Franklin, "Autobiography," 82, 85–86.

61. Ibid., 86.

62. Ibid., 86–87.

63. Pangle adopts this view, writing that Franklin "simply did not conceive of obligation and duty" as something good for its own sake; instead, Franklin believed that "concern for the welfare of others might reasonably be grounded in or grow out of a properly educated hedonistic or utilitarian self-love, and that such self-love might be said to entail, or to be the only reasonable ground of, duties and obligations" (Pangle, *The Spirit of Modern Republicanism,* 18, 19).

64. This interpretation becomes plausible once one realizes that Franklin's purpose in his autobiography was to discourse, not on why virtue is good, but on how to acquire it. Like Aristotle, Franklin agreed that the virtuous life involved habituation; that is, one must practice the virtues in order to become moral; see Franklin, "Autobiography," 78, and Aristotle, *Nicomachean Ethics,* trans. Martin Otswald (Indianapolis: Bobbs-Merrill, 1962), bk. 2, 1103a15–20. Unlike Artistotle, however, Franklin was not primarily concerned with people who had already achieved moral virtue. Aristotle wrote for grown men of comfortable means, assuming that they had already obtained most of the moral virtues; he sought to provide them a better understanding of what they already practiced, and perhaps to point the way to the higher

nobility of the intellectual virtues (Aristotle, *Nicomachean Ethics*, bk. 1, 1094b25–1095a10; bk. 6, bk. 10). Franklin sought to influence people who had not yet chosen the road to virtue—the young and the poor. In other words, he was concerned with how to *start* the process of habituation. Hence the question Franklin sought to answer is logically prior to the one discussed by Aristotle.

One might paraphrase Franklin's argument this way: Convince the young that moral virtue is in their interest so they will begin to practice it; there will be time enough for them to realize that virtue is good for its own sake once they become properly habituated. This argument comes out in the passage cited above, in which Franklin initially says that vicious actions are hurtful "the nature of man alone considered" and that virtue leads to "happiness," a term that is not synonymous with simple material well-being, even for Franklin. It is only when Franklin discusses how he plans to persuade the young to practice virtue that he substitutes "fortune" for "happiness." For more on the distinction between fortune and happiness in Franklin, read "On True Happiness" (*Pennsylvania Gazette*, November 20, 1735), *Works*, 2:72. Although Franklin probably did not write this article (see *Papers*, 1:170), it still may reflect his views because he regarded even his reprints of articles on morality as part of his "communicating instruction" to the public ("Autobiography," 92).

Interestingly, a much more explicit example of this same rhetorical approach (by which one ascends from self-interest to true virtue) can be found in two dialogues Franklin reprinted in the *Pennsylvania Gazette* in 1730. In the first dialogue, Philocles persuades Horatio to practice self-denial in his pleasure-seeking because such temperance will in fact lead to the greatest material pleasure in the long term by safeguarding his "health, convenience, or circumstances in the world." In the second dialogue, however, after Horatio has learned to behave temperately, Philocles leads him away from material pleasures to the "rational and moral good" that consists of "doing all the good we can to others, by acts of humanity, friendship, generosity, and benevolence; this is that constant and durable good which will afford contentment and satisfaction always alike, without variation or dimunition." Philocles continues that "the foundation of all virtue and happiness is thinking rightly. He who sees an action is right, that is, naturally tending to good, and does it because of that tendency, he only is a moral man; and he alone is capable of that constant, durable, and invariable good, which has been the subject of this conversation" ("Dialogue Between Philocles and Horatio, meeting accidentally in the fields, concerning virtue and pleasure," *Pennsylvania Gazette*, June 23, 1730, and "A Second Dialogue Between Philocles and Horatio, concerning virtue and pleasure," *Pennsylvania Gazette*, July 9, 1730, both in *Works*, 2:46–57).

65. Franklin, "Autobiography," 86, 90–91. This statement assumes that the society was not one of Franklin's fanciful creations, something that is not at all clear.

66. Franklin to Samuel Mather (May 12, 1784), *Writings* (Library of America ed.), 1092.

67. Franklin's appropriation of religious themes during the ratification struggle is also apropos. See "A Comparison of the Conduct of the Ancient Jews and of the Anti-Federalists in the United States of America," *Works*, 5:158–62.

68. Franklin to ? (December 13, 1757), *Writings* (Library of America ed.), 749.

69. See, for example, John Witherspoon, *The Absolute Necessity of Salvation Through Christ* (Edinburgh: Miller, 1758).

70. Jack Scott, "Biographical Sketch," in John Witherspoon, *Annotated Edition of Lectures on Moral Philosophy,* ed. Jack Scott (Newark: University of Delaware Press, 1982), 7-8.

71. Ibid., 16-25.

72. See John Maclean, *History of the College of New Jersey,* 2 vols. (Philadelphia: Lippincott, 1877), 1:359-61.

73. The list of subscribers to the editions of Witherspoon's *Works* appears at the end of the fourth volume. For George Washington's correspondence about subscribing to Witherspoon's *Works,* see Washington to secretary of state (November 24, 1799) and Washington to William W. Woodward (November 24, 1799), *Writings of George Washington,* ed. John Fitzpatrick, 39 vols. (Washington, D.C.: United States George Washington Bicentennial Commission, 1931-1944), 37: 439-40.

74. Witherspoon, "[Sermon] Delivered at a Publick Thanksgiving," *The Works of Reverend John Witherspoon,* 2d. ed., 4 vols. (Philadelphia: Woodward, 1802), 3:81.

75. Witherspoon, *Lectures,* lecture 14, Jurisprudence, 159.

76. Ibid., 160-61; also see "A Pastoral Letter from the Synod of New York and Philadelphia," in Witherspoon, *Works,* 3:14. Witherspoon drafted this letter from the synod.

77. Witherspoon, *Lectures,* lecture 8, 111; lecture 10, Of Politics, 123.

78. Ibid., lecture 14, 160.

79. Ibid. This passage is an implicit attack on John Locke, who ruled out toleration for papists. See John Locke, *A Letter Concerning Toleration* (Indianapolis: Bobbs-Merrill, 1955), 50-51.

80. "Pastoral Letter," in Witherspoon's *Works,* 3:14.

81. Witherspoon, *Lectures,* lecture 14, 160.

82. Ibid., 161.

83. Ibid.

84. Leonard W. Levy, *The Establishment Clause: Religion and the First Amendment* (New York: Macmillan, 1986), 20, 22, 23-24. After the Revolution the exemption system was gradually replaced with multiple establishments, which allowed religious adherents to pay taxes to the church of their choice (ibid., 25-26).

85. See Leonard W. Levy, *Emergence of a Free Press* (New York: Oxford University Press, 1985), in particular xii, 16-88.

86. Witherspoon, *Lectures,* lecture 8, 111.

87. These lectures unfortunately exist in rather incomplete form. Witherspoon apparently delivered them from brief notes, which he expanded in class. As he never prepared an edition of his lectures for publication, the only remnants are copies of the notes themselves, apparently transcribed from Witherspoon's originals by some of his students. Despite the fragmentary nature of the notes, they do provide the fundamental contours of Witherspoon's thoughts in this area, and when coupled with

his other writings, one may gain a fairly complete comprehension of his views (see Scott, "Biographical Sketch," 29).

88. Witherspoon, *Lectures,* lecture 1, 64.

89. Witherspoon is referring here to Cotton Mather; see ibid., 64, 68 n. 1.

90. Ibid., 64.

91. Ibid., 65.

92. See, for example, Witherspoon's discussion in lecture 4 of the foundation of virtue (ibid., 85-87). Witherspoon concludes, with regard to the various opinions on the subject, "that there is something true in every one of them, but that they may be easily pushed to an error by excess" (86). Also see the discussion of the grounds of divine dominion in lecture 7, 104; Witherspoon's harmonization of Hobbes and Hutchinson-Shaftsbury on the state of nature in lecture 10, 122; and Witherspoon's recapitulation at the end, 186-87.

93. Witherspoon, "Christian Magnanimity, Sermon 46," *Works,* 3:87-99, and "An Address to the Students of the Senior Class" (September 23, 1775), *Works,* 3: 101-20.

94. For example, moderation in drink and eating facilitates health, and noble actions bring praise and fame from one's peers. Hence, certain virtues are universally approved, even by the impious. These virtues include "truth and integrity in speech, honesty in dealing, humanity and compassion to persons in distress" (Witherspoon, "Address to Senior Class," *Works,* 3:104, and "Christian Magnanimity," *Works,* 3:83).

95. Witherspoon, "Address to Senior Class," *Works,* 3:104.

96. Aristotle, *Nicomachean Ethics,* bk. 4, 1124a1-5.

97. Ibid., 1124b.

98. Ibid., 1123b1-4, 15-20.

99. Witherspoon, "Christian Magnanimity," *Works,* 3:88.

100. Ibid., 89. See, for example, Niccolò Machiavelli, *The Discourses,* trans. Leslie J. Walker, ed. Bernard Crick (Harmondsworth, Eng.: Penguin, 1983), bk. 2, discourse 2, 278.

101. Aquinas similarly tried to square magnanimity with Christianity by reinterpreting it; see Aquinas, *Summa Theologiae,* ed. Anthony Ross and P. G. Walsh (New York: McGraw-Hill, 1966), II-II, question 129.

102. Witherspoon, "Christian Magnanimity," *Works,* 3:94-97.

103. Ibid., 95.

104. Ibid., 98-99.

105. Ibid., 99.

106. Witherspoon, "[Sermon] Delivered at a Publick Thanksgiving," *Works,* 3:84.

107. Ibid.

108. See Anson Phelps Stokes, *Church and State in the United States,* 3 vols. (New York: Harper and Brothers, 1950), 149-53, and Leonard W. Levy, *Treason Against God: A History of the Offense of Blasphemy* (New York: Schocken Books, 1981), 333-34.

109. Witherspoon, "Address to Senior Class," *Works,* 3:104.

110. Witherspoon, "[Sermon] Delivered at a Publick Thanksgiving," *Works,* 3:82.

111. Ibid., 83.

112. Witherspoon, "On the Georgia Constitution," *Works,* 3: 421–23.

113. John Witherspoon, *The Dominion of Providence over the Passions of Men,* 2d ed. (Glasgow, 1777), and "[Sermon] Delivered at a Publick Thanksgiving," in *Works,* 3:62.

114. Witherspoon, "Address to Senior Class," *Works,* 3:104–5.

115. Washington to Reformed German Congregation, New York (November 23, 1783), *Writings,* 27:249.

116. Washington to William Pearce (May 25, 1794), *Writings,* 33:375.

117. Washington to Henry Knox (March 2, 1797), *Writings,* 35:408–9.

118. See Benson J. Lossing, *The Pictorial Field-Book of the Revolution,* 2 vols. (New York: Harper and Brothers, 1859), 2:215 n. 2.

119. Washington, "Circular to the States," (June 8, 1783), *Writings,* 26:496.

120. See Boller, *George Washington and Religion,* 24–44.

121. Washington to Marquis de LaFayette (August 15, 1787), *Writings,* 29:259.

122. Washington to Hebrew Congregation in Newport, Rhode Island (August 17, 1790), *George Washington on Religious Liberty and Mutual Understanding: Selections from Washington's Letters,* ed. Edward Frank Humphrey (Washington, D.C.: National Conference of Catholics, Jews, Protestants, 1932), 22.

123. Washington to General Assembly of the Presbyterian Church (May 1789), ibid., 15.

124. See Washington's letter to the Religious Society Called Quakers (October 1789), ibid., 11.

125. Washington, "Farewell Address" (September 19, 1796), *Writings,* 35:229.

126. See Washington, "General Orders" (July 4, 1775), *Writings,* 3:309; "General Orders" (July 9, 1776), 5:245; "General Orders" (August 3, 1776), 367; and "General Orders" (July 29, 1779), 16:13.

127. See, for example, Washington's appointment of a day of thanksgiving after America's victory in the battle of Monmouth (Washington, "General Orders" [June 30, 1778], *Writings,* 12:131).

128. Washington to Reverend John Rodgers (June 11, 1783), *Writings,* 27:1.

129. Washington to George Mason (October 3, 1785), *Writings,* 28:285.

130. Washington, "Thanksgiving Proclamation" (October 3, 1789), *Writings,* 30:427–28, and "A Proclamation" (January 1, 1795), in *Compilation of the Messages and Papers of the Presidents,* ed. James D. Richardson (Washington, D.C.: Bureau of National Literature, 1897), 1:171.

131. Washington, "General Orders" (July 29, 1779), *Writings,* 16:13.

132. See, for example, Washington, "General Orders," (July 4, 1775), *Writings,* 3:309; Washington to major and brigadier generals (September 8, 1775), 483; "General Orders" (July 9, 1776), 5:245; "General Orders" (August 3, 1776), 367; "General Orders" (July 29, 1779), 16:13; Washington to General Assembly of the Presby-

terian Church (May 1789), *George Washington on Religious Liberty,* 15; Washington to the Religious Society Called Quakers (October 1789), ibid., 11; Washington to the Roman Catholics in the United States (December 1789), ibid., 10; Washington to New Church, Baltimore (January 27, 1793), *Writings,* 32:315; "A Proclamation" (January 1, 1795), in *Complilation of Messages of the Presidents,* 1:171.

133. Washington to the Roman Catholics in the United States (December 1789), *George Washington on Religious Liberty,* 10.

134. Presbyterians, like most Protestants of the reformed tradition, stressed the necessity of God's blessing to secure civil as well as personal happiness. They also stressed the need for public morality and piety. Hence Washington's letter to them emphasizes these very points: "While I reiterate the professions of my dependence upon Heaven as the source of all public and private blessings; I will observe that the general prevalence of piety, philanthropy, honesty, industry and economy seems, in the ordinary course of human affairs, particularly necessary for advancing and confirming the happiness of our country" (Washington to General Assembly of the Presbyterian Church [May 1789], *George Washington on Religious Liberty,* 15).

135. Methodists were known for the vitality and enthusiasm of their religious meetings, so Washington's choice of words in his letter to them was particularly appropriate: "I shall always strive to prove a faithful and impartial patron of *genuine, vital* religion" (Washington to the bishops of the Methodist Episcopal Church in the United States [May 29, 1789], *George Washington on Religious Liberty,* 7; emphasis added).

136. "May the Children of the Stock of Abraham, who dwell in this land, continue to merit and enjoy the good will of the other Inhabitants, while every one shall sit in safety under his own vine and fig-tree, and there shall be none to make him afraid" (Washington to Hebrew Congregation in Newport, Rhode Island, 22). The latter half of the sentence is taken from Micah 4:4.

137. Washington to the Roman Catholics in the United States, 10.

138. See Boller, *George Washington and Religion,* 24-25.

139. Washington to General Assembly of the Presbyterian Church, 15.

140. Washington to the Religious Society Called Quakers, 11; emphasis added.

141. Ibid.

142. See, for example, *West Virginia State Board of Education* v. *Barnette,* 319 U.S. 624 (1943); *Sherbert* v. *Verner,* 374 U.S. 398 (1963); *Gillette* v. *United States,* 401 U.S. 437 (1971); *Wisconsin* v. *Yoder,* 406 U.S. 205 (1972); *Hobbie* v. *Unemployment Appeals Commission of Florida,* 480 U.S. 136 (1987). The Supreme Court abandoned this approach for free exercise claims in *Employment Division, Department of Human Resources of Oregon* v. *Smith,* 110 S. Ct. 1595 (1990) .

143. Washington to George Mason (October 3, 1785), *Writings,* 28:285.

144. Pierce, "Character Sketches," 92.

145. See "James Wilson," *Dictionary of American Biography,* ed. Allen Johnson and Dumas Malone (New York: Charles Scribner's Sons, 1931), 20:326-30; *The Works of James Wilson,* ed. Robert Green McCloskey (Cambridge, Mass.: Belknap

Press, 1967), 1:1-48; and Geoffrey Seed, *James Wilson* (Millwood, N.Y.: KTO Press, 1978).

146. See Wilson's attack on Blackstone in his inaugural law lecture and his statement that "the elements of a law education [in America] ought to be drawn from our own constitutions and governments and laws." Of course, this was precisely what Wilson himself was attempting to do with his course of lectures (James Wilson, "Lectures on Law" in *Works,* 1:76-81).

147. Ibid., 123, 146.

148. Ibid., 123.

149. Ibid., 123-24.

150. Ibid., 124.

151. Ibid., 143-44.

152. Ibid., 144.

153. Ibid., 199-200.

154. In a lecture on "Man, as an Individual," for example, Wilson introduced one part of his discussion of the faculties of the human mind by paraphrasing Psalm 139: "Nay, as the mind is of an order higher than that of the body, even more of the wisdom and skill of the divine Architect is displayed in its structure. In all respects, fearfully and wonderfully are we made" (ibid., 102). Similarly, Wilson began his lecture on "Man, as a Member of Society" with a reference to the book of Genesis: " 'It is not fit that man should be alone,' said the all-wise and all-gracious Author of our frame, who knew it, because he made it; and who looked with compassion on the first solitary state of the work of his hands" (ibid., 227). Wilson likewise prefaced his discussion of the natural equality of men with an implied reference to Adam as the source of the whole human race: "In civil society, previously to the institution of civil government, all men are equal. Of one blood all nations are made; from one source the whole human race has sprung" (ibid., 240; Acts 17: 26 [KJV]). Also see Wilson's discussion of the common law doctrine that husband and wife become one person in the sight of the law. "They twain shall be one flesh" ("Lectures on Law," 2:601).

155. Wilson occasionally brings to view the importance of religion alone in maintaining—and reforming—social mores. In his discussion of marriage, he first described the oppression and dehumanization of wives in pagan cultures and then added: "By the precepts of christianity, and the practice of the christians, the dignity of marriage was, however, restored" (ibid., 1:240). In a somewhat similar vein, Wilson's argument against suicide demonstrates how some public arguments must inevitably be framed in religious terms. Wilson began by noting a seeming discrepancy between the natural law as applied to nations and as applied to individuals. A nation, being a voluntary compact of persons, may rightfully terminate itself, but a human being may not. "What can be the reasons of this difference?" asks Wilson. "Several may be given. By the voluntary act of the individuals forming the nation, the nation was called into existence: they who bind, can also untie: by the voluntary act, therefore, of the individuals forming the nation, the nation may be reduced to its original nothing. But it was not by his own voluntary act that the man made his appearance upon the theatre of life; he cannot, therefore, plead the right of the nation,

by his own voluntary act to make his exit. He did not make; therefore, he has no right to destroy himself. He alone, whose gift this state of existence is, has the right to say when and how it shall receive its termination (ibid., 1:155). We owe our earthly existence to God alone, says Wilson; therefore God alone has the right to end that existence.

156. "The arts, the sciences, philosophy, virtue, and religion, all contribute to the happiness, all, therefore, ought to receive the encouragement, of the nation. In this manner, public and private felicity will go hand in hand, and mutually assist each other in their progress" (ibid., 1:146). "A third means for augmenting the number of inhabitants is, to preserve the rights of conscience inviolate. The right of private judgment is one of the greatest advantages of mankind; and is always considered as such. To be deprived of it is insufferable. To enjoy it lays a foundation for that peace of mind, which the laws cannot give, and for the loss of which the laws can offer no compensation" (159). Also see Wilson's comments on religious freedom in America as established by Lord Baltimore in Maryland (71).

157. For a much fuller description of this criticism, as well as a more thorough rebuttal, see West, "The Politics of Revelation and Reason," 86–95.

158. Wilson, "Lectures on Law," 1:232–33.

159. Ibid., 2:694.

160. Ibid. Wilson is quoting Beccaria almost verbatim; see Cesare Beccaria-Bonesana, *An Essay on Crimes and Punishments* (Stanford: Academic Reprints, 1953), 72–73.

161. See Forrest McDonald, *Alexander Hamilton, a Biography* (New York: Norton, 1979), 29–30, 74–79, 112–13.

162. Ibid., 14.

163. See Hamilton, "Letters from Phocion," in *Works of Alexander Hamilton,* ed. Henry Cabot Lodge (New York: Putnam's Sons, 1904), 4:230–90.

164. Hamilton, "Printed version of the 'Reynolds Pamphlet,' " in *The Papers of Alexander Hamilton,* ed. Harold C. Syrett (New York: Columbia University Press, 1961–), 21:238–85.

165. See James Hamilton, *Reminiscences of James A. Hamilton* (New York: Charles Scribner, 1869), 3–5.

166. Hamilton to the *Royal Danish-American Gazette* (September 6, 1772, published on October 3, 1772), *Papers,* 1:34–38; also see "The Soul Ascending into Bliss," ibid., 38–39.

167. McDonald, *Alexander Hamilton,* 10–11.

168. See Douglass Adair and Marvin Harvey, "Was Alexander Hamilton a Christian Statesman?" in *Fame and the Founding Fathers: Essays by Douglass Adair,* ed. Trevor Colbourn (New York: Norton, 1974), 146–48.

169. Ibid., 149–56.

170. Hamilton, "Draft of Washington's Farewell Address," *Papers,* 20: 265–88.

171. Plutarch as paraphrased by Hamilton in the second section of his "Pay Book of the State Company of Artillery" (1777), *Papers,* 1:405; Adair and Harvey draw

the connection between this quote and Hamilton's view on the civil use of religion (Adair and Harvey, "Was Alexander Hamilton a Christian Statesman?" 149).

172. Hamilton to William L. Smith (April 10, 1797), *Papers,* 21:41.

173. Hamilton, "The Stand No. III" (April 7, 1798), ibid., 402–5.

174. Hamilton, "Draft of Washington's Farewell Address," ibid., 201. Hamilton, "The Stand No. III" (April 7, 1798), *Papers,* 21: 405

175. As an example of the partisan tome of "The Stand," consider: "The attempt by the rulers of a nation to destroy all religious opinion, and to pervert a whole people to Atheism, is a phenomenon of profligacy reserved to consummate the infamy of the unprincipled reformers of France" (Hamilton, "The Stand No. III" [April 7, 1798], *Papers,* 21:402–3.

176. See John M. Mason, "The Voice of Warning to Christians on the Ensuing Election of a President of the United States" (1800), in *Complete Works of John M. Mason,* ed. Ebenezer Mason (New York: Baker and Scribner, 1849), 4:533–79.

177. Hamilton to James A. Bayard (April 16–21, 1802), *Papers,* 25:605–10.

178. Adair and Harvey, "Was Alexander Hamilton a Christian Statesman?" 156–57.

179. God "has constituted an eternal and immutable law, which is indispensably obligatory upon all mankind, prior to any human institution whatever" but he has also "endowed [man] with rational faculties, by the help of which, to discern and pursue such things, as were consistent with his duty and interest" (Hamilton, "The Farmer Refuted," *Papers,* 1:87–88).

180. Aaron Burr to Hamilton (June 18, 1804), ibid., 26:242–46.

181. Hamilton to Burr (June 20, 1804), ibid., 248.

182. Hamilton, quoted in "Nathaniel Pendleton's Second Account of Alexander Hamilton's Conversation at John Tayler's House" (June 25, 1804), ibid., 263.

183. Burr's position as described by his second in William P. Van Ness to Nathaniel Pendleton (June 26, 1804), ibid., 268.

184. Hamilton's position as described by his second in Nathaniel Pendleton to William P. Van Ness (June 26, 1804), ibid., 270.

185. See Hamilton, "Statement on Impending Duel with Aaron Burr," (June 28–July 10, 1804), ibid., 280.

186. Ibid., 279.

187. Hamilton to Elizabeth Hamilton (July 10, 1804), ibid., 308.

188. See "Nathaniel Pendleton's Amendments to the Joint Statement Made by William P. Van Ness and Him on the Duel Between Alexander Hamilton and Aaron Burr" (July 19, 1804), ibid., 338, 339.

189. See "William P. Van Ness's Amendments to the Joint Statement Made by Nathaniel Pendleton and Him on the Duel Between Alexander Hamilton and Aaron Burr" (July 21, 1804), ibid., 340–41.

190. See "Nathaniel Pendleton's Amendments," ibid., 337–39; "Benjamin Moore to William Coleman" (July 12, 1804), ibid., 316; and "David Hosack to William Coleman" (August 17, 1804), ibid., 344–47.

191. Adams to Benjamin Rush (August 28, 1811), in *Works of John Adams,* ed. Charles Francis Adams (Boston: Little, Brown, 1856), 9: 640.

192. Adams, "Proclamation for a National Fast" (March 23, 1798), ibid., 169–70; and "Proclamation for a National Fast" (March 6, 1799), ibid., 172–74.

193. Adams to Thomas Jefferson (December 3, 1813), *Adams-Jefferson Letters,* ed. Lester J. Cappon (Chapel Hill: University of North Carolina Press, 1959), 2:403.

194. Adams to F. A. Vanderkemp (December 27, 1816), *Works,* 10:234.

195. Adams to Thomas Jefferson (December 25, 1813), *Adams-Jefferson Letters,* 2:412. In another letter to Jefferson Adams similarly wrote, "The human Understanding is a revelation from its Maker, which can never be disputed or doubted" (September 14, 1813; ibid., 373).

196. Adams's diary (March 2, 1756), *Diary and Autobiography of John Adams,* ed. L. H. Butterfield (Cambridge, Mass.: Belknap Press, 1961), 1:11.

197. Adams to Thomas Jefferson (September 14, 1813), *Adams-Jefferson Letters,* 2:373.

198. Adams's diary (August 14, 1796), *Diary,* 3:240–41.

199. Adams to Samuel Miller (July 8, 1820), *Works,* 10:390.

200. Adams wrote to John Taylor in 1814: "A large proportion of *'the wars, rebellions, persecutions, and oppressions,'* in England have arisen from ecclesiastical artifices, and the intoxication of religious enthusiasm. Are you sure that any form of government can at all times secure the people from fanaticism? Although this country has done much, are you confident that our moral, civil, or political liberties are perfectly safe on this quarter?" (*Works,* 6:489).

201. "Addressed to the Inhabitants of the Province of Massachusetts Bay" (December 19, 1774), in *Novanglus, and Massachusettensis; or, Political Essays Published in the Years 1774 and 1775* (Boston: Hews and Goss, 1819), 151.

202. "To the Inhabitants of the Colony of Massachusetts-Bay" (February 13, 1775), in *Papers of John Adams,* ed. Robert Taylor (Cambridge, Mass.: Belknap Press, 1977–), 2:266.

203. Ibid., 266–67. Once America officially separated itself from England, however, Adams became as intolerant of Tory ministers as Massachusettensis had been of patriot clergy. Upon learning from his wife that a minister in Massachusetts continued to offer prayers for the king, Adams commented, "This practice is Treason against the State and cannot be long tolerated." The minister in question was eventually forced to flee. See Abigail Adams to John Adams (September 29, 1776), *Adams Family Correspondence,* ed. L. H. Butterfield (Cambridge, Mass.: Belknap Press, 1963), 2:135, 136 n. 4; John Adams to Abigail Adams (October 7, 1776), ibid., 141; and Abigail Adams to John Adams (April 2, 1777), ibid., 194.

204. Although the statement cited was made early in Adams's career, Adams republished the essays in which this passage appears in 1819, and in his preface to the collection he indicated that the essays still reflected his views: "More conscious than ever of the faults in the style and arrangement, if not in the matter of my part of the following papers, I shall see them in print with more anxiety than when they were first published. The principles however are those on which I then conscientiously

acted, and which I now most cordially approve" (Adams, *Novanglus, and Massachu-settensis,* vii).

205. See "John Jay," in *Dictionary of American Biography,* 10:5–10.

206. Jay to John Murray, Jr. (April 15, 1818), in *Correspondence and Public Papers of John Jay,* ed. Henry Johnston (New York: Putnam's Sons, 1890–1893), 4:403.

207. Ibid., 403–4.

208. Ibid.

209. Jay to Edward Livingston (July 28, 1822), ibid., 465.

210. Jay to John Murray, Jr. (April 15, 1818), ibid., 406.

211. Ibid., 408.

212. Hamilton implied this same idea in "The Stand No. III" (April 7, 1798), *Papers,* 21:403, 405.

213. Jay, "Jay's Charge to the Grand Jury of Ulster County," *Papers,* 1:162–63.

214. Quoted by Richard B. Morris in *John Jay: The Making of a Revolutionary, Unpublished Papers, 1745–1780,* ed. Richard B. Morris (San Francisco: Harper and Row, 1975), 392.

215. Ibid.

216. Ibid.

217. Ibid.

218. Ibid., 15.

219. See, for example, G. W. Musgrave, *A Vindication of Religious Liberty* (Baltimore, John W. Woods, 1834). When a Catholic was selected as a Senate chaplain in 1832, he felt obliged to state in a speech: "I acknowledge no allegiance of the Pope's temporal power—I am no subject of his dominions—I have sworn no fealty to his throne—but I am, as all American Catholics glory to be, independent of all temporal authority—devoted to freedom, to unqualified toleration, to republican institutions" (quoted in Stokes, *Church and State,* 3:130). More recently, one might also think of John F. Kennedy's famous speech during the presidential campaign of 1960.

220. See Anson Phelps Stokes and Leo Pfeffer, *Church and State in the United States* (Westport, Conn: Greenwood Press, 1975), 83.

221. Article 39 of the New York Constitution of 1777 stated: "And whereas the ministers of the gospel are, by their profession, dedicated to the service of God and the cure of souls, and ought not to be diverted from the great duties of their function; therefore, no minister of the gospel or priest of any denomination whatsoever, shall at any time hereafter, under any pretence or description whatever, be eligible to, or capable of holding, any civil or military office of place within this State" (quoted in Stokes and Pfeffer, *Church and State,* 159). Note, however, that the exclusion is justified in terms of its benefits to religion, not as an attempt to reduce the influence of religion on government.

222. This incident is reported by James Hamilton, who commented that it was "so characteristic of Mr. Jay's Huguenot prejudice, that it will bear repetition" (Hamilton, *Reminiscences,* 43–44).

223. Jay to Edward Livingston (July 28, 1822), *Papers,* 4:465.

224. Jay to Jedidiah Morse (January 1, 1813), ibid., 365–66.

225. See letters to William Short (August 4, 1820), in *Jefferson's Extracts from the Gospels,* ed. Dickinson W. Adams (Princeton: Princeton University Press, 1983), 394–99; Jared Sparks (November 4, 1820), ibid., 401–2; and Timothy Pickering (February 27, 1821), ibid., 402–3. Also see letter to William Short on October 19, 1819, in which Jefferson lists the "artificial systems" grafted onto Christianity that he rejects: "The immaculate conception of Jesus, his deification, the creation of the world by him, his miraculous powers, his resurrection and visible ascension, his corporeal presence in the Eucharist, the Trinity; original sin, atonement, regeneration, election, orders of Hierarchy, &c." (Jefferson, *Writings* [New York: Library of America, 1984], 1431).

226. Jefferson, *Notes on the State of Virginia,* ed. William Peden (New York: Norton, 1954), 147.

227. See Jefferson to Reverend Samuel Miller (January 23, 1808), *Writings* (Library of America ed.), 1186–87.

228. See "A Bill for Punishing Disturbers of Religious Worship and Sabbath Breakers" and "A Bill Appointing Days of Public Fasts and Thanksgiving," in *Papers of Thomas Jefferson,* ed. Julian Boyd (Princeton: Princeton University Press, 1950–), 2:555–56.

229. Robert Cord, *Separation of Church and State* (New York: Lambeth Press, 1982), 38–39, 190, 224; Daniel Dreisbach, *Real Threat and Mere Shadow* (Westchester, Ill.: Crossway Books, 1987), 127–29, 130; James O'Neill, *Religion and Education Under the Constitution* (New York: Harper and Brothers, 1949), 77, 116–17.

230. See, for example, Jefferson, "Second Annual Message" (December 15, 1802), in *Writings of Thomas Jefferson,* ed. Andrew Lipscomb, 20 vols. (Washington, D.C.: Thomas Jefferson Memorial Association, 1903–1904), 3:340; "Second Inaugural Address" (March 4, 1805), ibid., 383; and "Eighth Annual Message" (November 8, 1808), ibid., 485.

231. Jefferson, "Second Inaugural Address" (March 4, 1805), ibid., 383.

232. Jefferson, *Notes on the State of Virginia,* 161.

233. Ibid., 160.

234. This argument was more fully developed (and more consistently maintained) by James Madison; see Madison to Thomas Jefferson (August 20, 1785), *Writings of James Madison,* ed. Gaillard Hunt (New York: Putnam's Sons, 1900–1910), 2:163–64; and *Federalist* no. 51, *Federalist Papers,* 324–25; also see *Federalist* no. 10, *Federalist Papers,* 79, 83–84; and Madison, speech before the Virginia Ratifying Convention (June 12, 1788), *Writings,* 5:176. Toward the end of his life, Jefferson appears to have abandoned the argument that sectarianism protects religious liberty, instead preferring to argue for the eventual triumph of Unitarianism over other sects.

235. Jefferson, "First Inaugural Address" (March 4, 1801), *Writings* (Lipscomb ed.), 3:320; also note the ritual invocation at the end of the speech, "And may that Infinite Power which rules the destinies of the universe lead our councils to what is best, and give them a favorable issue for your peace and prosperity" (ibid., 323).

236. We often forget what a strange and marvelous thing it was for the party in

power to quietly leave office after losing the election. As Harry Jaffa points out, "The election of 1800 in the United States was the first time that the losers gave up their offices peacefully and the winners did not proscribe their defeated opponents by death, imprisonment, loss of property, exile, or even the lost of civil or political rights" (Jaffa, *American Founding,* 9). Given the unprecedented nature of the occasion, it was all the more incumbent upon Jefferson to try to bind the nation's wounds and allay the fears of those who opposed him.

237. Jefferson, "First Inaugural," *Writings* (Lipscomb ed.), 3:319.

238. For an example of the clergy's attack on Jefferson, see John M. Mason, "The Voice of Warning to Christians," *Works,* 4:533-79.

239. Jefferson to Peter Carr (August 10, 1787), *Papers,* 12:14-15; to Thomas Law (June 13, 1814), *Jefferson's Extracts,* 355-58.

240. Jefferson to Peter Carr (August 10, 1787), *Papers,* 12:16.

241. Jefferson opposed incorporating the Bible into the education of young children, and he did not think public universities should have professors of divinity (Jefferson, *Notes on the State of Virginia,* 147).

242. See Eugene R. Sheridan, "Introduction," *Jefferson's Extracts,* 3-4, 12-16, 20-42; and Jefferson to Joseph Priestly (April 9, 1803), ibid., 327-29.

243. Jefferson to John Adams (May 5, 1817), *Adams-Jefferson Letters,* 2:512; Jefferson's letter was a response to a letter Adams had sent; see John Adams to Thomas Jefferson (April 19, 1817), ibid., 509.

244. Jefferson to William Short (April 13, 1820), *Jefferson's Extracts,* 392.

245. Jefferson to William Short (August 4, 1820), ibid., 396.

246. Jefferson to James Smith (December 8, 1822), ibid., 409.

247. Jefferson to Thomas Cooper (November 2, 1822), *Writings* (Library of America ed.), 1464.

248. Jefferson to Benjamin Waterhouse (June 26, 1822), *Jefferson's Extracts,* 405.

249. Ibid.

250. Jefferson to Thomas Cooper (November 2, 1822), *Writings* (Library of America ed.), 1464.

251. Jefferson to William Short (April 13, 1820), *Jefferson's Extracts,* 393.

252. "We have most unwisely committed to the hierophants of our particular superstition, the direction of public opinion. . . . We have given them stated and privileged days to collect and catechise us" (ibid).

253. "To suffer the civil magistrate to intrude his powers into the field of opinion and to restrain the profession or propagation of principles on supposition of their ill tendency is a dangerous fallacy, which at once destroys all religious liberty, because he being of course judge of that tendency will make his opinions the rule of judgment, and approve or condemn the sentiments of others only as they shall square with or suffer from his own" ("A Bill for Establishing Religious Freedom," *Writings of Thomas Jefferson,* ed. Paul Leicester Ford, 10 vols. [New York: Putnam's Sons, 1892-1899], 2:239).

254. Jefferson to William Short (April 13, 1820), *Jefferson's Extracts,* 393.

255. "Review: Memoirs of Dr. Joseph Priestly . . . and Observations on His Writings, by Thomas Cooper," *Virginia Evangelical and Literary Magazine* (February 1820): 63-74.

256. Dumas Malone, *Jefferson and His Time* (Boston: Little, Brown, 1981), 6:377; Nathaniel Francis Cabell, ed., *Early History of the University of Virginia, as Contained in the Letters of Thomas Jefferson and Joseph C. Cabell* (Richmond, Va.: Randolph, 1856), 234, editor's note.

257. "Review: Memoirs of Dr. Joseph Priestly," 70-72.

258. Ibid., 68, 72.

259. Ibid., 70, 72.

260. Cooper, quoted in ibid., 69; emphasis by Rice deleted.

261. Ibid., 69.

262. "We . . . think that Dr. C. wants some of the most important requisites in the character of a true philosopher. He who has been disciplined in the school of 'the child-like sage' Newton is modest, is humble, is patient in investigation, and slow to form general conclusions. But Dr. C. appears in his book rash, dogmatical, and peremptory. The intrepidity of his conclusions is really appalling; his hardihood is fearful. At the same time his prejudices appear to us violent; and all his liberality is reserved for his own party. Hobbes, and Collins, and Lindsey and Disney, and men of their stamp, are the true philosophers; while Reid and Beattie and Horsley and Porteus, are feeble and sophistical—mere lady philosophers. Now we do not think it good for the republic or for the interests of sound learning that our young citizens should go forth teeming with arrogance and self conceit, despising all others, and thinking that 'they are the men and that wisdom will die when they die' " (ibid., 72-73).

263. Malone, *Jefferson and His Time,* 6:377.

264. Jefferson to Thomas Cooper (November 2, 1822), *Writings* (Library of America ed.), 1464.

265. Cabell to Jefferson (August 5, 1821), *Early History of the University of Virginia,* 215.

266. Ibid.; Malone, *Jefferson and His Time,* 6:397; Sadie Bell, *The Church, the State, and Education in Virginia* (Philadelphia: Science Press Printing, 1930), 373-74.

267. Cabell to Jefferson (January 14, 1822), *Early History of the University of Virginia,* 233.

268. Jefferson to William Short (April 13, 1820), *Jefferson's Extracts,* 393.

269. See Report of the Board of Visitors of the University of Virginia (October 7, 1822), *Writings* (Lipscomb ed.), 19:414.

270. Jefferson to Benjamin Waterhouse (June 26, 1822), *Jefferson's Extracts,* 406. For similar predictions, see letters to James Smith (December 8, 1822), ibid., 409, and Timothy Pickering (February 27, 1821), ibid., 402-3.

271. Jefferson to Jared Sparks (November 4, 1820), ibid., 402.

272. Jefferson to James Smith (December 8, 1822), ibid., 409.

273. Report of the Board of Visitors (October 7, 1822), 415, 416.

274. Ibid., 414.

275. Ibid., 415.

276. Ibid., 415-16.

277. Ibid., 416.

278. "Regulations" (October 4, 1824), *The Complete Jefferson,* ed. Saul K. Padover (New York: Duell, Sloan, and Pearce, 1943), 1110.

279. Ibid., 1111.

280. Leonard W. Levy, *Jefferson and Civil Liberties: The Darker Side* (New York: Quadrangle, 1973), 12.

281. Ibid., 13. Jefferson's policy on religion at the University of Virginia did not long survive his death, however. In 1828, James Madison cleared the way for the university rotunda to be used for worship services conducted by local ministers, and by the 1830s the room was being used for weekly services presided over by a college chaplain. The chaplain was elected annually by the faculty, though his salary was paid for from private funds. Religion at the university received another boost in 1845 when evangelical clergyman William McGuffy joined the faculty as professor of moral philosophy. "In the decade before the Civil War students were often caught up in such religious activities as the Bible classes taught by Professor McGuffey, and they also did missionary work in the Ragged Mountains" (Virginius Dabney, *Mr. Jefferson's University: A History* [Charlottesville: University Press of Virginia, 1981], 12-13, 20; Bell, *The Church, the State, and Education in Virginia,* 379-91).

282. The political nature of Jefferson's proposal is underscored in a letter to Jefferson from Joseph Cabell: "I think also that your suggestions respecting the religious sects has had great influence. It is the Franklin that has drawn the lightning from the cloud of opposition. I write you, dear sir, with a heart springing up with joy, and a cheeck bedewed with tears of delight" (Cabell to Jefferson [February 3, 1823], Cabell, ed., *Early History of the University of Virginia,* 273).

283. "A Bill for Establishing Religious Freedom," *Writings* (Ford ed.), 2:238.

284. Jefferson to Jeremiah Moor (August 14, 1800), *Writings* (Ford ed.), 7:455.

285. See Jefferson's letters to Benjamin Rush (September 23, 1800), *Jefferson's Extracts,* 320-21; Moses Robinson (March 23, 1801), ibid., 324-25; William Short (April 13, 1820), ibid., 392-93; Thomas Cooper (November 2, 1822), *Writings* (Ford ed.), 12:272.

286. Jefferson to Jeremiah Moor (August 14, 1800), *Writings* (Ford ed.), 7:455.

287. Madison to Bradford (November 9, 1772), *Papers of James Madison,* ed. William T. Hutchinson and William M. Frachal (Chicago: University of Chicago Press, 1962-), 1:74-75; and (September 25, 1775), ibid., 96. In the same volume, also see Bradford to Madison (November 5, 1773), 98; and (October 17, 1774), 127.

288. Madison to Frederick Beasley (November 20, 1825), *Writings,* 9:230; also see Madison's letter to Jefferson supplying a list of theology books to include in the library of the University of Virginia (ibid., 202-7) and the second paragraph of Madison's letter to Reverend Jaspar Adams in 1832 (ibid., 485).

289. Madison, "Notes of a Speech Against Assessments for Support of Religion to Virginia Assembly" (November 1784), ibid., 2:88-89.

290. *Federalist* no. 10, *Federalist Papers,* 81.

291. Madison to Edward Everett (March 19, 1823), *Writings,* 9:126-27.

292. Madison to Beasley (November 20, 1825), ibid., 230.

293. Madison to unidentified (March 1836), ibid., 610.

294. For Madison's opposition to state-sponsored prayer days, see Madison to Edward Livingston (July 10, 1822), ibid., 100–103; and the "Detached Memoranda" (560–62). Although he opposed state prayer days later in life, Madison, while president, issued four prayer-day proclamations—more than any preceding president; see "A Proclamation" (July 9, 1812), *Compilation of Messages of the Presidents,* 1:498; "A Proclamation" (July 23, 1813), ibid., 517–18; "A Proclamation" (November 16, 1814), ibid., 543; and "A Proclamation" (March 4, 1815), ibid., 545–46.

295. Madison, "Detached Memoranda," 555.

296. Ibid., 558–60.

297. Ibid., 560.

298. See, for example, *Bowen* v. *Kendrick,* 487 U.S. 589 (1988).

299. Madison, veto message, February 21, 1811; see also statement in "Memorial and Remonstrance" that it is "an unhallowed perversion of the means of salvation" to "employ religion as an engine of civil policy" ("Memorial and Remonstrance Against Religious Assessments," *Writings,* 2:187).

300. "Memorial and Remonstrance," remonstrance seven, ibid.; for similar argument also see Madison's letter to Jasper Adams (1832), ibid., 9:485.

301. "Memorial and Remonstrance," remonstrance five, ibid., 2:187.

302. See Thomas E. Buckley, *Church and State in Revolutionary Virginia, 1776–1787* (Charlottesville: University Press of Virginia, 1977); Levy, *Establishment Clause,* 55–58; Thomas J. Curry, *First Freedoms: Church and State in America to the Passage of the First Amendment* (New York: Oxford University Press, 1986), 143–46.

303. Buckley, *Church and State,* 181.

304. Ibid., 178.

305. Robert M. Calhoon, *Evangelicals and Conservatives in the Early South, 1740–1861* (Columbia:University of South Carolina Press, 1988), 89.

306. Ibid.

307. See Madison to Robert Walsh (March 2, 1819), *Writings,* 8:430–32, and Jasper Adams (1832), ibid., 9:486.

308. Madison, "Detached Memoranda," 560–61.

309. Madison to William Bradford (January 24, 1774), *Papers,* 1:106. Also see Madison to Bradford (December 1, 1773), ibid., 100–101; and (April 1, 1774), ibid., 112–13.

310. See Madison, "Detached Memoranda," 557–58. In a similar vein, Madison wrote to Reverend Jasper Adams in 1832: "There may be less danger that Religion, if left to itself, will suffer from a failure of the pecuniary support applicable to it than that an omission of the public authorities to limit the duration of their Charters to Religious Corporations, and the amount of property acquirable by them, may lead to an injurious accumulation of wealth from the lavish donations and bequests prompted by a pious zeal or by an atoning remorse. Some monitory examples have already appeared" (Madison to Jasper Adams [1832], *Writings,* 9:487).

311. If "Detached Memoranda" was written before 1833, Massachusetts would be the sole remaining state with an establishment.

312. In 1788, Madison criticized Jefferson's draft of a new constitution for Virginia be-

cause it excluded the clergy from public office:"Does not the exclusion of Ministers of the Gospel as such violate a fundamental principle of liberty by punishing a religious profession with the privation of a civil right? does it [not] violate another article of the plan itself which exempts religion from the cognizance of Civil power? does it not violate justice by at once taking away a right and prohibiting a compensation for it? does it not in fine violate impartiality by shutting the door [against] the Ministers of one Religion and leaving it open for those of every other?" (Madison, "Observations on the 'Draft of a Constitution for Virginia,' " *Writings,* 5:288).

313. Madison to Edward Everett (March 19, 1823), ibid., 9:127.

314. Madison to Jasper Adams (1832), ibid., 487; emphasis is Madison's.

315. Madison, "Detached Memoranda," 552, 556.

316. Ibid., 556.

317. Bell, *The Church, the State, and Education in Virginia,* 379–80.

318. Madison to Thomas Jefferson (August 20, 1785), *Writings,* 2:163–64.

319. *Federalist* no. 51, *Federalist Papers,* 324–25; also see *Federalist* no. 10, ibid., 79, 83–84.

320. "If there were a majority of one sect, a bill of rights would be a poor protection for [religious] liberty. Happily for the states, they enjoy the utmost freedom of religion. This freedom arises from that multiplicity of sects, which pervades America, and which is the best and only security for religious liberty in any society. . . . The United States abound in such a variety of sects, that it is a strong security against religious persecution, and it is sufficient to authorize a conclusion, that no one sect will ever be able to outnumber or depress the rest" (Madison, speech before the Virginia Ratifying Convention, June 12, 1788, *Writings,* 5:176).

321. Madison, "Memorial and Remonstrance," ibid., 2:185.

322. Washington to different denominations residing in and near Philadelphia (March 3, 1797), ibid., 35:416.

323. Washington to Henry Knox (March 2, 1797), ibid., 35:409.

324. Washington, "General Orders" (July 29, 1779), ibid., 16:13.

325. Washington to Benedict Arnold (September 14, 1775), ibid., 3:492.

326. Washington, "Farewell Address," ibid., 35:229.

327. Adams, "A Dissertation on the Canon and the Feudal Law, No. 2" (August 1765), *Papers,* 1:115.

328. Adams, "A Dissertation" (August 1765), ibid., 116.

329. Ibid.

330. Adams, "Discourses on Davila" (1790), *Works,* 6:397.

331. Jay, "Address to the American Bible Society" (May 8, 1823), *Papers,* 4:488.

332. Madison, "Detached Memoranda," 560–61.

333. Hamilton, "The Farmer Refuted," *Papers,* 1:87.

334. Jefferson to James Fishback (September 27, 1809), *Jefferson's Extracts,* 343.

335. Berns, *First Amendment,* 15.

336. The need for moral virtue as a guide for politics is evident even in *The Federalist,* for all its discussion of the "inventions of prudence." According to Publius, the sheer multiplicity of interests in the extended republic, supplemented by the checks and balances built into

the structure of its government, will help guarantee that ruling coalitions cannot be founded on narrow interests or the passions of a few. The "inventions of prudence," then, are defense mechanisms. They are intended make it harder for unjust factions to rule—so that those ruling coalitions that do form will tend to be based on "principles . . . of justice and the general good." But there is the rub. The inventions of prudence may indeed stifle the creation of *unjust* ruling coalitions, but they provide no guarantee that *just* ruling coalitions will form. If a nation and its rulers are predominantly selfish and dominated by private interests, then even if the inventions of prudence succeed, there will not be just government. Instead, there will be government by gridlock—for no interest will be willing to sacrifice its own interest to further the greater good. Hence, there is a need to forge a societal consensus on the "principles . . . of justice and the general good" (*Federalist* no. 51, *Federalist Papers,* 322, 325).

## CHAPTER 2. EVANGELICALS AND THE POLITICS OF REVELATION AND REASON, 1800–1835

1. Thomas Robbins, cited in John A. Andrew III, *New England Congregationalists and Foreign Missions, 1800–1836: Rebuilding the Christian Commonwealth* (Lexington: University Press of Kentucky, 1976), 33.

2. Cited in John C. Miller, *The Federalists, 1789–1801* (New York: Harper and Row, 1960), 265 n. 34.

3. "Mason, John Mitchell," *Encyclopedia Americana* (New York: Americana, 1948), 18:381–82; Charles I. Foster, *An Errand of Mercy: The Evangelical Front, 1790–1837* (Chapel Hill: University of North Carolina Press, 1960), 143.

4. John M. Mason, "The Voice of Warning," in *Complete Works of John M. Mason,* ed. Ebenezer Mason (New York: Baker and Scribner, 1849), 4:538–45, 549–53.

5. Mason, "The Voice of Warning," 545–47.

6. Thomas Jefferson, *Notes on the State of Virginia,* ed. William Peden (New York: Norton, 1954), 143; Mason, "The Voice of Warning," 546–48.

7. Mason, "The Voice of Warning," 559.

8. Ibid., 566–67, 572–73.

9. Baptists and Methodists tended to be Jeffersonians. See Mark A. Noll, *One Nation Under God? Christian Faith and Political Action in America* (San Francisco: Harper and Row, 1988), 76–77, 81.

10. See Jedidiah Morse, *A Sermon, Exhibiting the Present Dangers and Consequent Duties of the Citizens of the United States of America* (Charlestown, Mass.: 1799); Vernon Stauffer, *New England and the Bavarian Illuminati* (New York: Columbia University Press, 1918).

11. Timothy Dwight, "The Duty of Americans, at the Present Crisis" (1798), in *Political Sermons of the American Founding Era, 1730–1805,* ed. Ellis Sandoz (Indianapolis: Liberty Press, 1991), 1374.

12. See Nathanael Emmons, "Obedience to Civil Magistrates," in *Works of Nathanael Emmons,* ed. Jacob Ide (Boston: Crocker and Brewster, 1842), 2:129.

13. Thomas Robbins, cited in Andrew, *New England Congregationalists,* 33.

14. Cited in Frank Luther Mott, *American Journalism:A History, 1690-1960,* 3d ed. (New York: Macmillan, 1962), 169.

15. See, for example, Thomas Jefferson, "Second Annual Message" (December 15, 1802), "Second Inaugural Address" (March 4, 1805), and "Eighth Annual Message" (November 8, 1808), in Thomas Jefferson, *The Writings of Thomas Jefferson,* ed. Andrew Lipscomb and Albert Ellery Bergin (Washington, D.C.: Thomas Jefferson Memorial Association, 1904), 3:340, 383, 485; Robert Cord, *Separation of Church and State: Historical Fact and Current Fiction* (New York: Lambeth Press, 1982), 38-39, 190, 224.

16. Dumas Malone, *Jefferson and His Time* (Boston: Little, Brown, 1981), 4:192; Thomas Jefferson to Reverend Samuel Miller (January 23, 1808), in *Writings* (New York: Library of America, 1984), 1186-87.

17. Nathanael Emmons, "Jeroboam," in *Works,* 2:200-201.

18. John MacLean, *History of the College of New Jersey* (Philadelphia: Lippincott, 1877), 2:32-33. In 1796 Federalists similarly blamed Jeffersonian Jacobins for devastating fires that ravaged Baltimore, Philadelphia, and New York. See John Bach McMaster, *A History of the People of the United States,* 8 vols. (New York: Appleton, 1892-1919), 2:538-39.

19. Samuel Stanhope Smith to Jedidiah Morse, cited in Samuel Holt Monk, "Samuel Stanhope Smith: Friend of Rational Liberty," in *The Lives of Eighteen from Princeton,* ed. Willard Thorp (Princeton: Princeton University Press, 1946), 103.

20. MacLean, *History of the College of New Jersey,* 2:34.

21. Andrew, *New England Congregationalists,* 4. For general background on religion and society in America during the eighteenth century and before, see Anson Phelps Stokes, *Church and State in the United States* (New York: Harper and Brothers, 1950), vol. 1; Edwin Gaustad, *Great Awakening in New England* (New York: Harper and Row, 1957); Perry Miller, *The New England Mind: From Colony to Province* (Cambridge: Harvard University Press, 1953); Thomas E. Buckley, *Church and State in Revolutionary Virginia, 1776-1787* (Charlottesville: University Press of Virginia, 1977); Sacvan Bercovitch, *The Puritan Origins of the American Self* (New Haven: Yale University Press, 1975); Jon Butler, *Awash in a Sea of Faith: Christianizing the American People* (Cambridge: Harvard University Press, 1990); William C. McLoughlin, *New England Dissent, 1630-1883: The Baptists and the Separation of Church and State* (Cambridge, Mass.: Harvard University Press, 1971); Alan Heimert, *Religion and the American Mind: From the Great Awakening to the Revolution* (Cambridge: Harvard University Press, 1966); John B. Boles, *The Great Revival, 1787-1805: The Origins of the Southern Evangelical Mind* (Lexington: University Press of Kentucky, 1972).

22. For coverage and discussion of the Second Great Awakening and its various revivals, see Nelson R. Burr, *A Critical Bibliography of Religion in America* (Princeton: Princeton University Press, 1961), 4:155-56; Boles, *The Great Revival;* Whitney R. Cross, *The Burned-Over District: The Social and Intellectual History of Enthusi-*

*astic Religion in Western New York, 1800–1850* (New York: Harper Torchbooks, 1965); Garth M. Rosell, "Charles G. Finney: His Place in the Stream of American Evangelicalism," in *The Evangelical Tradition in America,* ed. Leonard I. Sweet (Macon, Ga.: Mercer University Press, 1984), 131–47; Paul E. Johnson, *A Shop-keeper's Millennium: Society and Revivals in Rochester, New York, 1815–1837* (New York: Hill and Wang, 1978); Mary P. Ryan, *Cradle of the Middle Class: The Family in Oneida County, New York, 1790–1865* (New York: Cambridge University Press, 1981); William G. McLoughlin, *Modern Revivalism: Charles Grandison Finney to Billy Graham* (New York: Ronald Press, 1959); Timothy L. Smith, *Revivalism and Social Reform in Mid-Nineteenth-Century America* (New York: Abingdon Press, 1957); Charles Roy Keller, *The Second Great Awakening in Connecticut* (Hamden, Conn.: Archon Books, 1968); Donald G. Mathews, *Religion in the Old South* (Chicago: University of Chicago Press, 1977). See also the final chapter in Heimert, *Religion and the American Mind,* esp. 540–52.

23. William Gore Ouseley, *Remarks on the Statistics and Political Institutions of the United States* (London: Rodwell, 1832), 189.

24. Robert Baird, *Religion in America: or an Account of the Origin, Relation to the State, and Present Condition of the Evangelical Churches in the United States with Notices of the Unevangelical Denominations* (New York: Harper and Brothers, 1856), 531–32.

25. See charts in Roger Finke and Rodney Stark, *The Churching of America, 1776–1990: Winners and Losers in Our Religious Economy* (New Brunswick, N.J.: Rutgers University Press, 1992), 16, 55.

26. Leonard W. Levy, *Establishment Clause: Religion and the First Amendment* (New York: Macmillan, 1986), 40, 44.

27. Anson Phelps Stokes and Leo Pfeffer, *Church and State in the United States* (Westport, Conn.: Greenwood Press, 1975), 530–31.

28. Levy, *The Establishment Clause,* 35–37.

29. Thomas J. Curry, *The First Freedoms: Church and State in America to the Passage of the First Amendment* (New York: Oxford University Press, 1986), 218–19; McLoughlin, *New England Dissent,* 2:1280; [Favorably notes newspapers that have closed on the Sabbath], *Christian Advocate and Journal* [of the Methodist Episcopal Church], January 30, 1827, 87, col. 3; [Announcement of upcoming public fast declared by Governor of Connecticut], *Christian Advocate and Journal,* March 24, 1827, col. 4; "Thoughts on the Christian Sabbath," *Christian Advocate and Journal,* March 31, 1827, 117, col. 3.

30. Elwyn A. Smith, "The Voluntary Establishment of Religion," in *The Religion of the Republic,* ed. Elwyn A. Smith (Philadelphia: Fortress Press, 1971), 155.

Some might question the prominent place given to Lyman Beecher in the following pages. Certainly he was a controversial figure, and some of his theological views cannot be taken as representative of all (or even most) evangelicals during the period. If the subject of this work was revivalism (or theological movements within evangelicalism), the reliance on Beecher might pose difficulties. However, as noted previously in the Introduction, the subject here is evangelical political reformers and how they articulated their political views. In this arena Beecher was unquestionably one of the most important and respected evangelical leaders during the years 1800–1835. As a practical matter, he inaugurated the first great national reform campaign by evangelicals (against dueling); he also helped instigate the Sunday mails campaign. Even more important from the standpoint of this book, Beecher had one of the keenest theoretical grasps of the opportunities supplied by disestablishment and how to turn to the evangelicals' advantage the new language of religious liberty and voluntary associations. He was quoted not only by those within his own theological tradition but also by Baptists and others. In any case, though Beecher is used to frame the narrative that follows, the overview of evangelical reform presented here draws on many other sources, as does the chapter's concluding discussion of evangelical political theory.

31. For biographical treatments, see Stuart C. Henry, *Unvanquished Puritan: A Portrait of Lyman Beecher* (Grand Rapids, Mich.: William B. Eerdmans, 1973); Vincent A. Harding, *A Certain Magnificence: Lyman Beecher and the Transformation of American Protestantism, 1775–1865* (Brooklyn, N.Y.: Carlson, 1991). Stephen H. Snyder, *Lyman Beecher and His Children* (Brooklyn, N.Y.: Carlson, 1991).

32. Unattributed comment cited in "Beecher Family," *Encyclopedia Americana*, 1948 ed., 3:427.

33. "Beecher Family," "Beecher, Catherine," "Beecher, Charles," "Beecher, Edward," "Beecher, Henry Ward"; "Hooker, Isabella Beecher"; and "Stowe, Harriet Beecher," *Encyclopedia Americana,* 1948 ed., 3:423–27, 14:362–63, 25:705–6; "Beecher, Catharine," "Beecher, Charles," "Beecher, Edward," "Beecher, Henry Ward," "Beecher, Lyman," "Beecher, Thomas," and "Stowe, Harriet Beecher," *Dictionary of American Biography,* ed. Allen Johnson and Dumas Malone (New York: Charles Scribner's Sons, 1931), 2:125–37, 17:115–20. See also Snyder, *Lyman Beecher and His Children.*

34. Lyman Beecher, *Autobiography of Lyman Beecher,* ed. Barbara M. Cross (Cambridge, Mass: Belknap Press, 1961), 2:425–26.

35. Barbara M. Cross, Introduction to *Autobiography,* by Beecher, 1:xi.

36. Beecher, *Autobiography,* 1:12–23.

37. Ibid., 1:27.

38. Ibid., 2:170. The words mimicked a popular evangelical hymn.

39. Ibid., 2:244–49, 261–72, 414–19.

40. "The Moral Society was not an original idea with Beecher, but it was he, more than any other single person in America, who helped to popularize the idea that the nation might be won to the Kingdom of Christ through the means of such societies, for Beecher's gifts lay primarily in the tasks of focusing, shaping, and popularizing already existent movements" (Harding, *A Certain Magnificence,* 43). For an earlier proposal of reform, see Nathanael Emmons, "The Evil Effects of Sin," in *Works,* 2:42–58. Beecher was aware of Emmons's earlier effort and mentioned it; see Lyman Beecher, *The Practicality of Suppressing Vice by Means of Societies Instituted for That Purpose* (New London, Conn.: Samuel Green, 1804), 14.

41. Beecher, "Autobiography," 1:126.

244    NOTES TO PAGES 85-91

42. Ibid., 1:125-26.

43. Ibid., 1:126.

44. [Constitution of the Moral Society in East Hampton], reprinted as an appendix in Beecher, *The Practicality of Suppressing Vice.*

45. Ibid., 27.

46. Ibid., 6.

47. Ibid., 8.

48. Ibid., 8-10.

49. Ibid., 12, 15.

50. Ibid., 19.

51. Ibid., 17.

52. Ibid., 19.

53. Washington, cited in ibid., 18.

54. Ibid., 17.

55. Records for this period are fragmentary, so it is possible that numerous associations existed about which we know nothing. Nevertheless, given the records that do exist, it appears that most, if not all, voluntary associations formed by evangelicals from 1803 to 1811 were evangelistic rather than reform-minded. Bible societies were begun in Massachusetts and Pennsylvania in 1809; in Connecticut, New Jersey, New York, and South Carolina in 1810; and in New Hampshire in 1811. The Western Foreign Missionary Society was started in 1805, the Maine Missionary Society in 1807, the American Board of Commissioners for Foreign Missions in 1810, and the Auxillary Foreign Mission Society of Franklin County, Massachussetts, in 1811. The Philadelphia Religious Tract Society and the Episcopal Tract Society were both established in 1810. One of the few associations established to combat a social problem was the Philadelphia Dispensary, established around 1805. See list of societies supplied in Foster, *An Errand of Mercy,* 275-79.

56. See "Nathaniel Pendleton's Amendments," "Benjamin Moore to William Coleman" (July 12, 1804), and "David Hosack to William Coleman" (August 17, 1804), in Alexander Hamilton, *The Papers of Alexander Hamilton,* ed. Harold C. Syrett (New York: Columbia University Press, 1961-), 26:337-39, 316, 344-47.

57. A. W. Patterson, *The Code Duello with Special Reference to the State of Virginia* (Richmond: Richmond Press, 1927), 72.

58. John W. Mason, "Funeral Oration on the Death of General Hamilton," in *Complete Works,* 4:520-22.

59. Richard Furman, *Death's Dominion over Man Considered, a Sermon Occasioned by the Death of the Honorable Major General Alexander Hamilton* (Charleston, S.C.: Young, 1804), 18-20.

60. Timothy Dwight, *A Sermon on Duelling* (New York: Collins, Perkins, 1805), 4.

61. Ibid., 7-10, 13, 16.

62. Ibid., 17.

63. Ibid., 14-15.

64. Ibid., 33-35.

65. Ibid., 37-38.

66. "Burr, Aaron [1716-1757]," "Burr, Aaron [1756-1836]," *Encyclopedia Americana*, 1948 ed., 5:63-64.

67. Philanthropos, *Letter to Aaron Burr, Vice-President of the United States of America, on the Barbarous Origin, the Criminal Nature, and the Baneful Effects of Duels* (New York: John Low, 1804), 3-4, 6, 14, 19-24.

68. Beecher, "Autobiography," 1:105-7.

69. Lyman Beecher, "The Remedy for Duelling," in *Works of Lyman Beecher* (Boston: Jewett, 1852), 2:35, 56.

70. Ibid., 2:36.

71. Ibid., 2:36, 38.

72. Ibid., 2:38, 43-44.

73. Ibid., 2:44.

74. Ibid., 2:47-48.

75. Ibid., 2:50, 54.

76. Ibid., 2:63.

77. Ibid., 2:64.

78. See Don C. Setz, *Famous American Duels* (New York: Thomas Crowell, 1929), 123-68, 176-250; James A. Hamilton, *Reminiscences of James A. Hamilton* (New York: Charles Scribner, 1869), 41.

79. See, for example, "Literary Notice: Dr. Dwight's Sermon on Duelling," *The Panoplist* 1 (July 1805): 28-29; "Religious Intelligence," *Panoplist* 1 (July 1805): 76-77; Nathaniel Bowen, *A Sermon . . . on the Occasion of the Melancholy Death of Arthur Smith, and Thomas Hudson, Esq's, Who Fell in a Duel* (Charleston, S.C.: Gabriel M. Bounethead, 1807); "Memorial Against Duelling," *Panoplist* 2 (June 1809): 21-23; "On Human Depravity," *Panoplist* 3 (April 1811): 495-502; "Duelling," and "An Act to Suppress Duelling," *Panoplist* 5 (January 1813): 358-63; "Thoughts on Duelling," *Panoplist* 16 (July 1820): 303-4; Mason Locke Weems, *God's Revenge Against Duelling; or, the Duellist's Looking Glass*, 2d ed. (Philadelphia: Bioren, 1821); John Black, *A Sermon on National Righteousness and Sin* [along with antidueling resolutions adopted at a public meeting] (Pittsburgh: Pittsburgh Recorder Office, 1827); [Review of *Personal Sketches of His Own Times*, with reference to the portions of the book relating to dueling], *North American Review* (April 1828): 498-514; Jasper Adams, *Elements of Moral Philosophy* (Cambridge, Mass.: Folsom, Wells, and Thurston, 1837), 428-32; William H. Barnwell, *The Impiety and Absurdity of Duelling—a Sermon* (Charleston: Walker and Burke, 1844); Arthur Wigfall, *A Sermon upon Duelling* (Charleston, S.C.: Miller, 1856).

80. Beecher, "Autobiography," 1:107.

81. Ibid., 1:107-8.

82. "Religious Intelligence"; "Memorial Against Duelling." See also "An Act to Suppress Duelling"; Patterson, *The Code Duello*, 75; Stokes, *Church and State*, 2:10-11.

83. "An Act for Establishing Rules and Articles for the Government of the Ar-

mies of the United States," sess. 1, chap. 20, Articles 25–28 (1806), in *Public Statutes at Large* (Boston: Little, Brown, 1861), 2:363.

84. See remarks of Mr. Morril, February 8, 1819, February 9, 1819, remarks of Mr. Morril, April 12, 1820, and remarks of Mr. Morril, April 24, 1820, in *Debates and Proceedings in the Congress of the United States* (Washington, D.C.: Gales and Seaton, 1855), 218–23, 597, 630–36.

85. Remarks of Mr. Foot, December 30, 1819, report of Mr. Smyth, April 11, 1820, remarks of Mr. Moore, December 6, 1821, and January 3, 1822, in *Debates,* 830, 1820, 524, 633–34.

86. See February 17, 1831, February 24, 1831, and February 25, 1831, in *Register of the Debates in Congress* (Washington, D.C.: Gales and Seaton, 1831), 209–13, 260, 292. The two who fought the duel in 1838 were William Graves of Kentucky and Jonathan Cilley of Maine. Cilley was the one who was killed. An extensive account of the legislative debates spurred by the Graves-Cilley duel can be found in the *Congressional Globe* (Washington, D.C.: Globe Office, 1838), ed. Blair and Rives, vols. 6, 7. See also "William Jordan Graves," *Appleton's Cyclopædia of American Biography,* ed. James Grant Wilson and John Fiske (New York: Appleton, 1888), 2:727; "Jonathan Cilley," *Appleton's Cyclopædia,* 1:615; "An Act to Prohibit the Giving or Accepting, Within the District of Columbia, of a Challenge to Fight a Duel, and for the Punishment Thereof," sess. 3, chap. 30 (1839), in *Public Statutes at Large* (Boston: Charles C. Little and James Brown, 1846), 5:318–19; Setz, *Famous American Duels,* 251–82.

87. To be specific, popular opposition to dueling proved detrimental to both Andrew Jackson (a Democrat) and Henry Clay (a Whig). See Beecher, "Autobiography," 1:108, and the note by Dr. Leonard Bacon on the same page.

88. Nott on pagan Rome and Greece, in Patterson, *Code Duello,* 72; Mason on dueling, in Mason, "Funeral Oration on the Death of General Hamilton," in *Works,* 4:521; Furman on dueling, in Furman, *Death's Dominion over Man Considered,* 20; Dwight on dueling, in Dwight, *A Sermon on Duelling,* 7; Philanthropos, *Letter to Aaron Burr,* 6.

89. Beecher, *Autobiography,* 1:191.

90. Ibid., 1:185–87.

91. Ibid., 1:191; Lyman Beecher, "A Reformation of Morals Practicable and Indispensable," in *Works,* 2:75–113.

92. Beecher, "A Reformation of Morals," 99–100.

93. Ibid., 77–80.

94. Benjamin Franklin, "Poor Richard Improved" (1758), in *The Papers of Benjamin Franklin,* ed. Leonard W. Labaree (New Haven: Yale University Press, 1959–), 7:341.

95. Beecher, "A Reformation of Morals," 81.

96. Ibid., 79.

97. Ibid., 84.

98. Ibid., 88–89.

99. Ibid., 90.

100. Ibid., 90–93.

101. Ibid., 93.

102. Ibid., 95.

103. Stokes and Pfeffer, *Church and State*, 258–59; Baird, *Religion in America*, 345–46; Frank Luther Mott, *A History of American Magazine, 1741–1850* (New York: Appleton, 1930), 135–39, 262–65; Frederic Hudson, *Journalism in the United States, from 1600 to 1872* (New York: Harper and Brothers, 1872), 289–98. It is well recognized that evangelicals provided the main impetus for many of the reform movements in America during this period. See Foster, *An Errand of Mercy;* Clifford Griffin, *Their Brothers' Keepers: Moral Stewardship in the United States, 1800–1865* (New Brunswick, N.J.: Rutgers University Press, 1960); Baird, *Religion in America*, 308–67. Nevertheless, evangelicals were the only proponents of reform in the early nineteenth century. The focus of this book is American evangelicals, however; hence, reform movements sponsored by other groups are not covered.

104. Foster, *An Errand of Mercy*, 133.

105. Ibid., 134.

106. Beecher, *Autobiography*, 1:337.

107. Johnson, *A Shopkeeper's Millennium*, 118–119.

108. Beecher laid the groundwork for these larger single-issue groups by noting that they could serve a vital coordination function by "collect[ing] facts, and extend[ing] information, and, in a thousand nameless ways . . . exert[ing] a salutary general influence. . . . Associations of this general nature, for the promotion of the arts and sciences, have exerted a powerful influence; and no reason, it is presumed, can be given, why the cause of morals may not be equally benefited by similar associations" ("A Reformation of Morals," 96).

109. Foster, *An Errand of Mercy*, 144.

110. Ibid., 130–31, 146–54; Griffin, *Their Brothers' Keepers*, 66.

111. See, for example, Francis Wayland, "Duties of an American Citizen: Discourse II," in *Occasional Discourses* (Boston: Loring, 1833), 71–78.

112. Foster, *An Errand of Mercy*, appendix, 275–79; Timothy Dwight, "On Doing Good," in *Sermons by Timothy Dwight* (New Haven: Hezekiah Howe and Durrie and Peck, 1828), 1:549. See also American Bible Society, *Constitution of the American Bible Society . . . Together with Their Address to the People of the United States* (New York: Hopkins, 1816); American Bible Society, *First Annual Report of the Board of Managers of the American Bible Society* (New York: Seymour, 1817); "John Jay," *Dictionary of American Biography*, 10:10.

113. Baird, *Religion in America*, 334.

114. Other associations with similar purposes included the American Bible Class Society (established in 1827), the Baptist General Tract Society (established in 1824), the Episcopal Tract Society (established in 1810), the First Day Society (1790–1817), the Massachusetts Sabbath School Society (established about 1830), the Massachusetts Sunday School Union (c. 1828–1835), the Methodist Sunday School Association of New York City (c. 1820–1827), the Methodist Sunday School Union (1827–1836), the New England Tract Society (established in 1824), the New York City Tract

Society (established in 1827), the New York Protestant Episcopal Sunday School Society (established in 1817), the New York Religious Tract Society (1812-1826), the Philadelphia Religious Tract Society (c. 1810-1824), the Philadelphia Sunday and Adult School Union (1817-1824), the Revival Tract Society (established about 1830), and the Tract Society of the Methodist Episcopal Church (1828-1826). See Foster, *An Errand of Mercy,* appendix, 275-79; Baird, *Religion in America,* 308-16, 336-41.

115. American Sunday School Union, *First Report of the American Sunday School Union* (Philadelphia: Ashmead, 1825), 21-22; Baird, *Religion in America,* 313-14.

116. Baird, *Religion in America,* 314; American Sunday School Union, *Sixth Report of the American Sunday School Union* (Philadelphia: n.p., 1830), 13-15; American Sunday School Union, *Seventh Annual Report of the American Sunday School Union,* 2d ed. (Philadelphia: American Sunday School Union, 1831), 17-24.

117. Missionary societies included the New York Missionary Society (established in 1796); Missionary Society of Connecticut (established in 1800); the Western Foreign Missionary Society (established in 1805); the American Board of Commissioners for Foreign Missions (established in 1810); Auxilliary Foreign Mission Society of Franklin County, Massachusetts (established in 1811); the Philadelphia Missionary Society (established in 1813); the New York Evangelical Missionary Society (established in 1816); the United Foreign Missionary Society (established in 1816); the New York Evangelical Missionary Society of Young Men (1817-); the Northern Missionary Society of the State of New York (established in 1817); the Missionary Society of Philadelphia (established in 1818); the Auxiliary Foreign Mission Society in the Western District of Fairfield County, Conn. (established in 1824); the Methodist Missionary Society (established about 1824); and the Eastern Auxiliary Foreign Missionary Society of Rockingham County, New Hampshire, (established in 1825).

118. See, for example, John Price Durbin, *Substance of a Sermon in Favor of Aiding the Greeks in Their Present Contest* (Cincinnati: Looker and Reynolds, 1824); William Miller, *Address for the Benefit of the Greeks, Delivered in Trinity Church, Newark* (Newark, N.J.: Tuttle, 1824); Ezekiel G. Gear, *A Sermon Delivered at the Taking up of a Collection, for the Benefit of the Greeks, in the Congregation of St. John's Church* (Ithaca, N.Y.: Mack and Morgan, 1824); Nathaniel Bouton, *The Responsibilities of Rulers: A Sermon* (Concord, N.H.: Henry F. Moore, 1828), 17. For a good secondary discussion of American support for the Greek rebels, see James A. Field, *America and the Mediterranean World* (Princeton: Princeton University Press, 1969), 121-33.

119. Hiram Bingham, *A Residence of Twenty-one Years in the Sandwich Islands; or the Civil, Religious, and Political History of Those Islands: Comprising a Particular View of the Missionary Operations Connected with the Introduction and Progress of Christianity and Civilization Among the Hawaiian People,* 2d ed. (Hartford, Conn.: Hezekiah Huntington, 1848), 283-89; Joseph Tracy, *History of the American Board of Commissioners for Foreign Missions,* 2d ed. (New York: Dodd, 1842), 182-84; Office of the Judge Advocate General (Navy). Case file of the Court of Inquiry concerning Lt. John Percival, Records of General Courts-Martial and Courts of In-

NOTES TO PAGES 104-6    249

quiry of the Navy Department, 1799-1867. National Archives, Washington, D.C.; microfilm; Harold Whitman Bradley, *The American Frontier in Hawaii: The Pioneers, 1789-1843* (Stanford: Stanford University Press, 1942), 178-79; Charles Oscar Paullin, *Diplomatic Negotiations of American Naval Officers, 1778-1883* (Baltimore: Johns Hopkins Press, 1912), 337-39; Clifton Jackson Parker, *Protestant America and the Pagan World: The First Half Century of the American Board of Commissioners for Foreign Missions, 1810-1860* (Cambridge, Mass.: East Asian Research Center, Harvard University, 1969), 103-4.

120. See Ray Allen Billington, *The Protestant Crusade, 1800-1860: A Study of the Origins of American Nativism* (Chicago: Quadrangle, 1964), 53-70, 94-98.

121. Samuel Elliot Morison, *The Oxford History of the American People* (New York: Oxford University Press, 1965), 479-83.

122. Lyman Beecher, *A Plea for the West* (Cincinnati: Truman and Smith, 1835; reprint, New York: Arno Press, 1977), 49-50, 158.

123. "Mirari Vos," August 15, 1832, in *The Papal Encyclicals, 1740-1878,* ed. Claudia Carlen Ihm (n.p.: McGrath, 1981), 238.

124. Ibid. See the attacks on this encyclical in Beecher, *A Plea for the West,* 156; H. A. Boardman, "Is There Any Ground to Apprehend the Extensive and Dangerous Prevalence of Romanism in the United States?" (Philadelphia: Hooker and Agnew, 1841), reprinted in *Anti-Catholicism in America, 1841-1851: Three Sermons* (New York: Arno Press, 1977). Future papal encyclicals did nothing to curb evangelical fears of Catholic intolerance. In 1844 Pope Gregory XVI condemned Protestant missionary societies in Europe that were trying to propagate their doctrines. He called on civil authorities to suppress these societies because "experience shows that there is no more direct way of alienating the populace from fidelity and obedience to their leaders than through that indifference to religion propagated . . . under the name of religious liberty." The pope argued that it was in the civil authorities' best interest to curtail religious liberty because "as complete liberty of conscience . . . spreads among the Italian people, political liberty will result of its own accord" ("Inter Praecipuas," May 8, 1844, in ibid., 270-71).

125. Morton Borden, *Jews, Turks, and Infidels* (Chapel Hill: University of North Carolina Press, 1984), 54; Billington, *The Protestant Crusade,* 57; Arthur M. Schlesinger Jr., *The Age of Jackson* (Boston: Little, Brown, 1945), 139.

126. Billington, *The Protestant Crusade,* 70-76.

127. Beecher, *A Plea for the West,* 61.

128. Ibid., 170-71.

129. Beecher, "Autobiography," 2:250-51.

130. Samuel F. B. Morse, *Foreign Conspiracy Against the Liberties of the United States* (New York: Leavitt, Lord, 1835; reprint, New York: Arno Press, 1977).

131. See "The Cry of Charity," *Christian Watchman,* August 15, 1834, 129.

132. "It is scarcely necessary to say, that all good men view the proceeding of the mob with abhorrence" (*Boston Recorder,* August 15, 1834, 131). "It is well known that we have no sympathy with the general principles of the denomination of protesters that have suffered on this occasion, but we detest the spirit and the conduct that

would persecute any sect, who yield ready obedience to good and wholesome laws. It cannot but be immediately discerned, that if a mob may be tolerated in executing vengeance on one class of citizens, the oppressed have an equal right to organize against their oppressors and execute steady retribution. If we do not take means to bring to disgrace and punishment, those who have been the authors and actors in this riotous conflagration, can we complain should the thousands of Roman Catholics in our city and vicinity retaliate?" (*Christian Watchman,* August 15, 1834, 131).

133. "The Convent," *Boston Recorder,* August 22, 1834, 133; reprinted in *Christian Watchman,* August 29, 1834, 140. Contrary to some accounts, there is little, if any, evidence that Lyman Beecher played a role in inciting the burning of the convent. On the Sunday before the violence, he did preach three sermons in Boston that included general attacks on Catholicism. But these sermons were part of his stock fund-raising appeal for Lane Seminary (later printed as *A Plea for the West*), and there is no indication that the sermons even mentioned the Ursline convent. A contemporary account of these sermons published by the *Christian Watchman* did not mention the convent; nor did the revised text published as *A Plea for the West,* except for a condemnation of the mob violence at Charlestown. See *Christian Watchman,* August 15, 1834, 130; Beecher, *A Plea for the West,* 61–62. At any rate Beecher denied that he was responsible for the violence (*Autobiography,* 2:251), and Ray Allen Billington agreed: "In this contention Beecher was probably correct, for the respectable persons who listened to his sermons would scarcely take an open part in the rioting that took place, no matter what their personal sentiments might have been" (*The Protestant Crusade,* 83 n. 112).

The most immediate cause of the conflagration was probably a nun who had run away from the convent at the end of July. Her flight seemed to give substance to wild rumors about dark doings at the convent that had been circulating for some time. When the nun in question decided to return to the convent, new rumors started that she had been compelled to go back. These tales grew still more outrageous when the convent initially declined to allow city officials to inspect its facility. Secular newspapers then fueled the hysteria by publishing irresponsible—and false—reports about the "disappearance" of the nun. See Billington, *The Protestant Crusade,* 71–74.

134. See Billington, *The Protestant Crusade,* 90–94, 98–108.

135. E. C. Tracy, *Memoir of the Life of Jeremiah Evarts, Esq.* (Boston: Crocker and Brewster, 1845), 75; Beecher, "Autobiography," 1:179–84; 2:22–25; Luyman Beecher, "Lectures on Intemperance," in *Works,* 1:347–425; Stokes, *Church and State,* 2:40–41; American Society for the Promotion of Temperance, *Second Annual Report of the Executive Committee of the American Society for the Promotion of Temperance* (Andover, Mass.: Flagg and Gould, 1829), 9.

136. American Society for the Promotion of Temperance, *Second Annual Report,* 12, 15.

137. Ibid., 3–4, 27–28.

138. Foster, *An Errand of Mercy,* 275–79; Theodore Frelinghuysen, *Address, Delivered in the Orange Church, on the Evening of the 18th of December, 1826, Before*

*the Members of the Society for the Education of Poor and Indigent Children of the Parish of Orange* (Newark: Tuttle, 1827); Beecher, "Autobiography," 1:253-56.

139. Beecher, "Autobiography," 1:255. Timothy Dwight similarly argued that charitable efforts for the poor ought to help them support themselves ("On Doing Good," *Sermons,* 543).

140. Johnson, *A Shopkeeper's Millennium,* 118, 124-25.

141. Ibid., 123.

142. Ibid.

143. Foster, *An Errand of Mercy,* 188-89, 275-79.

144. Ryan, *Cradle of the Middle Class,* 118-19.

145. Winton U. Solberg, *Redeem the Time: The Puritan Sabbath in Early America* (Cambridge, Mass.: Harvard University Press, 1977), esp. 27-58.

146. Ibid., 3.

147. Ibid., 293-97.

148. Beecher, "Autobiography," 1:196; Richard John, "Taking Sabbatarianism Seriously: The Postal System, the Sabbath, and the Transformation of the American Political Culture," *Journal of the Early Republic* 10 (Winter 1990): 522.

149. Figure derived from petitions received, 1811-1816, House Committee on the Post Office and Post Roads, which are now contained in the Records of the House of Representative, Record Group 233, National Archives and Records Administration, Washington, D.C. The 13,000 figure underrepresents the actual number of subscribers because many petitions were adopted by town meetings without individual signatures, preventing any numerical count of the number of people supporting the petition.

150. See report of Mr. Mills, March 1, 1817, *American State Papers,* Class 7: Post Office Department (Washington, D.C.: Gales and Seaton, 1834), 1:357-59.

151. General Union for Promoting the Observance of the Christian Sabbath, *The Address of the General Union for Promoting the Observance of the Christian Sabbath, to the People of the United States* (New York: Daniel Fanshaw, 1828), 11.

152. Ibid.,; see also General Union for Promoting the Observance of the Christian Sabbath, *Proceedings in Relation to the Formation of the Auxillary Union of the City of Boston, for Promoting the Observance of the Christian Sabbath* (Boston: Marvin, 1828); General Union for Promoting the Observance of the Christian Sabbath, *Annual Report of the General Union for Promoting the Observance of the Christian Sabbath* (New York: Collord, 1829); General Union for Promoting the Observance of the Christian Sabbath, *Third Annual Report of the General Union for Promoting the Observance of the Christian Sabbath, and the Proceeding of the Annual Meeting* (New York: Sleight and Robinson, 1831).

153. Paul Goodman, *Towards a Christian Republic: Antimasonry and the Great Transition in New England, 1826-1836* (New York: Oxford University Press, 1988), 3-19; Stokes, *Church and State,* 2:20-25.

154. "Freemasonry," *Boston Recorder,* May 14, 1829, 78. Following this article, the *Recorder* printed a petition from evangelicals who were members of Masonic lodges. However, by the end of the year the *Recorder* had added a caveat to its policy

of not covering anti-Masonry, lest its policy be construed as support for Masonry: "We are not Free Masons, and never were; we have no predilections for Masonry, and never had. It is our honest belief that the institution, whatever it once was, is not adopted to this age and this country" ("Anti-Masonic Christian Herald," *Boston Recorder,* December 30, 1829, 210). On the division among evangelicals over antimasonry, see also Goodman, *Towards a Christian Republic,* 60–79, 236.

155. Goodman, *Towards a Christian Republic,* 64; Lyman Beecher to William Beecher, September 3, 1830, in Beecher, "Autobiography," 2:169.

156. For a history of the development of Liberia, see Amos J. Beya, *The American Colonization Society and the Creation of the Liberian State: A Historical Perspective, 1822–1900* (Lanham, Md.: University Press of America, 1991).

157. See William Jay, *Inquiry into the Character and Tendency of the American Colonization, and American Anti-Slavery Societies,* 6th ed. (New York: Williams, 1838; reprint, Miami: Mnemosyne, 1969), 11–20.

158. In a eulogy to Henry Clay in 1852, Abraham Lincoln noted that Clay, a strong supporter of the American Colonization Society, "considered it no demerit in the society, that it tended to relieve slave-holders from the troublesome presence of the free negroes; but this was far from being its whole merit in his estimation" ("Eulogy on Henry Clay at Springfield, Illinois," in *Abraham Lincoln: Speeches and Writings, 1832–1858* [New York: Library of America, 1989], 271).

159. George Dangerfield, *The Awakening of American Nationalism, 1815–1828* (New York: Harper and Row, 1965), 138–39.

160. Theodore Frelinghuysen, *An Oration: Delivered at Princeton, New Jersey, Nov. 16, 1824, Before the New Jersey Colonization Society* (Princeton: Princeton Press, 1824), 7. See also Nathaniel Bouton, *Christian Patriotism* (Concord, N.H.: Shepard and Bannister, 1825), 14–24. About Frelinghuysen, see "Frelinghuysen, Theodore," *Dictionary of American Biography,* 7:17; Talbot W. Chambers, *Memoir of the Life and Character of the Late Hon. Theodore Frelinghuysen* (New York: Harper and Brothers, 1863), 222–25.

161. Frelinghuysen, *An Oration,* 7–8.

162. Ibid., 9.

163. See Lincoln, "Eulogy on Henry Clay," 270–71; Abraham Lincoln, "Speech on the Dred Scott Decision at Springfield, Illinois" (June 26, 1857), in *Abraham Lincoln,* 402–3; Abraham Lincoln, "Mr. Lincoln's Reply," (August 21, 1858), in *Abraham Lincoln,* 510–11; Harry v. Jaffa, *Crisis of the House Divided: An Interpretation of the Issues in the Lincoln-Douglas Debates* (Chicago: University of Chicago Press, 1982), 384–86.

164. Foster, *An Errand of Mercy,* 201. For information on the early growth of the American Anti-Slavery Society and its harsh criticisms of the American Colonization Society, see American Anti-Slavery Society, *First Annual Report of the American Anti-Slavery Society* (New York: Dorr and Butterfield, 1834; reprint, New York: Kraus, 1972); American Anti-Slavery Society, *Second Annual Report of the American Anti-Slavery Society* (New York: William S. Dorr, 1835; reprint, New York: Kraus, 1972); American Anti-Slavery Society, *Third Annual Report of the American*

*Anti-Slavery Society* (New York: William S. Dorr, 1836; reprint, New York: Kraus, 1972); American Anti-Slavery Society, *Fourth Annual Report of the American Anti-Slavery Society* (New York: William S. Dorr, 1837; reprint, New York: Kraus, 1972); Jay, *Inquiry into the Character and Tendency.*

Antislavery philanthropist Gerrit Smith, a vice president of the American Colonization Society, initially sought to defend the society from its critics even while conceding many of their criticisms. By 1836 he had become a vice president of the American Anti-Slavery Society. See "Mr. Gerrit Smith on Colonization," *African Repository and Colonial Journal* 11 (March 1835): 65-76, and 11 (April 1835): 105-19; "Gerrit Smith, esq.," *African Repository and Colonial Journal* 12 (January 1836): 35-37; American Anti-Slavery Society, *Third Annual Report,* 11-19, 24. Vigorous defenses of the American Colonization Society can be found in its publication *African Repository and Colonial Journal.* See, for example, "Judge Jay Against Colonization" 11 (May 1835): 132-33; "The Excitement" 11 (October 1835): 289-92; "Mr. Key on the Colonization Society" 12 (November 1836): 339-51.

165. Lyman Beecher to Arthur Tappan, April 23, 1833, in Beecher, "Autobiography," 2:242.

166. Ibid. .

167. Beecher was further insistent that the black student attend social functions along with the other students (*Autobiography,* 2:243). Beecher regarded prejudice against blacks as purely a social creation, not as something arising from nature. "The prejudices of color is doubtless the result of condition and character. Had Africans been the oppressors, and Americans the slaves, white complexion and straight hair would have been the badges of servitude and the occasions of prejudice" ("Colonization and Emancipation," *Boston Recorder,* August 8, 1834, 124).

168. Beecher, *Autobiography,* 2:244-49. For an abolitionist account of the controversy at Lane, see American Anti-Slavery Society, *Second Annual Report,* 40-43; see also Lawrence Thomas Lesick, *The Lane Rebels: Evangelicalism and Antislavery in Antebellum America* (Metuchen, N.J.: Scarecrow Press, 1980), esp. 121-66.

169. See Lesick, *The Lane Rebels,* 122-23, 125; "American Union for the Relief and Improvement of the Colored Race," *African Repository and Colonial Journal,* 11 (May 1835): 137-40; Bertram Wyatt-Brown, *Lewis Tappan and the Evangelical War Against Slavery* (Cleveland: Press of Case Western Reserve University, 1969), 132-42. For an example of the material published by the union, see Ethan Allen Andrews, *Slavery and the Domestic Slave-Trade in the United States: In a Series of Letters Addressed to the Executive Committee of the American Union for the Relief and Improvement of the Colored Race* (Boston: Light and Stearns, 1836; reprint, Freeport, N.Y.: Books for Libraries Press, 1971).

170. Report of the Executive Committee of the American Union for the Relief and Improvement of the Colored Race, cited in "American Union," 138.

171. Wyatt-Brown, *Lewis Tappan,* 142.

172. See, for example, Jasper Adams's delicate treatment of the issue in *Elements of Moral Philosophy,* 174-76.

173. Sydney E. Ahlstrom, *A Religious History of the American People* (New Ha-

ven: Yale University Press, 1972), 659. For further discussion of the position embraced by southern Christians on slavery, see Robert M. Calhoon, *Evangelicals and Conservatives in the Early South, 1740-1861* (Columbia: University of South Carolina Press, 1988), 185-91; Donald G. Mathews, *Slavery and Methodism: A Chapter in American Morality, 1780-1845* (Princeton: Princeton University Press, 1965); John Boles, ed., *Masters and Slaves in the House of the Lord: Race and Religion in the American South, 1740-1870* (Lexington: University Press of Kentucky, 1988); Mathews, *Religion in the Old South;* J. R. Balme, *American States, Churches, and Slavery* (Edinburgh: William P. Nimmo, 1862; reprint, New York: Negro Universities Press, 1969), esp. 268-76; Fredrick Douglass, "Narrative of the Life of Frederick Douglass, an American Slave," in *Norton Anthology of American Literature,* 2d ed. (New York: Norton, 1985), 1:1940-45.

174. See discussion of the popular constraints against antislavery preachers in John Dixon Long, *Pictures of Slavery in Church and State* (1857; reprint, New York: Negro Universities Press, 1969), esp. 152-57.

175. Ibid.

176. As late as 1857 a Baptist church in Georgia could claim: "We, Baptists of the South, have no hesitation in avowing our belief that God 'hath made of one blood all nations.' We maintain . . . that the negro is a man . . . and when converted, the negro is as gladly welcomed into our churches as a brother, as if he were of pure Anglo-Saxon blood" (ibid., 162).

177. John Mason, "Considerations on Lots," in *Complete Works,* 1:503-57; Stokes, *Church and State,* 2:25-28. Other evangelicals critical of lotteries included Jaspar Adams and Lyman Beecher. See Adams, *Elements of Moral Philosophy,* 419-28; Henry, *Unvanquished Puritan,* 141.

178. Baird, *Religion in America,* 355; Griffin, *Their Brothers' Keepers,* 39-41; Tracy, *Memoir,* 76-79. Wayland at one point served as president of the American Peace Society, though by the Civil War his opinions had changed. See Charles C. Cole Jr.,*The Social Ideas of the Northern Evangelists, 1826-1860* (New York: Columbia University Press, 1954), 163; see also Thomas S. Grimké, "On Peace," in *Correspondence on the Principles of Peace, Manual Labor Schools* (Charleston, S.C.: Observer Office Press, 1833), 3-10. Information on the campaign for a world court can be found in Massachusetts Peace Society, *Sixteenth Report of the Executive Committee of the Massachusetts Peace Society* (Boston: Samuel N. Dickinson, 1832), 5-7.

179. Baird, *Religion in America,* 351-65. For a graphic account of the condition of American prisons at the time, see McMaster, *History of the People of the United States,* 7: 96-100.

180. Nathan O. Hatch, *The Democratization of American Christianity* (New Haven: Yale University Press, 1989), 64; more generally, see 62-66.

181. "The most profound religious debates in the early republic followed social and class lines rather than merely intellectual ones. For understanding the long-term course of American religious history, the debate between Lyman Beecher and

Lorenzo Dow looms larger than the one between Beecher and, say, William Ellery Channing" (ibid., 35).

182. Rice, cited in ibid., 21.

183. See David Rice, *A Second Epistle to the Citizens of Kentucky, Professing the Christian Religion* (Lexington, Ky.: Bradford, 1808), 3-7, 14-15, 35-36.

184. See Harding, *A Certain Magnificence,* 228-29, 239-45, 263-64.

185. Johnson, *A Shopkeeper's Millennium,* 116.

186. Carroll Smith-Rosenberg, "Women and Religious Revivals: Anti-Ritualism, Liminality, and the Emergence of the American Bourgeoisie," in Sweet, ed., *The Evangelical Tradition in America,* 200; see also Ryan, *Cradle of the Middle Class.*

187. Smith-Rosenberg, "Women and Religious Revivals," 201. Although Smith-Rosenberg's comment on the male leadership of revivalism is generally true, see Nathan Hatch's description of women evangelists in *The Democratization of American Christianity,* 78-79.

188. Benjamin Franklin to Messrs. The Abbe's Chalut and Arnaud (April 17, 1787), in *Writings of Benjamin Franklin,* ed. Albert Henry Smyth (New York: Macmillan, 1907), 9:569.

189. Eliphalet Nott, *Discourse Delivered in the Presbyterian Church, in Albany, the Fourth of July* (Albany: Charles R. and George Webster, 1801), 21-22.

190. Wayland, "The Duties of an American Citizen," 69.

191. Emmons, "The Evil Effects of Sin," 2:46-47. See also John M. Mason, "Divine Judgments" (September 20, 1793), in *Complete Works,* 2:59-60; Bishop James Madison, "Manifestations of the Beneficence of Divine Providence Towards America" (1795), in *Political Sermons of the American Founding Era, 1730-1805,* ed. Ellis Sandoz (Indianapolis: Liberty Press, 1991), 1319-20; Zephaniah Swift Moore, "An Oration on the Anniversary of the Independence of the United States of America" (1802), in *American Political Writing During the Founding Era, 1760-1805,* ed. Charles S. Hyneman and Donald S. Lutz (Indianapolis: Liberty Press, 1983), 2:1212-13; Samuel Kendal, "Religion the Only Sure Basis of Free Government" (1804), in *American Political Writing,* ed. Hyneman and Lutz, 2:1241-63; Bouton, *Christian Patriotism,* 6; Phinehas Cooke, *Reciprocal Obligations of Religion and Civil Government* (Concord, N.H.: Jacob B. Moore, 1825), 13; Bouton, *The Responsibilities of Rulers,* 24-27; Daniel Dana, *An Election Sermon* (Concord, N.H.: Jacob Moore, 1823), 17-18; Nathan Lord, *A Sermon Preached at the Annual Election* (Concord, N.H.: Hill and Barton, 1831); Beecher, "A Reformation of Morals," 79-80, 99-101; Francis Wayland, *The Elements of Moral Science,* ed. Joseph L. Blau (Cambridge, Mass.: Belknap Press, 1963), 320-21.

192. Francis Wayland, "Duties of an American Citizen," in *Occasional Discourses* (Boston: Loring, 1833), 77-78.

193. John M. Mason, "Hints on the Insufficiency of the Light of Nature," in *Complete Works,* 2:583-84.

194. John M. Mason, "Non-Conformity to the World," in *Complete Works,* 4:106, 109.

195. See Samuel Stanhope Smith, *A Comprehensive View of the Leading and*

*Most Important Principles of Natural and Revealed Religion,* 2d ed. (New Brunswick, N.J.: Deare and Myer, 1816), 11–71; Samuel Stanhope Smith, *Lectures . . . on the Subjects of Moral and Political Philosophy* (Trenton, N.J.: Daniel Fenton, 1812), 1:184–88, 300–321, 2:10–116; Wayland, *The Elements of Moral Science,* 39, 42–75; Adams, *Elements of Moral Philosophy,* 1–37.

196. Nathanael Emmons, "Dignity of Man," in *Complete Works,* 2:27–28.

197. Dwight, as transcribed in Theodore Dwight Jr., *President Dwight's Decisions and Questions Discussed by the Senior Class in Yale College, in 1813 and 1814* (New York: Jonathan Leavitt, 1833), 347; Timothy Dwight, "The Nature and Danger of Infidel Philosophy: Sermon I," in *Sermons,* 1:334, see also comments on 317.

198. Mason, "Non-Conformity to the World," 108.

199. Adams, *Elements of Moral Philosophy,* 37–60; Wayland, *The Elements of Moral Science,* 100–106, 132–33; George Bush, *Lack of Vision the Ruin of the People* (Indianapolis: Gazette Office, 1826), 4, 9, 18; Cooke, *Reciprocal Obligations,* 17; Thomas S. Grimké, *Address on the Expediency and Duty of Adopting the Bible: As a Class Book* (Charleston, S.C.: Observer Office Press, 1830); Thomas S. Grimké, *An Essay on the Appropriate Use of the Bible in Common Education* (Charleston, S.C.: Observer Office Press, 1833); Dana, *An Election Sermon,* 6; Archibald Alexander, *Brief Outline of the Evidences of the Christian Religion* (Princeton: Princeton University Press, 1825), 264.

200. Wayland, "Duties of an American Citizen: Discourse II," in *Occasional Discourses,* 72, and generally, 71–78.

201. Alexander, *Brief Outline,* 5, 7, 17–18.

202. Ibid., 7–9; Daniel Dana, *Evangelical Preaching Is Rational Preaching* (Concord, N.H.: Isaac Hill, 1826), 5–6; Timothy Dwight, "The Nature and Danger of Infidel Philosophy: Sermon II," in *Sermons,* 1:343–49; Smith, *A Comprehensive View,* 72–228, 238–55; Tobias Spicer, *Sermon* (Concord: n.p., 1833), 13–14.

203. Acts 17:26 (KJV); see citation of this passage by Mason, "The Voice of Warning," 548.

204. Mason,"The Voice of Warning," 545–49; Nathanael Emmons, "The Origin of Mankind," in *Works,* 2:9–22; Smith, *An Essay on the Causes of the Variety of Complexion and Figure in the Human Species,* 2d ed. (New Brunswick, N.J.: Simpson, 1810), esp. 265–78; Dwight, *President Dwight's Decisions,* 117–28. It is worth noting that Dwight was willing to apply his ideas on equality to women. In answering the question "Are the Abilities of the sexes equal?" he chastised male arrogance on the subject: "In determining this question we are prone to be prejudiced. We are like the man who showed a lion a statue of a man treading upon a lion's neck, to prove to him the superiority of his own species. 'Ah!' said the lion, 'let us be painters, and we will soon show you a lion with a man at his feet.'" After condemning the sorry state of education for women in America, Dwight observed that, despite "all the disadvantages under which they suffer, females have not only become good . . . but great. Elizabeth was better than any other sovereign that ever sat on the English throne, except Alfred the Great. Catherine of Russia, though in some respects bad, was better than the other monarchs of that country. . . . Women on thrones have generally ex-

celled men in that station." But his highest praise was that women surpass men "in moral excellence. . . . It may be set down as a strong probability, that many more women than men will go to heaven" (cited in Dwight, *President Dwight's Decisions*, 42–43).

205. Smith, *Lectures*, 2:171–76. Smith did not favor immediate emancipation, but he did favor a scheme that would allow slaves to earn money and buy their freedom. He also advocated a homestead law for freed blacks, which would give them land in the western territories. As an incentive for interracial marriages, white men married to black women and black men married to white women would be given a double portion of land.

206. Lyman Beecher, "The Republican Elements of the Old Testament," in *Works*, 1:176–90.

207. Cited in Stokes, *Church and State*, 3:149–50.

208. Leonard W. Levy, *Treason Against God: A History of the Offense of Blasphemy* (New York: Schocken Books, 1981), 335.

209. For an evangelical view of what could be known through natural religion, see Smith, *A Comprehensive View*.

210. James Madison, "Memorial and Remonstrance," in *Writings of James Madison*, ed. Gaillard Hunt (New York: Putnam's Son, 1900), 2:185.

211. See Emmons's highly partisan fast day sermon, "Obedience to Civil Magistrates," 129. In 1832 the issue of a national fast again sparked partisan strife. See congressional debates on the subject, *Register of the Debates*, 8:1130–32, 3833–35, 3858–87. Also relevant are Alexander Hamilton's comments on the political utility of a national fast in his letter to William L. Smith, April 10, 1797, *The Papers*, 21:41.

212. Cited in Stokes, *Church and State*, 3:150. See also Levy, *Treason Against God*, 334–35.

213. Thomas Jefferson to Joseph Priestly (April 9, 1803), in *Jefferson's Extracts from the Gospels*, ed. Dickinson W. Adams (Princeton: Princeton University Press, 1983), 327–29.

214. Lyman Beecher, *The Faith Once Delivered to the Saints*, 2d ed. (Boston: Crocker and Brewster, 1824), 16; Madison, "Manifestations," 1317–18; Kendal, "Religion the Only Sure Basis," 1249, 1253–54; Nott, *Discourse*, 22–23.

215. Alexander, *Brief Outline*, 257–60; Wayland, *The Elements of Moral Science*, 161–62; Adams, *Elements of Moral Philosophy*, 78–79; Smith, *A Comprehensive View*, 205–6; Beecher, "A Reformation of Morals," 108; Beecher, *Faith Once Delivered to the Saints*, 17–19; Dana, *Evangelical Preaching*, 8–10; Dana, *An Election Sermon*, 19; Spicer, *Sermon*, 16; Dwight, "The Duty of Americans, at the Present Crisis," 1378.

216. Bush, *Lack of Vision*, 12; Beecher, *The Faith Once Delivered to the Saints*, 17–19; Spicer, *Sermon*, 18; Mason, "The Voice of Warning," 556–57.

217. Bush, *Lack of Vision*, 12; Beecher, *The Faith Once Delivered to the Saints*, 16–17; Lyman Beecher, "Reply to a Review of the Sermon Entitled 'The Faith Once Delivered to the Saints,'" in *Works*, 2:382–406.

218. Spicer, *Sermon,* 18; "Review: Memoirs of Dr. Joseph Priestly . . . and Observations on His Writings, by Thomas Cooper," *Virginia Evangelical and Literary Magazine* (February 1820): 74.

219. When faced with a choice between any religion or no religion at all, evangelicals partially conceded the Founders' point and acknowledged that a false religion would be better than no religion at all as far as civic society was concerned. See Bush, *Lack of Vision,* 7; William Jay, *An Essay on the Importance of the Sabbath Considered Merely as a Civil Institution* (Geneva, N.Y.: James Bogert, 1826), 5.

220. Lyman Beecher, "The Memory of Our Fathers," in *Works,* 1:325–26.

221. Jedidiah Morse, *A Sermon Delivered at Charlestown, July 23, 1812* (Charlestown, Mass.: Samuel Etheridge, 1812), 30; Dwight, *President Dwight's Decisions,* 111–16.

222. Beecher, "Autobiography," 1:196.

223. Beecher, "A Reformation of Morals," 105; General Union for Promoting the Observance of the Christian Sabbath, *Address of the General Union,* 11–14.

224. Morse, *A Sermon,* 30–31; Ezra Stiles Ely, *The Duty of Christian Freemen to Elect Christian Rulers* (Philadelphia: William F. Geddes, 1828), esp., 8–14.

225. Beecher, "The Memory of Our Fathers," 341.

226. Beecher, *The Faith Once Delivered to the Saints;* John Witherspoon, "[Sermon] Delivered at a Publick Thanksgiving," in *The Works of Rev. John Witherspoon* (Philadelphia: Woodward, 1802), 2d ed., 3:83.

227. Timothy Dwight, "On Doing Good," in *Sermons,* 1:540–41.

228. Beecher, "The Memory of Our Fathers," 339.

229. Francis Wayland, "On the Death of the Ex-Presidents," in *Occasional Discourses,* 90–91.

230. Ibid., 93.

231. Beecher, *The Faith Once Delivered to the Saints,* 25.

232. Ibid.

233. Winfrid Ernest Garrison and Alfred T. DeGroot, *The Disciples of Christ: A History* (St. Louis: Christian Board of Publication, 1948), 175–77.

234. Cited in Hatch, *Democratization of American Christianity,* 100.

235. Ibid., esp. 17–46.

236. Garrison and DeGroot, *The Disciples of Christ,* 177.

237. George P. Hays, *Presbyterians* (New York: Hill, 1892), 413–24, esp. 417–20; Charles L. Thompson, "Presbyterian Church in the United States of America," *Encyclopedia Americana,* 1948 ed., 538. In 1833, the denomination split over the question of whether American Christians could vote and hold national office in good conscience.

238. Ely, *The Duty of Christian Freemen,* 8. Lois W. Banner comments that Ely's proposal "found little open support among the ecclesiastical community" ("Religious Benevolence as Social Control: A Critique of an Interpretation," in *Religion in American History: Interpretive Essays,* ed. John M. Mulder and John F. Wilson [Englewood Cliffs, N.J.: Prentice-Hall, 1978], 222).

239. Ely, *The Duty of Christian Freemen*, 8–11; and "Appendix, Designed to Vindicate the Liberty of Christians, & c," 30–32.

240. See, for example, *Trumpet and Universalist Magazine*, August 30, 1828, 34; Robert L. Jennings, "Religion Necessary to Make and Keep People Virtuous," *Free Enquirer*, December 24, 1828, 71; "Orthodox Attack on Congress," *Trumpet and Universalist Magazine*, February 4, 1829, 130; Frances Wright, "Address," *Free Enquirer*, October 18, 1829, 3–4; A Layman, "To Any Member of Congress," *Free Enquirer*, February 27, 1830, 138–40; "Plots and Masks," *Working Man's Advocate*, October 30, 1830, 3.

241. See Lyman Beecher's account of Wright's meetings in "The Perils of Atheism to the Nation," in *Works*, 1:92–94.

242. Frances Wright D'Arusmont, "Lecture IV. Religion," "Lecture III. Of the More Important Divisions and Essential Parts of Knowledge," in *Life, Letters, and Lectures, 1834–1844* (New York: Arno Press, 1972), 65–66, 45–46.

243. Wright's associate Robert L. Jennings made similar comments, deriding the clergy as "those, whose pecuniary advantage is increased by the crimes of society; nay, whose official existence depends upon the dissentions and hatred, the animosity, the strife, the vice, and misery, which they generate, or which is otherwise generate, among their fellow beings" ("Religion Necessary," 71).

244. D'Arusmont, "Lecture III," 46.

245. Frances Wright D'Arusmont, "Lecture VII. Of Existing Evils, and their Remedy," in *Life, Letters, and Lectures,* 102.

246. Robert Owen, "Mr. Owen's Second Discourse on a New System of Society," and "Oration, Containing a Declaration of Mental Independence," in *Robert Owen in the United States*, ed. Oakley C. Johnson (New York: Humanities Press, 1970), 55, 61–62, 7.

247. "Sunday School Union, or Union of Church and State"; remarks of Senator J. Hare Powell, as reported by the *Harrisburgh Chronicle*. Despite the harshness of his attack, Powell maintained that he supported Sabbath schools; remarks of Senator Brown, as reported by the *Pennsylvania Reporter;* also remarks of Senator Duncan, as reported by the *Harrisburgh Chronicle,* all in Ely, *The Duty of Christian Freemen,* 18–19, 22–26, 28, 19–22.

## CHAPTER 3. EVANGELICALS AND THE SUNDAY MAILS

1. The issue had already been litigated in Massachusetts in 1808. The state had tried to prosecute a mail coach for operating on Sunday, but the Massachusetts Supreme Court ruled that the indictment could not be sustained on the facts. The state law restricting Sunday travel allowed an exception for acts of "necesssity," and the court held that operating a mail coach under a contract with the Postmaster General fit this exception because such a contract was authorized by the postal authority granted to the federal government by the Constitution (*Commonwealth* v. *Knox,* 6 Tyng [Mass.] 76 [1809]).

2. For the best account of the entire incident, see "Stopping the Mail at Princeton," *Daily National Intelligencer,* June 23, 1829, 2.

3. "Arrest of the Mail," *Nile's Weekly Register,* May 2, 1829, 148.

4. "Stopping the Mail at Princeton," 2.

5. Richard John, "Taking Sabbatarianism Seriously: The Postal System, the Sabbath, and the Transformation of the American Political Culture," *Journal of the Early Republic* 10 (Winter 1990): 522.

6. Arthur M. Schlesinger Jr., *The Age of Jackson* (Boston: Little, Brown, 1945), 143.

7. Figures derived from petitions received, House Committee on the Post Office and Post Roads, Records of the U.S. House of Representatives, Record Group 233, National Archives and Records Administration, Washington D.C. (Unless otherwise specified, all other petitions listed in Notes are from this source.)

8. This figure was calculated by dividing 66,945 by the U.S. population in 1830 (12.9 million) and then multiplying the result by the estimated U.S. population in 1990 (248.7 million). Since the 1830 figure includes slaves, the comparison is a conservative one. With the nonslave population in 1830 (10.7 million), the adjusted number of petitions would be more than 1.5 million. Population figures were taken from the *Statistical Abstract of the United States, 1991* (Washington, D.C.: Bureau of the Census, 1991), 7; *Historical Statistics of the United States, Colonial Times to 1970* (Washington, D.C.: Bureau of the Census, 1975), 1:24–36.

9. Opinion Distribution of Sunday Mails Petitions Sent to the U.S. House of Representatives, 1827–1830

|  | Anti–Sunday | % of Total | Pro–Sunday | % of Total |
|---|---|---|---|---|
| 1827 | 8 | 100 | | |
| 1828 | 48 | 94 | 3 | 6 |
| 1829 | 504 | 98 | 17 | 2 |
| 1830 (through Feb.) | 275 | 70 | 118 | 30 |
| 1830 (after Feb.) | 33 | 32 | 71 | 68 |
| 1830 (total) | 308 | 62 | 189 | 38 |
| 1827–1830 | 868 | 81 | 209 | 19 |

Opinion Distribution of Signatures on Sunday Mails Petitions Sent to the U.S. House of Representatives, 1827–1830

|  | Anti–Sunday | % of Total | Pro–Sunday | % of Total |
|---|---|---|---|---|
| 1827 | 874 | 100 | | |
| 1828 | 7,012 | 95 | 340 | 5 |
| 1829 | 26,133 | 90 | 2,866 | 10 |
| 1830 (through Feb.) | 16,728 | 56 | 12,992 | 44 |

Source: *Petition and signature counts derived from petitions received, House Committee on the Post Office, National Archives.*

**10.** Geographic Distribution of Anti–Sunday Mails Petitions Sent to the U.S. House of Representatives, 1827–1830

| | No. of Petitions | % of Total | No. of Signatures | % of Total | Population | % of Total* |
|---|---|---|---|---|---|---|
| *New England* | | | | | | |
| Connecticut | 29 | 5.78 | 2,352 | 6.91 | 298 | 2.79 |
| New Hampshire | 14 | 2.79 | 698 | 2.05 | 269 | 2.52 |
| Maine | 51 | 10.16 | 2,520 | 7.41 | 399 | 3.73 |
| Massachusetts | 69 | 13.75 | 5,368 | 15.78 | 610 | 5.71 |
| Rhode Island | 1 | .20 | 113 | .33 | 97 | .91 |
| Vermont | 17 | 3.39 | 787 | 2.31 | 281 | 2.63 |
| Total | 181 | 36.06 | 11,838 | 34.80 | 1,954 | 18.28 |
| *Mid-Atlantic* | | | | | | |
| Delaware | 3 | .60 | 150 | .44 | 77 | .72 |
| New York | 121 | 24.10 | 9,894 | 29.08 | 1,919 | 17.95 |
| New Jersey | 19 | 3.78 | 815 | 2.40 | 321 | 3.00 |
| Pennsylvania | 53 | 10.56 | 4,038 | 11.87 | 1,348 | 12.61 |
| Total | 196 | 39.04 | 14,897 | 43.79 | 3,665 | 34.28 |
| *South* | | | | | | |
| Alabama | 1 | 2.19 | 56 | .16 | 190 | 1.78 |
| Arkansas | | | | | 26 | .24 |
| District of Columbia | 1 | .20 | 105 | .31 | 21 | .20 |
| Florida | | | | | 18 | .17 |
| Georgia | 2 | .40 | 58 | .17 | 297 | 2.78 |
| Kentucky | 11 | 2.19 | 698 | 2.05 | 519 | 4.85 |
| Louisiana | | | | | 89 | .83 |
| Maryland | 7 | 1.39 | 793 | 2.33 | 291 | 2.72 |
| Missouri | | | | | 114 | 1.07 |
| Mississippi | | | | | 70 | .65 |
| North Carolina | 12 | 2.39 | 421 | 1.24 | 473 | 4.42 |
| South Carolina | 7 | 1.39 | 742 | 2.18 | 258 | 2.41 |
| Tennessee | 13 | 2.59 | 691 | 2.03 | 536 | 5.01 |
| Virginia | 30 | 5.98 | 1,684 | 4.95 | 701 | 6.56 |
| Total | 84 | 16.73 | 5,248 | 15.43 | 3,603 | 33.70 |
| *Northwest* | | | | | | |
| Ohio | 39 | 7.77 | 1,938 | 5.70 | 938 | 8.77 |
| Indiana | | | | | 343 | 3.21 |
| Illinois | 1 | .20 | 16 | .05 | 157 | 1.47 |
| Michigan | 1 | .20 | 82 | .24 | 32 | .30 |
| Total | 41 | 8.17 | 2,036 | 5.98 | 1,470 | 13.75 |

* *Population of state in thousands, excluding slaves, divided by total population of region.*
Sources: Petition and signature counts derived from petitions received, House Committee on the Post Office, National Archives; population figures taken from *Historical Statistics of the United States*, 1:24–36.

**11.** Frequency of occupations in selected Anti-Sunday Mails Petitions sent to the U.S. House of Representatives, 1827–1830: farmers 769; merchants 364; mechanics 173; physicians 94; postal workers 91; clergy 77; attorneys 73; innkeepers 31; manufacturers 27; teachers 23; judges 23; builders 6; masons 6; millers 6; police 6; tavern keepers 5; stage proprietors 4; journalists 3; bankers 1; merchant sailors 1; ferrymen 1 (from petitions received, House Committee on the Post Office, National Archives).

12. *An Account of Memorials Presented to Congress During the Last Session, by Numerous Friends of Their Country and Its Institutions; Praying That the Mails May Not Be Transported, nor Post-Offices Kept Open, on the Sabbath* (New York: T. R. Marvin, 1829), 13, 25–29.

13. See, for example, John R. Bodo, *The Protestant Clergy and Public Issues* (Princeton: Princeton University Press, 1954), 39–43; Clifford Griffin, *Their Brothers' Keepers: Moral Stewardship in the United States, 1800–1865* (New Brunswick, N.J.: Rutgers University Press, 1960), 119–23; Leland Winfield Meyer, *The Life and Times of Colonel Richard M. Johnson of Kentucky* (New York: AMS Press, 1967), 256–62; Charles M. Snow, *Religious Liberty in America* (Washington, D.C.: Review and Herald, 1914), 239–54; Anson Phelps Stokes, *Church and State in the United States* (New York: Harper and Brothers, 1950), 2:17–18; Anson Phelps Stokes and Leo Pfeffer, *Church and State in the United States* (Westport, Conn.: Greenwood Press, 1975), 254–55; Schlesinger, *The Age of Jackson,* 138–140; Bertram Wyatt-Brown, "Prelude to Abolitionism: Sabbatarian Politics and the Rise of the Second Party System," *Journal of American History* 58 (September 1971): 316–41. For a rare positive view of the Sunday mails campaign, see John, "Taking Sabbatarianism Seriously," 517–67. John also provides a helpful listing of other articles on the subject on 518–19 n. 3.

14. Report of Mr. Johnson (March 4–5, 1830), in *American State Papers,* Class 7: Post Office Department (Washington, D.C.: Gales and Seaton, 1834), 1:229.

15. Ibid., 230.

16. See, for example, petition from inhabitants of Philadelphia, Pennsylvania (received [rec.] January 29, 1827); petition from inhabitants of Elizabethtown, New Jersey (rec. December 22, 1828); petition from the grand jury of Washington County, Pennsylvania (rec. December 29, 1828).

17. Petition from inhabitants of Hartford, Connecticut (rec. December 18, 1828).

18. Petition from the grand jury of Washington County, Pennsylvania (rec. December 29, 1828).

19. See petition from merchants and other inhabitants of Utica, New York (signed, January 17, 1827); petitition from inhabitants of Elizabethtown, New Jersey (rec. January 29, 1827); petition from inhabitants of Virginia (rec. January 2, 1828); petition from inhabitants of Hartford, Connecticut (rec. December 18, 1828); petition from inhabitants of Elizabethtown, New Jersey (rec. December 22, 1828); petition from the grand jury of Washington County, Pennsylvania (rec. December 29, 1828); petition from inhabitants of Middlebury and vicinity, Virginia (rec. December 29, 1828); petition from inhabitants of Huntington County, Pennsylvania (rec. January 2, 1829); petition from citizens of Spartanburg District, South Carolina (signed January 3, 1829); petition from inhabitants of Norfolk, Connecticut (rec. January 12, 1829); petition from inhabitants of Grangerville, New York (rec. January 12, 1829); petition from inhabitants of Franklin County, Pennsylvania (rec. January 12, 1829); petition from inhabitants of York County, Maine (rec. January 12, 1829); petition from inhabitants of Perry County, Ohio (rec. January 12, 1829); petition from

inhabitants of Sharon, Connecticut (rec. January 12, 1829); petition from inhabitants of Bedford, New York (rec. January 19, 1829); petition from inhabitants of Tappan, New York (rec. February 2, 1829); petition from inhabitants of Washington County, Vermont (rec. Febuary 2, 1829); petition of inhabitants of Lempster and vicinity, New Hampshire (rec. February 9, 1829); petition from inhabitants of Lansing, New York (rec. January 11, 1830); petition of inhabitants of Vermont (rec. January 11, 1830); petition from inhabitants of Brown County, Ohio (rec. January 11, 1830); petition from inhabitants of East Haddam, Connecticut (rec. January 18, 1830); petition from inhabitants of Salisbury, Connecticut (rec. January 11, 1830); petition from inhabitants of Albany, Vermont (rec. January 11, 1830); petition from Blount County, Tennessee (rec. January 18, 1830); petition of inhabitants of Prattsburgh, New Jersey (rec. January 18, 1830); petition from inhabitants of Mecklinburg County, North Carolina (rec. February 1, 1830); petition from Manlius and vicinity, New York (February 22, 1830); petition of inhabitants of Pawlet, Vermont (rec. February 22, 1830); petition from inhabitants of Orange County, New York (rec. February 22, 1830).

20. See petition from inhabitants of Elizabethtown, New Jersey (rec. January 29, 1827); petition from inhabitants of Elizabethtown, New Jersey (rec. December 22, 1828); petition from inhabitants of Norfolk, Connecticut (rec. January 12, 1829); petition from inhabitants of Sharon, Connecticut (rec. January 12, 1829); petition of inhabitants of Lempster and vicinity, New Hampshire (rec. February 9, 1829); petition from citizens of Spartanburg District, South Carolina (signed, January 3, 1829); petition of inhabitants of Vermont (rec. January 11, 1830); petition from inhabitants of Salisbury, Connecticut (rec. January 11, 1830); petition from inhabitants of East Haddam, Connecticut (rec. January 18, 1830); petition from inhabitants of Erie County, New York (January 18, 1830); petition from Blount County, Tennessee (rec. January 18, 1830); petition of inhabitants of Prattsburgh, New Jersey (rec. January 18, 1830); petition of inhabitants of Pawlet, Vermont (rec. February 22, 1830).

21. See petition from merchants and other inhabitants of Utica, New York (signed January 17, 1827); petitition from inhabitants of Elizabethtown, New Jersey (rec. January 29, 1827); petition from inhabitants of Virginia (rec. January 2, 1828); petition from inhabitants of Hartford, Connecticut (rec. December 18, 1828); petition from inhabitants of Elbridge, New York (rec. December 22, 1828); petition from inhabitants of Elizabethtown, New Jersey (rec. December 22, 1828); petition from inhabitants of Salem, New York (rec. December 29, 1828); petition from the grand jury of Washington County, Pennsylvania (rec. December 29, 1828); petition from inhabitants of Huntington County, Pennsylvania (rec. January 2, 1829); petition from inhabitants of First Parish in West Springfield, Massachusetts (rec. January 5, 1829); petition from inhabitants of Franklin County, Pennsylvania (rec. January 12, 1829); petition from inhabitants of Grangerville, New York (rec. January 12, 1829); petition from inhabitants of Perry County, Ohio (rec. January 12, 1829); petition from inhabitants of Egremont [?], Massachusetts (January 19, 1829); petition from inhabitants of Prince Edward County, Virginia (rec. January 26, 1829); petition from

inhabitants of Tappan, New York (rec. February 2, 1829); petition from inhabitants of Washington County, Vermont (rec. Febuary 2, 1829); petition from merchants of Baltimore, Maryland (rec. February 9, 1829); petition from inhabitants of Albany, Vermont (rec. January 11, 1830); petition from inhabitants of Lansing, New York (rec. January 11, 1830); petition from inhabitants of Vermont (rec. January 11, 1830); petition from inhabitants of Brown County, Ohio (rec. January 11, 1830); petition from the inhabitants of Limerick, Maine (rec. January 11, 1830); petition from inhabitants of Blount County, Tennessee (rec. January 18, 1830); petition from inhabitants of Erie County, New York (rec. January 18, 1830); petition from inhabitants of East Haddam, Connecticut (rec. January 18, 1830); petition from citizens of Castleton and vicinity, Vermont (rec. January 25, 1830); petition from inhabitants of Mecklinburg County, North Carolina (rec. February 1, 1830); petition of inhabitants of Cumberland County, Pennsylvania (rec. February 1, 1830); petition from inhabitants of Pennsylvania (rec. February 22, 1830); petition from Manlius and vicinity, New York (February 22, 1830); petition of inhabitants of Pawlet, Vermont (rec. February 22, 1830); petition from inhabitants of Orange County, New York (rec. February 22, 1830); petition of citizens of Kittery, Maine (rec. 1830).

22. Petition from citizens of Castleton and vicinity, Vermont (rec. January 25, 1830).

23. Petition from the inhabitants of Pennsylvania (rec. February 22, 1830).

24. See Francis Wayland, *The Elements of Moral Science,* ed. Joseph L. Blau (Cambridge, Mass.: Belknap Press, 1963), 145–48.

25. Petition from the grand jury of Washington County, Pennsylvania (rec. December 29. 1828). The petition also cites another British jurist, Chief Justice Matthew Hale.

26. Petition from inhabitants of Hartford, Connecticut (rec. December 18, 1828).

27. Petition from inhabitants of First Parish in West Springfield, Massachusetts (rec. January 5, 1829); see also petition from inhabitants of Manlius and vicinity, New York (rec. February 22, 1830).

28. Thomas Jefferson to William Short (April 13, 1820), in *Jefferson's Extracts from the Gospels,* ed. Dickinson W. Adams (Princeton: Princeton University Press, 1983), 393; see also Frances Wright's attack on the Sabbath in Frances Wright D'Arusmont, "Lecture VI. Formation of Opinions," in *Life, Letters, and Lectures, 1834–1844* (New York: Arno Press, 1972), 98–100.

29. Petition from citizens of Castleton and vicinity, Vermont (rec. January 25, 1830).

30. See petition from inhabitants of Virginia (rec. January 2, 1828); petition from the grand jury of Washington County, Pennsylvania (rec. December 29, 1828); petition from inhabitants of Middlebury and vicinity, Virginia (rec. December 29, 1828); petition from postmaster and others of Mead County, New York (signed December 31, 1828); petition from citizens of Spartanburg District, South Carolina (signed January 3, 1829); petition from inhabitants of East Gilmanton, New Hampshire (rec. January 5, 1829); petition of postmasters and other inhabitants of Colum-

biana County, Ohio (rec. January 5, 1829); petition from inhabitants of Norfolk, Connecticut (rec. January 12, 1829); petition from inhabitants of York County, Maine (rec. January 12, 1829); petition from inhabitants of Perry County, Ohio (rec. January 12, 1829); petition from inhabitants of Bainbridge, Ohio (rec. January 12, 1829); petition from postmaster and other inhabitants of North Haverick (rec. January 19, 1829); petition from inhabitants of Bedford, New York (rec. January 19, 1829); petition of inhabitants of Lempster and vicinity, New Hampshire (rec. February 9, 1829); petition from inhabitants of Trumbull County, Ohio (signed January 1, 1830); petition from inhabitants of Lansing, New York (rec. January 11, 1830); petition from inhabitants of Albany, Vermont (rec. January 11, 1830); petition from inhabitants of Brown County, Ohio (rec. January 11, 1830); petition of inhabitants of Vermont (rec. January 11, 1830); petition from inhabitants of Salisbury, Connecticut (rec. January 11, 1830); petition from inhabitants of Brewer, Maine (rec. January 11, 1830); petition from inhabitants of Erie County, New York (January 18, 1830); petition from citizens of Castleton and vicinity, Vermont (rec. January 25, 1830); petition from inhabitants of Mecklinburg County, North Carolina (rec. February 1, 1830); petition from inhabitants of Pennyslvania (rec. February 1, 1830); petition of inhabitants of Cumberland County, Pennsylvania (rec. February 1, 1830); petition of inhabitants of Pawlet, Vermont (rec. February 22, 1830); petition of inhabitants of Sullivan County, Tennessee (March 2, 1830); petition of citizens of Kittery, Maine (rec. 1830).

31. Petition from inhabitants of Virginia (rec. January 2, 1828).

32. From 1827 to February 1830 at least ninety-one petitioners identified themselves as working for the post office; most of these were postmasters or junior postmasters. Figure derived from petitions received, House Committee on the Post Office.

33. Lewis Tappan, *The Life of Arthur Tappan* (New York: Hurd and Houghton, 1871; reprint, Westport, Conn.: Negro Universities Press, 1970), 101–2.

34. Petition from citizens of Castleton and vicinity, Vermont (rec. January 25, 1830).

35. Petition from inhabitants of Pennyslvania (rec. February 1, 1830).

36. Petition from citizens of Castleton and vicinity, Vermont (rec. January 25, 1830).

37. See, for example, memorial from citizens of Boston (March 23, 1830), in *American State Papers,* Class 7: Post Office, 1:237.

38. John, "Taking Sabbatarianism Seriously," 528–29.

39. Petition from the inhabitants of Pennsylvania (rec. February 1, 1830).

40. Petition from citizens of Philadelphia, Pennsylvania [1830], in *American State Papers,* Class 7: Post Office, 1:234.

41. See petition from merchants and other inhabitants of Utica, New York (signed January 17, 1827); petition from inhabitants of Elizabethtown, New Jersey (rec. January 29, 1827); petition from inhabitants of Philadelphia, Pennsylvania (rec. January 29, 1827); petition from inhabitants of Virginia (rec. January 2, 1828); petition from inhabitants of Elbridge, New York (rec. December 22, 1828); petition from

inhabitants of Salem, New York (rec. December 29, 1828); petition from the grand jury of Washington County, Pennsylvania (rec. December 29. 1828); petition from inhabitants of Bainbridge, Ohio (rec. January 12, 1829); petition from inhabitants of Bedford, New York (rec. January 19, 1829); petition from inhabitants of Prince Edward County, Virginia (rec. January 26, 1829); petition of inhabitants of Lempster and vicinity, New Hampshire (rec. February 9, 1829); petition from inhabitants of Mecklinburg County, North Carolina (rec. February 1, 1830).

42. See petition from inhabitants of Utica, New York (signed January 17, 1827); petition from inhabitants of Orange County, Virginia (rec. January 2, 1828); petition from inhabitants of Bedford, New York (rec. January 19, 1829).

43. Petition from merchants of Baltimore, Maryland (rec. February 9, 1829).

44. See petition from inhabitants of Norfolk, Connecticut (rec. January 12, 1829); petition of inhabitants of Trumbull County, Ohio (signed January 1, 1830); petition from Blount County, Tennessee (rec. January 18, 1830); petition of citizens of Kittery, Maine (rec. 1830).

45. See petition from inhabitants of Franklin County, Pennsylvania (rec. January 12, 1829); petition from inhabitants of Grangerville, New York (rec. January 12, 1829); petition from inhabitants of Prince Edward County, Virginia (rec. January 26, 1829); petition from the inhabitants of Limerick, Maine (rec. January 11, 1830).

46. See J. M. Foster, *Reformation Principles Stated and Applied* (Chicago: Fleming H. Revell, 1890), 133-34.

47. See, for example, William Jay, *An Essay on the Importance of the Sabbath Considered Merely as a Civil Institution* (Geneva, N.Y.: James Bogert, 1826), 10-12; General Union for Promoting the Observance of the Christian Sabbath, *Address of the General Union for Promoting the Observance of the Christian Sabbath* (New York: Fanshaw, 1828), 14-15.

48. John, "Taking Sabbatarianism Seriously," 541.

49. Ibid., 541-42.

50. See petition of inhabitants of Washington County, Pennsylvania (rec. November 13, 1811); petition of General Assembly of the Presbyterian Church in the United States of America (rec. June 13, 1812); petition of the Synod of Pittsburg (rec. 1812[?]); petition of inhabitants of Otisfield, Maine (rec. December 22, 1814); petition of the members of the Congregational Church in Monson, Massachusetts (rec. January 11, 1815); petition of inhabitants of Springfield, Ohio (rec. December 12, 1815); petition of Congregational ministers of Massachusetts (rec. December 18, 1815); petition of inhabitants of Concord, Vermont (December 29, 1815); petition of the Convention of Congregational Ministers, Massachusetts (rec. January 16, 1816). See also petition of inhabitants of Waterbury, Connecticut (rec. December 26, 1814); petition of inhabitants of Hollis, New Hampshire (rec. January 25, 1815), petitions received, Senate Committee on the Post Office and Post Roads, Records of the U.S. Senate, Record Group 46, National Archives and Records Administration, Washington, D.C.

51. Petition of inhabitants of Washington County, Pennsylvania (rec. November 13, 1811).

52. Petition of the Covention of Congregational Ministers, Massachusetts (rec. January 16, 1816).

53. See petition of inhabitants of Washington County, Pennsylvania (rec. November 13, 1811); petition of the General Assembly of the Presbyterian Church in the United States (rec. June 13, 1812); petition of the members of the Congregational Church in Monson, Massachusetts (rec. January 11, 1815); petition of inhabitants of Concord, Vermont (December 29, 1815); petition of the Convention of Congregational Ministers, Massachusetts (rec. January 16, 1816).

See also petition of inhabitants of Waterbury, Connecticut (rec. December 26, 1814), petitions received, Senate Committee on the Post Office.

54. See, for example, petition of inhabitants of Washington County, Pennsylvania (rec. November 13, 1811); petition of Association of Ministers in and around Boston (signed January 9, 1812).

55. Petition of inhabitants of Concord, Vermont (December 29, 1815); petition of the Convention of Congregational Ministers, Massachusetts (rec. January 16, 1816); petition of inhabitants of Washington County, Pennsylvania (rec. November 13, 1811); petition of the General Assembly of the Presbyterian Church in the United States (rec. June 13, 1812).

56. Petition from inhabitants of York, Maine (rec. January 12, 1829).

57. Petition of inhabitants of East Haddam, Connecticut (rec. January 18, 1830).

58. Circular signed by Lyman Beecher, Justin Edwards, John Tappan, Jerimiah Evarts, and others, attached to petition from inhabitants of Brighton, Massachusetts (rec. February 2, 1829).

59. See, for example, petition from Salem Association of Baptists, Kentucky (rec. January 11, 1830); petition from inhabitants of Alstead, New Hampshire (rec. January 11, 1830); petition from inhabitants of Poughkeepsie, New York (rec. January 18, 1830); petition from inhabitants of Pennsylvania (rec. February 1, 1830); petition from inhabitants of Nantuckett, Massachusetts (rec. February 10, 1830); petition from inhabitants of Darrtown, Ohio (rec. February 22, 1830); petition from citizens of Third Congressional District of North Carolina (rec. February 15, 1830); petition from inhabitants of Sehigh, Pennsylvania (rec. March 1, 1830); petition from inhabitants of Hanover, Pennsylvania (rec. March 1, 1830); petition from inhabitants of Pennsylvania (rec. March 1, 1830); resolutions from inhabitants of Cincinnati, Ohio (rec. March 2, 1830).

60. See petition from inhabitants of Sussex, Delaware (rec. February 15, 1830); petition from inhabitants of Chester County and parts adjacent, Pennsylvania (rec. February 22, 1830); petition from inhabitants of Pennsylvania (rec. March 1, 1830); petition from inhabitants of Hanover, Pennsylvania (rec. March 1, 1830); petition from inhabitants of Madison County, New York (rec. March 1, 1830).

61. Petition from inhabitants of Dutchess County, New York (rec. January 25, 1830); see also report of Mr. Johnson (January 19, 1829), in *American State Papers,* Class 7: Post Office, 1:225.

62. Petition from inhabitants of Madison County, New York (rec. March 1, 1830).

63. Petition from the citizens of Windham County, Vermont (signed January 19, 1831), in *American State Papers,* Class 7: Post Office, 1:264. A more charitable dismissal of the religious liberty claims of postal workers was offered by petitioners from New York: "We have reason to expect that very many Post Masters will be in favor of stopping the Mails on sundays[,] some no doubt from pure motives[,] and many in order that they may not be compelled to serve the community on that Day— Yet we conceive the inconvenience to them to be small when compared with the Interests of the community in general[,] and it is well known that no one is compelled to serve as Post Master and any one can resign the Office when he pleases" (Petition of inhabitants of Trumansburgh and vicinity, New York [rec. January 19, 1829]).

64. See petition from inhabitants of Trumansburgh and vicinity, New York (January 19, 1829); petition from inhabitants of Darrtown, Ohio (rec. February 22, 1830); petition from inhabitants of Wheeling, Virginia (rec. March 1, 1830); petition from inhabitants of Hanover, Pennsylvania (rec. March 1, 1830); petition from inhabitants of Orange County, New York (rec. March 1, 1830); petition from inhabitants of Ohio (March 2, 1830).

65. Petition of inhabitants of Hanover, Pennsylvania (rec. March 1, 1830).

66. Petition of inhabitants of Wheeling, Virginia (rec. March 1, 1830).

67. Ibid; see also petition from inhabitants of Brown County, Ohio (rec. March 2, 1830).

68. Petition from the inhabitants of Alstead, New Hampshire (rec. January 11, 1830).

69. Alexis de Tocqueville, *Democracy in America,* trans. George Lawrence, ed. J. P. Mayer (Garden City, N.Y.: Anchor Books, 1969), 291.

70. Petition from inhabitants of Alstead, New Hampshire (rec. January 11, 1830).

71. See petition from inhabitants of Rochester, New York (rec. January 14, 1829); petition from inhabitants of Broome County, New York (rec. January 26, 1829); petition from businessmen of Lewiston, New York (rec. January 14, 1829); petition from inhabitants of Penobscott County, Maine (rec. February 2, 1829); petition from inhabitants of Poughkeepsie, New York (rec. January 18, 1830); petition from inhabitants of Dutchess County, New York (rec. January 25, 1830); petition from citizens of Third Congressional District of North Carolina (rec. February 15, 1830); petition from inhabitants of Chester County and adjacent parts, Pennsylvania (rec. February 22, 1830); petition from inhabitants of Hanover, Pennsylvania (rec. March 1, 1830); petition from the Alabama Baptist Association (rec. December 28, 1831).

72. For memorials from religious groups or those professing Christianity, see petition from inhabitants of Penobscott County, Maine (rec. February 2, 1829); petition from Salem Association of Baptists, Kentucky (rec. January 11, 1830); petition from inhabitants of Salinas, New York, who hold the seventh day as Sabbath (January 11, 1830); petition from inhabitants of Madison County, New York, who hold

the seventh day as Sabbath (rec. March 1, 1830); petition from the Alabama Baptist Association (rec. December 28, 1831). For memorials supporting voluntary Sabbath observance but opposing efforts to end Sunday mails, see petition from inhabitants of Poughkeepsie, New York (rec. February 2, 1829); petition from inhabitants of Tennessee (rec. February 26, 1829); resolutions from public meeting in Buffalo, New York (meeting held December 26, 1829[?]); petition from citizens of Third Congressional District of North Carolina (rec. February 15, 1830); petition from inhabitants of Darrtown, Ohio (rec. February 22, 1830); resolutions from inhabitants of Cincinnati, Ohio (rec. March 2, 1830).

73. Meyer, *The Life and Times,* 352–53, 379–85.

74. Petition from the Alabama Baptist Association (rec. December 28, 1831).

75. The *Kentucky Observer and Lexington Reporter* called Johnson "the mere slave and tool of Jackson, Van Buren and others of the party" (cited in Meyer, *The Life and Times,* 272). Johnson himself provided plenty of ammunition for such criticisms. After John Quincy Adams was elected president instead of Andrew Jackson in 1825, Johnson told an editor of the *National Intelligencer* that "even if they [those in the administration] act as pure as the angels that stand at the right hand of the throne of God, we'll put them down" (cited in Meyer, *The Life and Times,* 221).

76. Ibid., 343–92.

77. Ibid., 263.

78. Ibid., 301–2.

79. Ibid., 328–31, 339–40.

80. John, "Taking Sabbatarianism Seriously," 559; Robert Dale Owen, "Clerical Assurance in America," *Free Enquirer,* October 31, 1829, 6.

81. For examples of petitions that praised Johnson's first report, see petition from Salem Association of Baptists, Kentucky (rec. January 11, 1830); petition from inhabitants of Poughkeepsie, New York (rec. January 18, 1830); petition from inhabitants of Sussex County, Delaware (rec. February 15, 1830); petition from inhabitants of Darrtown, Ohio (rec. February 22, 1830); petition from inhabitants of Hampden County, Massachusetts (rec. March 2, 1830); resolutions from inhabitants of Cincinnati, Ohio (rec. March 2, 1830).

82. Report of Mr. Johnson (January 19, 1829), 225.

83. Ibid., 226.

84. Ibid., 225.

85. Report of Mr. McKean (February 3, 1829), in *American State Papers,* Class 7: Post Office, 1:226.

86. Ibid., 227.

87. See, for example, petition from inhabitants of New York (rec. February 11, 1811); petition of Association of Ministers in and about Boston, Massachusetts (signed January 9, 1812); petition from inhabitants of Otisfield, Maine (rec. December 22, 1814).

88. See petition from inhabitants of Poughkeepsie, New York (rec. February 2, 1829); petition from inhabitants of the City of New York (rec. January 11, 1830); petition from inhabitants of Poughkeepsie, New York (rec. January 18, 1830); resolu-

tions from inhabitants of Cincinnati, Ohio (rec. March 2, 1830). See also resolution and memorial from Windham County, Vermont (rec. February 24, 1831), in *American State Papers*, Class 7: Post Office, 1:263–65.

89. Petition from inhabitants of the City of New York (rec. January 11, 1830). For the continuing controversy over how the signatures were obtained, see *Free Enquirer*, April 3, 1830, 177–78.

90. Petition from inhabitants of Poughkeepsie, New York (rec. January 18, 1830).

91. Meyer, *The Life and Times*.

92. Report of Mr. Johnson (March 4–5, 1830), in *American State Papers*, Class 7: Post Office, 1:229.

93. Ibid., 230.

94. Ibid., 230–31.

95. Report of Mr. McCreery (March 5, 1830), in *American State Papers*, Class 7: Post Office, 1:231.

96. *Review of a Report of the Committee . . . by the Hon. Richard Johnson* (Washington, D.C.: n.p., 1829), 21.

97. Ibid., 21–22.

98. *The Logic and Law of Col. Johnson's Report to the Senate on Sabbath Mails* (Utica, N.Y.: Wilson, 1829), 4.

99. *Review of a Report*, 20–21.

100. Ibid., 19.

101. Ibid., 16.

102. Ibid., 18.

103. Ibid., 16.

104. Ibid., 19–20, 22.

105. Ibid., 12–13; *The Logic and Law*, 10–24.

106. General Union for Promoting the Observance of the Christian Sabbath, *Address of the General Union*, 7.

107. Ibid., 7–8, 12–13.

108. See list of officers, ibid., 8.

109. *Trumpet and Universalist Magazine*, August 30, 1828, 34.

110. Talbot W. Chambers, *Memoir of the Life and Character of the Late Hon. Theodore Frelinghuysen* (New York: Harper and Brothers, 1863), 81–82, 213–51.

111. Ibid., 46–47.

112. Ibid., 174–181

113. Ibid., 84–87, 95–113.

114. Ibid., 87–95.

115. Theodore Frelinghuysen to Jeremiah Evarts (February 1, 1830), Jeremiah Evarts Collection, Library of Congress.

116. Frelinghuysen to Evarts (February 22, 1830), Jeremiah Evarts Collection, Library of Congress.

117. Theodore Frelinghuysen, *Speech of Mr. Frelinghuysen on His Resolution*

*Concerning Sabbath Mails in the Senate of the United States, May 8, 1830* (Washington, D.C.: Rothwell and Ustick, 1830), 4–5, 8–12.

118. Ibid., 14.

119. See ibid., 11–13.

120. Frelinghuysen, *Speech of Mr. Frelinghuysen,* 6–7.

121. See list of officers in General Union for Promoting the Observance of the Christian Sabbath, *Address of the General Union,* 8.

122. Evarts's journal cited in E. C. Tracy, *Memoir of the Life of Jeremiah Evarts, Esq.* (Boston: Crocker and Brewster, 1845), 369.

123. Ibid., 371.

124. Schlesinger, *The Age of Jackson,* 143.

125. John, "Taking Sabbatarianism Seriously," 562–63.

126. Chambers, *Memoir,* 77.

127. John, "Taking Sabbatarianism Seriously," 563.

128. Petition from inhabitants of Poughkeepsie, New York (rec. January 18, 1830).

129. Report of Mr. Johnson (January 19, 1829), 226.

130. See memorial from citizens of Philadelphia, Pennsylvania ([1830?]), in *American State Papers,* Class 7: Post Office, 1:234–35.

131. Report of Mr. McCreery (March 5, 1830), 231.

132. See, for example, petition of inhabitants of York County, Maine (rec. January 12, 1829); petition of inhabitants of Bainbridge, Ohio (rec. January 12, 1829); petition of inhabitants of Bedford, New York (rec. January 19, 1829); petition of inhabitants of East Haddam, Connecticut (rec. January 18, 1830). See also memorial of citizens of North Carolina (December 1829), in *American State Papers,* Class 7: Post Office, 1:232–33.

133. "Article VII. [Review of the] Report of the Committee of the House of Representatives of the United States on Post-Offices and Post-Roads," *North American Review* (July 1830): 157.

134. "It is the opinion of the committee that the subject should be regarded simply as a question of expediency, irrespective of its religious bearing" (Report of Mr. Johnson [January 19, 1829], 225).

135. See the discussion of these men in Chapter 1.


## CHAPTER 4. EVANGELICALS AND CHEROKEE REMOVAL

1. Samuel Worcester to David Greene (May 31, 1831), American Board of Commissioners for Foreign Missions, Papers, Houghton Library, Harvard (Woodbridge, Conn.: Research Publications, microfilm), ABC 18.3.1, 7, item 140.

2. "Worcester, Samuel Austin," *Encyclopedia Americana,* 1948 ed., 29:511.

3. Joseph Tracy, *History of the American Board of Commissioners for Foreign Missions* (New York: Dodd, 1842), 2d ed., 249-50.

4. Ibid., 250.

5. Worcester to Greene (May 31, 1831).

6. [Postscript dated June 2, 1831], ibid.

7. *Cherokee Nation* v. *State of Georgia* 5 Peters 1 (1831); Richard Peters, *The Case of the Cherokee Nation Against the State of Georgia* (Philadelphia: John Grigg, 1831), 163-64.

8. Peters, *The Case of the Cherokee Nation,* 159.

9. [Postscript dated June 2, 1831], Worcester to Greene (May 31, 1831).

10. "Resolutions of the Legislature of Georgia," February 4, 1828, in *New American State Papers, Indian Affairs* (Wilmington, Del.: Scholarly Resources, 1972), 9:52.

11. See, for example, Treaty of Tellico (October 2, 1798), sec. 6, which guaranteed that the United States "will continue the guarantee of the remainder of their country forever, as made and contained in former treaties" (Peters, *The Case of the Cherokee Nation,* 256).

12. See reply of General Council of Cherokee Nation to U.S. Commissioners (October 11, 1827), in *New American State Papers, Indian Affairs,* 9:39.

13. "Resolutions of the Legislature of Georgia," 9:51-62.

14. "Constitution of the Cherokee Nation [July 1827]," reprinted in *Starr's History of the Cherokee Indians,* ed. Jack Gregory and Rennard Strickland (Fayetteville, Ark.: Indian Heritage Association, 1967), 60-61. The Cherokee constitution was reminiscent of the U.S. Constitution, guaranteeing a bicameral legislature, a supreme court, and an executive branch whose chief officer would be called the "Principal Chief." It also protected basic civil rights, including trial by jury, freedom from unreasonable search and seizure, the right to bail in most cases, and the absolute security of private property from public appropriation without the owner's consent (61-63).

There were some notable divergences from the American Constitution, however. Perhaps most obvious was the explicit denial of rights to blacks and mulattoes (56). Given that Cherokee lands were in the heart of the South and included cotton plantations, the protection of slavery was understandable, though unfortunate. Slaveholding among the Cherokees posed a moral dilemma for northern missionaries, one that they never really confronted satisfactorily. Some missionaries of the ABCFM did purchase slaves to emancipate them; but they did not urge Cherokee slaveholders to do likewise. (See Charles K. Whipple, *Relation of the American Board of Commissioners for Foreign Missions to Slavery* [n.p.: Wallcut, 1861; reprint, New York: Negro Universities Press, 1969], esp., 3-5, 37-48, 86-106.)

The Cherokee constitution also differed from its American counterpart in the treatment of religion. Unlike the U.S. Constitution, the Cherokee charter appealed to God, "acknowledging with humility and gratitude the goodness of the sovereign Ruler of the Universe, in offering us an opportunity so favorable to the design, and imploring His aid and direction in its accomplishment" ("Constitution," 55). The document also prescribed a religious test: "No person who denies the being of a God, or a future state of rewards and punishment, shall hold any office in the civil department of the nation" (62).

At the same time, the Cherokees guaranteed the freedom of worship and stipulated that "no minister of the Gospel, or public preacher of any religious persuasion, whilst he continues in the exercise of his pastoral functions, shall be eligible to the office of Principal Chief, or a seat in either house of the General Council" (62). The reasoning for this latter exclusion was avowedly religious: "Ministers of the Gospel are, by their profession, dedicated to the service of God and the care of souls, and ought not to be diverted from the great duty of their function" (62). This rationale closely followed that found in the New York state constitution, which had been drafted by evangelical John Jay.

15. R. Pierce Beaver, *Church, State, and the American Indians* (St. Louis: Concordia, 1966), 104–7.

16. Elias Boudinot, *An Address to the Whites* (Philadelphia: William F. Geddes, 1826), 8–11.

17. Ibid., 8.

18. William G. McLoughlin, *Cherokee Renascence in the New Republic* (Princeton: Princeton University Press, 1986), 414–42.

19. William G. McLoughlin, *Cherokees and Missionaries, 1789–1839* (New Haven: Yale University Press, 1984), 240.

20. John Ehle, *Trail of Tears: The Rise and Fall of the Cherokee Nation* (New York: Doubleday, 1988), 220.

21. See J. Orin Oliphant, ed., *Through the South and the West with Jeremiah Evarts in 1826* (Lewisburg, Penn.: Bucknell University Press, 1956).

22. For a recent biography, see John A. Andrew III, *From Revival to Removal: Jeremiah Evarts, the Cherokee Nation, and the Search for the Soul of America* (Athens: University of Georgia Press, 1992).

23. E. C. Tracy, *Memoir of the Life of Jeremiah Evarts, Esq.* (Boston: Crocker and Brewster, 1845), 428–29.

24. Ibid., 429.

25. Francis Paul Prucha, Introduction to *Cherokee Removal: The "William Penn" Essays and Other Writings of Jeremiah Evarts* (Knoxville: University of Tennessee Press, 1981), 8; Tracy, *Memoir,* 339, 347–49.

26. Prucha, Introduction, 11.

27. Tracy, *Memoir,* 339.

28. Cited in Tracy, *Memoir,* 347.

29. Jeremiah Evarts, "William Penn" Essay No. 1, in *Cherokee Removal,* 48.

30. Ibid., 49.

31. Ibid., 49–50.

32. Ibid., 50; the story of Naboth can be found in I Kings 21.

33. Ibid., 50–51.

34. Ibid., 51.

35. Ibid., 52; the end of this passage is a quote from Micah 6:8.

36. Ibid., 53.
37. Jeremiah Evarts, "William Penn" Essay No. 2, in *Cherokee Removal*, 53.
38. Ibid., 54.
39. Treaty of Holston, cited in Jeremiah Evarts, "William Penn" Essay No. 6, in *Cherokee Removal*, 80.
40. Evarts, "William Penn" Essay No. 7, in *Cherokee Removal*, 84-85.
41. Ibid., 84.
42. Jeremiah Evarts, citing Treaty of Tellico, "William Penn" Essay No. 8, in *Cherokee Removal*, 89.
43. Jeremiah Evarts, "William Penn" Essay No. 7, in *Cherokee Removal*, 86.
44. Jeremiah Evarts, "William Penn" Essay No. 15, in *Cherokee Removal*, 126-27.
45. Ibid., 127.
46. Jeremiah Evarts, "William Penn" Essay No. 16, in *Cherokee Removal*, 129.
47. Ibid., 129-30.
48. Jeremiah Evarts, "William Penn" Essays Nos. 16, 17, 18, in *Cherokee Removal*, 130-43.
49. Jeremiah Evarts, "William Penn" Essay No. 18, 143-45.
50. Jeremiah Evarts, "William Penn" Essay No. 20, in *Cherokee Removal*, 155.
51. Ibid.
52. Ibid., 156-57.
53. Ibid., 156.
54. Ibid.
55. Enacting clause of 1802 compact, cited in ibid., 158, Evarts's emphasis removed. Evarts added that through 1826 Georgia had respected the clear stipulations of not only the compact of 1802 but also the various treaties protecting Indian lands. The state's present contention that the Indians lived within its borders at its pleasure was both novel and new. Indeed, it was not until December 1827 that Georgia first openly declared "that the State might properly take possession of the Cherokee country by force; and that it was owing to her moderation and forbearance that she did not thus take possession" (Jeremiah Evarts, "William Penn" Essay No. 21, in *Cherokee Removal*, 161). This was legal theory created ex nihilo.
56. Act of Georgia (December 20, 1828), cited in Jeremiah Evarts, "William Penn" Essay No. 22, in *Cherokee Removal*, 173.
57. Ibid., 173-74.
58. Ibid., 174.
59. Ibid., 174, 176-77.
60. Ibid., 177.
61. Ibid., 177-78.
62. "Resolutions of the Legislature of Georgia," 9:55-56.
63. Jeremiah Evarts, "William Penn" Essay No. 23, in *Cherokee Removal*, 184.
64. Ibid., 185.
65. Jeremiah Evarts, "William Penn" Essay No. 24, in *Cherokee Removal*, 186-93.

66. Ibid., 192–93.

67. Ibid., 194; the passage cited by Evarts is Deuteronomy 27:17–19.

68. Ibid., 194.

69. Ibid., 194–95.

70. James Wilson, *The Works of James Wilson,* ed. Robert Green McCloskey (Cambridge, Mass.: Belknap Press, 1967), 1:125.

71. Evarts's rationalism did not end, however, with his articulation of the common ground shared by reason and revelation; it permeated his very conception of the political process. If human beings are morally accountable, and if morality is eminently reasonable, then men are obliged to act according to their nature and make all their decisions—political decisions, included—according to the reasonable principles of right and wrong. But this means that politics must be a process of deliberation by reflection and choice rather than passion and force. Accordingly, those citizens who want to participate in politics have a civic obligation to become properly informed about the great issues confronting them. Deciding issues by prejudice or passion is not enough; it is not even tolerable.

Evarts's emphasis on man's rationality helps explain the length and the exhaustiveness of his essays. He apologized to readers for going into such detail to prove his point, and he acknowledged that he risked losing his audience on account of his lengthy presentation of treaties ("William Penn" Essay No. 14, in *Cherokee Removal,* 120–21.) But he wanted to leave no reasonable doubts on the subject; and he hoped that those he was most trying to reach—the "members of the Amercan community, who may be justly denominated honest and intelligent"—would stick with him. According to Evarts, these were the people who were capable of deciding the Indian question "properly, if they will take the trouble to understand it, and will distinctly and loudly express their opinion upon it" (121).

Evarts's conception of a politics of reflection and choice closely resembled the working ideal of the judicial system: Evidence and argument must be freely presented on both sides; and then the judge or jury should carefully deliberate until a conclusion is reached. The judicial overtones of Evarts rhetoric was no accident, for he had been a practicing lawyer early in his career (Tracy, *Memoir,* 43–47). Now he realized he was bringing the most significant case of his career not before a literal court but before the court of public opinion. Evarts accordingly appealed to his readers as if they were members of a jury: "Let every intelligent reader consider himself a juryman in the case; and let him resolve to bring in such a verdict, as he can hereafter regard with complacency. It is not a single man, who is on trial, and who may lose his life by the carelessness of the jury. Sixty thousand men, women, and children, in one part of the United States, are now in constant expectation of being driven away from their country, in such a manner as they apprehend will result in their present misery and speedy extermination:—sixty thousand human beings, to whom the faith of the United States has been pledged in the most solemn manner, to be driven away—and yet is it possible that the people of the United States should be unwilling to hear their story, or even to require silence till their story can be heard? ("William Penn" Essay No. 14, 121).

72. Senator Theodore Frelinghuysen, who led the fight for the Cherokees in the Senate, told Evarts that nothing could have been done without the essays (Tracy, *Memoir,* 365).

73. Ibid., 349–53.

74. See, for example, memorial of inhabitants of New York (rec. January 4, 1830); memorial of inhabitants from Pennsylvania (rec. January 7, 1830); memorial of Religious Society of Friends, New York (rec. January 14, 1830); memorial of the Religious Society called Quakers of Pennsylvania, Delaware, and Maryland (rec. January 26, 1830); memorial of inhabitants of Pittsburgh, Pennsylvania (rec. February 19, 1830); memorial of sundry citizens of Farmington, Connecticut (rec. February 27, 1830), petitions and memorials received, Senate Committee on Foreign Relations and Indian Affairs, Records of the U.S. Senate, Record Group 46, National Archives and Records Administration, Washington, D.C.

75. Sometimes petitions for the two issues would be forwarded to Congress together, causing one of the petitions to be misfiled with the wrong committee. See, for example, the petitions of the inhabitants of Tallmadge, Ohio (signed January 19 [or 17], 1830); petition of inhabitants of Morgan, Ohio (rec. February 22, 1830). See also petitions of inhabitants of Kittery, Maine (rec. January 20, 1831), petitions received, Senate Committee on Foreign Relations and Indian Affairs.

76. See memorial of sundry ladies of Hallowell, Maine (rec. January 18, 1830), petitions received, Senate Committee on Foreign Relations and Indians Affairs. See also petition of female inhabitants of Lewis, New York (signed January 24, 1831); petition of the ladies of Monson, Massachusetts (rec. February 14, 1831); petition of female inhabitants of Hadley, Massachusetts (rec. February 15, 1831); petition of men and women of Nelson, Ohio (rec. March 3, 1831), House Committee on Indian Affairs, Records of the U.S. House of Representatives, Record Group 233, National Archives and Records Administration, Washington, D.C.

77. Memorial of sundry ladies of Hallowell, Maine (rec. January 18, 1830), petitions received, Senate Committee on Foreign Relations and Indians Affairs.

78. Thirty-eight petitions are on file for the Senate and sixteen for the House of Representatives during this period. Count is derived from records for the House Committee on Indian Affairs and Senate Committees on Foreign Relations and Indian Affairs, National Archives.

79. See, for example, the vitriolic House debate over the referral of one such petition on January 11, 1830, in *Register of the Debates in Congress* (Washington, D.C.: Gales and Seaton, 1830), 506–11.

80. Wilson Lumpkin, *The Removal of the Cherokee Indians from Georgia* (New York: Dodd, Mead, 1907), 47.

81. "Let it be remembered that weak minorities always made the most noise" (ibid., 67).

82. Ibid.

83. Evarts, cited in Tracy, *Memoir,* 358.

84. Speech of Senator Theodore Frelinghuysen (April 8, 1830), in *Register of the Debates,* 309.

85. Ibid., 311.

86. Ibid., 312.

87. Ibid., 312-20.

88. Talbot W. Chambers, *Memoir of the Life and Character of the Late Hon. Theodore Frelinghuysen* (New York: Harper and Brothers, 1863), 70.

89. Cited in ibid., 71.

90. Speech of Senator John Forsyth (April 15, 1830), in *Register of the Debates,* 325.

91. Ibid., 326-27.

92. Ibid., 329.

93. See Niccolò Machiavelli's praise of the founders of new cities in *The Prince,* trans. Harvey Mansfield Jr. (Chicago: University of Chicago Press, 1985), 6-16, 21-24, 68-71. Also note Machiavelli's comments on the origins of Rome in *The Discourses,* trans. Leslie J. Walker, ed. Bernard Crick (Harmondsworth, Eng.: Penguin, 1983), 102, 131-32.

94. Forsyth (April 15, 1830), 336.

95. Ibid., 334.

96. Ibid., 334-36.

97. Ibid., 334.

98. Ibid., 336.

99. John 8:7.

100. See the rebuttals offered by Senator Peleg Sprague (April 17, 1830), and Representative Henry R. Storrs (May 15, 1830), in *Register of the Debates,* 354-55, 1003-8.

101. Jeremiah Evarts, "William Penn" Essay No. 23, in *Cherokee Removal,* 184.

102. Forsyth (April 15, 1830), 336.

103. Speech of Congressman Henry Storrs (May 15, 1830), in *Register of the Debates,* 1005.

104. Ibid., 1007.

105. Ibid., 1015.

106. "I profess to admire that active spirit of christian benevolence which has done so much for our common country, in the cause of letters and morality. That religion which carries its saving influence into families, congregations, and society in general, adorns its professors" (ibid.). See also American Sunday School Union, *Seventh Annual Report of the American Sunday School Union* 2d ed. (Philadelphia: American Sunday School Union, 1831), 7.

107. Speech of Congressman Wilson Lumpkin (May 17, 1830), in *Register of the Debates,* 1020.

108. Ibid., 1022.

109. Ibid., 1020.

110. Ibid., 1019.

111. Ibid., 1021.

112. "If the wicked one himself can assume the form of an angel of light to de-

ceive and effect his diabolical purposes, then we need not be surprised to see the children walking in the footsteps of their parents" (ibid.).

113. Ibid., 1020.

114. Ibid., 1021.

115. Ibid., 1020.

116. Ibid., 1018-19.

117. Speech of Congressman George Evans (May 18, 1830), in *Register of the Debates,* 1038.

118. Prucha, Introduction, 7-8.

119. Evans (May 18, 1830), 1038.

120. Tracy, *Memoir,* 371.

121. Ibid., 364.

122. David Crockett, *A Narrative of the Life of David Crockett of the State of Tennessee* (Knoxville: University of Tennessee Press, 1973), 205-6.

123. Ibid., 206.

124. See May 18, 1830, *Register of the Debates,* 1049; and speech of Edward Everett (May 19, 1830), in *Register of the Debates,* 1058.

125. Text of bill as enacted, May 26, 1830, in *Register of the Debates,* 1136.

126. Speech of Edward Everett (May 19, 1830), in *Register of the Debates,* 1053.

127. Tracy, *Memoir,* 374.

128. Ibid., 372-73.

129. May 24, 1830, in *Register of the Debates,* 1131.

130. Speech of Congressman Hemphill (May 24, 1830), in *Register of the Debates,* 1132.

131. Tracy, *Memoir,* 375-76.

132. Ibid., 376-77.

133. Ibid., 377-79.

134. Ibid., 382-83.

135. Ibid., 380.

136. Ibid., 381.

137. From the end of the twenty-first Congress in May 1830 to March 1832, at least 79 petitions on behalf of the Indians came into the Senate, and from the end of the twenty-first Congress through the first quarter of 1831 at least 138 petitions came into the House. These figures likely understate the total number of petitions received since they are derived from the number of petitions filed with the House and Senate Committees on Indian Affairs.

138. Both the opinion of the court by Chief Justice John Marshall and the dissenting opinion by Justice Smith Thompson (and joined by Justice Joseph Story) recognized the validity of the Cherokees' treaty rights. The concurring opinions filed by Justices William Johnson and Henry Baldwin were much more ambiguous, tending toward Georgia's reading of the law. See Peters, *The Case of the Cherokee Nation,* 159-221, esp. 160-61, 192-94, 218-21.

139. For an account of Evarts's last days, see Tracy, *Memoir,* 408-17.

140. D. S. Butrick to Evarts (May 25, 1831), ABCFM, Papers, ABC 18.3.1, 7, item 7.

141. Butrick to Greene (June 9, 1831), ABCFM, Papers, ABC 18.3.1, 7, item 8.

142. Ibid.

143. Butrick to Greene (May 25, 1831), ABCFM, Papers, ABC 18.3.1, 7, item 7.

144. Worcester to Greene (June 29, 1831), ABCFM, Papers, ABC 18.3.1, 7, item 144.

145. [Postscript dated July 8, 1831, by Elias Boudinot], Worcester to Greene (July 5, 1831), ABCFM, Papers, ABC 18.3.1, 7, item 145.

146. Worcester to Greene (July 18, 1831), ABCFM, Papers, ABC 18.3.1, no. 146. Unless noted otherwise, the account that follows is derived from this letter by Worcester.

147. Joseph Tracy, *History of American Board of Commissioners for Foreign Missions,* 2d ed. (New York: Dodd, 1842), 252–53.

148. *Worcester* v. *Georgia* 6 Peters 515, 561 (1832).

149. Ehle, *Trail of Tears,* 255.

150. See Worcester to Greene (December 7, 1832), ABCFM, Papers, ABC 18.3.1, 7, item 180; McLoughlin, *Cherokee Renascence,* 446.

151. William G. McLoughlin, *Cherokees and Missionaries,* 307–10.

152. Ibid., 313–14.

153. Ibid., 312–13.

154. Ehle, *Trail of Tears,* 322–46.

155. Ibid., 389–92.

156. Ibid., 371–81.

157. Prucha, Introduction, 40.

158. Lumpkin, *The Removal of Cherokee Indians,* 2:202–3.

159. Ibid., 2:252.

160. Ibid., 2:222–25.

161. McLoughlin, *Cherokees and Missionaries,* 299.

162. Worcester to Greene (January 23, 1833), ABCFM, Papers, ABC 18.3.1, 7, item 209.

163. For a similar expression of this view, see "Prudential Committee Opinions," (December 25, 1832), ABCFM, Papers, ABC 18.3.1, 7, item 189.


## EPILOGUE

1. "Georgia to Pardon Two in 1831 Case," *New York Times* (national ed.), November 11, 1992, A-7.

2. Lyman Beecher, *The Practicality of Suppressing Vice by Means of Special Societies Instituted for That Purpose* (New London, Conn.: Samuel Green, 1804), 17.

3. Nathaniel Hawthorne, "Young Goodman Brown," in *Tales and Sketches* (New York: Library of America, 1982), 276–89.

4. Nathaniel Hawthorne, "The Gray Champion," in *Tales and Sketches*, 236-43.

5. Ibid., 243.

6. See Paul Goodman, *Towards a Christian Republic: Antimasonry and the Great Transition in New England, 1826-1836* (New York: Oxford University Press, 1988), 29-30, 137-39, 150, 190, 237. Everett did not join the antimasons, but he cultivated their support and espoused some of their doctrines.

7. Ibid., 239-45.

8. Louis W. Banner, "Religious Benevolence as Social Control: A Critique of an Interpretation," in *Religion in American History: Interpretive Essays*, ed. John M. Mulder and John F. Wilson (Englewood Cliffs, N.J.: Prentice-Hall, 1978), 222.

9. Leonard W. Levy, *The Law of the Commonwealth and Chief Justice Shaw: The Evolution of American Law, 1830-1860* (New York: Harper Torchbooks, 1967), 57.

10. Cited in Morton Borden, *Jews, Turks, and Infidels* (Chapel Hill: University of North Carolina Press, 1984), 99, 151 n. 4.

11. Nativism did not become a major political issue until the mid-1830s and early 1840s. See Glyndon G. Van Deusen, *The Jacksonian Era, 1828-1848* (New York: Harper Torchbooks, 1963), 16-17. The fight over public education began to take shape in Massachusetts in 1837 and 1838 with Horace Mann. See Anson Phelps Stokes, *Church and State in the United States* (New York: Harper and Brothers, 1950), 2:47-72, esp. 55-64. The effort to amend the Constitution to recognize Christ arose midcentury. Reformed Presbyterians—many of whom refused to vote because the Constitution did not recognize Christ—were at the head of this movement. See George P. Hays, *Presbyterians* (New York: Hill, 1892), 420-21; Leo Pfeffer, *Church, State, and Freedom*, rev. ed. (Boston: Beacon Press, 1967), 241-42.

12. Lyman Beecher, *The Faith Once Delivered to the Saints*, 2d ed. (Boston: Crocker and Brewster, 1824), 25.

13. Lyman Beecher, *A Plea for the West* (Cincinnati: Truman and Smith, 1835; reprint, New York: Arno Press, 1977), 163.

14. F. Freeman, *Religious Liberty: A Discourse* (Plymouth, Mass.: Benjamin Drew Jr., 1832), 23.

15. Ibid., 17.

16. Ibid., 17-18.

17. David Longworth Ogden, "Second Discourse: On the Misrepresentation of Benevolent Actions," in *Two Discourses* (Hartford, Conn.: Hudson and Skinner, 1830), 28.

18. Ibid., 26, 31-32.

19. James Madison, *Federalist* no. 51, *Federalist Papers*, 322, 325.

20. James Davison Hunter, *Culture Wars: The Struggle to Define America* (New York: Basic Books, 1991).

21. Patrick Buchanan, Speech presented to the Republican National Convention, Houston, Texas, August 17, 1992; emphasis added.

# BIBLIOGRAPHY

*Abington School District* v. *Schempp* 374 U.S. 203 (1963).

Abzug, Robert. *Cosmos Crumbling: American Reform and the Religious Imagination*. New York: Oxford University Press, 1994.

*An Account of Memorials Presented to Congress During the Last Session, by Numerous Friends of Their Country and Its Institutions; Praying That the Mails May Not Be Transported, nor Post-Offices Kept Open, on the Sabbath*. New York: T. R. Marvin, 1829.

Adair, Douglass, and Marvin Harvey. "Was Alexander Hamilton a Christian Statesman?" In *Fame and the Founding Fathers: Essays by Douglass Adair*, ed. Trevor Colbourn, pp. 141–59. New York: Norton, 1974.

Adams, Jaspar. *Elements of Moral Philosophy*. Cambridge, Mass.: Folsom, Wells, and Thurston, 1837.

———. *The Relation of Christianity to Civil Government in the United States*. 2d ed. Charleston, S.C.: Miller, 1833.

Adams, John. *Diary and Autobiography of John Adams*. 4 vols. Ed. L. H. Butterfield. Cambridge, Mass.: Belknap Press, 1961.

———. *Novanglus, and Massachusettensis; or, Political Essays Published in the Years 1774 and 1775*. Boston: Hews and Goss, 1819.

———. *Papers of John Adams*. 8 vols. to date. Ed. Robert Taylor. Cambridge, Mass.: Belknap Press, 1977–.

———. *Works of John Adams*. 10 vols. Ed. Charles Francis Adams. Boston: Little, Brown, 1856.

Adams, John, and Thomas Jefferson. *Adams-Jefferson Letters*. Ed. Lester J. Cappon. Chapel Hill: University of North Carolina Press, 1959.

Adams, John, and others. *Adams Family Correspondence*. 6 vols. Ed. L. H. Butterfield. Cambridge, Mass.: Belknap Press, 1963.

Ahlstrom, Sydney E. *A Religious History of the American People*. New Haven: Yale University Press, 1972.

Aldridge, Alfred Owen. *Man of Reason: The Life of Thomas Paine*. Philadelphia: Lippincott, 1959.

Alexander, Archibald. *Brief Outline of the Evidences of the Christian Religion*. Princeton: Princeton University Press, 1825.

Alley, Robert S. *So Help Me God: Religion and the Presidency, Wilson to Nixon*. Richmond, Va.: John Knox Press, 1972.

*American Anti-Slavery Reporter, Nos. 1–8, 1834*. Westport, Conn.: Negro Universities Press, 1970.

American Anti-Slavery Society. *First Annual Report of the American Anti-Slavery Society.* New York: Dorr and Butterfield, 1834. Reprint, New York: Kraus, 1972.

_____. *Fourth Annual Report of the American Anti-Slavery Society.* New York: William S. Dorr, 1837. Reprint, New York: Kraus, 1972.

_____. *Second Annual Report of the American Anti-Slavery Society.* New York: William S. Dorr, 1835. Reprint, New York: Kraus, 1972.

_____. *Third Annual Report of the American Anti-Slavery Society.* New York: William S. Dorr, 1836. Reprint, New York: Kraus, 1972.

American Bible Society. *Constitution of the American Bible Society . . . Together with Their Address to the People of the United States.* New York: Hopkins, 1816.

_____. *First Annual Report of the Board of Managers of the American Bible Society.* New York: Seymour, 1817.

American Board of Commissioners for Foreign Missions. Papers. Houghton Library, Harvard University. Woodbridge, Conn.: Research Publications, microfilm.

American Society for the Promotion of Temperance. *Second Annual Report of the Executive Committee of the American Society for the Promotion of Temperance.* Andover, Mass.: Flagg and Gould, 1829.

*American State Papers.* Class 7: Post Office Department. Vol. 1. Washington, D.C.: Gales and Seaton, 1834.

American Sunday School Union. *First Report of the American Sunday School Union.* Philadelphia: Ashmead, 1825.

_____. *Seventh Annual Report of the American Sunday School Union.* 2d ed. Philadelphia: American Sunday School Union, 1831.

_____. *Sixth Report of the American Sunday School Union.* Philadelphia: n.p., 1830.

Andrew, John A., III. *From Revivals to Removal: Jeremiah Evarts, the Cherokee Nation, and the Search for the Soul of America.* Athens: University of Georgia Press, 1992.

_____. *New England Congregationalists and Foreign Missions, 1800–1830: Rebuilding the Christian Commonwealth.* Lexington: University Press of Kentucky, 1976.

Andrews, Ethan Allen. *Slavery and the Domestic Slave-Trade in the United States: In a Series of Letters Addressed to the Executive Committee of the American Union for the Relief and Improvement of the Colored Race.* Boston: Light and Stearns, 1836. Reprint, Freeport, N.Y.: Books for Libraries Press, 1971.

*Appleton's Cyclopædia of American Biography.* 7 vols. Ed. James Grant Wilson and John Fiske. New York: Appleton, 1887–1900.

Aquinas, Thomas. *Summa Theologiae.* Ed. Anthony Ross and P. G. Walsh. New York: McGraw-Hill, 1966.

_____. *Treatise on Law.* Chicago: Regnery Gateway, n.d.

Aristotle. *Nicomachean Ethics.* Trans. Martin Otswald. Indianapolis: Bobbs-Merrill, 1962.

"Arrest of the Mail." *Nile's Weekly Register,* May 2, 1829, 148.

"Article VII. [Review of the] Report of the Committee of the House of Representatives of the United States on Post-Offices and Post-Roads." *North American Review* (July 1830): 154–67.

Augustine, Saint. *The Political Writings of St. Augustine.* Ed. Henry Paolucci. Chicago: Regnery Gateway, 1962.

Baird, Robert. *Religion in America; or, an Account of the Origin, Relation to the State, and Present Condition of the Evangelical Churches in the United States with Notices of the Unevangelical Denominations.* New York: Harper and Brothers, 1856.

Balme, J. R. *American States, Churches, and Slavery.* Edinburgh: William P. Nimmo, 1862. Reprint, New York: Negro Universities Press, 1969.

Banner, Louis W. "Religious Benevolence as Social Control: A Critique of an Interpretation." In *Religion in American History: Interpretive Essays,* ed. John M. Mulder and John F. Wilson, 218–35. Englewood Cliffs, N.J.: Prentice-Hall, 1978.

Barnwell, William H. *The Impiety and Absurdity of Duelling—a Sermon.* Charleston: Walker and Burke, 1844.

Beaver, R. Pierce. "The Missions and Indian Removal." In *Church, State, and the American Indians,* 85–122. Saint Louis: Concordia, 1966.

Beccaria-Bonesana, Cesare. *An Essay on Crimes and Punishments.* Stanford: Academic Reprints, 1953.

Beecher, Lyman. *Autobiography of Lyman Beecher.* Ed. Barbara M. Cross. Cambridge, Mass.: Belknap Press, 1961.

_____. *The Faith Once Delivered to the Saints.* 2d ed. Boston: Crocker and Brewster, 1824.

_____. *A Plea for the West.* Cincinnati: Truman and Smith, 1835. Reprint, New York: Arno Press, 1977.

_____. *The Practicality of Suppressing Vice by Means of Societies Instituted for That Purpose.* New London, Conn.: Samuel Green, 1804.

_____. *Works of Lyman Beecher.* 3 vols. Boston: Jewett, 1852.

Bell, Sadie. *The Church, the State, and Education in Virginia.* Philadelphia: Science Press Printing, 1930.

Berns, Walter. *The First Amendment and the Future of American Democracy.* New York: Basic Books, 1976.

Beya, Amos J. *The American Colonization Society and the Creation of the Liberian State: A Historical Perspective, 1822–1900.* Lanham, Md.: University Press of America, 1991.

Bingham, Hiram. *A Residence of Twenty-one Years in the Sandwich Islands; or the Civil, Religious, and Political History of Those Islands: Comprising a Particular View of the Missionary Operations Connected with the Introduction and Progress of Christianity and Civilization Among the Hawaiian People.* 2d ed. Hartford, Conn.: Hezekiah Huntington, 1848.

Boardman, H. A. *Is There Any Ground to Apprehend the Extensive and Dangerous Prevalence of Romanism in the United States?* Philadelphia: Hooker and Agnew, 1841. Reprinted in *Anti-Catholicism in America, 1841–1851: Three Sermons.* New York: Arno Press, 1977.

Bodo, John R. *The Protestant Clergy and Public Issues.* Princeton: Princeton University Press, 1954.

Boles, John B. *The Great Revival, 1787–1805: The Origins of the Southern Evangelical Mind.* Lexington: University Press of Kentucky, 1972.

Boles, John, ed. *Masters and Slaves in the House of the Lord: Race and Religion in the American South, 1740–1870.* Lexington: University Press of Kentucky, 1988.

Boller, Paul F. *George Washington and Religion.* Dallas: Southern Methodist University Press, 1963.

Borden, Morton. *Jews, Turks, and Infidels.* Chapel Hill: University of North Carolina Press, 1984.

Boudinot, Elias. *An Address to the Whites.* Philadelphia: William F. Geddes, 1826.

Bouton, Nathaniel. *The Responsibilities of Rulers: A Sermon.* Concord, N.H.: Henry F. Moore, 1828.

*Bowen* v. *Kendrick* 487 U.S. 589 (1988).

Bowen, Nathaniel D. *A Sermon; Preached October, 1807, in St. Michael's Church, Charleston.* Charleston, S.C.: Privately printed, 1823.

Bradford, William. "History of Plimoth Plantation." In *The Puritans: A Sourcebook of Their Writings,* ed. Perry Miller and Thomas H. Johnson, vol. 1, 91–117. Rev. ed. New York: Harper and Row, 1963.

Bradley, Harold Whitman. *The American Frontier in Hawaii: The Pioneers, 1789–1843.* Stanford: Stanford University Press, 1942.

Buchanan, Patrick. Speech presented to the Republican National Convention, Houston, Texas, August 17, 1992.

Buckley, Thomas E. *Church and State in Revolutionary Virginia, 1776–1787.* Charlottesville: University Press of Virginia, 1977.

Burr, Nelson R. *A Critical Bibliography of Religion in America.* Princeton: Princeton University Press, 1961.

Bush, George. *Lack of Vision the Ruin of the People.* Indianapolis: Gazette Office, 1826.

Cabell, Nathaniel Francis. *Early History of the University of Virginia, as Contained in the Letters of Thomas Jefferson and Joseph C. Cabell.* Richmond, Va.: Randolph, 1856.

Calhoon, Robert M. *Evangelicals and Conservatives in the Early South, 1740–1861.* Columbia: University of South Carolina Press, 1988.

Calvin, John. *John Calvin on God and Political Duty,* ed. John T. McNeill. 2d ed. Indianapolis: Bobbs-Merrill, 1956.

Carwardine, Richard. Evangelicals and Politics in Antebellum America. New Haven: Yale University Press, 1993.

Chambers, Talbot W. *Memoir of the Life and Character of the Late Hon. Theodore Frelinghuysen.* New York: Harper and Brothers, 1863.

*Church of the Holy Trinity* v. *United States* 143 U.S. 457 (1892).

Cole, Charles C., Jr. *The Social Ideas of the Northern Evangelists, 1826–1860.* New York: Columbia University Press, 1954.

*Compilation of the Messages and Papers of the Presidents. 20 vols.* Ed. James D. Richardson. Washington, D.C.: Bureau of National Literature, 1897–1917.

Congressional Temperance Society. *First Annual Report.* Washington, D.C.: Jacob Gideon, 1834.

Cooke, Phinehas. *Reciprocal Obligations of Religion and Civil Government.* Concord, N.H.: Jacob B. Moore, 1825.

Cord, Robert. *Separation of Church and State: Historical Fact and Current Fiction.* New York: Lambeth Press, 1982.

Cousins, Norman, ed. *"In God We Trust": The Religious Beliefs and Ideas of the American Founding Fathers.* New York: Harper and Brothers, 1958.

Crockett, David. *A Narrative of the Life of David Crockett of the State of Tennessee.* Ed. James A. Shackford and Stanley J. Folmsbee. Knoxville: University of Tennessee Press, 1973.

Cross, Whitney R. *The Burned-Over District: The Social and Intellectual History of Enthusiastic Religion in Western New York, 1800–1850.* New York: Harper Torchbooks, 1965.

Curry, Thomas J. *The First Freedoms: Church and State in America to the Passage of the First Amendment.* New York: Oxford University Press, 1986.

Dabney, Virginius. *Mr. Jefferson's University: A History.* Charlottesville: University Press of Virginia, 1981.

Dana, Daniel. *An Election Sermon.* Concord: Jacob Moore, 1823.

_____. *Evangelical Preaching Is Rational Preaching.* Concord, N.H.: Isaac Hill, 1826.

Dangerfield, George. *The Awakening of American Nationalism, 1815–1828.* New York: Harper and Row, 1965.

D'Arusmont, Frances Wright. *Life, Letters, and Lectures, 1834–1844.* New York: Arno Press, 1972.

DeMar, Gary. *God and Government.* Atlanta: American Vision Press, 1984.

Dennis, Lane T., ed. *Francis A. Schaeffer: Portraits of the Man and His Work.* Westchester, Ill.: Crossway Books, 1986.

Douglass, Frederick. "Narrative of the Life of Frederick Douglass, an American Slave." In *Norton Anthology of American Literature,* vol. 1, 1940–45. 2d ed. New York: Norton, 1985.

Dreisbach, Daniel. *Real Threat and Mere Shadow: Religious Liberty and the First Amendment.* Westchester, Ill.: Crossway Books, 1987.

"Duelling." *North American Review* 17 (April 1828): 498–514.

Durbin, John Price. *Substance of a Sermon in Favor of Aiding the Greeks in Their Present Contest.* Cincinnati: Looker and Reynolds, 1824.

Dwight, Theodore, Jr. *President Dwight's Decisions and Questions Discussed by the Senior Class in Yale College, in 1813 and 1814.* New York: Jonathan Leavitt, 1833.

Dwight, Timothy. *Folly, Guilt, and Mischief of Duelling.* Hartford, Conn.: Hudson and Goodwin, 1805.

_____. *A Sermon on Dueling.* New York: Collins, Perkins, 1805.

_____. *Sermons by Timothy Dwight.* 2 vols. New Haven: Hezekiah Howe and Durrie and Peck, 1828.

Eidsmoe, John. *Christianity and the Constitution: The Faith of Our Founding Fathers.* Grand Rapids, Mich.: Baker Book House, 1987.

Ely, Ezra Stiles. *The Duty of Christian Freemen to Elect Christian Rulers.* Philadelphia: William F. Geddes, 1828.

Emmons, Nathanael. *Works of Nathanael Emmons.* 6 vols. Ed. Jacob Ide. Boston: Crocker and Brewster, 1842.

*Employment Division, Department of Human Resources of Oregon v. Smith* 110 S. Ct. 1595 (1990).

*Engel v. Vitale* 370 U.S. 421 (1962).

Evarts, Jeremiah. *Cherokee Removal: The "William Penn Essays" and Other Writings by Jeremiah Evarts.* Ed. Francis Paul Prucha. Knoxville: University of Tennessee Press, 1981.

_____. Correspondence. Jeremiah Evarts Collection, Library of Congress.

*Everson v. Board of Education* 330 U.S. 1 (1947).

Farris, Michael Farris. Remarks before Baptist youth gathering. Olympia, Washington, March 19, 1983.

Field, James A. *America and the Mediterranean World.* Princeton: Princeton University Press, 1969.

Fortin, Ernest. "Did the Separation of Church and State Benefit Religion? The Pros and Cons of Disestablishment." Paper presented at the American Political Science Association Annual Convention for the Claremont Institute for the Study of Political Philosophy and Statesmanship, San Francisco, Calif.: August 1990.

Foster, Charles I. *An Errand of Mercy: The Evangelical United Front, 1790–1837.* Chapel Hill: University of North Carolina Press, 1960.

Foster, J. M. *Reformation Principles Stated and Applied.* Chicago: Fleming H. Revell, 1890.

Franklin, Benjamin. "Autobiography," In *Benjamin Franklin's Autobiography and Selected Writings,* 1–164. New York: Holt, Rinehart and Winston, 1959.

_____. *The Papers of Benjamin Franklin.* 30 vols. to date. Ed. Leonard W. Labaree. New Haven: Yale University Press, 1959–.

_____. *Works of Benjamin Franklin.* 10 vols. Ed. Jared Sparks. Philadelphia: Childs and Peterson, 1840.

_____. *Writings.* New York: Library of America, 1987.

_____. *Writings of Benjamin Franklin.* 10 vols. Ed. Albert Henry Smyth. New York: Macmillan, 1905–1907.

Freeman, F. *Religious Liberty: A Discourse.* Plymouth, Mass.: Benjamin Drew Jr., 1832.

Frelinghuysen, Theodore. *Address, Delivered in the Orange Church, on the Evening of the 18th of December, 1826, Before the members of the Society for the Education of Poor and Indigent Children of the Parish of Orange.* Newark, N.J.: Tuttle, 1827.

_____. [Authorship uncertain but sometimes attributed to Frelinghuysen.] *An In-*

*quiry into the Moral and Religious Character of the American Government*. New York: Wiley and Putnam, 1838.

_____. *An Oration: Delivered at Princeton, New Jersey, Nov. 16, 1824, Before the New Jersey Colonization Society*. Princeton: Princeton Press, 1824.

_____. *Speech of Mr. Frelinghuysen on His Resolution Concerning Sabbath Mails in the Senate of the United States, May 8, 1830*. Washington, D.C.: Rothwell and Ustick, 1830.

Furman, Richard. *Death's Dominion over Man Considered, a Sermon Occasioned by the Death of the Honorable Major General Alexander Hamilton*. Charleston, S.C.: Young, 1804.

Fustel de Coulanges, Numa Denis. *The Ancient City: A Study on the Religion, Laws, and Institutions of Greece and Rome*. Baltimore: Johns Hopkins University Press, 1980.

Garrison, Winfrid Ernest, and Alfred T. DeGroot. *The Disciples of Christ: A History*. St. Louis: Christian Board of Publication, 1948.

Gaustad, Edwin S. *Faith of Our Fathers: Religion and the New Nation*. San Francisco: Harper and Row, 1987.

Gear, Ezekiel G. *A Sermon Delivered at the Taking up of a Collection, for the Benefit of the Greeks, in the Congregation of St. John's Church*. Ithaca, N.Y.: Mack and Morgan, 1824.

General Union for Promoting the Observance of the Christian Sabbath. *Address of the General Union for Promoting the Observance of the Christian Sabbath*. New York: Fanshaw, 1828.

_____. *Annual Report of the General Union for Promoting the Observance of the Christian Sabbath*. New York: Collord, 1829.

_____. *Proceedings in Relation to the Formation of the Auxillary Union of the City of Boston, for Promoting the Observance of the Christian Sabbath*. Boston: Marvin, 1828.

_____. *Proceedings of the Pennsylvania Branch of the General Union for Promoting the Observance of the Christian Sabbath*. Philadelphia: Martin and Boden, 1828.

_____. *Third Annual Report of the General Union for Promoting the Observance of the Christian Sabbath, and the Proceedings of the Annual Meeting*. New York: Sleight and Robinson, 1831.

"Georgia to Pardon Two in 1831 Case." *New York Times* (national ed.), November 11, 1992, A-7.

*Gillette* v. *United States* 401 U.S. 437 (1971).

Goldwin, Robert, and Art Kaufman, eds. *How Does the Constitution Protect Religious Freedom?* Washington, D.C.: American Enterprise Institute, 1987.

Goodman, Paul. *Towards a Christian Republic: Antimasonry and the Great Transition in New England, 1826–1836*. New York: Oxford University Press, 1988.

Griffin, Clifford. *Their Brothers' Keepers: Moral Stewardship in the United States, 1800–1865*. New Brunswick, N.J.: Rutgers University Press, 1960.

Grimké, Thomas S. *Address on the Expediency and Duty of Adopting the Bible: As a Class Book.* Charleston, S.C.: Observer Office Press, 1830.

_____. *Correspondence on the Principles of Peace, Manual Labor Schools.* Charlestown, S.C.: Observer Office Press, 1833.

_____. *An Essay on the Appropriate Use of the Bible in Common Education.* Charleston, S.C.: Observer Office Press, 1833.

_____. *Oration on the Principal Duties of Americans.* Charleston, S.C.: William Estill, 1833.

Hamilton, Alexander. *The Papers of Alexander Hamilton.* 26 vols. Ed. Harold C. Syrett. New York: Columbia University Press, 1961–1979.

_____. *Works of Alexander Hamilton.* 12 vols. Ed. Henry Cabot Lodge. New York: Putnam's Sons, 1904.

Hamilton, Alexander, James Madison, and John Jay. *The Federalist Papers.* New York: New American Library, 1961.

Hamilton, James. *Reminiscences of James A. Hamilton.* New York: Charles Scribner, 1869.

Hanley, Mark. *Beyond a Christian Commonwealth.* Chapel Hill: University of North Carolina Press, 1994.

Harding, Vincent. *A Certain Magnificence: Lyman Beecher and the Transformation of American Protestantism, 1775–1865.* Brooklyn, N.Y.: Carlson, 1991.

Harris, Patricia Roberts. "Religion and Politics: A Commitment to a Pluralistic Society." *Vital Speeches* 47 (November 1, 1980): 50–53.

Hatch, Nathan O. *The Democratization of American Christianity.* New Haven: Yale University Press, 1989.

Hawthorne, Nathaniel. *Tales and Sketches.* New York: Library of America, 1982.

Hays, George P. *Presbyterians.* New York: Hill, 1892.

Heimert, Alan. *Religion and the American Mind: From the Great Awakening to the Revolution.* Cambridge, Mass.: Harvard University Press, 1966.

Henry, Stuart C. *Unvanquished Puritan: A Portrait of Lyman Beecher.* Grand Rapids, Mich.: William B. Eerdmans, 1973.

Hill, Robert. "Is Locke America's Philosopher? James Wilson Answers." Paper presented at the American Political Science Association Annual Meeting for the Georgetown Institute for the Study of Politics, San Francisco, Calif., August 30, 1990.

*Historical Statistics of the United States, Colonial Times to 1970.* 2 vols. Washington, D.C.: Bureau of the Census, 1975.

*Hobbie* v. *Unemployment Appeals Commission of Florida* 480 U.S. 136 (1987).

Horowitz, Robert H., ed. *The Moral Foundations of the American Republic.* 3d ed. Charlottesville: University Press of Virginia, 1986.

House Committee on Indian Affairs. Petitions and Memorials. Records of the U.S. House of Representatives. Record Group 233. Center for Legislative Archives, National Archives and Records Administration, Washington, D.C.

House Committee on the Post Office and Post Roads. Petitions and Memorials. Records of the U.S. House of Representatives. Record Group 233. Center for Legislative Archives, National Archives and Records Administration, Washington, D.C.

Howe, John R. Jr., *The Changing Political Thought of John Adams.* Princeton: Princeton University Press, 1966.

Hudson, Frederic. *Journalism in the United States, from 1600 to 1872.* New York: Harper and Brothers, 1872.

Hunter, James Davison. *Culture Wars: The Struggle to Define America.* New York: Basic Books, 1991.

Charles S. Hyneman and Donald S. Lutz, eds. *American Political Writing During the Founding Era, 1760-1805.* Indianapolis: Liberty Press, 1983.

Ihm, Claudia Carlen, ed. *The Papal Encyclicals, 1740-1878* N.p.: McGrath, 1981.

Jaffa, Harry V. *The American Founding as the Best Regime: The Bonding of Civil and Religious Liberty.* Montclair, Calif.: Claremont Institute for the Study of Political Philosophy and Statesmanship, 1990.

———. *Crisis of the House Divided: An Interpretation of the Issues in the Lincoln-Douglas Debates.* Chicago: University of Chicago Press, 1982.

———. "Crisis of the Strauss Divided." Claremont, Calif., April 22, 1987. Unpublished paper.

———. *Thomism and Aristotelianism: A Study of the Commentary by Thomas Aquinas on the Nicomachean Ethics.* Chicago: University of Chicago Press, 1952.

Jay, John. *Correspondence and Public Papers of John Jay.* 4 vols. Ed. Henry Johnston. New York: Putnam's Sons, 1890-1893.

———. *John Jay: The Making of a Revolutionary, Unpublished Papers, 1745-1780.* Ed. Richard B. Morris. San Francisco: Harper and Row, 1975.

Jay, William. *An Essay on Duelling.* Savannah, Ga.: Savannah Anti-Duelling Association, 1829.

———. *An Essay on the Importance of the Sabbath Considered Merely as a Civil Institution.* Geneva, N.Y.: James Bogert, 1826.

———. *Inquiry into the Character and Tendency of the American Colonization, and American Anti-Slavery Societies.* 6th ed. New York: Williams, 1838. Reprint, Miami: Mnemosyne, 1969.

Jefferson, Thomas. *The Complete Jefferson.* Ed. Saul K. Padover. New York: Duell, Sloan, and Pearce, 1943.

———. *Jefferson's Extracts from the Gospels.* Ed. Dickinson W. Adams. Princeton: Princeton University Press, 1983.

———. *Notes on the State of Virginia.* Ed. William Peden. New York: Norton, 1954.

———. *Papers of Thomas Jefferson.* 25 vols. to date. Ed. Julian P. Boyd. Princeton: Princeton University Press, 1950-.

———. *Writings.* New York: Library of America, 1984.

———. *Writings of Thomas Jefferson.* 10 vols. Ed. Paul Leicester Ford. New York: Putnam's Sons, 1892-1899.

John, Richard. "Taking Sabbatarianism Seriously: The Postal System, the Sabbath, and the Transformation of the American Political Culture." *Journal of the Early Republic* 10 (Winter 1990): 517–67.

Johnson, Paul E. *A Shopkeeper's Millennium: Society and Revivals in Rochester, New York, 1815–1837*. New York: Hill and Wang, 1978.

Johnson, William J. *George Washington the Christian*. New York: Abingdon Press, 1919.

Keller, Charles Roy. *The Second Great Awakening in Connecticut*. Hamden, Conn.: Archon Books, 1968.

Kelly, George Armstrong. *Politics and Religious Consciousness in America*. New Brunswick, N.J.: Transaction Books, 1984.

Lesick, Lawrence Thomas. *The Lane Rebels: Evangelicalism and Antislavery in Antebellum America*. Metuchen, N.J.: Scarecrow Press, 1980.

Levy, Leonard W. "Cherokee Indian Cases." In *Encyclopedia of the American Constitution,* ed. Leonard W. Levy, Kenneth L. Karst, and Dennis J. Mahoney, vol. 1, 241. New York: Macmillan, 1986.

_____. *Emergence of a Free Press*. New York: Oxford University Press, 1985.

_____. *The Establishment Clause: Religion and the First Amendment*. New York: Macmillan, 1986.

_____. *Jefferson and Civil Liberties: The Darker Side*. New York: Quadrangle, 1973.

_____. *The Law of the Commonwealth and Chief Justice Shaw: The Evolution of American Law, 1830–1860*. New York: Harper Torchbooks, 1967.

_____. *Treason Against God: A History of the Offense of Blasphemy*. New York: Schocken Books, 1981.

Lichtman, Allan J. "The New Prohibitionism." *Christian Century* 97 (October 29, 1980): 1029–30.

Lincoln, Abraham. *Abraham Lincoln: Speeches and Writings, 1832–1858*. 2 vols. New York: Library of America, 1989.

Locke, John. *A Letter Concerning Toleration*. Indianapolis: Bobbs-Merrill, 1955.

_____. *The Reasonableness of Christianity, as Delivered in the Scriptures*. Ed. George W. Ewing. Washington, D.C.: Regnery Gateway, 1965.

_____. *Two Treatises of Government*. Ed. Peter Laslett. Rev. ed. New York: New American Library, 1965.

*The Logic and Law of Col. Johnson's Report to the Senate on Sabbath Mails*. Utica, N.Y.: G. Wilson, 1829.

Long, John Dixon. *Pictures of Slavery in Church and State*. 1857. Reprint, New York: Negro Universities Press, 1969.

Lord, Nathan. *A Sermon Preached at the Annual Election*. Concord, N.H.: Hill and Barton, 1831.

Lossing, Benson J. *The Pictorial Field-Book of the Revolution*. 2 vols. New York: Harper and Brothers, 1859.

Lumpkin, Wilson. *The Removal of the Cherokee Indians from Georgia*. New York: Dodd, Mead, 1907.

McBrien, Richard P. *Caesar's Coin: Religion and Politics in America.* New York: Macmillan, 1987.

McClellan, James. "The Making and Unmaking of the Establishment Clause." In *A Blueprint for Judicial Reform,* ed. Patrick McGuigan and Randall Rader, 295–325. Washington, D.C.: Free Congress Research and Education Foundation, 1981.

*McCollum v. Board of Education* 333 U.S. 203 (1948).

McConnell, Michael W. "The Origins and Historical Understanding of the Free Exercise of Religion," *Harvard Law Review* 103 (1990): 1409–1517.

McDonald, Forrest. *Alexander Hamilton, a Biography.* New York: Norton, 1979.

McDonald, John. *Sermon on the Premature and Lamented Death of General Alexander Hamilton.* Albany: John Barber, 1804.

M'Elroy, Joseph. *A Sermon, Delivered . . . on the Occasion of the Death of the Rev. John M. Mason, D.D.* New York: John P. Haven, 1830.

McGuire, Edward Charles. *The Religious Opinions and Character of Washington.* New York: Harper and Brother, 1836.

Machiavelli, Niccolò. *The Discourses.* Trans. Leslie J. Walker. Ed. Bernard Crick. Harmondsworth, Eng.: Penguin, 1983.

_____. *The Prince.* Trans. Harvey Mansfield Jr. Chicago: University of Chicago Press, 1985.

Maclean, John. *History of the College of New Jersey.* 2 vols. Philadelphia: Lippincott, 1877.

McLoughlin, William G. *Cherokee Renascence in the New Republic.* Princeton: Princeton University Press, 1986.

_____. *Cherokees and Missionaries, 1789–1839.* New Haven: Yale University Press, 1984.

_____. *New England Dissent, 1630–1883: The Baptists and the Separation of Church and State.* Cambridge, Mass.: Harvard University Press, 1971.

McMaster, Gilbert. *The Moral Character of Civil Government, Considered with Reference to the Political Institutions of the United States.* Albany: Little, 1832.

Madison, James. "Madison's 'Detached Memoranda.'" *William and Mary Quarterly* 3 (1946): 534–68.

_____. *Notes of Debates in the Federal Convention of 1787.* New York: Norton Company, 1987.

_____. *Papers of James Madison.* 16 vols. Ed. William T. Hutchinson and William M. Frachal. Chicago: University of Chicago Press, 1962–.

_____. *Writings of James Madison.* 9 vols. Ed. Gaillard Hunt. New York: Putnam's Sons, 1900–1910.

Malbin, Michael. *Religion and Politics: The Intentions of the Authors of the First Amendment.* Washington, D.C.: American Enterprise Institute, 1978.

Malone, Dumas. *Jefferson and His Time.* 6 vols. Boston: Little, Brown, 1981.

Maring, N. H. "Evangelical." "Evangelicalism." In *Encyclopediac Dictionary of Religion,* 1268, 1270–1271. Philadelphia: Sisters of St. Joseph of Philadelphia, 1979.

Marshall, Peter, and David Manuel. *From Sea to Shining Sea*. Old Tappan, N.J.: Fleming H. Revell, 1986.

_____. *The Light and the Glory*. Old Tappan, N.J.: Fleming H. Revell, 1977.

Mason, John M. *Complete Works of John M. Mason*. 4 vols. Ed. Ebenezer Mason. New York: Baker and Scribner, 1849.

Massachusetts Peace Society. *Sixteenth Report of the Executive Committee of the Massachusetts Peace Society*. Boston: Samuel N. Dickinson, 1832.

Mathews, Donald G. *Religion in the Old South*. Chicago: University of Chicago Press, 1977.

_____. *Slavery and Methodism: A Chapter in American Morality, 1780–1845*. Princeton: Princeton University Press, 1965.

Meyer, Leland Winfield. *The Life and Times of Colonel Richard M. Johnson of Kentucky*. New York: AMS Press, 1967.

McGuire, Edward Charles. *The Religious Opinions and Character of Washington*. New York: Harper and Brothers, 1836.

Miller, John C. *The Federalists, 1789–1801*. New York: Harper and Row, 1960.

Miller, William. *Address for the Benefit of the Greeks, Delivered in Trinity Church, Newark*. Newark, N.J.: Tuttle, 1824.

*Minersville School District* v. *Gobitis* 310 U.S. 586 (1940).

Monk, Samuel Holt. "Samuel Stanhope Smith: Friend of Rational Liberty." In *The Lives of Eighteen from Princeton*, ed. Willard Thorp, 86–110. Princeton: Princeton University Press, 1946.

Morison, Samuel Elliot. *The Oxford History of the American People*. New York: Oxford University Press, 1965.

Morse, Jedediah. *A Sermon Delivered at Charlestown, July 23, 1812*. Charlestown, Mass.: Samuel Etheridge, 1812.

Morse, Samuel F. B. *Foreign Conspiracy Against the Liberties of the United States*. New York: Leavitt, Lord, 1835. Reprint, New York: Arno Press, 1977.

Mott, Frank Luther. *American Journalism: A History, 1690–1960*. 3d ed. New York: Macmillan, 1962.

_____. *A History of American Magazine, 1741–1850*. New York: Appleton, 1930.

Musgrave, G. W. *A Vindication of Religious Liberty*. Baltimore: John W. Woods, 1834.

*New American State Papers, Indian Affairs*. Vol. 9. Wilmington, Del.: Scholarly Resources, 1972.

Newmyer, R. Kent. *Supreme Court Justice Joseph Story: Statesman of the Old Republic*. Chapel Hill: University of North Carolina Press, 1985.

Niebuhr, H. Richard. *The Kingdom of God in America*. New York: Harper Torchbooks, 1959.

_____. *The Social Sources of American Denominationalism*. New York: New American Library, 1975.

Noll, Mark A. *One Nation Under God? Christian Faith and Political Action in America*. San Francisco: Harper and Row, 1988.

Noll, Mark A., George Mardsen, and Nathan Hatch. *The Search for a Christian America.* Westchester, Ill.: Crossway Books, 1983.

Nott, Eliphalet. *A Discourse.* Salem, Mass.: Cushing, 1804.

_____. *Discourse Delivered in the Presbyterian Church, in Albany, the Fourth of July.* Albany: Charles R. and George Webster, 1801.

Office of the Judge Advocate General (Navy). Case file of the Court of Inquiry concerning Lt. John Percival. Records of General Courts-Martial and Courts of Inquiry of the Navy Department, 1799–1867. National Archives, Washington, D.C. Microfilm.

Ogden, David Longworth. "Second Discourse: On the Misrepresentation of Benevolent Actions." In *Two Discourses,* 4–49. Hartford, Conn.: Hudson and Skinner, 1830.

*O'Lone* v. *Estate of Shabazz* 482 U.S. 342 (1987).

O'Neill, James. *Religion and Education Under the Constitution.* New York: Harper and Brothers, 1949.

Oliphant, J. Orin, ed. *Through the South and the West with Jeremiah Evarts in 1826.* Lewisburg, Penn.: Bucknell University Press, 1956.

Ouseley, William Gore. *Remarks on the Statistics and Political Institutions of the United States.* London: Rodwell, 1832.

Pangle, Thomas. *The Spirit of Modern Republicanism: The Moral Vision of the American Founders and the Philosophy of Locke.* Chicago: University of Chicago Press, 1988.

Parker, Clifton Jackson. *Protestant America and the Pagan World: The First Half Century of the American Board of Commissioners for Foreign Missions, 1810–1860.* Cambridge, Mass.: East Asian Research Center, Harvard University, 1969.

Patterson, A. W. *The Code Duello, with Special Reference to the State of Virginia.* Richmond: Richmond Press, 1927.

Paullin, Charles Oscar. *Diplomatic Negotiations of American Naval Officers, 1778–1883.* Baltimore: Johns Hopkins Press, 1912.

Peters, Richard. *The Case of the Cherokee Nation Against the State of Georgia.* Philadelphia: John Grigg, 1831.

Pfeffer, Leo. *Church, State, and Freedom.* Rev. ed. Boston: Beacon Press, 1967.

Philanthropos. *A Letter to Aaron Burr, Vice-President of the United States of America, on the Barbarous Origin, the Criminal Nature, and the Baneful Effects of Duels.* New York: John Low, 1804.

Prucha, Francis Paul. Introduction to *Cherokee Removal: The "William Penn" Essays and Other Writings of Jeremiah Evarts,* by Jeremiah Evarts, 3–40. Knoxville: University of Tennessee Press, 1981.

"Review: Memoirs of Dr. Joseph Priestly . . . and Observations on His Writings, by Thomas Cooper." *Virginia Evangelical and Literary Magazine* (February 1820): 63–74.

*Review of a Report of the Committee . . . by the Hon. Richard Johnson.* Washington, D.C.: n.p., 1829.

[Review of *Personal Sketches of His Own Times,* with reference to the portions of the book relating to dueling]. *North American Review* (April 1828): 498–514.

*Reynolds* v. *United States* 98 U.S. 145 (1878).

Rice, David. *A Second Epistle to the Citizens of Kentucky, Professing the Christian Religion.* Lexington, Ky.: Bradford, 1808.

Rosell, Garth M. "Charles G. Finney: His Place in the Stream of American Evangelicalism." In *The Evangelical Tradition in America,* ed. Leonard I. Sweet, Macon, Ga.: Mercer University Press, 1984.

Ryan, Mary P. *Cradle of the Middle Class: The Family in Oneida Country, New York, 1790–1865.* New York: Cambridge University Press, 1981.

Sandoz, Ellis, ed. *Political Sermons of the American Founding Era, 1730–1805.* Indianapolis: Liberty Press, 1991.

Scanzoni, John. "Resurgent Fundamentalism: Marching Backward Into the '80s?" *Christian Century* 97 (September 10–17, 1980): 847ff.

Schaeffer, Edith. *The Tapestry: The Life and Times of Francis and Edith Schaeffer.* Waco, Tex.: Word Books, 1981.

Schaeffer, Francis A. *A Christian Manifesto.* Westchester, Ill.: Crossway Books, 1981.

_____. *Complete Works of Francis A. Schaeffer: A Christian Worldview.* Westchester, Ill.: Crossway Books, 1982.

Schaff, Philip. *History of the Christian Church.* 5th ed. 5 vols. Grand Rapids, Mich.: Eerdmans, 1910.

Schlesinger, Arthur M., Jr. *The Age of Jackson.* Boston: Little, Brown, 1945.

Schriver, Peggy. *The Bible Vote: Religion and the Right.* New York: Pilgrim Press, 1981.

Seed, Geoffrey. *James Wilson.* Millwood, N.Y.: KTO Press, 1978.

Sega, Giacomo. *An Essay on the Practice of Duelling.* Philadelphia: Privately printed, 1830.

Senate Committee on Foreign Relations and Indian Affairs. Petitions and Memorials. Records of the U.S. Senate. Record Group 46. Center for Legislative Archives, National Archives and Records Administration, Washington, D.C.

Senate Committee on Post Office and Civil Service. Petitions and Memorials. Records of the U.S. Senate. Record Group 46. Center for Legislative Archives, National Archives and Records Administration, Washington, D.C.

Setz, Don C. *Famous American Duels.* New York: Thomas Crowell, 1929.

Shelley, B. L. "Evangelicalism." In *Dictionary of Christianity in America,* 413–16. Downer's Grove, Ill.: Intervarsity Christian Fellowship, 1990.

*Sherbert* v. *Verner* 374 U.S. 398 (1963).

Smith, Elwyn A. "The Voluntary Establishment of Religion." In *The Religion of the Republic,* ed. Elwyn A. Smith, 154–82. Philadelphia: Fortress Press, 1971.

Smith, Samuel Stanhope. *A Comprehensive View of the Leading and Most Important Principles of Natural and Revealed Religion.* 2d ed. New Brunswick, N.J.: Deare and Myer, 1816.

——. *An Essay on the Causes of the Variety of Complexion and Figure in the Human Species.* 2d ed. New Brunswick, N.J.: Simpson, 1810.

——. *Lectures . . . on the Subjects of Moral and Political Philosophy.* 2 vols. Trenton, N.J.: Daniel Fenton, 1812.

Smith, Timothy L. *Revivalism and Social Reform in Mid-Nineteenth-Century America.* New York: Abingdon Press, 1957.

Smith-Rosenberg, Carroll. "Women and Religious Revivals: Anti-Ritualism, Liminality, and the Emergence of the American Bourgeoisie." In *The Evangelical Tradition in America,* ed. Leonard I. Sweet, Macon, Ga.: Mercer University Press, 1984.

Snow, Charles M. *Religious Liberty in America.* Washington, D.C.: Review and Herald, 1914.

Snyder, Stephen H. *Lyman Beecher and His Children: The Transformation of a Religious Tradition.* Brooklyn, N.Y.: Carlson, 1991.

Solberg, Winton U. *Redeem the Time: The Puritan Sabbath in Early America.* Cambridge, Mass.: Harvard University Press, 1977.

*Speeches on the Passage of the Bill for the Removal of the Indians, Delivered in the Congress of the United States, April and May, 1830.* Boston: Perkins and Marvin, 1830. Reprint, Millwood, N.Y.: Kraus, 1973.

*Statistical Abstract of the United States, 1991.* Washington, D.C.: Bureau of the Census, 1991.

Stokes, Anson Phelps. *Church and State in the United States.* 3 vols. New York: Harper and Brothers, 1950.

Stokes, Anson Phelps, and Leo Pfeffer. *Church and State in the United States.* Westport, Conn.: Greenwood Press, 1975.

"Stopping the Mail at Princeton." *Daily National Intelligencer,* June 23, 1829, 2.

Storing, Herbert J. *What the Anti-Federalists Were For.* Chicago: University of Chicago Press, 1981.

Story, Joseph. *Commentaries on the Constitution of the United States.* Boston: Hilliard, Gray, 1833. Reprint, New York: Da Capo Press, 1970.

Strauss, Leo. *Natural Right and History.* Chicago: University of Chicago Press, 1953.

——. "Preface to Hobbes *Politische Wissenschaft.*" *Interpretation* 8 (January 1979): 1.

——. "Progress or Return?" In *The Rebirth of Classical Political Rationalism: An Introduction to the Thought of Leo Strauss,* ed. Thomas L. Pangle, 227–70. Chicago: University of Chicago Press, 1989.

Tappan, Lewis. *The Life of Arthur Tappan.* New York: Hurd and Houghton, 1871. Reprint, Westport, Conn.: Negro Universities Press, 1970.

Thomas, Cal. *Book Burning.* Westchester, Ill.: Crossway Books, 1983.

Tocqueville, Alexis de. *Democracy in America.* Trans. George Lawrence. Ed. J. P. Mayer. Garden City, N.Y.: Anchor Books, 1969.

Tracy, E. C. *Memoir of the Life of Jeremiah Evarts, Esq.* Boston: Crocker and Brewster, 1845.

Tracy, Joseph. *History of the American Board of Commissioners for Foreign Missions.* 2d ed. New York: Dodd, 1842.

U.S. Congress. House Committee on the Post Office and Post Roads. *See under* House.

U.S. Congress. Senate Committee on Foreign Relations and Indian Affairs. *See under* Senate.

U.S. Navy. *See* Office of the Judge Advocate General (Navy).

Wall, James M. "Bringing Back the Conscience Vote." *Christian Century* 97 (December 17, 1980) 1235.

_____. "A Changing Political Climate," *Christian Century* 97 (September 24, 1980): 867–68.

_____. "The New Right Exploits Abortion." *Christian Century* 97 (July 30–August 6, 1980): 747–48.

*Wallace* v. *Jaffree* 472 U.S. 38 (1985).

Washington, George. *George Washington on Religious Liberty and Mutual Understanding: Selections from Washington's Letters.* Ed. Edward Frank Humphrey. Washington, D.C.: National Conference of Catholics, Jews, Protestants, 1932.

_____. *Writings of George Washington.* 39 vols. Ed. John Fitzpatrick. Washington, D.C.: United States George Washington Bicentennial Commission, 1931–1944.

Wayland, Francis. *The Elements of Moral Science.* Ed. Joseph L. Blau. Cambridge, Mass.: Belknap Press, 1963.

_____. *Occasional Discourses.* Boston: Loring, 1833.

Weems, Mason Locke. *God's Revenge Against Duelling; or the Duellists Looking Glass.* 2d ed. Philadelphia: Bioren, 1821.

*West Virginia State Board of Education* v. *Barnette* 319 U.S. 624 (1943).

"What's Wrong with Born-Again Politics? A Symposium." *Christian Century* 97 (October 22, 1980): 1002–4.

Whipple, Charles K. *Relation of the American Board of Commissioners for Foreign Missions to Slavery.* Wallcut, 1861. Reprint, New York: Negro Universities Press, 1969.

Whitehead, John W. *The Second American Revolution.* Elgin, Ill.: David C. Cook, 1982.

Wigfall, Arthur. *A Sermon upon Duelling.* Charleston, S.C.: Miller, 1856.

Williams, Jack K. *Dueling in the Old South (1775–1865).* Houston: Texas A&M University Press, 1980.

Wills, Gary. "Evangels of Abortion." *New York Review of Books,* June 15, 1989, 18–19.

Wilson, James. *The Works of James Wilson.* 2 vols. Ed. Robert Green McCloskey. Cambridge, Mass.: Belknap Press, 1967.

*Wisconsin* v. *Yoder* 406 U.S. 205 (1972).

Witherspoon, John. *The Absolute Necessity of Salvation Through Christ.* Edinburgh: Miller, 1758.

_____. *Annotated Edition of Lectures on Moral Philosophy.* Ed. Jack Scott. Newark: University of Delaware Press, 1982.

_____. *The Dominion of Providence over the Passions of Men.* 2d ed. Glasgow, 1777.

_____. *The Works of Rev. John Witherspoon.* 2d ed. 4 vols. Philadelphia: Woodward, 1802.

Wolfe, Gregory. "The Abolition of Man Revisited: College Textbooks in the Social Sciences." *University Bookman* (Summer 1982).

Woodward, Kenneth L. "Guru of Fundamentalism." *Newsweek,* November 1, 1982, 88.

*Worcester v. State of Georgia* 6 Peters 515 (1832).

Wuthnow, Robert. "The Political Rebirth of American Evangelicals." In *The New Christian Right: Mobilization and Legitimation,* eds. Robert C. Liebman and Robert Wuthnow, 149–60. New York: Aldine, 1983.

Wyatt-Brown, Bertram. *Lewis Tappan and the Evangelical War Against Slavery.* Cleveland: Press of Case Western Reserve University, 1969.

Zwier, Robert, and Richard Smith. "Christian Politics and the New Right." *Christian Century* 97 (October 8, 1980): 937–41.

# INDEX